The Logic of Liberal Rights

Rights are becoming more complicated every day. A unified theory seems unimaginable. Yet that is what this book proposes.

The Logic of Liberal Rights uses basic logic to develop a model of argument presupposed in all disputes about civil rights and liberties. No prior training in logic is required, as each step is explained. This analysis does not merely apply general logic to legal arguments. It is specifically tailored to the issues of civil rights and liberties. It shows that all arguments about civil rights and liberties presuppose one fixed structure. There can be no original argument in rights disputes, except within the confines of that structure. Concepts arising in disputes about rights, like 'liberal' or 'democratic', are not mere abstractions. They have a fixed and precise character.

This book integrates themes in legal theory, political science and moral philosophy, as well as the philosophy of logic and language. For the advanced scholar, it provides a model presupposed by leading theoretical schools (liberal and critical, positivist and naturalist). For the student, it provides a systematic theory of civil rights and liberties. Examples are drawn from the European Convention on Human Rights but no special knowledge of the Convention is assumed, as the issues analysed arise throughout the world. Such issues include problems of free speech, religious freedom, privacy, torture, unlawful detention and private property.

Eric Heinze (JD, Harvard; PhD, Leiden) is Senior Lecturer in Law, University of London, Queen Mary. He has held fellowships from the Fulbright Foundation and the French and German governments. He teaches Legal Theory, Constitutional Law, Human Rights and Public International Law. In addition to articles in those fields, his books include *The Logic of Equality* and *Sexual Orientation: A Human Right*.

Routledge studies in twentieth-century philosophy

1 **The Story of Analytic Philosophy**
Plot and heroes
Edited by Anat Biletzki and Anat Matar

2 **Donald Davidson**
Truth, meaning and knowledge
Edited by Urszula M. Zeglén

3 **Philosophy and Ordinary Language**
The bent and genius of our tongue
Oswald Hanfling

4 **The Subject in Question**
Sartre's critique of Husserl in *The Transcendence of the Ego*
Stephen Priest

5 **Aesthetic Order**
A philosophy of order, beauty and art
Ruth Lorland

6 **Naturalism**
A critical analysis
Edited by William Lane Craig and J.P. Moreland

7 **Grammar in Early Twentieth-century Philosophy**
Richard Gaskin

8 **Rules, Magic and Instrumental Reason**
A critical interpretation of Peter Winch's philosophy of the social sciences
Berel Dov Lerner

9 **Gaston Bachelard**
Critique of science and the imagination
Cristina Chimisso

10 **Hilary Putnam**
Pragmatism and realism
Edited by James Conant and Urszula M. Zeglén

11 **Karl Jaspers**
Politics and metaphysics
Chris Thornhill

12 **From Kant to Davidson**
The idea of the transcendental in twentieth-century philosophy
Edited by Jeff Malpas

13 **Collingwood and the Metaphysics of Experience**
A reinterpretation
Guiseppina D'Oro

14 **The Logic of Liberal Rights**
A study in the formal analysis of legal discourse
Eric Heinze

15 **Real Metaphysics**
Edited by Hallvard Lillehammer and Gonzalo Rodriguez-Pereyra

The Logic of Liberal Rights

A study in the formal analysis of legal discourse

Eric Heinze

Routledge
Taylor & Francis Group
LONDON AND NEW YORK

For Evert Alkema

First published 2003
by Routledge
11 New Fetter Lane, London EC4P 4EE

Simultaneously published in the USA and Canada
by Routledge
29 West 35th Street, New York, NY 10001

Routledge is an imprint of the Taylor & Francis Group

Typeset in Times New Roman by
Florence Production Ltd, Stoodleigh, Devon
Printed and bound in Great Britain by
The Cromwell Press, Trowbridge, Wiltshire

British Library Cataloguing in Publication Data
A catalogue record for this book is available from
the British Library

Library of Congress Cataloging in Publication Data
Heinze, Eric.
The logic of liberal rights: a study in the formal analysis of legal discourse/Eric Heinze.
p. cm
Includes bibliographical references and index.
1. Law – Methodology. 2. Natural law. 3. Human rights.
I. Title.
K258.H45 2003
340′.112 – dc21 2003037067

ISBN 0–415–30056–8

Contents

Acknowledgements

This book sets forth a full account of a topic first examined in an article published several years ago (Heinze 1999a). The analysis here is in all respects overriding. A number of scholars have provided valuable comments on various chapters. I would particularly like to thank Wilfred Hodges, Matthew Kramer, Istvan Pogany, Stephen Read, Mark Sainsbury, Jefferey Seitzer and Wayne Sumner. Valuable support was provided by Brian Littlechild and Tom Wormgoor. Many thanks also to Joe Whiting and Amritpal Bangard, and to their colleagues at Routledge including Yeliz Ali, Julia Davis, Tara Demetriou, Neil Dowden and Annabel Watson, as well as to Susan Leaper, Vicky Squires and the staff at Florence Production.

Cases and sources

Cases brought under the European Convention on Human Rights

Cases from other jurisdictions

Sources

AC	Appeal Cases (United Kingdom)
AJDA	*Actualité juridique, droit administrative*
All ER	*All England Reports*
BverfGE	*Entscheidungen des Bundesverfassungsgerichts*
CE	Conseil d'État (France)
Dalloz	*Recueil Dalloz*
ECHR	European Convention on Human Rights
EHRR	European Human Rights Reports
Eur. Comm'n H.R. Dec. and Rep.	*Decisions and Reports of the European Commission of Human Rights*
Eur. Ct H.R. (ser. A)	*Publications of the European Court of Human Rights, Series A*
GG	Grundgesetz (Germany)
GW	Grondwet (Netherlands)
HR	Hoge Raad (Netherlands)
ICCPR	International Covenant on Civil and Political Rights
NJ	*Nederlandse Jurisprudentie*
UDHR	Universal Declaration of Human Rights
US	*United States Reports*

Because it is logically incoherent . . .
rights discourse is a trap.

Duncan Kennedy

Introduction

In 1987, several men were arrested in Britain for engaging in acts of sadomasochism. The acts included application of hooks and needles to the genitalia, hot-iron branding and beatings with implements such as nettles and spiked belts. Although the acts resulted in flow of blood and scarring, there was no evidence of serious injuries. Several of the participants were convicted on charges of criminal misconduct.[1] Three of them then brought a complaint against the conviction under the European Convention of Human Rights. In the case of *Laskey, Jaggard and Brown v. United Kingdom*,[2] the European Court of Human Rights found that their right to privacy had not been violated.

How would a roomful of legal scholars analyse that case? A libertarian might argue that freely consenting adults ought to be able to do with their bodies whatever they please. A Christian conservative might argue that homosexual acts of any kind violate God's law. A black-letter lawyer might distinguish sexual sadomasochism from lawful sexual activity not involving violence, or from lawful violent activity not involving sex. An exponent of critical legal studies might argue that the very process of inscribing the controversy within an individual-versus-the-state idiom alienates from law the very persons whose interests the law should embrace. A feminist might argue that even exclusively male participants perpetuate a culture of brutality which reinforces violence against women. A critical race theorist might argue that sadomasochism recapitulates questionable practices of domination and servitude. A postmodernist might argue that, far from promoting a culture of oppression, sexual sadomasochism parodies and subverts it. A practitioner of law and economics might argue that the question of the acts' legality should be decided on the basis of the total cost incurred by society when such acts are illegal, discounted by the costs incurred when they are legal.

What might these scholars agree on? Of course, it is possible that there is no genuine discussion taking place at all – that they are just talking past each other. But let's assume they are not. Let's assume that all participants believe the remarks of all other participants to be pertinent. In that case, the possibility of meaningful disagreement among them already presupposes some agreement about the terms of their disagreement. The participants must already, if only tacitly, have agreed on something, before any coherent disagreement can take place. Consider some analogies. The claim 'The earth revolves around the sun' can be pitted against the claim 'The sun revolves around the earth' only if there is already prior agreement on the possibility of one celestial body travelling around another. The claim 'Hamlet ought to have killed Claudius' can be meaningfully pitted against the claim 'Hamlet ought not to have killed Claudius' only on the prior assumption that the conduct of this fictional character can be evaluated in ethical terms.

For *Laskey*, or any other case, we could postulate P_1, P_2, P_3, . . . P_n, as the set of prior propositions without which no coherent disagreement about the case can take place. What elements would that set contain? One might think that it must include some purely factual information: the acts committed, the arrests, the trial, the convictions, the sentencing, the appeals. Yet our question is not 'What would this roomful of scholars agree about?' Rather, we are asking 'What must they agree that they *dis*agree about?' Assuming agreement on the facts, what is their normative disagreement?

We might say that their disagreement is about 'interpretation'. The libertarian interprets the case in secular terms; the Christian conservative interprets it in theological terms; the black-letter lawyer interprets it in doctrinal terms, and so on. We could then postulate the propositions P_1, P_2, P_3, . . . P_n as a body of *Urtheorie* – of 'anterior' or 'background' or 'pre-interpretative' theory – which must be assumed in order for any coherent disagreement to emerge. Our search is not for ethically defensible or rhetorically persuasive concepts, but for those concepts which make arguments recognisable as arguments about liberal rights – concepts without which liberal rights discourse[3] would be unthinkable.

Assuming the existence of background concepts P_1, P_2, P_3, . . . P_n, we would want to know how many there are. By the end of the book, we will arrive at the answer $n = 6$. But why is rights discourse closed in that way, and how closed is it? What does that closure mean about what can and cannot be said? Do lawyers, judges or legal scholars forever delude themselves into thinking that they are inventing new arguments, when in fact they are just reproducing different versions of P_1, P_2 . . . P_6? Do they *only* recapitulate those background concepts, or do they also go further? What does it mean to 'go further'? In what sense have the background concepts already decided how much further an argument can go? How determinate are the background concepts?

The early years of the European Convention found the Court with a docket barely thick enough to provide a few weeks' work. Its case law through the mid-1960s amounted to a meagre bundle of intellectually vacuous reports. Decisions were delivered with the slightest *ratio decidendi*, and rarely with significant concurring or dissenting opinions. Yet, by the 1990s, the Court was regularly issuing long, complex judgments. Individual judges were writing separate opinions, often staging lively disagreements. That development has been part of a broader historical pattern. Since the 1970s, civil as well as common law countries, such as Britain, Germany, France and the Netherlands, have witnessed the same growth of judicial activity in civil rights and liberties. That expansion in the quantity and complexity of decisions has not delivered a progressive refinement of the case law; it remains as difficult as ever to identify principles linking past decisions or providing guidance for future ones. The leading treatises[4] reveal not a code of lucid principles, but a maze of tenuous results. Adding the great variety of claims which are now brought, one might conclude that no organising principles could ever be found. Yet the background theories will show that such a conclusion is not entirely accurate. We will see that even contradictory results continue to presuppose a fixed, determinate, formal coherence. Most importantly, we will see that the model represents a common structure presupposed by disagreements not only between litigants, or across cases, but also across theoretical schools: liberal and critical, positivist and naturalist. We will find a common structure presupposed by approaches as different as Kelsenian positivism and critical legal studies.

Law and logic

The aim of this book will be to develop a method of formal-logical analysis as a means of identifying the background concepts. As such techniques will be unfamiliar to some scholars, the method assumes no prior familiarity with logic or the philosophy of language.

Western logic derives largely from Aristotle, and from scholastic philosophy of the Middle Ages. In the nineteenth and twentieth centuries, philosophers and mathematicians such as Frege, Russell, Carnap and Tarski revised classical approaches, augmenting the power of logical analysis through symbolic notation forms. Yet lawyers and legal scholars are often ambivalent about logic. Certainly, no one doubts the logical character of an ordinary, law-applied-to-fact deduction, for example:

(1) If Croft has omitted to pay her employee at or above the minimum wage, she is subject to a fine of €10,000.
(2) Croft has omitted to pay her employee at or above the minimum wage.
∴ Croft is subject to a fine of €10,000.

But many have doubted whether logic can illuminate the subtler or more ambiguous elements of law. In the early nineteenth century, during the German codification debates, Savigny frowned on the ideal of deducing law from a system of abstract norms.[5] Oliver Wendell Holmes ushered in

American legal realism, proclaiming that 'the life of the law has not been logic: it has been experience'.[6] By 1935, the philosopher Alfred Ayer would trumpet to a broader readership that the truths of logic are 'a mere body of tautologies',[7] 'entirely devoid of factual content'.[8] Jurists could hardly be blamed for concluding that a heap of tautologies must be of little use to law.

Of course, Ayer never meant to be dismissive. While conceding that principles of logic cannot fulfil our search for knowledge about the world, he maintained that they do 'guide us' in that search:[9]

> A being whose intellect was infinitely powerful would take no interest in logic and mathematics. For he would be able to see at a glance everything that his definitions implied, and, accordingly, could never learn anything from logical inference which he was not fully conscious of already. But our intellects are not of this order. It is only a minute proportion of the consequences of our definitions that we are able to detect at a glance. Even so simple a tautology as '91 × 79 = 7189' is beyond the scope of our immediate apprehension.[10]

Similarly, a complex legal corpus does not reveal its conceptual scheme at a glance. That is where formal analysis can help. Today, the subtlety of symbolic techniques allows a degree of precision that was unknown in Savigny's or Holmes's day.

It was once thought that the goal of logic in legal theory would be the elaboration of a distinct legal logic – a model that would distinguish legal reasoning from, say, moral, political, sociological, or other kinds of reasoning.[11] That ambition mirrored the aim of traditional legal positivists to describe law as a distinct and autonomous system. Yet the recent tendency to renounce 'totalising' approaches to law[12] is reflected in the general agreement that no clear line can be drawn around any distinct sphere of legal reasoning.[13] Consider again the syllogism about Croft. Although the subject matter is ostensibly legal, that general form of reasoning is not specific to law. Even Kelsen, whose work exemplifies the search for characteristics unique to law, agreed that there is no distinct legal logic, but only general logical forms applied to law.[14]

If logic is unable to elicit a distinct form of legal reasoning, can it nevertheless illuminate the theory or practice of law? Three principal approaches have emerged. The first and oldest draws upon *traditional logic*: legal argument is analysed with reference to syllogistic structures familiar from classical logic, like the foregoing syllogism. Once maligned as 'mechanical',[15] the versatility of that approach has again drawn attention in studies such as those by Soeteman,[16] Rhodes and Pospesel,[17] and Meier.[18] The second approach involves *deontic logic*. Deontic logic sets forth fundamental relationships among concepts of obligation, permission and prohibition.[19] It has been developed in its most useful form only in recent decades, notably by von Wright.[20] The third approach, and the most influential in

Anglo-American scholarship, is *Hohfeldian analysis*.[21] Hohfeld found that the one word 'right' was being used in ways so divergent as to produce errors in legal reasoning. He sought to ascertain precise distinctions among such concepts as 'claim' (now commonly called 'claim-right'), 'privilege' (now commonly called 'liberty'), 'power' and 'immunity'. Subsequent scholars have refined Hohfeld's system to the point of making it a cornerstone of analytic jurisprudence.[22] These three approaches are not mutually exclusive. Some scholars have wedded deontic and Hohfeldian approaches[23]; and the traditional approach commonly hovers in the background of deontic and Hohfeldian analyses.[24]

This book proposes a fourth method, and can perhaps be understood by situating it with respect to the others. In view of our focus on rights, Hohfeld might at first seem to be of particular importance. Yet Hohfeld does not provide the only formal analysis of rights discourse. (No knowledge of Hohfeld is assumed in this book. The following remarks are intended only for those who might be wondering how the model will resemble or depart from Hohfeld.) In order to focus on certain distinct elements of rights discourse, Hohfeld must bracket out other ones. Following Hohfeld, the men in *Laskey* might have argued that a given man X possessed the 'power' to create a 'liberty' in another man Y for Y to hit X, which in turn endowed both X and Y with an 'immunity' from state intervention. The state might then have responded that X never had any such original power, and thus failed to create any subsequent liberty in X, or immunity in X and Y against the state. On that reading, the dispute turns on *whether* that original power exists in X, and not on how that power is distinct from a right, liberty or immunity.

Hohfeld asks: What is a right? What is a liberty? What is a duty? He responds by inter-defining, and ascertaining the links among, those and related terms. In this study, the question will be: What is a 'liberal right'? What does it mean for a norm to count as a right within a 'liberal regime'? We will seek a systematic, formal account of those concepts, principally through a formal account of the elements of harm and consent. The questions posed about our roomful of scholars can, then, be stated in more general terms: What concepts must be present for them to be discussing *Laskey* as a dispute about 'liberal' rights? Of course, those issues have preoccupied liberal theorists from Locke and Kant to Rawls and Nozik. In two ways, however, this study will differ from theirs. First, those theorists seek a 'macro' account of liberal government and society. By contrast, this study undertakes a 'micro' analysis. It identifies only concepts of 'liberalism', 'paternalism' and 'democracy' generated within a designated legal corpus, and which liberal rights discourse presupposes. Second, this study only examines those theories. It does not advocate or challenge them. It is descriptive, not prescriptive.

It is easy to believe that courts are forever confronted with new disputes, which raise unforeseen issues and require original arguments. It is easy to believe that law is always changing, and legal argument always changing with it, such that creativity on the part of lawyers, judges or scholars can provide illuminating insights. Yet those impressions are only partly accurate. In this study, it will be suggested that arguments about liberal rights, however novel or unusual they may appear, are constrained within the fixed set of background concepts. Those concepts can be stated in definitive terms. We cannot alter them without destroying the very conditions for a jurisprudence of liberal rights.

This book is introductory, but does not provide a general introduction to the field of law and logic. Its purpose is to answer the question initially posed: What body of *Urtheorie* can we discover in liberal rights discourse? It does not ask whether the background concepts are good or bad. It asks only what they are. It is not a 'logic of the better result': it does not propose a model of how controversies should be decided. Indeed, we will see that bad decisions, in so far as they remain within the formally liberal bounds of the background theories, are identical in structure to good ones.[25]

In view of that aim, one might question whether the analysis undertaken in this study is really logic at all, particularly if we understand logic to consist in the analysis of the validity of inferences drawn from premises to conclusions. This study will be concerned with the translation of arguments about rights into precise symbolic language, with the relationships between components of that language, and with the way those arguments then serve as premises to conclusions about whether an asserted right has been violated. It will not, however, require any elaborate calculus for validity testing, for the simple reason that that would not be the most interesting feature of the model. This book could be understood as a preliminary formalisation, which would then pave the way for further refinement, with a view towards a detailed calculus for validity testing. In my view, however, it is those preliminary structures which are the most important. Once the background theories have been ascertained, the ways in which they are then used by jurists or scholars to reason from premises to conclusions will ordinarily be clear through common intuition, without the need for a formal calculus.[26] Although a 'mini-calculus' will be developed, it will serve the limited goal of ascertaining relationships among elements of the model, and will not provide a full-blown technique for validity testing.

If that preliminary function accurately describes this book, then it might be argued that this study is more an exercise in semantics than in logic. I do not entirely disagree. Yet a study of *The Semantics of Liberal Rights* would raise broader questions of rhetoric, hermeneutics or speech pragmatics. The model proposed in this book is limited to the identification of formal concepts presupposed by arguments adduced, in any given case, in favour of, or in opposition to, an assertion that a liberal right should be recognised or applied. It is that relationship of presupposition which, in my view, justifies an understanding of the model as 'logical'.

Overview

By the time of the framing of the Universal Declaration of Human Rights in 1948, concepts of human rights had grown to include economic, social and cultural rights, such as rights to minimum levels of food, employment or education. Since that time, additional concepts of rights have gained ground, such as concepts of peoples' and minorities' rights.[27] This study will focus on individual civil rights and liberties, with particular attention to the case law of the European Convention. That restriction will be imposed for the practical reason that even that more limited corpus is enormous. Social, economic, cultural or group rights may indeed be amenable to formal analysis, but that project will have to wait for another day. Of course, it is now widely accepted that no clear distinctions can be drawn among these various sets of rights. Civil rights and liberties are widely construed to impose affirmative obligations on states.[28] We will consider the consequences.

The earlier and middle parts of the book are largely concerned with the translation of basic components of rights discourse into symbolic form. In the final chapters, the background theories are represented as combinations of those symbols. The results will not be surprising. The six background theories presented in the final chapters are formal concepts of liberalism, paternalism and democracy – concepts already familiar in rights theory. It is generally accepted that rights discourse 'implies' such concepts in a common-sense way. Our task will be to see how, and to what degree, they are implied as a logical matter. Throughout much of the book, readers unfamiliar with formal analysis may wonder why the search for background theories requires a symbolic language. In the final chapters it will become clear that the background theories could not be expressed with ease or precision in ordinary language.[29]

This study contains no analysis of discrimination law. Discrimination raises questions not about whether a right is enjoyed at all, but rather whether it should be enjoyed equally. As I have argued in *The Logic of Equality*,[30] that feature entails a formal structure which, while compatible with the one examined in this book, contains distinctive elements of its own. Also, there is no analysis of the jurisprudence of US constitutional law. That omission may come as a surprise, in view of this book's emphasis on judicial balancing. However, it is precisely because US constitutional law is so complex that it requires a study of its own.[31]

In Parts I to III, as the overall structure and constituents of the model are introduced, special attention is paid to a relatively small number of cases decided under the European Convention of Human Rights.[32] As many of the cases to be examined originated from the UK, the later chapters include a few examples from domestic French, German and Dutch law.[33] However, no familiarity with any of these jurisdictions will be required, as the issues analysed are already widely familiar, including freedom of expression, freedom of religion, privacy, torture, unlawful detention and private property. This book's hypothesis will be that identical forms of argument are to be found in any corpus conventionally recognised as a system of civil rights and liberties, despite the fact that different corpuses may include different rights, or may offer variable degrees of actual protection. As already noted, our roomful of scholars could agree upon factual matters, such as the acts committed or the circumstances of the arrest. But that is not the level of anterior agreement we are seeking. An examination of appellate-level cases will allow us to assume matters of fact to be stipulated, so as to focus on normative disagreements.

A summary of the contents is as follows. Part I examines persons and entities who will be called the *agents* of rights discourse. Chapter 1 prepares the way by introducing some preliminary concepts, beginning with the familiar idea that rights must be balanced against restrictions. The contentious case – court A adjudicating complaint X brought by party *p* against party *q* – is adopted as an exemplar of that balancing process. In Chapter 2, an initial schema of agents is adopted to distinguish between the persons or entities who make arguments, who will be called *parties*, and the persons or entities about whom arguments are made, who will be called *actors*. In Chapters 3 and 4, we examine how the arguments of two kinds of parties – *the claimant*, who asserts a right, and *the respondent*, who seeks a restriction on the right – provide a framework for the model. Chapters 5 to 8 are concerned with actors. Chapters 5 to 7 explore one kind of actor, who will be called *the individual actor*. The focus is on the relationship between individual actors who desire to exercise rights and individual actors who are thereby affected. In Chapter 8, another kind of actor is introduced, namely, all of *society*. We consider what it means to treat such a vast entity as an 'actor'. The relationships among actors, and among arguments about them, are examined in greater detail in Chapters 9 and 10.

In Parts II and III, we turn to two kinds of *interests* which are commonly understood to be attributed to actors in rights arguments: *harm* and *consent*. Part II introduces a formal concept of harm. Chapters 11 and 12, by means of two *harm axioms*, examine how every rights argument presupposes some concept of harm. In Chapters 13 to 16, the various components of the harm axioms are translated into symbolic form. By the time we reach Chapters 15 and 16, the language is sufficiently developed to allow comparisons with standard rights discourse. Part III introduces a formal concept of consent. Chapter 17 examines various meanings of the concept of consent, with particular attention to the traditional distinction between consent in fact and consent in law. In Chapter 18, it is argued that any assertion about harm implies some corresponding assertion about consent, thus generating strict 'pairings' between the harm and consent components of any argument. In Chapter 19, we return to the distinction between consent in fact and in law, in order to refine the concept of consent.

In Parts IV and V, the elements of agents, harm and consent are situated within larger schemes. Part IV prepares the way for identifying the background theories. In Chapter 20, assertions about actors, harm and consent are correlated to arguments about the *breach* or *non-breach* of a right. In Chapter 21, arguments about breach and non-breach are used as a basis for postulating a body of background theories which underlie all arguments. In Chapter 22, the background theories are divided into two general kinds: *individualist* and *collectivist.* In Part V, the background theories are developed in detail. In Chapters 23 and 24, we examine two *individualist* theories which are identified as *liberal.* In Chapter 25, we examine a third individualist theory which is identified as *paternalist.* In Chapter 26, we examine three *collectivist* theories, two of which are identified as *democratic*, and one as *anti-democratic.* Again, there is nothing new about such concepts. However, formal analysis allows us to express and to compare them in terms of a discrete number of shared components.

Part I

Agents

1 Rights and restrictions

Rights are subject to restrictions. This book will examine how arguments are used to strike that balance. Yet the concepts of 'right' and 'restriction' are broad. We begin by adopting a set of 'position axioms' governing the use of those terms. All axioms adopted in this book are compiled in Appendix 1.

1.1 Liberal rights

There is a core of norms which widely recur within regimes of liberal rights, governing such interests as freedom of expression or belief, fair arrest and trial, or humane conditions of detention.[1] Beyond that core, there is no obvious uniformity in the way rights are defined or ascertained. Uncertainty about what is meant by, or included within, 'liberal rights' raises questions about the scope of our analysis. Will it apply to *all* liberal rights? How could such a claim be tested, if there can be no clear agreement on what those rights are?

Consider the following provisions. Article 5 of the German Basic Law provides that 'freedom of reporting by radio and motion pictures is guaranteed. There shall be no censorship'.[2] Article 7 of the Dutch Constitution provides that '[t]here shall be no prior supervision of the content of a radio or television broadcast'.[3] Are those two passages different? Similar? Identical? How would we find out? Through a bilingual dictionary? Through an empirical study? Of what significance would be the fact that both states are parties to the European Convention of Human Rights, or to the International Covenant on Civil and Political Rights?

Generality

One response might be that the two provisions do not express two distinct rights, but rather express only two instances of one broader right, such as a right of free speech, or a right of free expression. But that response merely cloaks the same problem in a new guise, as we must then ask in what ways those two instances are similar or different.

The problem does not arise only with respect to comparisons between jurisdictions. Even within a single jurisdiction, it is not always clear which norm is at issue. In *Laskey*, what is the right sought by the men? A right to engage in certain sadomasochistic acts? Or a right to engage in certain *sexual* acts, which would include certain sadomasochistic acts? Or a still broader right of *intimate association*, which would include certain sexual acts, which would in turn include certain sadomasochistic acts? Or an even broader right of *privacy*, which would, in turn, include each of those? Such questions raise the familiar issue of the correct level of generality at which a legal norm is to be formulated.[4]

Of course, before the European Court, the men can invoke only norms set forth in the treaty and its protocols.[5] The answer to our question might then be: 'the men seek to have the article 8 right of privacy interpreted to protect certain sadomasochistic acts'. Yet that response is purely conventional. It relies on the language which the drafters of the instrument happened to adopt. Only certain historical and cultural circumstances, but nothing in principle, would have prevented the drafters from adopting, say, a more specific 'right of sexual conduct' or 'right of intimate association'. As a functional matter, there may be no difference between saying, in more specific terms, that the men seek 'a right to engage in certain sadomasochistic acts', and saying, more broadly, that the men seek 'protection for certain sadomasochistic acts, as part of the broader article 8 right to privacy'. Similarly, we could combine those two levels of generality by saying that the men seek 'a *right* to engage in certain sadomasochistic acts, as part of the broader article 8 *right* to privacy'.

The point is not that there are never differences among levels of generality. For example, one might want to say that the right at stake in *Laskey* is part of a broader right of 'self-expression'. That formulation, however, could raise issues of free expression under article 10, distinct from those raised under article 8. The point is only that different levels of generality do not *necessarily* comport differences in substance. There are some instances in which they are just two ways of stating the same thing. We therefore adopt:

> **Axiom of Generality**: There is no necessary distinction between a norm in itself and a norm enunciated as part of a broader norm.

By extension, for our purposes there will rarely be any relevant difference between 'recognising' and 'applying' a right. In most cases, those locutions merely reflect more general ('applying') or more specific ('recognising') levels of generality. A categorically distinct act of recognition would occur only where there is no higher level of generality.

Recognition

But we still have not answered the initial question: What norms will count as liberal rights for our analysis? For several reasons, it would be impossible to adopt an 'extensional' definition of liberal rights – a list which would be both exhaustive and unambiguous. No single list could provide a full account of all jurisdictions maintaining regimes of liberal rights. Even a list for one jurisdiction would be impossible. It would require clarity and agreement on the scope of each right, which is barely to be found in practice, and, in any event, shuns enumeration in list form, as any treatise will demonstrate. Moreover, such a list would exclude future developments. Nor is any 'intensional' definition imaginable – a definition which would provide a prior, fixed criterion for identifying which norms do and do not count as liberal rights. In view of endless ambiguities and disagreements surrounding many rather specific rights, we could hardly expect greater clarity or agreement at a higher level of abstraction.

Could we begin with Hohfeldian theory, drawing initial distinctions between concepts of 'claim-right', 'liberty', 'immunity' and 'power'? In *Laskey*, the two crucial sets of arguments are the men's arguments *favouring* an interpretation of article 8 so as to protect their sadomasochistic conduct, pitted against the state's arguments *opposing* that interpretation. It is *those* arguments which we will seek to examine. As noted in the Introduction, the difference between them does not turn on any Hohfeldian distinction. Similarly, we might want to begin with such deontic categories as 'obligation', 'permission' and 'prohibition'. Yet the question of how those terms apply to the interests at stake in a given case can be decided only after some determination of what those interests are.

None of the foregoing approaches provides a satisfactory starting point. Instead, we will adopt a conventional description:

> **Axiom of Recognition**: A right is liberal if it is recognised within a corpus conventionally regarded as a body of liberal rights.

We will examine specimens from an existing corpus of law generally regarded as a corpus of 'liberal rights' or 'civil rights and liberties', without assuming from the outset any conceptual link between those labels and that corpus. Ascertaining that link will be the aim of the book.

It may appear odd to use the term 'axiom' for a principle which depends on a conventionally defined corpus. Yet that step underscores two points. First, it would be difficult to frame a concept of an isolated or free-floating liberal right within an otherwise non-liberal regime. We will see that a right becomes liberal within a comprehensive body of norms. The background theories will arise as a unified network. We will have to analyse a variety of rights in order to identify them. Second, the word 'recognised' is key, as illustrated by a trivial example. Assume a legal rule that prohibits detonation of atomic bombs by civilians. Dexter challenges the rule, claiming that he can express his views on life only by detonating atomic bombs. Any arguments on the merits will then consist of Dexter's assertion that he has a right to detonate atomic bombs pitted against the state's assertion that he has no such right. For purposes of our model, the right exists as a liberal right in so far as Dexter's arguments succeed ('are recognised'), and does not exist in so far as they fail ('are not recognised'). Every other claim will be treated identically. The triviality or ludicrousness of Dexter's claim is irrelevant. Yet if the Axiom of Recognition is purely conventional, how can we hope to identify norms that are distinctly 'liberal'? How are 'liberal' rights to be distinguished, say, from 'ordinary', private-law rights? That question is examined in Section 1.4.

1.2 Restrictions

The only aim of this study is to ascertain the background theories. That point will be repeated on a number of occasions, as it will justify a series of simplifying assumptions which might otherwise be unwarranted. Those assumptions will include definitions of certain specified terms – like 'harm' or 'consent' – to allow them to cover a broader range of circumstances than would be customary in ordinary usage, and to do so in a way that will be free of the ambiguities of ordinary language. We can now turn to one example.

Rights can be obstructed in countless ways. In this study, all means of obstructing the exercise of rights will be called *restrictions*. Just as we are assuming no fixed criteria governing the content of rights, we will assume no fixed criteria governing the range of possible restrictions. Hence, a simplifying principle:

> **Axiom of Restrictions**: A restriction is any means by which a person or entity impedes the right-seeker in, or penalises the right-seeker for, the exercise of an asserted right.

That axiom raises a number of difficulties, which must be addressed in turn.

Variety of 'restrictions'

The term 'restriction', defined so broadly, embraces any number of familiar concepts: 'deprivation', 'denial', 'encroachment', 'incursion', 'infringement', 'interference', 'limitation', 'regulation'. Those terms commonly comport differences in meaning or nuance, and are not all interchangeable in standard legal usage. For example, a 'deprivation' may be distinguished from a 'limitation' or 'regulation' in order to denote a full denial of a right (e.g. where private property is wholly appropriated by the state without compensation) as opposed to a partial constraint (e.g. where discrete restrictions are imposed on the use of property which nonetheless remains profitably usable). Similarly, distinctions between acts and omissions can leave the blanket term 'restriction' sounding inapposite when applied to an omission: if a state is accused of not doing enough to give effect to a right, we would not colloquially refer to such inaction as a 'restriction'. Moreover, in a case of extreme abuse, such as extrajudicial killing or torture, it might sound banal to speak merely of a 'restriction' on the corresponding right. However, the term 'restriction' will be used to include all of those circumstances, in so far as they all comport *a purpose or effect of extinguishing or diminishing the right-seeker's enjoyment of an asserted right.* (The only significant distinction which will be drawn will be between that concept of 'restriction' and the concept of 'breach' or 'violation'. The terms 'breach' or 'violation' will be used to denote a judicial determination about the *legality* of the restriction.[6]) Such an axiom may seem unwelcome, in so far as it obliterates subtleties which one would have thought to be useful in law. It must be stressed that we are seeking to eliminate that variety of terms not for all purposes, but only for the very narrow purposes of a formal model, for which any distinctions among them are irrelevant.

Completed and prospective acts and omissions

In some cases, a restriction may literally mean that the party seeking to exercise a right is prevented from doing so. For example, people may refrain altogether from committing acts of sadomasochism, fearing the legal consequences. Or a prior restraint may be imposed on a newspaper to prohibit publication of an article. In other cases, as in *Laskey*, the right-seekers' acts or omissions have already been completed, but have then resulted in a legal penalty. In this study, the term 'restriction' will be used in both senses. For our purposes, terms such as 'seeking recognition of' or 'seeking exercise of' a right will apply equally to past and future conduct. Similarly, we will speak of persons or entities 'seeking a restriction' on an asserted right, referring not only to prospective attempts to impede the relevant acts or omissions, but also to attempts to uphold sanctions already imposed.

'Restriction' as non-existence of a right

In some cases, there may be agreement between disputing parties that a given right is *relevant* to the act or omission in question – their disagreement being about whether the scope of that right should be extended to protect *that* act or omission. As we have seen, that disagreement may depend merely on the level of generality at which a right is articulated. If *Laskey* is understood as a dispute about a right to engage in certain acts of sadomasochism, then the dispute between the men and the state is categorical. If it is understood more broadly in terms of the right to privacy, then the British government does not disagree about the existence of the right, but only on whether it should be construed to protect certain acts of sadomasochism.

In some cases, however, the existence of any relevant right is denied. That denial could be construed as an assertion that no restriction is being placed on any right, since there is no right to restrict. For example, the case of *Johnston v. Ireland*[7] was brought by individuals complaining about provisions of Irish law which prohibited divorce. They argued that article 12 of the European Convention, which sets forth a right to marry,[8] must also include the right to obtain a divorce.[9] The Court, however, finding that article 12 did not encompass the right to obtain a divorce, concluded that the Convention did not include any right under which the complaint could be heard.[10] That finding could be construed to mean that Irish law did not restrict any right to obtain a divorce under the European Convention, as no such right existed. For our purposes, however, a denial that a right exists will be treated as a restriction, i.e. as a restriction on an asserted right. For *Johnston*, we can say, again depending merely on our chosen level of generality, that Irish law restricted the exercise either (1) of an asserted right to obtain a divorce, under article 12; or (2) of the right to marry under article 12, interpreted to encompass a right to divorce. On either reading, we will say that the Court upheld the restriction – and not that there was no relevant right.

'Restriction' as derogation

It is widely accepted in liberal regimes that rights may be suspended during declared states of emergency.[11] For example, article 15(1) of the European Convention provides in part:

> In time of war or other public emergency threatening the life of the nation any High Contracting Party may take measures derogating from its obligations under this Convention to the extent strictly required by the exigencies of the situation.

Under article 15(2), derogation shall not apply to certain rights:

> No derogation from Article 2, except in respect of deaths resulting from lawful acts of war, or from Articles 3, 4 (paragraph 1) and 7 shall be made under this provision.[12]

States could seek to rebut complaints brought under Convention articles which are not excluded under article 15(2) by arguing that the obligation in question was not binding during a declared state of emergency – that, during that period, the state's obligation, and the correlative individual right, temporarily 'ceased to exist'. It might not be customary to speak of the suspension of rights as a 'restriction', as that term ordinarily connotes a limit on a right which *is* in effect. However, as nothing in our analysis will be affected by that distinction, we will understand the concept of 'restriction' to include derogation.

'Restriction' as a countervailing right

In some cases, what we are calling a restriction might be the assertion of a countervailing right. Consider the case of John, who brings a private suit to enjoin, or to seek compensation for, the publication of a newspaper article written by another individual, Mary, on grounds of invasion of privacy. Depending on the facts which give rise to the dispute, it might be John who asserts a right of privacy, and Mary who seeks a restriction on that right by asserting her interest in free expression (e.g. where John sues for a prior restraint). Alternatively, it might be Mary who asserts a right of free expression, and John who seeks a restriction on that right by asserting his interest in privacy (e.g. where Mary subsequently appeals against a prior restraint successfully procured by John).

These scenarios also show how a case may start out as a dispute about one right, but then turn into a dispute about another. If John wins a prior restraint based on his asserted right of privacy, the litigation could continue – say, in an appellate forum, or in an international forum, such as the European Court – as a claim about Mary's right of free expression. (Indeed, there are cases in which the *same kind* of interest could be adduced both for asserting the right *and* for asserting the restriction. In a child custody dispute, for example, two disputing parents might both base their opposing claims on an interest in privacy or family life.) In such cases, how should we decide whose claim to treat as an assertion of a right, and whose claim to treat as seeking a restriction on that right?

One solution is simply to examine a dispute as it was in fact litigated. Meanwhile, as to hypothetical cases, such as the dispute between John and Mary, we can simply stipulate whose claim will be treated as asserting a right and whose claim will be treated as asserting a restriction on that right. In fact, for the most part, that is the solution we will adopt. However, a new problem then arises. If we wish to analyse more than one phase of litigation, our notation system would become untidy – that is, still feasible in principle, but unnecessarily complex – if the roles reverse when the case passes to another stage of litigation. As our aim is only to record the structure of substantive arguments about the merits of the dispute, our job will be easier if we can assign roles which remain fixed throughout all stages of the litigation.

Consider an example from the 1986 case of *Lingens v. Austria*.[13] In 1975, Lingens, an Austrian journalist, published two articles accusing the

State Chancellor, Bruno Kreisky, of having expressed sympathy with persons or events of the Nazi past. Kreisky then brought a private criminal prosecution for defamation against Lingens in the Austrian courts. (Be sure to keep these facts of *Lingens* in mind, as this case will be discussed frequently in the next few chapters.) In the abstract, such an action could, with equal plausibility, be construed in terms of Kreisky's civil rights (right to protection of reputation) or in terms of Lingens's civil rights (freedom of speech, freedom of the press).

We must nevertheless choose *some* distribution of roles. If we wanted to focus our attention on the litigation in the national courts, we could choose a distribution under which it would be Kreisky who asserts the right, and Lingens who seeks the restriction. That would be a perfectly valid distribution, and our model would apply without difficulty. However – for no reason other than a desire to use a corpus which will be familiar, and easily available, to a greater number of readers – we will use the distribution which reflects the litigation of the dispute in the judgment of the European Court. At that stage of the dispute, it was Lingens who asserted a right of freedom of expression under article 10(1), while the Austrian state, under article 10(2), defended a restriction on that right[14] that had been upheld in Kreisky's favour in the national courts.[15]

Although our overall focus in *Lingens* is, then, on the European Court, we may nevertheless wish to refer to arguments which were made in the national courts. Therefore, for the sole purpose of consistency in the recording of arguments, we will apply that same role distribution throughout all stages of the litigation. We will analyse even the phase of the dispute in the national courts in terms of Lingens's asserted right to free expression and Kreisky's assertion of a restriction on that right. In later chapters, we will examine a few cases from national courts which did not go before the European Commission or Court. In those cases, we will choose the role distribution relevant to the particular judgment we are examining.

'Restriction' as a benefit

Assume that a group of prisoners is offered the following choice: either to accept severe corporal punishment along with a chance of parole, or to forgo corporal punishment, by waiving any chance of parole. The prisoners choose the former. On their behalf, a complaint of torture or inhuman or degrading treatment is then brought under article 3 of the Convention. The state responds: 'The prisoners freely chose corporal punishment, and are receiving a benefit for it. Nothing can be both a benefit and a restriction. Therefore, no restriction has been placed on their article 3 rights.' Of course, the state's argument is fallacious. Perhaps no *one* thing can be both a benefit and a restriction. In this case, however, two things are involved. One of them (the chance of parole) may indeed be a benefit, but the other (the corporal punishment) remains a restriction on the article 3 right. Even if we were to accept that the benefit *justifies* the restriction, that in no way means that the benefit obliterates the restriction. For our model, we will refer to *all* restrictions as such, regardless of whether they are ultimately held to be justified. (As to justifications for a 'benefit-restriction' of this type, we will see later on how they use concepts of harm and consent.[16])

1.3 Contentious character

Balances between rights and restrictions are struck in several ways. Sometimes attempts to strike the balance are worked into an authoritative text. For example, in several articles of the European Convention, as in many international and national instruments, the general statement of a right is followed by limiting provisions, as we have just seen in article 10.[17] Evidence about the intended balance between rights and restrictions may also be sought in records of the discussions and debates (*travaux préparatoires*) leading to the drafting of such a text.[18] In some jurisdictions, another means of striking the balance is through advisory opinions, whereby a court is asked to provide a general statement about the interpretation of the right, without reference to a dispute between particular parties.[19]

In the present study, the focus will be on the *contentious case*,[20] brought by one party against another within a judicial[21] forum. Two objections might be raised to that approach. First, readers from civil-law traditions may suspect that such a choice assumes a common law bias, disproportionately emphasising the judicial function. However, the analysis will treat contentious cases only as examples of rights balancing, without regard to the legal status of judicial holdings in any given jurisdiction. Questions of judicial precedent, often prominent in common-law scholarship, will assume no special role. By the end of the book, it should be clear that the same general forms of arguments about the balance between rights and restrictions are identical in common-law and civil-law jurisdictions, and structure debate in other fora, such as legislative or administrative bodies, and among the broader public. To be sure, the focus on cases of the European Court of Human Rights arises largely from the fact that they provide detailed reasons for the decisions reached,[22] as well as separate opinions of individual judges,[23] some of which will come under scrutiny in our analysis. Nevertheless, we will see that, even in jurisdictions where it is common for a judicial decision to be issued with no extensive *ratio decidendi* (*jugement non motivé*), the relevant substantive controversies and corresponding arguments are rarely difficult to surmise.

Second, it might be objected that such an approach is unduly confrontational, neglecting processes such as negotiation or alternative dispute resolution. Yet the fact that our framework is conflictual does not mean that the parties to a dispute are precluded from friendly settlement – which, indeed, may still proceed in the shadow of prospective litigation. The means chosen to resolve a dispute is important, but is distinct from questions about the structure of liberal rights discourse. One consequence of adopting a contentious framework is that some degree of stasis is assumed. All kinds of dialogue, negotiation, compromise and evolution of arguments may transpire around a dispute; but, ultimately, the contentious framework presupposes that there is some stand-off, that there is some insuperable disagreement as to the recognition or application of some right. That disagreement will be assumed to provide the central structure of the case.

Disputes about rights do not arise in a vacuum. They commonly arise with other legal issues. For example, if a subordinate unit of government, such as a municipality, imposes a restriction on some individual's freedom of expression, questions might arise not only about the substantive legitimacy of the restriction, but also about whether that unit of government acted within its powers. A finding that that the restriction was imposed *ultra vires* might dispose of the case, obviating the need for argument on substantive grounds.[24] In this analysis, however, we will examine only arguments about the substantive merits of claims.[25]

A further element can now be added to our conventional concept of the liberal right:

> **Axiom of Contentious Character**: A right is liberal only if it can in principle conflict with some ascertainable restriction.

That axiom does not state that any norm which can in principle conflict with some ascertainable restriction *is* a liberal right (as the sheer ability to conflict with some restriction can also be predicated of many ordinary norms in contract, property or tort which may not be incorporated within systems conventionally recognised as liberal rights regimes). Rather, more modestly, the axiom states that *if* a right is formally liberal, then it can in principle conflict with some ascertainable restriction. The axiom sets forth a necessary, not a sufficient condition for a right to qualify as liberal.

Such an axiom may seem questionable in extreme cases. Surely we can concoct nightmare scenarios in which we could imagine no possible restriction on a right. For example, it would seem that there are no grounds on which a government of a healthy and prosperous state could authorise the mass killing of children. It would seem that the right of children to be protected in that situation must be absolute, subject to no *conceivable* restriction. Here, however, we must be careful in the use of language. That scenario may preclude *plausible* restrictions on rights; it cannot, however, preclude *possible,* i.e. *conceivable* or *imaginable* ones – which, arguably, are infinite in number. *Conceivably*, it could be argued that the government wants to commit the act for purposes of controlling a contagious disease, or as a secondary effect of bombing a separatist insurgency in areas near schools. Those rationales are horrific because they *are* conceivable. Conceivable restrictions are possible for any liberal right, and that is all that is meant by the requirement that the right be able to conflict, in principle, with some ascertainable restriction. (It is also a reason why the model will apply to hypothetical or non-judicial contexts. In legislative or popular debate, speculation about possible restrictions, with or without prior real-world precedents, is not unusual.) The axiom requires, as a minimum ingredient, a regime in which the question of balancing rights against restrictions can always arise as a formal matter, even where, as a substantive matter, everyone agrees on how certain cases would be decided.

1.4 The liberal element of legal argument

The goal of ascertaining a distinctly liberal element in rights discourse raises some preliminary questions. The term 'liberal' is commonly used to denote a set of political ideals, but can it be made precise enough to represent distinct structural components of legal argument? (The discussion in this section is not essential to the structure of the model and can be read later on.)

The 'liberal' right

In view of the conventionally defined Axiom of Recognition and the broadly defined Axiom of Restriction, can we ascertain a characteristically liberal element that would distinguish argument about civil rights and liberties from argument about other legal norms? Can argument about 'liberal' rights be distinguished categorically from argument about 'ordinary' rights in contract, property or tort? Consider a run-of-the-mill private-law dispute. Farmer Fatima has struck a deal to deliver 500 litres of fresh but perishable cream to baker Bernard. Before delivery, Bernard attempts to rescind the deal, and refuses to accept the cream when it arrives. Failing to sell the cream elsewhere, Fatima sues Bernard for her losses. What is to stop farmer Fatima from bringing a claim against baker Bernard as a 'civil' right? Indeed, if Fatima loses that suit, what is to stop her from bringing a claim against the state to the European Court?

For our purposes, nothing. Barring any procedural, jurisdictional or other non-merit-based issue,[26] the Court could accept or dismiss the complaint only on the *substantive* grounds of its 'well-foundedness'.[27] In other words, trivially, the Court must follow the Axiom of Recognition, by deciding which rights will and will not be recognised, either at the admissibility stage or through adjudication. In fact, it is perfectly plausible that a body of civil rights and liberties could include certain rights between private parties.[28] There are notorious historical precedents for the elevation of private-law rights to higher-law status, even if some have fallen into disfavour today.[29]

The question then arises as to the substantive basis for accepting or rejecting Fatima's claim. Consider the following objection. It could be contended that all individual rights, including rights in contract, property or tort, are by definition liberal. On that view, there can be no concept of liberal rights as distinct from individual rights generally. Civil rights and liberties might have a distinct moral or political status, but no legal character different from that of other rights. Let's call that argument a *theory of the implicit liberalism of rights* (in short, *the liberal theory*). It could run as follows:

1 An individual right protects an individual interest.
2 Yet an individual right protects an individual interest only if it is subject to the rule of law.
3 If an individual right, subject to the rule of law, protects an individual interest, then that individual right is a liberal right.

From those premises it follows that any individual right is *ipso facto* a liberal right.[30]

Let us assume that thesis 1 is uncontroversial.[31] What is the justification for thesis 2? Here is one example. If it is found in court that Fatima has a right to compensation from Bernard, then, under the rule of law, government may not, except in accordance with law, prevent her from collecting damages. Her right to collect compensation from Bernard is a bundle of rights. One of its strands is a right against arbitrary government interference, which presupposes the rule of law. As to thesis 3, in so far as Fatima's bundle of rights to compensation includes that right against arbitrary government interference, it is formally indistinguishable from any 'civil' right which Fatima may have against government. If government were to annul the judgment against Bernard willy-nilly, Fatima would have legal recourse, just as she would have if government imprisoned her for her religious or political beliefs. Fatima's 'public' suit against government for annulling the judgment does not meaningfully differ from her 'private' suit against Bernard: a structurally identical concept of right is maintained, but is now merely directed against government, rather than Bernard. In *Fatima v. Bernard*, the duty correlative to the asserted right is upon Bernard; in *Fatima v. State*, it is upon government.

In rebuttal, one might propose a *theory of the non-implicit liberalism of rights* (in short, *the classical-positivist theory*[32]). One could reject thesis 2 by arguing that, under an absolute Hobbesian or Austinian sovereign, Fatima could lawfully win a judgment against Bernard, even if it were possible that government might abrogate it willy-nilly. The specific content of the right would be modified so as to include that eventuality, but its overall right-duty structure would otherwise remain intact. Accordingly, a legal norm can protect an individual interest – less securely, perhaps, but still effectively – without the rule of law. (It might also be noted in passing that the 'individual' referred to in thesis 2 could be an absolute monarch, whose 'individual interests' could by definition be protected, indeed would be better protected, without recourse to the rule of law.)

Hohfeldian analysis can accommodate either theory, as long as the assumptions made in each case are clear. On behalf of the liberal theory, it could be said that the configuration of claim-rights, liberties, powers or immunities which constitute a given right are plausible – are saved from becoming impossible fictions – only in so far as they are not subject to sudden and arbitrary abrogation. After all, what kind of claim-right, liberty, power or immunity do I have if the legal system can never assume its effectiveness? Hohfeldian analysis requires the liberal theory if we assume that the Hohfeldian categories are meaningful only when secured by some measure of settled expectations.

By contrast, the Hohfeldian categories can accommodate the positivist theory if they *are* stipulated to be perpetually subordinated to any contrary act of government. Fatima then has both (a) a claim against Bernard, subject to any contrary act of government, and (b) a claim against government, subject to the government's contrary act. To the liberal theorist's objection that the Hohfeldian concepts are eviscerated by that stipulation, the positivist will respond that the sheer possibility of arbitrary negation does not equal its actuality. To the extent that the norm is *not* abrogated by government, to the extent that (any form of) government is willing to assure execution of Fatima's judgment against Bernard, that private-law judgment operates fully to secure an individual right. The positivist sees a liberal regime as one possible legal order, but not as a necessary condition for individual rights. If Fatima can bring a suit against government for arbitrarily annulling the judgment against Bernard, that distinct strand within the bundle is indeed secured by the rule of law. However, that strand is distinct from her right to compensation vis-à-vis Bernard, which does not presuppose the rule of law. Accordingly, there can be individual rights which do not presuppose the rule of law. So there can be individual rights which are not liberal. A search for the distinguishing features of those rights which *are* liberal is, then, entirely plausible.

As that positivist challenge to thesis 2 suffices to illuminate the controversy for our immediate purposes, we need not further examine thesis 3. Our present concern is with the effects of the two theories on the background theories. If the positivist theory were correct, then we could continue in the hope of ascertaining an essential character distinct to the discourse of civil rights and liberties. If the liberal theory were correct, the fact that all individual rights are liberal would make the particular designation of a civil rights and liberties corpus within the legal system as 'liberal' appear purely conventional. Of course, a thorough confrontation between these two theories would take us well beyond the scope of this study. Moreover, in view of the already wide scope of civil rights and liberties, this study cannot undertake a systematic analysis of private-law disputes. However, in the final chapters an intermediate position between the two approaches will be suggested. The point of the model will not be to draw a bright line between 'liberal' and 'ordinary' rights. We will see that some ordinary rights disputes can indeed be explained in terms of the background theories. To that extent, the background theories elicit elements of a private-law dispute which raise problems distinct to the concerns of liberal society. Nevertheless, the *Urtheorie* will serve as a paradigm for civil rights and liberties disputes in a more rigorous and pervasive way than it would do for private law.[33]

The 'liberal' regime

A question also arises about the possibility of a sham regime. A sham liberal regime, a regime liberal in name only, can be said to be liberal *in form* only, e.g. by maintaining charters of rights which, in practice, are not observed because restrictions (e.g. appeals to 'public order' or 'national security') are maintained willy-nilly. The analysis will assume that a formal distinction can be drawn between that kind of sham-liberal regime and a regime which raises no pretence of respecting rights (even if no functional distinction can be drawn between the two). Indeed, in today's world, the latter kind of regime has almost disappeared. The model will apply to all contemporary states, in so far as all states today do maintain at least nominal regimes of individual rights. North Korea and Libya have both acceded to the International Covenant on Civil and Political Rights, even if outside observers would find that citizens of those states enjoy little real protection.

The result is that this study would be boring – repetitively predictable – as applied to North Korea or Libya, not that it is precluded in principle. Western European jurisdictions provide fertile terrain because they have generated and published a more intricate web of conflicts between rights and restrictions. The difference between a liberal regime and an expressly non-liberal regime is that legal argument presupposes the background theories in the liberal regime, but not in the non-liberal regime. By contrast, the difference between a genuine liberal regime and a sham one runs along different lines. The more a regime is a genuine liberal democracy, the more all six background theories will play robust roles in litigation, and in public and legislative debate. All of the background theories will have vocal and effective advocates over a wide variety of issues. The earmark of a controversial case will be the difficulty in determining which background theory will or should prevail. Where a regime is only a sham liberal democracy, the background theories are detectable, but it will usually be easy to predict which will prevail, namely, the one which favours government interests.[34] (It is also worth noting a sociological, anthropological or historiographic role for the model: the model might serve to ascertain genuinely liberal elements in a system which does not expressly purport to be liberal. Past or present societies having had minimal or no contact with Western liberalism might be found to reflect the model in their systems for resolving disputes, through their manner of weighing and balancing conflicting interests. But that possibility is mentioned here only in passing. It will not be pursued.)

1.5 The model in context

If the background concepts will represent the locus of agreement presupposed by any disagreement, then they cannot themselves be committed to any particular doctrinal or theoretical viewpoints. Although some well-known themes in legal theory pertain to the model, from traditions as diverse as classical positivism and American legal realism, analytic jurisprudence and critical legal studies, their influence nevertheless leaves the model's purely formal character intact. Those schools will not receive detailed attention, as that would require a different kind of work; but a brief review of them will help to place the remainder of the work in a more familiar context. (Readers not immediately concerned with these issues can skip this section.)

Law and morals

One role of the model will be to suggest a rewriting of John Stuart Mill's theory of individual rights, as set forth in *On Liberty*,[35] and as modified through the famous Hart–Devlin debate, including Hart's concept of paternalism.[36] Mill correctly understood that the decisive elements of civil rights and liberties are concepts of harm and consent. It is within a framework set by those concepts that the roomful of scholars is conducting its discussion. The book's aim is to see how liberal rights disputes can be understood entirely in terms of harm and consent, as long as those terms remain purely formal – as long as they are defined such that no consensus about their substantive content need ever be reached.

Of course, Mill did not seek to define harm and consent in exclusively formal terms, and attempts to win agreement on substantive concepts of harm and consent have forever after gone awry: *Who's to say what 'harm' is? What is 'consent'?*[37] We cannot blame Mill, Hart or Devlin for failing to adopt purely formal concepts of harm and consent, as they were concerned with specific legal reform, which required substantive concepts. Our concern is different. Through formal concepts of harm and consent, we will be able to dissect rights discourse without having to commit ourselves to any substantive position on the nineteenth-century Mill–Stephen debate or its twentieth-century Hart–Devlin analogue. Those controversies commonly centred on such issues as alcohol consumption or sexual morality; but we will see how every liberal rights dispute is structured in terms that are formal analogues of the concepts of liberalism, paternalism or community interest, which emerged from those debates.

Open texture

Another central theme in legal theory concerns open texture and indeterminacy in legal norms. For Hart, the two terms are related:

> Whichever device, precedent or legislation, is chosen for the communication of standards of behaviour, these, however smoothly they work over the great mass of ordinary cases, will, at some point where their application is in question, prove indeterminate; they will have what has been termed an *open texture*.[38]

For other scholars the two concepts are distinct. In Dworkin's work, open texture in controversial cases – the point at which no one rule clearly or unambiguously governs – is where deeper principles inherent in the legal order can and do operate to avoid the thoroughgoing indeterminacy which would make the judge an *ad hoc* legislator.[39]

The issue of open texture serves to stake out divisions among a number of theoretical schools,[40] even schools which, on other points, strongly diverge. We can use the broad term *analytic-positivist* to denote an approach to open texture running through Bentham, Austin, Kelsen, Hart and *Begriffsjurisprudenz*. By contrast, the term *critical-realist* can be used to denote an approach found in American legal realism and the *Freirechtsschule*, and continuing through to critical legal studies, deconstructionism and postmodernism. A familiar dichotomy can then be sketched as follows. The analytic-positivist approaches depict law as sufficiently autonomous and self-contained to be able to operate straightforwardly upon 'the great mass of ordinary cases'. On that view, open texture is exceptional, incidental or peripheral. By contrast, for the critical-realist schools, open texture becomes central – a key indicator of (depending on the particular school) law's disjointed, improvised or even arbitrary and internally contradictory character.

From the critical-realist approach, the analysis will adopt the hypothesis that open texture in liberal rights discourse does indeed entail a fundamental element of indeterminacy – the crucial difference being that the model here will be concerned solely with the *formally* determinate and indeterminate elements of liberal rights discourse.[41] That difference prevents it from having to adopt a concept of *substantive* indeterminacy, thus avoiding the need to compare concepts of open texture in, say, the theories of Holmes, Frank, Kennedy or Unger.

Yet that distinction between the analytic-positivist and the critical-realist approaches must not be drawn too tightly, lest we overlook an important area of agreement between them. The analytic-positivist movements may downplay open texture, but cannot ignore it. It remains crucial to their project of renouncing natural law. Open texture is one of the key moments at which the natural-law theorist wants to show that higher moral principles can serve to resolve controversial cases. The analytic-positivist schools need an explanation of open texture which will show that the filling of gaps need not be explained through reference to transcendental, extra-legal norms. Yet that position holds just as strongly for critical-realist schools. It is hardly controversial to note an important point of agreement between the analytic-positivist and the critical-realist schools, namely, a rejection of any thesis that the very concepts of law or justice must implicitly assume a thoroughgoing set of preordained norms or principles.

The model presented here will emerge at that narrow intersection of the analytic-positivist and the critical-realist approaches. Again, from the critical-realist schools, this study will adopt the view that a fundamental element of determinacy and indeterminacy underlies liberal rights discourse. But that is precisely where an analytic-positivist element also kicks in: it would be a mistake to think that the *fact* of open texture means that any *analysis of it* must itself be fundamentally open-ended, or that a theory of indeterminacy must itself be indeterminate.[42] A rigorous *analysis of* open texture need not thereby leave open texture less open. It can simply pinpoint the extent and limits of open texture. And that is the aim of this study: an analysis of formal elements of open texture is undertaken in order to chart the extent and limits of formal determinacy in liberal rights discourse. From analytic-positivism, then, and notably from Kelsen, this study adopts the view that there is a determinate, underlying structure to the corpus in question – that even substantive indeterminacy, and a fortiori substantive determinacy, presuppose a formal determinacy.

Yet if the common locus within which this study emerges is an attack on classical natural law, does that mean that the book must at least assume an anti-naturalist position? No. The attack on natural law which unites critical-realist and analytic-positivist schools is substantive, and thus goes a step further than is required for the study: it entails the substantive rejection of a higher-law regime beyond positive law. The model presented here will draw from the common locus of analytic-positivist and critical-realist positions only the more modest (arguably obvious) thesis that, in a conflict between right and restriction, even an 'easy' one, no result is dictated as formal matter. That more modest view is fully compatible with natural-law theory, or indeed with Fullerian or Dworkian jurisprudence. The model will only display the formal structure of arguments, not their substantive strength or weakness, plausibility or implausibility. The aim is to identify the background theories upon which the schools proffering various theses about liberal rights must agree if they are all to be talking about the same thing.

Review these terms

1 liberal right (*conventional concept*)
2 restriction
3 contentious character

2 Overview of agents

In the next few chapters, we will encounter a variety of persons and entities who populate rights discourse. Collectively, they will be called *agents*. They will be divided into two kinds: *parties* and *actors*. While those words are familiar in English. Meanings will be assigned to them for purposes of the analysis, as has just been done with the terms 'right' and 'restriction'.

2.1 Definitions

Arguments adduced in contentious cases have two basic features: they are *about* certain persons or entities, and they are *made by* certain persons or entities:

1 The term *actors* will be used to designate the persons or entities *about whom arguments are made* – the persons or entities to whom interests are attributed in arguments about rights.
2 The term *parties* will designate the persons or entities *who make* those arguments within the context of a contentious case. (We will see that a party and an actor can be, but are not always, the same person or entity.[1])
3 Accordingly, the term *agents* will encompass the entire set of *parties* and *actors*.

The task throughout these initial chapters will be to refine the concept of 'agents' by refining the concepts of 'actors' and 'parties'.

2.2 Basic schema: the 'tree diagram'

To distinguish between the two basic kinds of agents, we will arrange them within a simple schema. The lower-case Greek letter ψ (psi) will represent the possible agents. The letter θ (theta) will represent the possible parties. The letter α (alpha) will represent the possible actors. The relationships among those three elements is illustrated in the tree diagram in Figure 2.1.

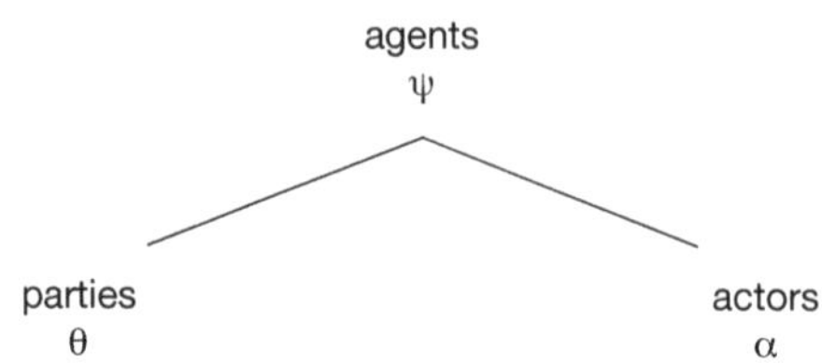

Figure 2.1

The letter ψ in Figure 2.1 is a *variable* – a symbol which can individually represent more than one of the elements within the system – as it can represent θ or α. We will see that θ is also a variable, in so far as it can represent more than one kind of party, and α is a variable, in so far as it can represent more than one kind of actor. As the analysis progresses, refinement of the schema will mean that new branches will be added. In symbolic languages, any figure at all can be used as a symbol, and will mean nothing more than what it is defined to mean. For our model, the two alphabets will be used only as a rough-and-ready code for recording overall relationships among symbols. As a rule of thumb, Roman variables will be used to represent more specific, or 'concrete', elements, while Greek variables will be used to represent more general, or abstract, elements.[2] But that distinction should be seen only as a convenience. All symbols, along with important formulas, are compiled in Appendix 2.

2.3 Postulates

A more concise means of stating relationships among elements of the model will also be used. The term *formula* will be used to denote *a statement expressed in symbolic form.* The term *postulate* (Ps) will be used to denote *a formula that defines a set of possible values of a symbol by means of other symbols.* In order to denote the set of *values* which can be assumed by a variable, the symbol '$\subset$' will be placed after that variable, followed by the possible values. A postulate can be used to define the set of possible values of the variable ψ,

$$\text{Ps}(\psi) \quad \psi \subset \theta, \alpha$$

All postulates introduced in the book are compiled in Appendix 2.

Review these terms

1. actor
2. party
3. agent
4. variable
5. postulate

3 Parties

This chapter introduces the two *parties* to disputes in contentious cases. They are called the *claimant* and the *respondent.* Those terms are assigned symbols which provide a framework for recording arguments in symbolic form. Further features of the symbolic language are then examined.

3.1 Claimant and respondent

Legal systems assign all kinds of names to parties in dispute: plaintiff and defendant, *requérant* and *défendeur, Kläger* and *Beklagte.* Even within one system, various names appear, depending on the type, or stage, of the litigation: plaintiff, defendant, appellant, respondent, petitioner. . . . For our purposes, all of those variations will be cast aside. The term *claimant* will designate *the party asserting a right.* The claimant seeks recognition or application of, and thereby challenges some restriction on, a right, regardless of the jurisdiction in which, or the stage of litigation at which, or the rules of legal personality or judicial standing under which, the claim is brought. The claimant may be a lone individual, but also an organisation, business enterprise or any other entity entitled, within a given jurisdiction, to bring a complaint.[1] In many cases, claimants bring the dispute on their own behalf: it is *their* right that they are asserting. But that is not always the case. Liberal regimes generally provide for claims to be brought on someone else's behalf, as in the case of minors or persons deemed incompetent.[2]

The term *respondent* will be used to designate *the party seeking a restriction on the right.* The respondent opposes recognition or application of a right, seeking to maintain or to procure some restriction on it. In many disputes, the respondent is a state government. For example, the European Court of Human Rights is authorised to hear complaints only against states.[3] Where no such condition applies, the respondent can also be a private party.[4]

In some cases, that use of the terms 'claimant' and 'respondent' will run contrary to familiar usage. Recall that, in *Lingens*, it was the former Chancellor Kreisky who had brought the original suit against the journalist in the national courts. In that initial action, we would ordinarily think of Kreisky as being in the 'claimant' (e.g. 'plaintiff') role, and Lingens as being in the 'respondent' (e.g. 'defendant') role. That is, the term 'claimant' might be understood to refer to a party bringing a claim; and 'respondent', to the defending party. But recall that we have already decided to examine all stages of the case in terms of Lingens's asserted right of free expression. Therefore, we will say that, even in the national courts, Lingens was the party whom we are now calling the 'claimant', and Kreisky was the party whom we are now calling the 'respondent'. Accordingly, we will say that when the dispute passed to the European Commission and Court, Lingens remained in the role of claimant, and the role of respondent passed to the Austrian state.

Another feature of an international body like the European Court is that it may provide the possibility of an inter-state complaint procedure. That is a procedure which allows a state party to a human rights treaty to bring a complaint against another state party. (Such a procedure can be useful where the alleged abuses are widespread, particularly if the gravity of the situation prevents victims from litigating effectively on their own behalf.[5]) For our purposes, the roles would be distributed as in any other case: the state asserting a right acts as claimant, and the accused state defending the restriction acts as respondent.

Notation

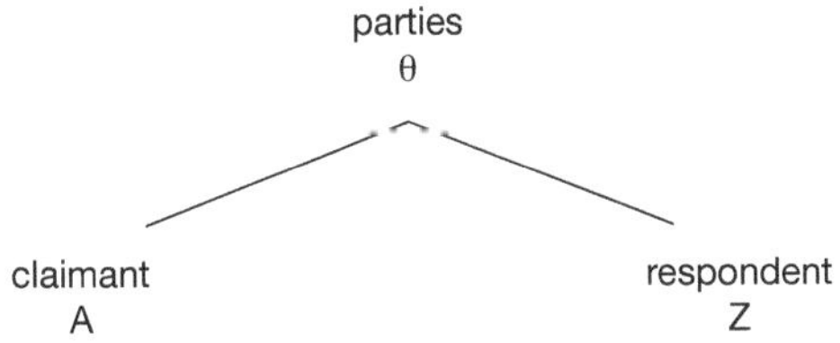

Figure 3.1

We can now state the two possible values for the θ variable. The claimant will be designated by the upper-case, Roman letter 'A'. The respondent will be designated with the letter 'Z'. A schema of parties appears in Figure 3.1. The letters A and Z may, too, appear to be variables, in so far as A will range over claimants, and Z will range over respondents, in an unlimited number of disputes. Within the confines of the model, however, they will serve as *constants*. The letter A will have one and only one meaning ('claimant') and the letter Z will have one and only one meaning ('respondent'). In that respect, they differ from a symbol like θ, which can take as a value either A or Z; or ψ, which can take as a value either θ or α (hence, either A, Z or α). A postulate can be used to define the set of possible values of the variable θ,

Ps(θ) $\theta \subset$ A, Z

Exercise set 3.1

(Answers for exercise sets appear in the Answers section beginning on p. 282.)

Draw a tree diagram incorporating Figure 3.1 into Figure 2.1.

Formulas

In order to record that a party makes an assertion, the letters A or Z will be followed by a colon, which will in turn be followed by symbols representing the assertion. For example, to say 'The claimant asserts *x*', we write,

F 3.1 A: *x*

All such notations will be called *formulas* (F). As noted in Section 2.3, the term *formula* will denote *any statement expressed in symbolic terms.* Similarly, to say 'The respondent asserts *y*', we write,

F 3.2 Z: *y*

Positions

This study uses different kinds of formulas. The term *position* will be used to refer specifically to formulas consisting of *the party symbol which precedes the colon together with the assertion which follows the colon.* We will say that A: *x* represents a *claimant position* or *A position*, and Z: *y* represents a *respondent position* or *Z position.* Where reference need simply be made to *some* party, without specification as to whether that party is the claimant or the respondent, the θ variable will be used. To say 'Some party asserts *p*', we write,

F 3.3 θ: *p*

A formula using θ to represent the party will be called a *party position* or *θ position.* In the formula A: *x*, we would say that θ takes the value of A. In the formula Z: *x*, we can say that θ takes the value of Z. The aim of the book will be to ascertain all possible formal structures of θ positions.

Of course, if our concern is with the formal structure of arguments, then why bother noting the party? Why not just analyse the argument *p*? That technique already signals a departure from other formal approaches. Hohfeldian or deontic analyses, for example, can frequently be applied to arguments without regard to the identity of the party making the argument. In our model, however, the question whether an argument is made by a claimant or a respondent will sometimes affect its structure. Some arguments can be made only by claimants – those seeking recognition of the right. Others can be made only by respondents – those challenging recognition of the right.[6]

Utterances in θ positions

The statements represented by the letters *x* and *y* are being referred to as *assertions*. Yet that term is not straightforward. Imagine a case like *Laskey*, where an attorney representing the government, in a sarcastic caricature of the claimant position, exclaims, 'So the state can place no limits on what adults do in private!' In other words, let us say that there is one respondent position Z_1: y_1, such that,

y_1 = 'So the state can place no limits on what adults do in private!'

Literally, of course, the attorney wants the court to believe some opposite statement Z_2: y_2, where, e.g.

y_2 = 'So the state *can* place limits on what adults do in private.'

It is Z_2, then, that we wish to analyse. But with what justification? The respondent has literally asserted the opposite. Can we say that the respondent 'argues' y_2 through implicit premises? Or that the respondent ironically 'suggests' or 'intimates' y_2?

A phrase like 'the claimant asserts' or 'the respondent asserts' cannot always be taken to mean that a position is stated in a concise utterance. It must often be reconstructed and, indeed, as is common in standard treatises, can ordinarily be reconstructed uncontroversially. Similarly, parties do not always set forth their arguments according to prescribed formulas or rigorous logical canons. Sometimes a position is stated as an eloquent conclusion scrupulously derived from lucid premises, but sometimes it is stated in utterly haphazard or conclusory fashion. Moreover, it is often artificial, even impossible, to draw clear lines between a party's premises and conclusions. (By contrast, the background theories will take the form of 'arguments' – distinct premises and conclusions – in a stricter sense, but are understood to be presupposed, and not consciously articulated.[7]) Accordingly, when referring to some *p* in a θ position, we will say that the party 'states', 'asserts', 'claims' or 'argues' *p* without attempting to differentiate those terms, and on the understanding that a (usually uncontroversial) reconstruction of the party's statements is at work. We will also use such terms – again, rarely having to distinguish them – to refer to the symbolic form of an utterance *p* made in a θ position (θ: *p*). In that context, they will refer to *statements, expressed in symbolic form, which are or could be made by parties* to a contentious case. The question whether natural-language utterances or symbolic θ positions are at issue will be clear from the discussion, and will sometimes refer to both, as we will be translating between natural and symbolic language.

The phrase 'could be' is crucial in that definition. It will allow a departure from common usage through a simplifying assumption. In examining arguments adduced in liberal rights discourse, there are several reasons why we cannot depend only on oral or written submissions. First, courts occasionally resolve cases in favour of a given party, but for reasons different from those actually adduced by that party. In some cases, the party may just not have thought of the argument. In other cases, the party, as a matter of principle, may have deliberately rejected it. For example, a court might release a religious dissident on grounds of procedurally defective arrest – grounds which the dissident had deliberately declined to raise, having preferred to be released solely on grounds of freedom of religion. Certainly, we would want the model to account for the arguments actually made by the claimant. But the model must also account for arguments not made by, but made on behalf of, a party. Second, it can happen that an argument never in fact adduced either by the party or by the court is nevertheless seen to be persuasive in a hypothetical vein. We, as scholars, may imagine a free speech argument which, for whatever reason, was raised neither by the party nor by the court. The model must be able to account for hypothetical as well as actual arguments.

In order to meet these problems, we will frequently say that some party *position* states *p* (i.e. that a claimant position states *x*, or that a respondent position states *y*). We will allow that phrase to mean that the party *could* assert *p*, or that *p* is or could be made on the party's behalf, as long as those stipulations are expressly stated. That usage is acceptable because the model's aim is not to ascertain or to verify whether a party does in fact make an argument, but only to set forth the argument's formal structure.[8] (Certainly, if we wanted to distinguish those various kinds of arguments, we could do so in our notation. For example, an argument actually made by a claimant could be written A: *x*. An argument made not by, but on behalf of, the claimant, could be written A′: *x*. An argument made neither by, nor on behalf of, the claimant, but which *could* or *might* have been made might be written A″: *x*, and so forth. For our limited purposes, however, such notation will be unnecessary.)

3.2 Corollaries to position axioms

Those basic forms for θ positions will allow us to adopt the following sets of *corollaries* to the axioms introduced in Chapter 1. The term 'corollary' is not used here according to strict usage, but more loosely to spell out consequences of axioms when viewed in terms of other fundamental constituents of the model, such as claimant and respondent positions. In Appendix 1, each corollary directly follows its corresponding axiom.

Corollaries to the Axiom of Recognition

Two corollaries to the Axiom of Recognition require little explanation: a 'claimant corollary', which characterises A positions, and a 'respondent corollary', which characterises Z positions:

> **Claimant Corollary**: Every claimant position asserts that the disputed right must be recognised.

> **Respondent Corollary**: Every respondent position asserts that the disputed right must *not* be recognised.

Some of the assumptions made thus far pertain to those corollaries. The Axiom of Generality allows the term 'recognised' to be construed to mean 'recognised or applied'. The use of the term 'asserts' can be construed to mean 'asserts or assumes': the idea is not that all statements out of the party's (lawyer's) mouth repeat that the right must or must not be recognised, but only that a party's statements, in sum and in context, ultimately serve that end.

Those corollaries also introduce a further simplifying assumption. It can sometimes happen that a party adduces mutually contradictory arguments – perhaps inadvertently, perhaps over a long course of litigation. If a party were to assert both *p* and *not-p*, we might be able to ascertain the formal structure of both arguments, but it is questionable how much that would tell us about what the party was in fact arguing. More importantly, there must be some limit to the kinds of arguments a party position can make if it is to be coherent at all – and if there is to be a dispute at all. Contradictions on minor points need not destroy a legal argument. At the outer limit, however, a claimant must ultimately be arguing for recognition of some right, and the respondent ultimately be arguing against it. We will limit the scope of θ positions, such that they represent not everything parties can conceivably say, but only that the disputed right must be recognised or that it must not be recognised. Hence:

> **Party Corollary**: Every party position asserts *either* that the disputed right must be recognised *or* that it must not be recognised.

That discrepancy between claimant and respondent positions might appear to preclude the hypothesis that there is background *agreement* underlying all disagreement in liberal rights disputes. But that contradiction is not real. Like the dispute about Hamlet, the parties' arguments may agree on certain background theses, even if they invoke those theories towards divergent ends. Accordingly, the corollaries must not be construed to mean that the two parties can never agree on anything. However, the parties must disagree about the recognition of the right in question. As to other points, they may agree or disagree. As in the dispute about Hamlet, the question as to whether there is agreement or disagreement may merely depend on the level of abstraction at which a point is pitched. We will see that agreement between the parties emerges at higher levels of abstraction, but always within the contentious framework.

Corollaries to the Axiom of Restrictions

We can adopt three similar corollaries to the Axiom of Restrictions:

> **Claimant Corollary**: Every claimant position *opposes* some means by which a person or entity impedes the right-seeker in, or penalises the right-seeker for, the exercise of an asserted right.
>
> **Respondent Corollary**: Every respondent position *favours* some means by which a person or entity impedes the right-seeker in, or penalises the right-seeker for, the exercise of an asserted right.
>
> **Party Corollary**: Every party position *either opposes or favours* some means by which a person or entity impedes the right-seeker in, or penalises the right-seeker for, the exercise of an asserted right.

The observation made about the corollaries to the Axiom of Recognition applies here. Parties may occasionally contradict themselves. Therefore, these three corollaries admit as claimant positions only those which *oppose* some means by which the right-seeker is impeded in, or penalised for, the exercise of the asserted right; and admit as respondent positions only those which *favour* some means by which the right-seeker is impeded in, or penalised for, the exercise of the asserted right.

Taken together, the six foregoing corollaries elicit a broader feature of the model, namely that it comports an inexorable element of 'dialogue stasis'. As already noted, there can be all kinds of dialogue about rights, where shifts in positions and compromises may occur (e.g. in legislation, negotiation or alternative dispute resolution). However, the possible mutations are not limitless. Once a dispute reaches the stage of formal adjudication, by definition there must be assumed to be some insuperable stand-off, some fundamental disagreement between the parties, without which they would have no reason to litigate at all. Despite possible agreement at a higher level of abstraction, there must be some essential stasis of the opposing parties' positions in relation to each other.

Corollaries to the Axiom of Contentious Character

We can adopt several corollaries to the Axiom of Contentious Character:

> **Claimant Corollary**: Every claimant position conflicts with some possible respondent position.
>
> **Respondent Corollary**: Every respondent position conflicts with some possible claimant position.
>
> **Party Corollary**: Every party position conflicts with some other possible party position.

The Party Corollary elicits a point which follows from the Axiom, but is worth stressing. If every θ position conflicts with some other possible θ position, then no θ position is non-rebuttable. Depending on the facts of a case, a given θ position may lack a *plausible* rebuttal (indeed, for easy cases that would be expected), but no θ position lacks some *possible* rebuttal. That distinction between plausible and possible rebuttals recapitulates the distinction between plausible and possible restrictions with which the Axiom of Contentious Character was introduced in Section 1.3. Hence:

> **Rebuttal Corollary**: Every party position can be rebutted by some other party position.

In fact, the model will allow a rebuttal to a given θ position to be ascertained systematically.[9]

From those four corollaries, a fifth can be surmised, which provides a formal concept of 'adjudication' (although its truth may only become clearer later on):

> **Adjudication Corollary**: A dispute about a liberal right is adjudicated if and only if some possible claimant position *or* some possible respondent position prevails.

The reference to 'some possible' position confirms that the prevailing position may not have been expressly articulated by the successful party. Moreover, the corollary is only 'weakly' ('inclusively') disjunctive: it does not preclude the possibility of a de jure or de facto compromise, where some possible claimant position *and* some possible respondent position are adopted. It only precludes a resolution which would adopt neither.

In Chapter 1, the Axiom of Recognition, the Axiom of Restrictions and the Axiom of Contentious Character provided three distinct principles for developing the model. Their corollaries, however, taken together, are rather redundant. The claimant corollaries to the Axiom of Recognition, the Axiom of Restrictions and the Axiom of Contentious Character seem to say the same or similar things, as do the respective respondent corollaries. In fact, that redundancy is strong. Under the model, there will be no difference between favouring a right and opposing a restriction, or between opposing a right and favouring a restriction. And if favouring a right entails opposing a restriction, then any position favouring a right conflicts with some position opposing a restriction, and any position favouring a restriction conflicts with some position opposing a right. Those redundancies place the contradictory relationship between claimant and respondent positions at the centre of the model. If one principle unites the corollaries introduced in this section, it is that liberal rights discourse is meaningful as such only in so far as it is inexorably confrontational. It emerges as sheer conflict between rights and restrictions, claimants and respondents. Only within that antagonistic framework does it move beyond the platitudes which characterise the literal wording of standard human rights instruments.

3.3 Truth value

(1) The chameleons at London Zoo are larger than the elephants.

(2) The guppies at London Zoo are chameleons.

∴ The guppies at London Zoo are larger than the elephants.

Figure 3.2

Logic is concerned with the validity of reasoning from premises to conclusions. Assuming the truth or falsehood of an argument's premises, logic examines the conclusions that follow. A question then arises about θ positions: will it be necessary, or possible, to say that statements in θ positions are true or false? Consider the argument in Figure 3.2. In deductive logic, one common criterion for the validity of an argument is as follows: *if* the premises are true, *then* the conclusion must be true.[10] By that standard the deduction in Figure 3.2 is valid. Assuming that London Zoo has all three species, we may disagree that the chameleons are larger than the elephants, or that the guppies are chameleons, but those objections are distinct from the question of the argument's validity. For the argument to be valid, it need only be the case that, *if* it were true that the chameleons are larger than the elephants, and *if* it were true that the guppies are chameleons, then it would be true that the guppies are larger than the elephants.

The first and second premises of the argument in Figure 3.2, and thus the conclusion, are assumed in traditional logic to be the kinds of statements to which a *truth value* can be assigned. In classical logic, the only truth values used are 'true' and 'false'.[11] It can be said to adopt the following criterion of validity: *if* a truth value of 'true' is assigned to the premises, *then* the conclusion also takes a value of 'true'. *Prima facie*, that criterion seems easy enough to accept. Logic does not require that we admit the truth of the premises. It merely examines the conditions under which a formally valid argument follows from those premises *if* they are true. But compare the argument in Figure 3.3. On the criterion just set forth, the argument in Figure 3.3 is valid. But is that argument entirely comparable to the one in Figure 3.2?

(1) Beautiful blondes have fun.

(2) Marilyn is a beautiful blonde.

∴ Marilyn has fun.

Figure 3.3

Consider the following objection. The argument in Figure 3.2 is acceptable because, assuming the standard meanings of its terms, statements like 'Chameleons at London Zoo are larger than elephants' and 'Guppies at London Zoo are chameleons' are subject to empirical investigation. A group of otherwise disputatious people, like our roomful of scholars, could go to London Zoo and reach agreement on assigning values of 'true' or 'false' to the premises. The premises in Figure 3.3, however, are not of that order. Even congenial people can disagree on what 'beautiful' means. It is debatable whether a statement about beauty is the kind to which a judgment of 'true' or 'false' can be assigned – leaving aside what is meant by 'fun', or how much of it is had, or whether bleaching counts.

If we admit values of 'true' and 'false' for Figure 3.3, their criteria arguably differ from those which govern in Figure 3.2. We might call those in Figure 3.3 'aesthetic', and those in Figure 3.2 'empirical'. It would then seem that there are as many concepts of truth as there are criteria for judging it. So how many criteria are there? Is it always clear which are to be applied in a given case? Are the criteria governing quantum mechanics 'empirical' in the same way as those governing the animal species in the zoo? Are the criteria governing beauty of a mathematical equation the same as those governing blondes? These are knotty questions, and classical logic proceeds by eschewing them. It says: 'Choose whatever criteria of truth you like. That is the concern of other branches of knowledge, not of logic. Logic merely examines the formal validity of reasoning from premises to conclusions once you have chosen your criteria for assigning truth values.' The question then arises whether a truth value can be ascribed to an argument p in a θ position.

Although *Laskey* and *Lingens* raise different sets of issues, we will see that they join with other liberal rights disputes in being structured by questions of harm and consent. In *Laskey*, the respondent state claims, and the claimants deny, that the men inflicted unacceptable harm on each other, and could not validly consent to do so. In *Lingens*, the respondent state claims that the claimant Lingens overstepped his rights to free expression by unacceptably harming Mr Kreisky, through defamation, without Kreisky's consent. Yet are those assertions, either by the claimants or by the respondents, the kinds of statements to which we would assign values of 'true' and 'false'? Are they to be assessed as a matter of empirical fact? Or of ethical judgement? Even if there are harms which everyone would describe as 'unacceptable', we easily find borderline cases, such as mild slapping of children or 'reasonable' self-defence. In those cases (but some would say, in *all* cases), it is doubtful whether there is a mere fact of the matter – a straightforward value of 'true' or 'false' – about what kind or level of harm is 'acceptable' or 'unacceptable'.[12]

Our only concern is with the formal structure of an argument p in a θ position, and not with its substantive truth or plausibility – those questions are examined elsewhere in legal scholarship. Therefore, we will take a further simplifying step, by stipulating that an argument p in a θ position can be assigned the value of 'true' or 'false', without asking which criteria would justify that ascription in any given case:

> **Axiom of Truth Value**: Every argument in a θ position is assumed to be true or false.

> **Claimant Corollary**: The claimant assumes some A position to be true, and any contradictory position to be false.

> **Respondent Corollary**: The respondent assumes some Z position to be true, and any contradictory position to be false.

Again, nothing in this study is concerned with the substantive truth or plausibility of assertions, but only with the formal structures of the background theories which are presupposed by those assertions.

And, again, parties may sometimes make arguments against their interests, including arguments which flatly contradict each other. A party who assumes the truth of his or her arguments would then be assuming the truth of contradictory propositions. However, we have ensured against that possibility through the corollaries to the Axiom of Recognition and the Axiom of Restrictions, which admit only claimant positions favouring the right and opposing the restriction, and only respondent positions favouring the restriction and opposing the right.

3.4 Opaque contexts

The Axiom of Truth Value and its corollaries thus allow us to eliminate ambiguity about the truth of an argument *p* in a θ position by allowing us to stipulate truth values. But there is a further problem. We are examining a given argument *p* not in isolation, but within a θ position. Does it matter? Consider the following *compound statement*:

1 The cup is red and the saucer is blue.

It can be broken down into two *simple* ('*atomic*') *statements*:

1.1 The cup is red.

1.2 The saucer is blue.

The atomic statements 1.1 and 1.2 can easily be assigned truth values, assuming we know all other relevant information, such as *which* cup, *which* saucer, *which* point in time. Statement 1, then, can also be assigned a truth value: if we know the truth value of 1.1 and 1.2, we can ascertain the truth value of 1. If 1.1 and 1.2 are both true, then 1 is true. If 1.1 is true and 1.2 is false, then 1 is false, and so on. Now compare statement 1 with the following one:

2 The fact is that the cup is red.

Statement 2 can also be broken down, albeit in a different way:

2.1 The fact is that *x*.

2.2 The cup is red.

Statement 2 can be formed by substituting sentence 2.2 for *x* in 2.1 (adjusting for punctuation). Accordingly, in so far as 2.2 can be assigned a truth value, so can 2. The same holds for such locutions as:

3 The truth is that the cup is red.

4 It is the case that the cup is red.

But consider,

5 Fatima believes that the cup is red.

Sentence 5 can be broken down just like 2:

5.1 Fatima believes *x*.

5.2 The cup is red.

However, the fact that the cup is red implies nothing about what colour Fatima believes it to be. Statements 2.1 and 5.1, respectively, illustrate what are commonly known as *transparent contexts* and *opaque contexts*. Statement 2.1 exemplifies a transparent context, as the truth or falsehood of 2 can be inferred from the truth or falsehood of 2.2. Statement 5.1 exemplifies an opaque context, as the truth or falsehood of 5 cannot be inferred from the truth or falsehood of 5.2.

The notation forms A: x and Z: y, and thus θ: p, create opaque contexts. From the truth value of an assertion p one cannot infer the truth value of the statement that a given party does in fact *assert p*.[13] Perhaps we would be better off avoiding opaque contexts altogether, by examining the structure of a given assertion p directly, abstracted from any θ position. As was noted in Section 1.3, however, the model is structured by the contentious character of liberal rights discourse. We will see that background theories underpinning arguments about liberal rights intrinsically assume either support for the right, as urged by a claimant, or support for the restriction, as urged by the respondent. The structure of each background theory will depend on whether it appears in an A position or a Z position. Further simplifying assumptions will now be adopted, so that opaque contexts will pose no unnecessary obstacles.

Assertion

As a practical matter, and particularly when disputes are examined in an appellate context, as there is rarely much dispute about what a party is asserting, either because that party's statements are clear on the face of it, or because they can be reconstructed in an uncontroversial way. When analysing a given position, we will do so *assuming* that it adequately represents the party's position, solely for the purpose of ascertaining the background theory underlying it. If it were later to appear that that position does not adequately reflect the party's view, we would then find some alternative position for purposes of ascertaining *its* background theory. The question whether a statement of a party's position fairly represents that party's view is certainly important, but is distinct from the question as to which background theory underlies it. Only the latter question concerns us. The difficulties posed by opaque contexts in a broader philosophical framework therefore raise no difficulties for our model, and we can adopt stipulations to that effect:

> **Axiom of Assertion**: A party is assumed to make an assertion attributed to that party in a θ position, subject to the Axiom of Recognition and the Axiom of Restrictions, and their corollaries.

In other words, we simply stipulate a value of 'true' for the proposition that the party makes the assertion, leaving to one side any controversy which might in theory arise about whether the assertion adequately represents the party's view. (Again, for purposes relevant to our model, such controversy rarely arises in practice.) Simply put, for A: *x*, we assume that the claimant does assert *x*. For Z: *y*, we assume that the respondent does assert *y*. Thus for all θ: *p*, we assume that the party does assert *p*. In itself, the axiom may create the appearance of allowing any statement at all to be attributed to any party, including self-contradictory statements. As explained in Section 3.2, however, that danger is precluded by the corollaries to the Axiom of Recognition and the Axiom of Restrictions.[14]

As noted in Section 3.1, some verbs could replace 'asserts' straightforwardly with no relevant change in meaning, such as 'argues', 'maintains' or 'insists'. Others might be more questionable, such as 'suggests', 'intimates that', 'appears to mean' or 'seems to feel'. Consider also the appearance of adjectives or adverbs, which would commonly arise in ordinary language:

6 The claimant emphatically states *x*.

7 The claimant never ceases to repeat *x*.

Here too, the linguistic and philosophical issues can become obscure, but pose no real problem for the model. We will accept the forms 'The claimant asserts', 'The respondent asserts' or 'The party asserts' as *paradigm locutions*. Other locutions will be deemed applicable to the extent that they could be substituted by one of these under prevailing linguistic usage, without any relevant change in meaning. In an unrestricted linguistic context, it is not always obvious to what extent such substitutions are possible, or what counts as prevailing linguistic usage. Within the restricted context of the model, however, those problems will not arise.

Note also that the following two statements exhibit a difference between active and passive grammatical voice:

8 The claimant asserts *x*.

9 *x is asserted* by the claimant.

For purposes of the model, those grammatical differences will generate no relevant semantic differences.

Indicative tenses

A formula like A: *x* may be amenable to various translations, depending on the verb tenses we are willing to admit. For example, we routinely use the past tense to discuss cases already decided:

10 The claimant *asserted x*.

11 The claimant had already *asserted x*.

For future litigation, we could use future tenses:

12 The claimant *will assert x*.

13 The claimant will have asserted x.

One might also distinguish between verbs denoting discrete moments in time (Fatima asserts *x* in response to the lawyer's question) and verbs used atemporally (Fatima asserts *x* as a rule of good business practice.) The latter can often be assumed to apply to all time frames relevant to a given case in question. Despite such differences, those examples all assume real cases. They use indicative, rather than conditional or subjunctive verb tenses. Accordingly, no problems arise if we extend the Axiom of Assertion to include them:

> **Indicative Tense Corollary to the Axiom of Assertion**: A party is assumed to make any past, present or future assertion attributed to that party in a θ position, subject to the Axiom of Recognition and the Axiom of Restriction, and their corollaries.

As applied to future statements, that corollary may seem questionable. Statements about the future have a contingent character. I may indeed predict that 'the claimant will assert *x*', but that does not mean it will happen. For our purposes, however, that prospect raises no issue distinct from that raised as applied to present or past tenses. In all three cases, a mistake of fact may certainly occur. The point of the Axiom of Assertion and its corollaries is to stipulate that the model proceeds irrespective of factual contingencies as to whether a given statement is in fact made by a party. Extension of the model to future assertions also raises the prospect of changes to parties' arguments in the course of litigation, but that possibility raises few real problems. Where such changes occur, it will be easy enough to distinguish arguments made at one time from those made at another.

Conditionals, modes and counterfactuals

Contingencies commonly arise in hypothetical cases, or in hypothetical arguments proposed for real cases:

14 The claimant *would assert x.*

15 The claimant *can assert x.*

16 The claimant *must* assert *x.*

17 The claimant *might have asserted x.*

18 The claimant *ought to have asserted x.*

Those statements involve conditionals (e.g. 'would'), modalities (e.g. 'can', 'must'), and conditional modalities (e.g. 'could', 'ought to'), as well as counterfactuals (e.g. 'could have', 'ought to have').

In the context of θ positions, such statements share with indicatives the characteristic of opacity. But they commonly possess two additional characteristics. First, they frequently presuppose that the assertions to which they refer are not in fact made.[15] Second, it may be unclear what it would mean to ascribe a truth value to them, as speculative questions of judgment may arise. One might therefore hesitate to extend the Axiom of Assertion to cover such cases. Once again, it is the limited scope of the analysis which will allow us to take that step without committing errors. The model is not concerned with what parties would, might, can, could or should assert, but only with the structure of an assertion on the assumption that it is in fact made. Depending on the context, it may be necessary to state or to stipulate from the outset whether an argument is meant to represent the views actually put forth by a party, or is merely hypothetical or counterfactual – those, again, are distinct questions. Our only concern is with the structure of a position on the assumption that a party makes it. Hence:

> **Hypothetical Case Corollary to the Axiom of Assertion**: A party is assumed to make any assertion attributable to that party in a θ position, subject to the Axiom of Recognition and the Axiom of Restrictions, and their corollaries.[16]

As with the axiom, the appearance of open-endedly allowing any statement at all to be attributed to any party is precluded by the corollaries to the Axiom of Recognition and the Axiom of Restrictions. More advanced versions of the model are certainly conceivable, such that additional components would be expressly introduced for the purpose of distinguishing temporality, conditionals, modalities, counterfactuals or multivalent truth values. However, that level of detail lies well beyond anything needed to analyse most real or hypothetical cases.

Exercise set 3.2

Translate into symbolic form.

Example: The claimant asserts x.

Answer: A: x

1 The claimants loudly asserted x.
2 The respondent could assert y.
3 p should have been asserted by the claimants.
4 Some party might have asserted p.

3.5 Formal and substantive determinacy

A formula such as θ: p provides the initial rudiments of formal structure – the first elements of what will be called *formal determinacy*. Most of this book will be concerned with the task of identifying structural elements to the right of the colon, such that variables like x, y or p can be replaced by more precise formulas. To the extent that such refinement is possible, a position will be called *formally determinate*. Hence:

> **Dispute Corollary to the Axiom of Contentious Character**: A dispute is about the adjudication of a liberal right only in so far as it is a dispute – between a claimant position and a respondent position – about the values to be ascribed to variables representing those respective positions.

Beyond that point – that is, where no additional formal structure can be ascertained – positions will be called *formally indeterminate*. Parallel to those concepts will be concepts of *substantive* determinacy and indeterminacy. We will say that an argument is *substantively determinate* in so far as it attributes determinate values to the variables comprising its respective θ position; and *substantively indeterminate* in so far as it fails to do so. That general framework will become clearer once a sufficient degree of formal structure has been developed to permit concrete examples.

Of course, questions about the substantive determinacy of legal discourse are well known: How malleable is legal language? To what degree can purportedly neutral concepts be manipulated to achieve unjust ends? That debate runs from legal realism through to rule scepticism, critical legal studies, feminism, critical race theory, deconstructionism and postmodernism. But it is not the object of this study. It is a debate which begins where this study ends. Our hypothesis will be that substantive determinacy in legal discourse, however great or small it may be, is only even possible within the confines of formal determinacy. Legal discourse can be no more precise, predictable or transparent than its formal structure allows it to be. Where there is formal determinacy, there may or may not be substantive determinacy; but where there is formal indeterminacy, then by definition there can be no substantive determinacy. Debates about substantive determinacy take place within the limits of formal determinacy. Our task will be to identify those limits. Once we have identified them, the study will end.

A hint of those characteristics of determinacy and indeterminacy can already be detected. The concept of 'party' is formally determinate to the extent that it divides into claimant and respondent. Yet substantive indeterminacy is still possible. For example, those formal concepts say nothing about who has standing in a given jurisdiction to appear in either role. Controversy can still arise around that question. A dispute about whether certain kinds of class actions should be allowed, or whether children above the age of ten ought to be able to bring cases on their own behalf, need not in itself reject the bipolar ascription of only A and Z values to the θ variable. It represents only a disagreement about the values which ought to be attributable to the θ variable. We will be able to make similar observations about other elements of the model, e.g. who qualifies as affected agents,[17] or what counts as harm or consent.[18] In each case, we will see that substantive indeterminacy can always arise, yet always within the confines of a fixed formal structure. Someone critical of the whole enterprise of liberal rights may criticise not only the substantive indeterminacy, but also the formal structure. For example, with reference to parties, a critic of liberal rights might argue that the idea of resolving conflicts within the binary claimant-versus-respondent framework fails to match human experience or to meet human needs. By contrast, someone content with liberal rights may object to particular applications of the binary party framework (e.g. barring or admitting certain kinds of claimants under a given set of rules governing standing to bring a claim), but must ultimately accept that overall binary structure.

Review these terms

1 claimant
2 respondent
3 constant
4 formula
5 assertion (argument)
6 position
7 transparent context
8 opaque context
9 formal determinacy
10 substantive determinacy

4 Quantification and reverse translation

In the last chapter we examined how the parties to the dispute provide the framework within which arguments about liberal rights will be examined. In this chapter, we examine more closely the means of representing claimant and respondent positions. We then examine questions arising from the translation of symbolic formulas back into ordinary language.

4.1 Quantification: inclusive and exclusive symbols

The claimant and respondent positions must disagree on at least one point, but, on other points, may agree or disagree. The formula θ: p states that 'Some party asserts p', yet the word 'some' can mean different things, depending on whether the claimant and the respondent agree or disagree about p. Three scenarios are possible:

1 It is possible that the A and Z positions agree. In that case, the phrase 'Some party asserts' would apply to either party.

2 It is possible that the A and Z positions disagree. In that case, the phrase 'Some party asserts' would apply only to one party.

3 It may be desirable to state 'Some party asserts' without specifying which party it is, and without stating anything one way or the other about what the other party asserts.

The element of quantification counts among the most important in logic, and will help us to distinguish among those scenarios. In ordinary language, there are many ways of indicating quantity, of varying degrees of precision ('a few', 'lots', 'seven'). Of particular importance in standard logic are the *universal quantifier* and the *existential quantifier*. The universal quantifier is used to make a statement about *all* members of a class, e.g. 'All lions are mammals'. Universally quantified statements can be freely instantiated by any member of the class. For example, if Cyrus is a lion, then we can infer that Cyrus is a mammal. The existential quantifier is used to make a statement about *some* members of a class (e.g. 'Some lions are brave'). Existentially quantified statements cannot be freely instantiated by any member of the class. The premise that *some* lions are brave does not mean that all lions are brave, so Cyrus may be cowardly. A thorough study of quantification would require far more detail, but that thumbnail sketch will suffice for now.

Let's begin with scenario 1. Applying the universal quantifier to θ in θ: p would yield the proposition that *all* parties assert p – both the claimant position and the respondent position assert p. We will use a notation different from those common in standard logic. The term *marker* will be used to denote *a superscript symbol attached to a principal symbol in order to give the latter a particular meaning*. We will attach a superscript dot ($^\circ$) to θ, and will call that symbol the *inclusive party symbol*, hence θ°: p. In ordinary language, that notation can mean:

All parties assert p.

Both party positions assert p.

From either of those we can infer through instantiation both of the following:

1.3 The claimant position asserts p.

1.4 The respondent position asserts p.

Now consider scenario 3. If we wish to state only that some party asserts p, without stating one way or the other what the other party asserts, we will leave θ unmodified. In that unmodified form, θ will serve as an *exclusive party symbol*, and we can continue, without ambiguity, to translate θ: p as 'Some party asserts p', where nothing is stated or implied about what the opposing party asserts. In some cases, it *may* also be true that both parties assert p (i.e. θ°: p), however that proposition would have to be established as a separate matter, and is never deducible solely from θ: p. Note that the unmodified θ is only 'weakly' exclusive. By contrast, scenario 2 is 'strongly' exclusive: it bars agreement by the opposing party, while the unmodified θ leaves the question of agreement between them unspecified. If we wanted, we could certainly invent a further symbol (e.g. another modification of θ) which would mean 'Some party asserts p, *but not both*'. However, for the applications falling within the model, the weaker symbol will suffice.

Now recall the postulate Ps(θ),

Ps(θ) $\quad \theta \subset$ A, Z

In a θ position (θ: *p*), the variable θ, as an exclusive party symbol, takes the values A and Z *disjunctively*: it must represent one party, and, depending on the assertion made, (*p*) may or may not represent the other. By contrast, the symbol θ° as the inclusive party symbol takes those values *conjunctively*: it must represent both parties.

Later in the book, further inclusive symbols carrying the superscript dot will be introduced. None of them, however, will appear in postulates or tree diagrams. While postulates or tree diagrams including them could be formulated, that would add considerable complexity without yielding much greater insight into liberal rights discourse. That omission poses no theoretical problem, as the model could be developed without recourse to inclusive symbols. For example, instead of writing 'θ°: *p*', it is perfectly feasible to write 'A: *p* and Z: *p*'. Nevertheless, inclusive symbols will have the advantage of expressive economy. That will be their role in the model.

4.2 Verbal uniformity

The Axiom of Assertion and its corollaries facilitate translation from ordinary language into symbolic language so as to avoid problems which might arise from constructs such as opaque contexts or hypothetical locutions. They are axiomatic, as they do not concern translation in a purely mechanical sense. They determine the status of assertions about rights within the model. But we must also consider translation in the other direction, from symbolic language into ordinary language, for which we will adopt *reverse translation rules*. They are called 'rules' rather than 'axioms', as they serve not to elucidate the structure of the model, but only to facilitate its application. The final background theories could be developed without them, but would be more complicated to use. The reverse translation rules are set forth in Appendix 3 in an integrated form which makes each rule applicable to all agents, as will become clearer after the chapters concerning the other agents have been completed.

We have seen that a formula like A: *x* can represent a variety of statements, for example:

1 The claimant would probably assert *x*.

2 The claimant timidly asserted *x*.

3 The claimant should have tried to assert *x*.

4 The claimant will no doubt assert *x*.

The Axioms of Truth Value and Assertion set forth the assumptions under which A: *x* admissibly symbolises them. But now suppose a translation in the other direction. We have encountered the symbolic formula A: *x*, and must translate it into natural language. Sometimes the appropriate translation will be suggested by the context. Arguments which have appeared in actual, completed cases will commonly be translated into the past tense. Arguments of a contingent or speculative character will commonly be recorded by means of conditional, subjunctive, modal or counterfactual locutions. A passive voice may be used when clarity would be served by referring to the interest in question as the grammatical subject of the sentence. However, in some cases, and particularly in the exercise sets, a translation will commonly be required without further information being provided about the facts of the case. Hence:

> **Rule of Verbal Uniformity**: Unless context or usage permit otherwise, verbs are translated into the present, simple, indicative tense and active voice.

To translate A: *x* into ordinary language, knowing nothing more about the case, we therefore say, 'The claimant asserts *x*.'

4.3 Identity of interest

Laskey involved three claimants (Mr Laskey, Mr Jaggard and Mr Brown). We can imagine hypothetical cases involving countless variations on *Laskey*, e.g. where one of the participants claims to have engaged in milder acts than the others, or one of the participants was under the legal age of consent, or was deemed incompetent to give valid consent, at the time the acts were committed. It would then be useful to distinguish different claimants, say, by enumerating them (A_1, A_2 . . . A_n). Similarly, we can imagine a case like *Lingens* in which the journalist had written about several politicians, who, in the national courts, might have brought a joint action, and whom we might then designate as Z_1, Z_2 . . . Z_n. Nevertheless, from now on, we will assume the opposite:

> **Rule of Identity of Interest (Parties)**: Unless context permits otherwise, the arguments of more than one claimant are assumed to be identical, and the arguments of more than one respondent are assumed to be identical.

That assumption will allow us to eliminate the enumeration of parties where there are no relevant differences in their substantive arguments. Accordingly, in translation from ordinary language into symbols, unless the facts are expressly stated or stipulated such as to require enumeration, multiple claimants will be represented by the single symbol A, and multiple respondents by the single symbol Z. In the next few chapters, we will see that the Rule of Identity of Interest applies to agents other than parties. Appendix 3 provides a concise, integrated statement of the rule.

4.4 Singular agents

For translating from natural language into symbolic language, the Rule of Identity of Interest tells us what to do only when we already know or have stipulated that there is more than one claimant or respondent. However, suppose we encounter the formula A: *x*, lacking such knowledge or stipulation. Two translations are possible:

a The claimant asserts *x*.

b The claimants assert *x*.

Hence:

> **Rule of Singular Agents (Party)**: Unless context permits otherwise, a party is assumed to be singular.

Accordingly, we translate A: *x* with version (a). We will see that this rule also applies to other agents. Appendix 3 provides an integrated statement.

4.5 Singular locutions

The assumption of a singular party does not perforce mean that party is expressly identified. Therefore more than one translation of A: *x* is still possible:

a The claimant asserts *x*.

b A claimant asserts *x*.

c Some claimant asserts *x*.

d A given claimant asserts *x*.

Even those minor differences are not entirely insignificant. In ordinary usage, version (a) might suggest that the claimant is some identified person or entity. Versions (b), (c) and (d) might more strongly suggest reference to a hypothetical claimant. As a practical matter, context and intuition will suffice. These variations would cause no confusion in any plausible application of the model. Hence:

> **Rule of Singular Locutions for Agents (Party)**: Unless context or usage dictate otherwise, choice of singular locution for a party is free.

This rule also applies to other agents, as set forth in the rule in Appendix 3.

4.6 Translation of θ

Recall the hypothetical case of *John v. Mary* from Section 1.2. Now assume (1) that John is only one of several individuals (including Jane, Jill and Jasper) about whom the article is written; and (2) that Mary is only one of several individuals (including Mark, Michael and Matilda) who have written and published it. That dispute, in which both parties are plural, might be denominated *John et al. v. Mary et al.* The formula $\theta°$: *p* arising in that dispute might fairly enough be translated as 'Both parties assert *p*', although the word 'both', tending to mean 'two', is slightly misleading. An alternative translation (still assuming identity of interest on both sides) would be 'All parties assert *p*'.

A somewhat trickier problem arises with the formula θ: *p*. The translation 'Some *parties* assert *p*' is acceptable, and will be used in this study, as long as we do not overlook the fact that the word 'some' implies nothing about which side the parties are on. The weakly exclusive status of θ means that one or more of the parties are certainly on *one* side, and may *or may not* also be on the other side. Hence:

> **Rule of θ Translation**: Unless context permits, plural translations of θ must not imply agreement between the claimant and respondent positions.

As a practical matter, the context will ordinarily be clear enough to avoid confusion. In the rare case where it is not, a more explicit translation might be required ('One or more of the parties on *one* side assert *p*, and one or more parties on the other side may or may not assert *p*'), but no such cases will arise in this study.

Exercise set 4.1

Translate into natural language.

Example: A: *x*

Answer: The claimant asserts *x*.

1 Z: *p*
2 θ: *y*
3 θ°: *y*

Exercise set 4.2

Redo Exercise set 4.1, assuming plural parties.

Example: A: x

Answer: The claimants assert x.

Review these terms

1 marker
2 inclusive symbol
3 weakly exclusive symbol
4 strongly exclusive symbol
5 verbal uniformity
6 identity of interest
7 singular agent
8 singular locution

5 The individual actor

Having situated *parties* on the left side of the colon (θ:), our task is now to identify the agents on the right side, who are being called *actors*. In this chapter, we examine one kind of actor: *the individual*.

5.1 Attribution

In Chapter 2, the term *actor* (α) was adopted to denote a person or entity to whom interests are attributed in arguments about liberal rights. For example, to say that the claimant attributes interest u to some actor, we write,

F 5.1 A: αu

To say that the respondent attributes some contrary interest v to that actor, we write,

F 5.2 Z: αv

More generally, to say that some party attributes some interest i to some actor, we write,

F 5.3 θ: αi

5.2 Notation

Throughout the next few chapters, we will encounter different kinds of actors. For example, we will see how all of society can be understood as an actor to whom interests are attributed in argument. In those arguments we will use the letter 'S' to represent 'society'. But we will begin with the concept of the *individual actor*. As with the persons or entities who can be parties, the actor whom we are calling the 'individual' may indeed be an individual human being, but may also be an entity such as an organisation or business enterprise. The variable 'I' will represent any individual actor to whom interests are attributed by a party. To say that the claimant attributes interest *u* to some individual, we write,

F 5.4 A: I*u*

To say that the respondent attributes some interest *v* to that individual, we write,

F 5.5 Z: I*v*

More generally, to say that some party attributes interest *i* to an individual, wc writc,

F 5.6 θ: I*i*

The content of those interests which we are calling *u, v* or *i* will be considered when we turn to the chapters on harm and consent. We can further chart our schema of agents by adding some new branches to the tree, as set forth in Figure 5.1. Although that diagram includes the letter 'S' to anticipate the addition of 'society' as an actor, we will not examine that term until Chapter 8.

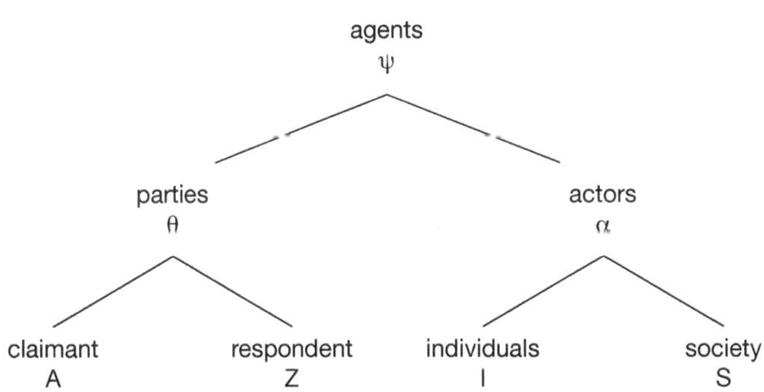

Figure 5.1

Exercise set 5.1

Translate into symbolic form.

Example: The claimant attributes interest *r* to some individual.
Answer: A: *Ir*

1 The claimants attributed interest *q* to Garbo.
2 The respondents could attribute interest *r* to *Barney's All Natural Fish and Chips.*

3 Some party should have attributed interest *s* to Mrs Perkins.
4 Interest *t* might have been attributed to some individual by some party.
5 The claimant could have attributed interest *v* to herself.
6 Both parties will ultimately attribute interest *v* to Marilyn.
7 The respondent would attribute interest *w* to himself.

5.3 Multiple individuals

We have been analysing *Lingens* in terms of a restriction on an asserted right of free expression. On the facts of the case, we can immediately identify two individual actors: the journalist and the former Chancellor. For now, we will use enumerated versions of the variable I to distinguish these two individuals: the symbol I_1 will represent the journalist, the symbol I_2 will represent the former Chancellor.

The journalist, complaining of a violation of his right of free expression, assumes the A position. In other words, as a *party* asserting the right in court, he is the claimant; as an *actor* seeking to exercise that right in the world, he is an individual actor. Why use two different symbols to represent the same person or entity? We will find out in a moment. Let's first see how a party in this case makes an assertion about an individual actor. In the journalist's view, the former Chancellor's interest in preventing defamation should not extend so far as to result in a penalty for the publication of the articles at issue. In other words, A attributes to I_2 an insufficient interest in securing the desired restriction on the right. Using the letter *a* to represent that 'insufficient interest', we can write,

F 5.7 A: $I_2 a$

While the dispute was still in the national courts, it was the former Chancellor, in the Z position, who sought the restriction. Before the European Court, the Z position passed to the Austrian state. In either case, the Z position attributes to I_2 a legitimate interest – let's call it a 'sufficient interest' – in restricting the journalist's right of free expression. We will represent that 'sufficient interest' with the letter *b*,

F 5.8 Z: $I_2 b$

In F 5.8, while the case is still in the national courts, two different symbols denote the former Chancellor: Z, as the *party* making the argument, and I_2, as the *actor* about whom the argument is made. In other words, he is making an argument about himself. Why not use just one symbol? The case's further progression provides one answer. It was *only* in the national courts that the Z position was assumed by the Chancellor talking about himself. When the dispute went to the European Court, the Z position passed to the Austrian state. By using two different symbols, the *actor* about whom the argument is made can remain the same, even if the *party* making that argument changes.

The journalist's interests can be represented in the same way. The journalist attributes to himself an interest in free expression which he deems sufficient to override the restrictions sought on defamation grounds. In other words, the A position attributes that interest to I_1. We can represent that interest with the letter *c*,

F 5.9 A: $I_1 c$

The Z position attributes to the journalist an interest in free expression which is insufficient to override the restrictions (*d*),

F 5.10 Z: $I_1 d$

5.4 Simple and compound positions

The A and Z positions have now each made two assertions. The A position has asserted $I_1 c$ and $I_2 a$. The Z position has asserted $I_1 d$ and $I_2 b$. Two or more 'simple' positions can be combined into a compound position by means of an 'operator' called a *conjunction*. The conjunction is often represented by a dot (·), and can be inserted between the two sets of symbols. We can thus fuse F 5.9 [A: $I_1 c$] and F 5.7 [A: $I_2 a$] into one compound A position,

F 5.11 A: $I_1 c \cdot I_2 a$

Similarly, we can fuse F 5.10 [Z: $I_1 d$] and F 5.8 [Z: $I_2 b$] into one compound Z position,

F 5.12 Z: $I_1 d \cdot I_2 b$

The term *simple position* will be used to designate a θ position consisting of only one assertion. The term *compound position* will designate a θ position in which assertions representing more than one simple position are conjoined.

Of course, compound positions are not always such a straightforward affair. A conjunction is not the only possible kind of relationship among propositions. Suppose, for example, that the claimant does not argue '$I_1 c$ *and* $I_2 a$', but rather '$I_1 c$ *or* $I_2 a$'. The latter position is a *disjunction*. A 'wedge' (v) is frequently used to record disjunctive propositions,

F 5.13 A: $I_1 c \vee I_2 a$

In standard logic, the distinction between conjunctive and disjunctive propositions is crucial. Confusion between them can lead to error.[1]

The distinction seems so clear that we would have every reason to adopt it. Simple though it may appear, however, it would make the model very complex. It is not always clear, and does not always need to be clear, whether a party or a court, proffering or examining a set of arguments, is adopting a conjunctive or disjunctive mode. For example, if a party prevails on one argument, the court, finding it unnecessary to examine the others, need not determine whether the winning argument prevails *along with* the others ('conjunctively') or *in spite of* the others ('disjunctively').[2] Distinguishing between conjunctive and disjunctive arguments would complicate the mechanics of the model without yielding useful insight into the character of rights discourse. Omission of that distinction will raise no computational problems for the kinds of computations used in this model, which, again, are not aimed at validity testing. Accordingly, we will simplify matters by using only conjunctions to form complex positions:

> **Axiom of Compound Positions**: All compound positions are assumed to be conjunctive.

(Of course, in any attempt to use the model for validity testing, one would have to decide whether any conjunctions in a given set of formulas must be changed into disjunctions.)

Exercise set 5.2

Translate.

> *Example:* The claimant attributes interest a to Arthur and interest b to Bertha.
>
> *Answer:* A: $I_1a \cdot I_2b$

1 The respondents might have attributed interest p to Garbo and interest q to Dietrich.
2 Some party should have attributed interest r to Bacall and to Bogart.
3 The claimant would attribute interests s, t and u to herself.
4 Both parties might plausibly attribute interest r to Leigh and interest s to Leigh and to Gable.

5.5 Personal and non-personal actors

We have now distinguished between two individual actors in *Lingens* by enumerating I symbols (I_1, I_2). Yet sheer enumeration does not reflect qualitative differences between them. Instead of distinguishing between the journalist and the former Chancellor in a purely quantitative way (I_1, I_2), let's describe their interests in qualitative terms. Observe that the interests (*c*, *d*) attributed to the journalist (I_1) concern the individual actor who seeks to exercise the right of free expression. By contrast, the interests (*a*, *b*) attributed to the former Chancellor (I_2) concern an individual actor who claims to be affected by the journalist's exercise of that right.

That is the way the difference looks from the outside. But now let's adopt the viewpoint of the journalist. His interest in free expression concerns both *himself* and the former Chancellor. We will say that his interest in free expression concerns both his *own person* and the *person of another*. More generally, we will say that the interests of the individual actor who seeks to exercise the right concern that individual's *own person*. By contrast, where the actual or purported effects of that personal actor's exercise of the right concern some other individual actor, we will say that they concern *the person of another*, whom we will call the *non-personal actor*. Those are the only two individual actors that will be formally recognised. Individuals who may be relevant to the litigation (lawyers, judges, certain witnesses) are not perforce individual actors for purposes of the model. Hence:

> **Axiom of Individual Actors**: An individual actor is either a personal actor or a non-personal actor, and nothing else.

In earlier chapters, the individual actor whom we are now calling the 'personal actor' had been called the 'right-seeker'. The two terms can be understood to be synonymous. the only reason for preferring the term 'personal actor' is to distinguish that actor from the non-personal actor.

Lingens illustrates the distinction between these two kinds of individual actors with reference to two men who are in head-on conflict: the journalist is the personal actor and the former Chancellor is the non-personal actor. However, the relationship between a personal actor and a non-personal actor need not be hostile. The non-personal actor is being defined as *any* individual other than the personal actor who may be affected by the personal actor's exercise of the right. That individual may or may not be in legal conflict with the personal actor. For example, *Laskey* includes three individuals: each man is a personal actor with respect to himself, seeking to exercise a right of sexual autonomy; *and* each man is simultaneously a non-personal actor, affected by the exercise of that right by one or more of the other participants. These relationships are examined further in Chapter 7. In *Laskey*, then, we are now calling each of the three men a claimant *and* a personal actor *and* a non-personal actor. Are three roles really necessary for each individual man? Yes. We will see that those roles remain distinct in liberal rights discourse.

We have now assumed the viewpoint of the individual seeking to exercise the asserted right as the basis for assigning the roles of personal and non-personal actor. As with the roles of claimant and respondent, the purely conventional nature of the roles of personal actor and non-personal actor must be emphasised. In *Lingens*, we will say that the journalist refers to himself as the personal actor and to the former Chancellor as the non-personal actor. But do not be confused by the fact that that usage consistently assumes the point of view of the individual seeking to exercise the right. We will say that, in the national courts, in so far as we are assuming the right at issue to be the journalist's freedom of expression, the former Chancellor, too, refers to the journalist as the personal actor, and to himself as the non-personal actor.

A non-personal actor need not actually have played any particular part in any phase of the litigation. It is true that, in *Laskey* and *Lingens*, non-personal actors are involved in at least some stage of the litigation. However, it is possible for a restriction to be imposed on the basis of the effects of the exercise of the asserted right upon some person or entity without that person or entity – that non-personal actor – becoming a party to the dispute. The non-personal actor may be involved in some other way, for example as a witness, or may play no role whatsoever in the litigation. For example, in the case of *Kokkinakis v. Greece*,[3] the European Court examined the legality of criminal penalties imposed for proselytising. Mr Kokkinakis had been imprisoned under the statute for having attempted to convince a woman to embrace the beliefs of the Jehovah's Witnesses. The woman contacted the police, but the criminal suit was not brought by her.

The *Lingens* and *Laskey* cases have helped to focus our attention on some differences between cases. *Lingens* involves only one personal actor and only one non-personal actor. *Laskey* involves more than one. In *Lingens*, those two kinds of actors are in head-on conflict. In *Laskey*, their interests coincide. In the next few chapters, we will keep our attention focused on these two cases, in order to elicit more information about basic elements of the model.

Review these terms

1	individual actor	2	multiple individuals
3	simple position	4	compound position
5	operator	6	conjunction
7	disjunction	8	dot
9	personal actor	10	non-personal actor

6 The personal actor

This chapter introduces a symbol for the personal actor, along with reverse translation rules governing its use.

6.1 Notation

In colloquial usage, reference to a 'personal actor' or to an individual's 'own person' are awkward. But those ideas are amenable to straightforward symbolic notation, through modification of the symbol I. The personal actor will be represented by means of the marker 'p', and will thus be written 'I^p'. The symbol I^p is a *constant*. Although it represents any personal actor in any case, it has no inferior formal values (unlike, e.g. θ, which can represent A or Z; or ψ, which can represent α or θ). In *Lingens*, the symbol I_1 had been used to represent the journalist, i.e. the personal actor. The formulas A: I_1c [F 5.9] and Z: I_1d [F 5.10] can now be rewritten, respectively,

F 6.1 A: I^pc

F 6.2 Z: I^pd

Exercise set 6.1

Translate.

Example: The claimant attributes interest *u* to the personal actor.
Answer : A: I^pu

1 The respondents have attributed interest *u* to the personal actor.
2 Some party would attribute interest *v* to the personal actor.
3 The claimants ought to attribute interests *a*, *b* and *c* to the personal actor.
4 Both parties could arguably attribute interests *b* and *c* to the personal actor.

6.2 Identity of interest

The p marker is qualitative, not quantitative in character. A case may involve several personal actors who could be enumerated (I^p_1, $I^p_2 \ldots I^p_n$). We could say that the three claimants in *Laskey* attribute to each of the three men – that is, to themselves – an interest u in being able to engage in sadomasochistic acts,

F 6.3 A: $I^p_1 u \cdot I^p_2 u \cdot I^p_3 u$

Similarly, we could say that the respondent, disagreeing, attributes to the three men an interest v in *not* engaging in the acts,

F 6.4 Z: $I^p_1 v \cdot I^p_2 v \cdot I^p_3 v$

An enumeration of personal actors I^p_1, $I^p_2 \ldots I^p_n$ is useful when differences among the actors affect their legal interests. Nevertheless, as with parties (θ_1, $\theta_2 \ldots \theta_n$), we will adopt a reverse translation rule assuming the contrary:

> **Rule of Identity of Interest (Personal Actors)**: Unless context permits otherwise, the interests of more than one personal actor are assumed to be identical.

All of the personal actors can then be represented collectively by I^p. F 6.3 and F 6.4 can thus be written, respectively, as,

F 6.5 A: $I^p u$

F 6.6 Z: $I^p v$

We would only reintroduce enumeration where some difference between the personal actors entails a difference in arguments about their substantive interests.

But note that the assumption of identity of interest applies to any *given* argument in a dispute, but not necessarily to any *other* argument in that dispute. For example, it may apply to a given argument made by a claimant, without applying to a counter-argument made by the respondent (who may want to rebut the argument by distinguishing between the interests of different personal actors). It may also apply to a given argument made by the claimant, without applying to another argument made by that claimant; that is, distinctions between the interests of personal actors may be irrelevant to the former argument, but relevant to the latter. That point is important, as it applies to all reverse translation rules: *the application of a reverse translation rule is distinct for each argument in a dispute*; the fact that a rule is applied in a particular way to one argument does not mean that it should be applied in the same way for other arguments. In any event, few cases are so complicated as to create real ambiguities of this kind.

Also, do not confuse *an interest attributed to more than one actor* with *more than one interest attributed to an actor*. The following formula cannot be simplified, as it reflects three distinct interests attributed to the personal actor, or to whichever set of personal actors I^p represents in the case (assuming of course, for interests u, s and t, that $u \neq s \neq t$),

F 6.7 $\theta: I^p u \cdot I^p s \cdot I^p t$

6.3 Singular agent

Before the question of identity of interest *among* plural personal actors even arises, a prior question must be answered: *Is* there in fact more than one personal actor? Suppose we encounter some formula A: $I^p u$, and want to translate it without knowing anything about the facts of the case. Recall from Section 3.3 that we are already applying the Rule of Singular Agents as applied to the party ('The claimant'). We are left, then, with two possibilities:

a The claimant attributes interest u to the personal actor.

b The claimant attributes interest u to the personal actors.

We will therefore adopt a further rule of singular agents,

Rule of Singular Agents (Personal Actor): Unless context permits otherwise, a personal actor is assumed to be singular.

Accordingly, unless some contrary fact is known or stipulated, the formula A: $I^p u$, is translated by version (a).

6.4 Singular locutions

We have seen that a singular translation can be rendered in a variety of ways:

c The claimant attributes interest u to the personal actor.

d The claimant attributes interest u to a personal actor.

e The claimant attributes interest u to some personal actor.

f The claimant attributes interest u to a given personal actor.

If, for example, the facts are known or stipulated such that an already identified actor is being discussed, version (c) will ordinarily be appropriate. Other versions will be appropriate where no such identification is known or required. In practice, the differences are minor and, for our model, will be irrelevant. Hence:

> **Rule of Singular Locutions for Agents (Personal Actor)**: Unless context or usage dictate otherwise, choice of singular locution for a personal actor is free.

In Section 4.2, it was noted that reverse translation rules are not axiomatic, as their role is purely to simplify translation, and not to contribute required elements to the model. Nevertheless, they are not equally dispensable. Some reverse translation rules, like those introduced thus far in this chapter, will be called *contingent*: they are applied unless the facts or context dictate otherwise. In the next section, however, we will see that some reverse translation rules are *absolute*: it is not possible for there to be a contrary fact or context, so the rule always applies. The absolute rules might therefore seem to have an axiomatic character, but they merely follow from already-adopted elements of the model, and add no new structure to it.

Exercise set 6.2

Translate.

Example: The claimant attributes interest *u* to the personal actors.

Answer : A: $I^{p}u$

1 The respondents would have attributed interest *u* to the personal actors.
2 Some party had attributed interest *v* to the personal actors.
3 Either party attributes interest *v* to the personal actors.
4 The claimant could have attributed interests *a*, *b* and *c* to the personal actors.

Exercise set 6.3

Redo problems 1–3 in Exercise set 6.2, assuming *no* identity of interest among the personal actors.

6.5 Rapport

As already noted, two agents represented in a θ position are sometimes the same, such as Mr Lingens, who is both claimant and personal actor. Hence:

1 The term *agent reflexivity* will refer to a relationship in which a person or entity represented by one symbol is the same as a person or entity represented by another symbol.
2 The term *agent non-reflexivity* will refer to a relationship in which a person or entity represented by one symbol is *not* the same as a person or entity represented by another symbol.

The term *rapport* will refer generally to the question of whether the relationship between persons or entities represented by two different symbols is reflexive or non-reflexive. In this and later chapters, we will discover great variety in the kinds of rapport which can arise in θ positions. Quite a few of the rules governing them will be introduced in this and subsequent sections, in order to ensure that the concept is clear. It would be both tedious and – as is evident from the integrated statement of the Rule of Rapport in Appendix 3 – unnecessary to remember all of them. In practice, it will usually be clear from context whether a given relationship within a θ position is reflexive or non-reflexive, so ordinary intuition will be reliable.

In this and the next few chapters, the focus is on the rapport between *parties* and *actors*. In F 6.1 [A: $I^p c$], Mr Lingens attributes interest *c* 'to the personal actor', but that means that he attributes interest *c* to himself. For *Laskey*, the same observation applies to F 6.5 [A: $I^p u$]. Accordingly:

3 The term *party–actor reflexivity* will refer to a relationship in which the party and the actor are the same person or entity.
4 The term *party–actor non-reflexivity* will refer to a relationship in which the party and the actor are *not* the same person or entity.

Suppose we encounter the formula A: $I^p u$, knowing nothing about the facts of the case. Even assuming singular agents, more than one translation is possible:

a The claimant attributes interest *u* to the personal actor.

b The claimant attributes interest *u* to (her-, him-) itself.

Hence:

Rule of Rapport (Claimant and Personal Actor): Unless context or usage permit otherwise, non-reflexivity is assumed between the claimant and the personal actor.

In other words, unless context or usage permit otherwise, the claimant and the personal actor are assumed to be different persons or entities. Barring contrary circumstances, the correct translation of A: $I^p u$ is then (a) rather than (b). At first, that presumption against reflexivity may appear unrealistic, as it is very common for agents to bring cases on their own behalf. For two reasons, however, a working assumption of non-reflexivity is preferable. First, being a contingent assumption, it can be suspended whenever the context dictates otherwise. More important, however, is that a non-reflexive translation of a reflexive θ position may be awkward in colloquial usage ('Mary Smith attributes interest *u* to Mary Smith'), but is never factually erroneous. By contrast, a reflexive rendering of a non-reflexive θ position would be factually incorrect. In *Laskey*, it would be factually correct to translate the formula A: $I^p u$ by saying 'The claimants attribute interest *u* to the personal actors.' By contrast, if the case had been brought by persons who were not personal actors, it would be factually false to say 'The claimants attribute interest *u* to themselves.' When in doubt, then, the non-reflexive rendering is preferable.

Under the Claimant and Respondent Corollaries to the Axioms of Recognition and Restrictions, the personal actor is the actor seeking to exercise a right, while the respondent seeks a restriction on the right. Therefore, it would never be possible to encounter a set of facts in which the respondent and the personal actor are the same person or entity. Hence:

> **Rule of Rapport (Respondent and Personal Actor)**: Non-reflexivity must be assumed between the respondent and the personal actor.

In other words, a claimant and a personal actor cannot in any context be the same person or entity. The formula Z: $I^p v$ must be translated non-reflexively (e.g. 'The respondent attributes interest *v* to the personal actor'). Again, the respondent could well play the role of personal actor in some related lawsuit, as in Mr Kreisky's suit against Mr Lingens in the national courts. However, within the framework in which the role of personal actor has been fixed with respect to an asserted right – in this case Mr Lingens's freedom of expression – there is no sense in which the respondent can be the same person or entity as the personal actor. In general, a reverse translation rule will be called *absolute* when it is applied in all circumstances, regardless of context or usage. By contrast, a reverse translation rule will be called *contingent* when it operates only as a default – when it is applied *unless* context or usage dictate or permit otherwise.

How do these principles affect the translation of θ, e.g. in a formula like θ: $I^p i$? If θ represents the respondent, reflexivity must be precluded, but θ could represent the claimant. Hence a contingent rule:

> **Rule of Rapport (θ and Personal Actor)**: Unless context or usage permit otherwise, non-reflexivity is assumed between θ and the personal actor.

In the absence of contrary facts, then, an acceptable translation of θ: $I^p i$ would be 'Some party attributes interest *i* to the personal actor.'

What about $\theta°$, e.g. in $\theta°$: $I^p j$? Again, it represents views agreed upon by both parties. Both parties may indeed agree on attributing an interest to a given actor, but that actor cannot simultaneously be the same person or entity as the claimant *and* the respondent, since the claimant and the respondent cannot be the same person or entity. Accordingly, an absolute rule of non-reflexivity would seem to be required between $\theta°$ and the personal actor. Note, however, that, where there is reflexivity between the claimant and the personal actor, a 'disaggregated' translation is easily imaginable, which would preserve both the personal actor's reflexivity with the claimant and the non-reflexivity with the respondent. For example, if the claimants in *Laskey* agree with the British state on attributing interest *j* to the personal actors, one certainly could translate $\theta°$: $I^p j$ non-reflexively as 'All parties attribute interest *j* to the personal actors'; however, through disaggregation of the parties, one could translate it just as plausibly by saying 'The claimants attribute *j* to themselves, and the state (also) attributes *j* to them.' Accordingly, a contingent rule of rapport suffices:

> **Rule of Rapport ($\theta°$ and Personal Actor)**: Unless context or usage permit otherwise, non-reflexivity is assumed between $\theta°$ and the personal actor.

That possibility of disaggregated translations warrants the inclusion of reference to 'usage', in addition to factual context, in the general formulation of the rule. All of the rules adopted in this section can now be consolidated into a more general version:

> **Rule of Rapport (Party and Personal Actor)**: Unless context or usage permit otherwise, non-reflexivity is assumed between the party and the personal actor. Except, non-reflexivity *must* be assumed between Z and I^p.

That consolidated version will be further elaborated in the coming chapters to include all possible relationships among persons or entities represented in θ positions, until reaching its final form, as set forth in Appendix 3.

6.6 Application and suspension of reverse translation rules

Contingent rules allow us to change our stipulations in order to change our translations, as in Exercise set 6.3. The only requirement is that facts which are known or stipulated to be contrary to the contingent rules must be expressly stated. Take, for example, the formula A: $I^p u$. Assuming no contrary facts, we translate it as:

The claimant attributes interest *u* to the personal actor.

However, as long as we do so expressly, we can suppose a singular claimant, but plural personal actors,

The claimant attributes interest *u* to the personal actors.

Or plural claimants and a singular personal actor:

The claimants attribute interest *u* to the personal actor.

Or party–actor reflexivity:

The claimant attributes interest *u* to (her-, him-) itself.

Or plural claimants, plural personal actors, and party–actor reflexivity,

The claimants attribute interest *u* to themselves.

Or a modal verb:

The claimant should attribute interest *u* to the personal actor.

Or plural claimants, plural personal actors, party–actor reflexivity and a modal verb, in which case all of the contingent rules are suspended:

The claimants should attribute interest *u* to themselves.

However, do not forget that only contingent rules can be suspended, not absolute ones. Given the formula Z: $I^p v$, we can, for example, suspend the Rule of Singular Agents as applied to the party:

The respondents attribute interest *v* to the personal actor.

Or the Rule of Singular Agents as applied to the actor:

The respondent attributes interest *v* to the personal actors.

Or both:

The respondents attribute interest *v* to the personal actors.

However, we can never suspend the Rule of Rapport as applied to the respondent and the personal actor. Those formulas must always be translated non-reflexively. In the exercise sets, you must ignore even an explicit instruction to assume given facts wherever it would result in a violation of an absolute rule.

Exercise set 6.4

Translate.

Example: A: I^pu

Answer: The claimant attributes interest *u* to the personal actor.

1 Z: $I^p t$
2 θ: $I^p k$
3 A: $I^p a \cdot I^p b \cdot I^p c$

Exercise set 6.5

Redo Exercise set 6.4, assuming plural actors.

Example: A: $I^p u$

Answer: The claimant attributes interest *u* to the personal actors.

Exercise set 6.6

Redo Exercise set 6.4, assuming plural parties.

Example: A: $I^p u$

Answer: The claimants attribute interest *u* to the personal actor.

Exercise set 6.7

Redo Exercise set 6.5, assuming *also* plural parties.

Example: A: $I^p u$

Answer: The claimants attribute interest *u* to the personal actors.

Exercise set 6.8

Redo Exercise set 6.4, assuming party–actor reflexivity.

Example: A: $I^p u$

Answer: The claimant attributes interest *u* to (her-, him-) itself.

Exercise set 6.9

Redo Exercise set 6.4, assuming plural agents.

Example: A: $I^p u$

Answer: The claimants attribute interest *u* to the personal actors.

Exercise set 6.10

Redo Exercise set 6.4, assuming plural agents and party–actor reflexivity.

Example: A: $I^p u$

Answer: The claimants attribute interest *u* to themselves.

Review these terms

1 reflexivity
2 non-reflexivity
3 rapport
4 party–actor reflexivity
5 party–actor non-reflexivity

7 The non-personal actor

In this chapter, we examine more closely the distinction between personal and non-personal actors. A symbol is introduced to represent the non-personal actor, along with reverse translation rules governing it.

7.1 Role distribution between the personal actor and the non-personal actor

Let's examine more closely what we mean by designating the men appearing in *Laskey* as being both personal actors and non-personal actors. The distinction might at first seem to correspond to a distinction between active and passive sexual roles, such that, when playing the 'active' role, inflicting the blows or wounds, the participants are exercising their asserted rights of sexual privacy or autonomy; and when playing the 'passive' role, receiving the blows or wounds, they are merely consenting to incur the effects of the 'active' participants' exercise of those rights.

In two senses, however, that characterisation would be inaccurate. First, all of the men purport to be pursuing rights of privacy or autonomy, regardless of their particular tastes or roles. One man may seek to exercise the right by receiving blows; another may seek to exercise the right by inflicting them; another may seek to exercise the right by doing both. In that sense, each of the men is a personal actor. Second, each of the men desires to incur the effects of the exercise of the right by at least one of the others. For the men playing sexually active roles, that may seem counter-intuitive: in colloquial usage, it sounds odd to say that the person who *inflicts* the blows is 'incurring' anything. However, to the extent that the man receiving the blows is doing so as an exercise of an asserted right, the man inflicting the blows is 'affected by' that passive man's exercise of *that* asserted right. In short, the distinction between personal actors and non-personal actors does not perforce correspond to a distinction between active and passive (sexual) roles. More generally, any individual is a personal actor when his or her conduct is the object of the asserted right, regardless of whether that conduct is 'active' or 'passive' with respect to the act in question. And any individual is a non-personal actor when he or she is affected by any act undertaken by a personal actor pursuant to the asserted right – again, regardless of whether that effect is active or passive in any conventional sense.

7.2 Mutual exclusion of the personal actor and the non-personal actor

If only trivially, the personal actor always incurs some effect of his or her *own* conduct. For example, Mr Lingens incurs any number of effects of his own exercise of the right of free expression, such as public notoriety, or the satisfaction of having spoken his mind. It could therefore be said that, merely by *being* a personal actor, that personal actor becomes *ipso facto* a non-personal actor – that any personal actor is always a non-personal actor with respect to his or her own conduct.

However, we will not adopt that usage. It is precisely because personal actors are by definition affected by their own conduct that no distinct role of non-personal actor need be created for them. Any effects incurred by a personal actor through his or her own conduct merely form part of the interests attributed to him or her in the role of personal actor. Thus, if the Austrian state attributes to Mr Lingens an insufficient interest *d* in procuring the satisfaction of speaking his mind, it does so merely by attributing that interest to him as a personal actor [Z: $I^p d$]. Similarly, in *Laskey*, we say that each man is a non-personal actor with respect to at least one of the *other* men; however, none of the men is denominated a non-personal actor with respect to the effects of his own conduct upon himself. Those effects are merely factored into each man's role as personal actor. Hence:

> **Axiom of Mutual Exclusion of Individual Actors**: For any given argument, an individual actor is either a personal actor or a non-personal actor, but not both.

Under that axiom, the roles of personal actor and non-personal actor, within the bounds of any given argument, are fixed into a *mutually exclusive* relationship: the personal actor cannot be the non-personal actor, and the non-personal actor cannot be the personal actor. That mutually exclusive relationship applies only within the confines of *that* argument, and does not preclude the possibility of the roles changing within the confines of some other argument (and regardless of whether that latter argument be made by the opposing party or by the same party).

If necessary, complex arguments can be broken down into several simpler arguments such that, within the parameters of any given argument, the roles remain fixed and mutually exclusive. For example, the argument 'Ned and Ted want to hit each other' can be treated as representing up to four simpler arguments, each maintaining mutual exclusivity of the roles of personal actor and non-personal actor within its own confines. Two of those arguments concern Ned's asserted rights:

1 'Ned wants to hit Ted.' *From the point of view of Ned's asserted right to hit Ted, Ned is the personal actor and Ted is the non-personal actor.*

2 'Ned wants to be hit by Ted.' *From the point of view of Ned's asserted right to be hit by Ted, Ned is the personal actor and Ted is the non-personal actor.*

And two of them would concern Ted's asserted rights:

3 'Ted wants to hit Ned.' *From the point of view of Ted's asserted right to hit Ned, Ted is the personal actor and Ned is the non-personal actor.*

4 'Ted wants to be hit by Ned.' *From the point of view of Ted's asserted right to be hit by Ned, Ted is the personal actor and Ned is the non-personal actor.*

Any simple argument about the effects of a personal actor's exercise of an asserted right upon some non-personal actor, *for the limited purposes of that assertion*, fixes the roles of personal actor and non-personal actor into place. The assertion that Ned seeks to exercise his asserted right by receiving a beating from Ted fixes Ned in the role of personal actor, and Ted in the role of non-personal actor; however, we see that that assertion does not preclude a second assertion, for example, that Ted seeks to exercise his asserted right by inflicting a beating upon Ned, which – solely within the confines of *that* assertion – fixes Ted in the role of personal actor, and Ned in the role of non-personal actor. Nor does either assertion preclude a third assertion that Ted seeks to exercise his asserted right by receiving a beating from Ned, which fixes Ted in the role of personal actor, and Ned in the role of non-personal actor. Nor are additional assertions precluded, which would involve, for example, further individuals, or different kinds of beatings, or activities other than beatings. A personal actor within one argument can become a non-personal actor within some other argument – made either by the opposing party or by the same party – but never within the same argument.

As a practical matter, the cases, like *Laskey*, in which a personal actor in one argument can also assume the role of non-personal actor in some other argument are fairly few. Nevertheless, such relationships do arise in controversial cases, as in the regulation of high-risk sports like boxing. Imagine two or more terminally ill individuals asserting a right to cooperate in killing each other. Each member asserts a right not merely to kill herself or himself individually – that would merely place each individual in the role of the personal actor, seeking to exercise a right to commit suicide – but rather to participate in killing one or more of the others. Similarly, perfectly healthy individuals could assert a right to conclude a suicide pact (perhaps as part of a religious ritual), in which each member does not merely kill herself or himself individually, but rather participates in killing one or more of the others. Note also that not every argument, or every dispute, need involve an identifiable non-personal actor. In the next chapter, we will see that arguments can also be made with reference to broader public concerns, without regard to identified non-personal actors.

7.3 Notation

What kind of marker might we attach to the symbol I in order to designate the non-personal actor? The joy of symbols is that we are free to choose any one we like. We could, for example, choose the marker ‘q’ (I^q). However, the economy of symbolic notation lies in its ability to display relationships between its components.

A basic operation in logic is the negating function, commonly represented by means of a symbol called a ‘tilde’ (~), which appears before some other symbol. Where X represents a proposition, ~X expresses a contradictory proposition. Accordingly, it cannot be the case that both X and ~X are true.[1] For example:

X: *Madrid is the capital of Spain.*

~X: *Madrid is not the capital of Spain.*

Similarly, rather than introducing a new letter, we will use the marker ‘~p’ to denote the non-personal actor as the individual actor who is not the personal actor,[2] but is affected by the conduct of the personal actor ($I^{\sim p}$).[3] In *Lingens*, the symbol I_2 had been used to represent the former Chancellor as the non-personal actor. The formulas A: I_2a [F 5.7] and Z: I_2b [F 5.8] can now be rewritten, respectively,

F 7.1 A: $I^{\sim p}a$

F 7.2 Z: $I^{\sim p}b$

Like I^p, the symbol $I^{\sim p}$ is a constant. Although it represents any non-personal actor in any case, it has no inferior formal values. Indeed, under the Axiom of Mutual Exclusion of Individual Actors, it is I^p and $I^{\sim p}$ which represent the two inferior values of I. Hence:

Ps(I) $I \subset I^p, I^{\sim p}$

7.4 Compound positions

Recall the earlier compound positions in *Lingens*,

F 5.11 A: $I_1c \cdot I_2a$

F 5.12 Z: $I_1d \cdot I_2b$

For the A position, we can now rewrite F 5.11, combining the claimant's position about the interests of the personal actor [A: $I^{p}c$, F 6.1] and the non-personal actor [A: $I^{\neg p}a$, F 7.1] as follows,

F 7.3 A: $I^{p}c \cdot I^{\neg p}a$

Similarly, we can rewrite F 5.12 by combining the respondent's positions in F 6.2 [Z: $I^{p}d$] and F 7.2 [Z: $I^{\neg p}b$],

F 7.4 Z: $I^{p}d \cdot I^{\neg p}b$

7.5 Rapport

Party–actor reflexivity involving the non-personal actor is possible with respect either to the claimant or the respondent. In this section, we will see that the consolidated statement of the rule in Section 6.5 easily expands to accommodate the non-personal actor. Consider some examples. In *Lingens*, at the national level, the Chancellor, in so far as he incurs the effects of Lingens's exercise of the right of expression, is a respondent who speaks about himself as non-personal actor. At the national level, then, F 7.2 [Z: $I^{\neg p}b$] can be translated as, 'The former Chancellor attributes interest b *to himself*'.[4] That reflexive relationship disappears when the Austrian state assumes the role of respondent before the European Court. At that point, F 7.2 translates as 'The respondent (state) attributes interest b to the former Chancellor'. Hence, more generally:

> **Rule of Rapport (Respondent and Non-personal Actor)**: Unless context or usage permit otherwise, non-reflexivity is assumed between the respondent and the non-personal actor.

In other words, unless context or usage permit otherwise, the respondent and the non-personal actor are assumed to be different persons or entities. Barring contrary facts, an acceptable translation of Z: $I^{\neg p}w$ would be 'The respondent attributes interest *w* to the non-personal actor.'

Similarly, in *Laskey*, in so far as each of the men claim to have consented to incur the effects of the exercise of the asserted right by any of the others, they are claimants speaking about themselves [A: $I^{\neg p}x$], but that, too, is only a possibility, since that or any similar case could just as easily be brought by a claimant who is not the personal actor. Hence:

> **Rule of Rapport (Claimant and Non-personal Actor)**: Unless context or usage permit otherwise, non-reflexivity is assumed between the claimant and the non-personal actor.

So, unless context or usage permit otherwise, the claimant and the non-personal actor are assumed to be different persons or entities. Barring contrary facts, an acceptable translation of A: $I^{\neg p}v$ would be 'The claimant attributes interest *v* to the non-personal actor'.

Those applications of the Rule can be extended to θ and θ°, where, again, we see no change in the consolidated statement set forth in Section 6.5. Whether θ represents the claimant or the respondent, reflexivity is always possible, but never necessary:

> **Rule of Rapport (θ and Non-personal Actor)**: Unless context or usage permit otherwise, non-reflexivity is assumed between θ and the non-personal actor.

In that case, unless context or usage permit otherwise, θ and the personal actor are assumed to be different persons or entities. In the absence of contrary facts, an acceptable translation of θ: $I^{\neg p}i$ would be 'Some party attributes interest *i* to the non-personal actor.'

What about θ°, for example, in θ°: $I^{\neg p}k$? Again, the claimant and the respondent cannot be the same person or entity, but a disaggregated translation is possible. For example, if the claimants in *Laskey* agree with the British state on attributing interest *k* to the non-personal actors, one certainly could translate θ°: $I^{p}k$ non-reflexively as, 'All parties attribute interest *k* to the non-personal actors'; however, through disaggregation of the parties, one could translate it just as plausibly by saying, 'The claimants attribute *k* to themselves, and the state (also) attributes *k* to them.' Accordingly, a contingent rule of rapport suffices:

> **Rule of Rapport (θ° and Non-personal Actor)**: Unless context or usage permit otherwise, non-reflexivity is assumed between θ° and the non-personal actor.

Barring contrary circumstances, an acceptable translation of θ°: $I^{p}j$ would be, 'Both parties attribute interest *j* to the non-personal actor.' The rules adopted in this section can be incorporated easily into the consolidated statement set forth in Section 6.5, yielding a more general statement of the relationship between the party and any individual actor:

Rule of Rapport (Party and Individual Actor): Unless context or usage permit otherwise, non-reflexivity is assumed between the party and an individual actor. Except, non-reflexivity *must* be assumed between Z and I^p.

> ***Exercise set 7.1***
>
> Add branches to the tree diagram of agents appearing in Figure 5.1 to reflect the different kinds of individual actors. Add dotted lines to connect parties and individual actors who can appear in relationships of party–actor reflexivity.

7.6 Identity of interest

As with personal actors, an enumeration of non-personal actors $I^{\sim p}{}_1$, $I^{\sim p}{}_2$ . . . $I^{\sim p}{}_n$ is possible when differences among them affect arguments on the merits. However, we will adopt the contrary assumption:

Rule of Identity of Interest (Non-personal Actors): Unless context permits otherwise, the interests of more than one non-personal actor are assumed to be identical.

Again, do not confuse *a particular interest attributed to more than one actor* with *more than one interest attributed to an actor*. The following formula cannot be simplified, as it reflects three distinct interests attributed to the non-personal actor (or to whichever non-personal actors $I^{\sim p}$ represents),

F 7.5 θ: $I^{\sim p}v \cdot I^{\sim p}m \cdot I^{\sim p}n$

7.7 Singular agent

Suppose we encounter some formula A: $I^{\sim p}v$, and want to translate it without knowing anything about the facts of the case. We are already assuming a singular party ('The claimant'). We are left, then, with two possibilities:

a The claimant attributes interest *v* to the non-personal actor.

b The claimant attributes interest *v* to the non-personal actors.

We will therefore adopt:

> **Rule of Singular Agents (Non-personal Actor)**: Unless context permits otherwise, a non-personal actor is assumed to be singular.

That is, unless some contrary fact is known or stipulated, the formula A: $I^{\sim p}v$, is translated by version (a).

7.8 Singular locutions

We will also adopt:

> **Rule of Singular Locutions for Agents (Non-personal Actor)**: Unless context or usage dictate otherwise, choice of singular locution for a personal actor is free.

Accordingly, depending on context, A: $I^{\sim p}v$ can also be translated:

c The claimant attributes interest *v* to the non-personal actor.

d The claimant attributes interest *v* to a non-personal actor.

e The claimant attributes interest *v* to some non-personal actor.

f The claimant attributes interest *v* to a given non-personal actor.

7.9 Application and suspension of assumptions

As with formulas involving personal actors, formulas involving non-personal actors can be translated in various ways, through the application and suspension of contingent rules, as long as any facts which are known or stipulated to be contrary to the contingent assumptions are expressly stated. For example, applying all the rules, the formula A: $I^{\sim p}v$ would be translated as:

> The claimant attributes interest *v* to the non-personal actor.

However, we can produce an alternative translation, say, by assuming plural non-personal actors:

> The claimant attributes interest *v* to the non-personal actors.

Or plural claimants:

> The claimants attribute interest *v* to the non-personal actor.

Or party–actor reflexivity:

> The claimant attributes interest *v* to (her-, him-) itself.

Or plural claimants, plural non-personal actors, party–actor reflexivity, and a modal verb, in which case all of the contingent assumptions are suspended:

> The claimants could attribute interest *v* to themselves.

7.10 Compound positions

Assume a position in which a claimant attributes interests *u* and *v* to a personal and non-personal actor, respectively [A: $I^{p}u \cdot I^{\neg p}v$]. Applying all the contingent rules, we would write:

> The claimant attributes interest *u* to the personal actor and interest *v* to the non-personal actor.

Once again, by variously applying and suspending our assumptions, a broad range of translations is possible. For example, we can suppose a singular personal actor, but plural non-personal actors:

> The claimant attributes interest *u* to the personal actor and interest *v* to the non-personal actors.

Or plural personal actors, but a singular non-personal actor:

> The claimant attributes interest *u* to the personal actors and interest *v* to the non-personal actor.

Or party–actor reflexivity with respect only to the personal actor (as Mr Lingens might do):

> The claimant attributes interest *u* to (her-, him-) itself and interest *v* to the non-personal actor.

Or party–actor reflexivity with respect only to the non-personal actor (imagine a case brought by the non-personal actor on behalf of the personal actor):

> The claimant attributes interest *u* to the personal actor and interest *v* to (her-, him-) itself.

Party–actor reflexivity cannot be assumed for both $I^{p} \cdot I^{\sim p}$ within a single argument, as that would violate the Axiom of Mutual Exclusion of Individual Actors. We could also assume plural claimants, plural non-personal actors and party–actor reflexivity with respect to the personal actor:

> The claimants attribute interest *u* to themselves and interest *v* to the non-personal actors.

In *Laskey*, where we know the facts of the case to be such that the personal and non-personal actors are the same persons, we can write:

> The claimants attribute interests *u* and *v* to themselves and to each other.

On any given distribution of roles, i.e. for any specific instance of such an argument (as explained in Section 7.2), that translation will not violate the Axiom of Mutual Exclusion of Individual Actors. In addition, the phrase 'to each other' in that sentence remains non-reflexive. We are using the concept of reflexivity to describe only arguments made by parties with reference to *themselves*, and not arguments made with reference to anyone else, even if – as in the case of plural individual actors who are both personal and non-personal actors – it is the same persons or entities who are signified.

We can also assume plural claimants, plural non-personal actors, and party–actor reflexivity with respect to the *non*-personal actors:

> The claimants attribute interests *u* and *v* to the personal actors and to themselves.

In *Laskey*, the personal and non-personal actors are the same persons, hence:

> The claimants attribute interests *x* and *y* to each other and to themselves.

Again, for any specific instance of such an argument, that translation will not violate the Axiom of Mutual Exclusion of Individual Actors.

Exercise set 7.2

Translate. (Two of the problems can have more than one correct answer. For those problems, provide both possible answers.)

Example: The claimant attributes interest x to the non-personal actor.

Answer: A: $I^{\sim p}x$

1 Interest s would be attributed to the non-personal actors by the respondents.
2 Some party should attribute interests m and n to the non-personal actor.
3 Some party has attributed interest m to the personal actors and to the non-personal actor.
4 Some party has attributed interest m to the personal actor and to the non-personal actors.
5 The claimants could attribute interest q to themselves.
6 The respondents could attribute interest r to themselves.
7 Some party could attribute interest s to itself.

Exercise set 7.3

Redo Exercise set 7.2, problems 5, 6 and 7, assuming that no other individual actor is affected by the conduct of the personal actor. (Is a response possible in each case?)

Exercise set 7.4

Translate.

Example: Z: $I^{\sim p}x$

Answer: The respondent attributes interest x to the non-personal actor.

1 A: $I^{p}y$
2 θ: $I^{\sim p}s$
3 Z: $I^{p}x \cdot I^{\sim p}y$
4 Z: $I^{\sim p}x \cdot I^{\sim p}y$
5 A: $I^{p}x \cdot I^{\sim p}x$
6 θ: $I^{p}s \cdot I^{\sim p}s$

Exercise set 7.5 *(Optional)*

Redo Exercise set 7.4 assuming plural parties.

Example: Z: $I^{\sim p}x$

Answer: The respondents attribute interest *x* to the non-personal actor.

Exercise set 7.6 *(Optional)*

Redo Exercise set 7.4 assuming plural personal actors.

Example: Z: $I^{\sim p}x$

Answer: The respondent attributes interest *x* to the non-personal actor.

Exercise set 7.7 *(Optional)*

Redo Exercise set 7.4 assuming plural non-personal actors.

Example: Z: $I^{\sim p}x$

Answer: The respondent attributes interest *x* to the non-personal actors.

Exercise set 7.8 *(Optional)*

Redo Exercise set 7.4 assuming plural actors.

Example: Z: $I^{\sim p}x$

Answer: The respondent attributes interest *x* to the non-personal actors.

Exercise set 7.9

Redo Exercise set 7.4 assuming plural agents.

Example: Z: $I^{\sim p}x$

Answer: The respondents attribute interest *x* to the non-personal actors.

Exercise set 7.10

Redo Exercise set 7.4 assuming reflexivity with respect only to the personal actor.

Example: Z: $I^{\sim p}x$

Answer: The respondent attributes interest *x* to the non-personal actor.

Exercise set 7.11

Redo Exercise set 7.4 assuming reflexivity with respect only to the non-personal actor.

Example: Z: $I^{\sim p}x$

Answer: The respondent attributes interest *x* to (her-, him-) itself.

Exercise set 7.12

Redo Exercise set 7.4 assuming plural agents and reflexivity with respect to the personal actor.

Example: Z: $I^{\sim p}x$

Answer: The respondents attribute interest *x* to the non-personal actors.

Exercise set 7.13

Redo Exercise set 7.4 assuming plural agents and reflexivity with respect to the non-personal actor.

Example: Z: $I^{\neg p}x$

Answer: The respondents attribute interest x to themselves.

8 Society

Arguments about rights are not only about individual interests. Broader public aims are also commonly cited as grounds for restricting, or respecting, rights. Those interests are adduced in ways which do not merely reduce to individual interests. Society itself becomes an actor.

8.1 Society as an actor

The famous case of *Handyside v. United Kingdom*[1] concerned the publication in the United Kingdom of a work for schoolchildren, entitled *The Little Red Schoolbook*. The book was first published in Denmark and, later, in translation, in a number of other European and non-European countries. It contained discussions of issues of interest to young people, including human sexuality.

In 1970, a British publisher, Richard Handyside, purchased the rights to issue the book in the United Kingdom. After an initial printing, he sent several hundred review copies to newspapers and journals. A number of British newspapers then launched a campaign critical of the book, drawing attention to the explicit nature of passages which encouraged children to explore their sexuality, and to disregard their parents' or teachers' guidance on matters such as sexual conduct or drug use.[2] Shortly thereafter, British officials, pursuant to the Obscene Publications Acts of 1959 and 1964, seized existing copies of the book and imposed a ban on future publication.[3] After losing challenges to government action in the British courts, Handyside brought an action under the European Convention. The European Court found that the British authorities had not violated the Convention.

How shall we characterise the actors in this case? The position of the claimant *and* personal actor, Mr Handyside, is similar to that of Mr Lingens. Mr Handyside attributes to himself some interest in free expression. The British government attributes to him an interest in free expression *in*sufficient to warrant publication of the book, in view of the potential harm to children. Can we identify a non-personal actor whose interests might be affected by the personal actor's exercise of the right? It is not obvious how we would do so. In *Lingens*, an identifiable individual, the former Chancellor, assumed that role. In *Handyside*, the UK government does not name any specific child who might be harmed by reading the book. The risk asserted by the government is not to any conclusively identifiable child, but to children generally. By extension, in so far as parents, schools and communities are affected, the government deems that risk to be of concern to the broader public.[4] Liberal rights jurisprudence routinely accepts the existence of public interests which need not be adduced with respect to any identifiable individual.[5] It includes a concept of society as an actor – as an entity to which interests are attributed in disputes about rights.

8.2 Notation

Society will be represented with the letter S. In *Handyside*, we can say that the claimant attributes to society an insufficient moral interest *e* in a prohibition of the book,

F 8.1 A: S*e*

The respondent state attributes to society a sufficient moral interest *f* in prohibiting the book's publication,

F 8.2 Z: S*f*

Like I^p and $I^{\sim p}$, the symbol S is a constant. It represents society in any case, and thus a great number of societies under an instrument like the European Convention, but has no inferior formal values. It completes the set of actors,

$Ps(\alpha) \quad \alpha \subset I, S$

(Hence, the set of actor constants, $\alpha \subset I^p, I^{\sim p}, S$, as examined in Section 9.3.)

Consider another example. In *Dudgeon v. United Kingdom*,[6] the European Court examined a Northern Irish prohibition on consensual, adult homosexual conduct. Although Mr Dudgeon had not been prosecuted for committing homosexual acts, police officials, in a search on an otherwise unrelated matter, had discovered his personal correspondence and diaries describing homosexual activity, which served as the basis for a subsequent police interrogation about his sexuality. The European Court found that the prohibition violated Mr Dudgeon's article 8 right to privacy.[7] Although reference was made to the question of 'vulnerable' individuals who might be harmed by homosexual activity,[8] this case, too, involved no identified non-personal actor whose interests could be specifically assessed. The arguments instead centred on the state's authority to legislate in the area of public morals. The British government noted a body of public opinion opposed to law reform,[9] significant enough, in its view, to represent an interest *g* of society as a whole in maintaining the prohibition in force,

F 8.3 Z: S*g*

The claimant used the same kind of argument, noting a substantial body of opinion, which, in his view, was favourable to law reform,[10] and thus attributing to society an interest *h* in abolishing the legislation,

F 8.4 A: S*h*

Even where non-personal actors are clearly identified, arguments about society's broader interests are common. Much of the discussion in *Laskey* is devoted not to the particular interests of the individuals concerned, but to society's broader interests in permitting or prohibiting sadomasochism, with regard to questions of public health or morals.[11]

8.3 State organs and state interests

If a unit of government imposes a restriction on a right, questions may arise not only about the substantive legitimacy of the restriction, but also about whether that unit of government acted within its powers. The dispute may then focus on the apparatus of government, such as questions of separation of powers or checks and balances. Specific government organs may have distinct interests in the outcome of the dispute. Recall that, in this analysis, we are examining only disputes about the substantive validity of restrictions, without regard to such questions.[12] However, that sidelining of intra-governmental elements does not render all interests of government bodies irrelevant to our analysis. If there is any sense in which the interests of government bodies are relevant to arguments about the *substantive merits* of the case, then they are relevant to our analysis.

In *Rees v. United Kingdom*,[13] *Cossey v. United Kingdom*[14] (and, more recently, *Sheffield and Horsham v. United Kingdom*[15]), post-operative transsexuals complained about the refusal of the government to effectuate adequate changes to personal identification documents reflecting their change of sex. They described that omission as a source of distress in situations in which proof of identity was required,[16] such as application for employment, judicial proceedings, or the procurement of passports and visas, insurance policies or access to personal details held by public authorities.[17] In *Rees* and *Cossey*, the dispute focused largely on the question of the state's positive obligations, the government arguing that a duty to modify certain personal identification documents would impose excessive administrative burdens on the responsible State bodies.[18] Such an argument identifies organs of state as entities having a distinct interest in the substantive validity of the restriction.

To which actor is that interest attributable? Among the actors we have identified, the one which seems most closely to match 'the state' – and, by extension, organs of the state – would be 'society'. But how close is that match? An interest in shielding the apparatus of the state from sheer administrative burden or expense seems different from an interest in promoting public morals or health, as asserted in *Laskey*, *Handyside* or *Dudgeon*. Of course, transsexualism *also* raises concerns of health or morals;[19] but those concerns are distinct from sheer questions of administrative onus. Surely there is a difference between the interests of the broader populace in health and morals and the interests of the internal machinery of state?

Under other kinds of analysis, there might be good reason to draw that distinction. But we will not do so here. We will draw no distinction between interests attributed to the broader public and interests attributed to the some organ of government. (Indeed, as a general matter, an interest in efficient and cheap government can just as credibly be attributed to society as a whole as an interest in health or morals, even if that is done implausibly in some individual cases.) We will therefore opt for a notation form within which the interests of state organs are understood to be asserted as interests of society. In *Rees* and *Cossey*, the attribution of an unjustifiable burden *j* to the state, will be recorded as the attribution of an unjustifiable burden *j* to society [Z: S*j*]. The claimant, in response, attributes to the state, and thus to society, a justifiable burden *k* [A: S*k*].

8.4 Rapport

Where it is some branch of government which assumes the respondent position, and, in that position, attributes to society interests of some organ of the state, then the state talks about itself. In such cases, Z positions taking the form Z: S*x* are reflexive. In *Rees* and *Cossey*, the state speaks of *its* interest in avoiding excessive administrative burdens.

Of course, it may not always be possible to draw a clear distinction between a general public interest and an interest of some organ of state. Consider, for example, disputes concerning national security or public order. The case of *Leander v. Sweden*[20] concerned an individual who was denied employment at a naval museum situated near a restricted military zone, on the basis of information compiled by the Swedish authorities about his private life, the content or sources of which were not disclosed to him. He brought a complaint under article 8 of the Convention, claiming that the use of such material to his detriment constituted a violation of his right to privacy. The government claimed that a duty to disclose such information would jeopardise the interests *l* of the state's security forces[21] [Z: S*l*]. Such an argument does not, and arguably *can*not, clearly distinguish between, on the one hand, state security as a general public safety issue, and, on the other hand, State security as a mere matter of internal government management or administration.

How shall we treat such ambiguities? Do not forget why the concept of rapport has been introduced in the first place. It is decisive in the structure of arguments. It serves only to facilitate translation from symbolic back to natural language. In order to avoid error, we have been applying background assumptions of non-reflexivity, which may produce awkward locutions in ordinary speech ('Mary Smith attributes interest *u* to Mary Smith'), but will not produce errors. That awkwardness barely arises when it is a more abstract entity, such as a government or a government body, that is speaking. It would be entirely accurate, and not particularly awkward, to record the Z positions in *Rees* and *Cossey* in non-reflexive terms, by saying that the state in each case attributes *to society* an interest in avoiding excessive burdens on government. Similarly, in *Leander,* it would be appropriate to say that the state attributes to society an interest in national security. The only point to examining reflexivity between respondents and state bodies is to note that a reflexive relationship *is possible.* Hence:

> **Rule of Rapport (Respondent and Society)**: Unless context or usage permit otherwise, non-reflexivity is assumed between the respondent and society.

Barring a contrary context, we would therefore translate the formula Z: Sx as, 'The respondent attributes interest x to society.'

Can there be reflexivity between a set of claimants and society as a whole [A: Sy]? As we will not encounter such a situation in this study, we need not be too concerned about it. Nevertheless, such a scenario is certainly conceivable. Claimants purporting to represent society in general would be accusing some respondent, such as a state, of committing human rights violations. A phenomenon coming close to that scenario would be a massive class action or an *actio popularis.* Such litigation might arise against states accused of committing widespread and systemic violations.[22] In such a case, it is conceivable that the claimants would plausibly refer to the interests of society as a first-person 'we'. As a point of sheer translation, then, the possibility of such an argument must be left open. Hence, the contingent rule:

> **Rule of Rapport (Claimant and Society)**: Unless context or usage permit otherwise, non-reflexivity is assumed between the claimant and society.

Unless contrary facts are known or stipulated, we would therefore translate the formula A: Sy as: 'The claimant attributes interest y to society.'

The effects of θ and $\theta°$ are straightforward. Whether θ represents the claimant or the respondent, reflexivity is always possible, but never necessary:

Rule of Rapport (θ and Society): Unless context or usage permit otherwise, non-reflexivity is assumed between θ and society.

In the absence of contrary facts, an acceptable translation of θ: S*k* would be, 'Some party attributes interest *k* to society.' As to θ°, the claimant and the respondent cannot be the same person or entity, but a disaggregated translation is possible (e.g. for θ°: *p* in *Rees* or *Cossey*, 'The respondent state attributes interest *p* to itself, the claimants attribute interest *p* to it'). Hence, a contingent rule:

Rule of Rapport (θ° and Society): Unless context or usage permit otherwise, non-reflexivity is assumed between θ° and society.

The rules adopted in this section can be incorporated into a further refinement of the consolidated statement, expressing the relationship between any party and any actor:

Rule of Rapport (Party and Actor): Unless context or usage permit otherwise, non-reflexivity is assumed between the party and an actor. Except, non-reflexivity *must* be assumed between Z and I^p.

Exercise set 8.1

Draw a tree diagram of all agents, adding dotted lines to connect agents who can appear in relationships of party–actor reflexivity.

Exercise set 8.2

Translate.

Example: The claimant attributes interest *x* to society.

Answer: A: S*x*

1 Some party had attributed interest *x* to the non-personal actor and interest y to society.
2 The respondents could attribute interest *x* to the personal actor and to the state.
3 The respondent, Mathilde, should have attributed interest *x* to the personal actor and to society.
4 The respondent government attributed interest *x* to itself.
5 The claimant attributed interests *x*, *y* and *z* to the state.
6 Both parties attributed interests *x* and *z* to the state.

8.5 Multiple societies

The relevant society in a given case will ordinarily be construed as limited to the jurisdiction in which the restriction is imposed. However, under international, federally structured, or devolved jurisdictions, the interests of more than one society may nevertheless be introduced into argument. Central to Mr Handyside's arguments was the view that the ban on *The Little Red Book* could not plausibly be deemed 'necessary' for the protection of morals, under article 8(2) of the European Convention, in so far as it already circulated freely in most states that were parties to the Convention.[23] He argued that the interests *e* of British society [A: S_1e] are similar in relevant respects to the interests *e* shared by other European societies [A: S_2e, S_3e, . . .]. The Court, however, agreed with the view of the British government that, even conceding the characterisation of interests *e* common to other European societies [Z: S_2e, S_3e, . . .], the interests *f* of British society [Z: S_1f] may not be similar.[24] Hence the Court's famous dictum that 'it is not possible to find in the domestic law of the various Contracting States a uniform European conception of morals',[25] which forms the basis of the 'margin of appreciation' doctrine as applied to the 'public morals' provisions of articles 8–11. (We will return to the margin of appreciation doctrine in our analysis of the concept of harm.)

In addition, Mr Handyside, noting that the book had not been the object of proceedings in Scotland, Northern Ireland, the Channel Islands or the Isle of Man, suggested a parity of relevant interests among various British 'societies', such that the interests *e* of society in England and Wales [A: S_1e] should be deemed similar in relevant respects to the interests *e* shared by those other British societies [A: $S_{1.1}e$, $S_{1.2}e$, . . .].[26] Here too, however, the Court agreed with view of the British government that, even conceding interests *e* common to those other British societies [Z: $S_{1.1}e$, $S_{1.2}e$, . . .], the interests *b* of England and Wales [Z: S_1b] should not be assumed to be similar.[27] Similarly, Mr Dudgeon assimilated the interests of Northern Irish society to those of European societies, and other societies within Britain, which had abolished sodomy laws,[28] while the British government distinguished those interests.[29]

It is possible, then, to enumerate multiple societies in order to account for their various interests. However, on closer inspection, we see that there is an important difference between enumerating multiple individual actors and enumerating multiple societies. In these examples from *Handyside* and *Dudgeon*, the enumeration of societies serves an inherently comparative function. The claimant seeks to elicit *similarities* between the interests of S_1 and the interests of S_2 and S_3 or $S_{1.1}$ or $S_{1.2}$; the respondent seeks to elicit *differences* between them and S_1. A given argument about the interests of societies S_2 or $S_{1.1}$ is made not for *their* sake, but for the sake of characterising the interests of S_1. The enumeration of societies serves only the purpose of characterising the interests of the society corresponding to the jurisdiction whose laws or practices are at issue in the dispute, and not to characterise the interests of those other societies as a distinct matter.

By contrast, suppose a case like *Laskey*, in which the individual actors' interests are distinct – say, one of them is a minor (I_1); another is recognised as incompetent to give consent (I_2); and another only filmed the acts without committing any of them (I_3). Those individual actors are enumerated because the norms governing each of them may be different. Each man is enumerated for the sake of characterising *his* interests and determining *his* rights, and not merely for the sake of discussing the rights or interests of some other individual actor. It is possible that one of the men might be found to have a right (say, a man who engaged only in physically harmless acts with another, competent and consenting, man), which another man did not have (say, a man who inflicted harm on a minor). Of course, like multiple societies, individual actors, too, *may* be enumerated merely for the purpose of drawing a comparison which does not ultimately bear on the adjudication of those actors' respective rights. However, the enumeration of individual actors is not restricted to a purely comparative function. It can also serve the purpose of distinguishing individual actors whose rights may be adjudicated in different ways.

The purely comparative role played by references to S_2 or S_3 does not mean that those societies have no interest whatsoever in the resolution of the dispute. Certainly, the way the European Court resolves a dispute for one society within its jurisdiction will have consequences for the way it decides similar disputes for any other society within its jurisdiction.[30] However, unlike enumerated individual actors, there is no sense in which those other societies' interests or powers are expressly adjudicated within the confines of the dispute at hand. The Rule of Identity of Interest thus applies with special force. Except in the occasional dispute having a specifically transnational, and thus trans-jurisdictional, element, rarely would distinct interests of more than one society be at issue in the adjudication of a dispute about civil rights or liberties. Hence:

> **Rule of Identity of Interest (Society)**: Unless context permits otherwise, the interests of more than one society are assumed to be identical.

Handyside and *Dudgeon* do nevertheless illustrate how multiple societies may be relevant for sheer purposes of comparison. While assuming the society to be singular, we will allow for the introduction of additional S symbols where express, comparative reference is made to other societies in argument. Nevertheless, the initial assumption will always be that only one society is at issue:

> **Rule of Singular Agents (Society)**: Unless context permits otherwise, a society is assumed to be singular.

As the society at issue is generally known (or stipulated), reference to 'the' society will suffice. In other contexts, however, other singular translations are admissible, such as 'a society' or 'a given society':

> **Rule of Singular Locutions for Agents (Society)**: Unless context or usage dictate otherwise, choice of singular locution for society is free.

8.6 Application and suspension of assumptions

A: $I^{p}x \cdot I^{\sim p}x \cdot Sx$	θ: $I^{p_1}p \cdot I^{\sim p_2}q \cdot Sr$
Z: $I^{p_1}p \cdot I^{\sim p_2}q \cdot Sr$	A: $I^{p}a \cdot I^{p}b \cdot Sc$
θ: $I^{p}p \cdot I^{\sim p}q \cdot Sr$	Z: $I^{p}y \cdot I^{\sim p}y \cdot Sy$
θ: $Sr \cdot Ss \cdot St$	Z: $I^{\sim p_1}p \cdot I^{\sim p_2}q \cdot I^{\sim p_3}r$

Figure 8.1

Our stock of agent symbols is now complete. It is large enough to generate a variety of combinations. Consider the random examples in Figure 8.1. If we contemplate the ways in which contingent assumptions can be variously applied and suspended in translation (singular or plural parties or actors, reflexivity and non-reflexivity, etc.), the range of possible translations becomes enormous.

In the past few chapters, we have seen that we must not underestimate the importance of translation. It is crucial to our ability to use the symbolic language with confidence. Yet it would be a mistake to exaggerate the role of translation. Throughout the remaining chapters of the book, we will see that θ positions appearing in actual cases are rarely as complicated as that random list would suggest. In most of the remaining chapters, the emphasis will be on actual cases, or rather straightforward hypothetical ones, where our ability to refer to specified individuals and societies (Mr Handyside, Mr Lingens; the UK, Austria . . .) will help to keep the various roles clear. More complicated combinations will occasionally appear – not in the case studies, but in the exercise sets, in the view that, if one can work with complicated configurations, then one can work all the more confidently and critically with easier ones. However, for the most part, little emphasis will be placed on complicated formulas which, while theoretically possible, would rarely arise in the analysis of actual cases.

Exercise set 8.3

Translate.

Example: A: $I^p x \cdot Sx$

Answer: The claimant attributes interest x to the personal actor and to society.

1 Z: Sp
2 Z: $Sa \cdot Sb \cdot Sc$
3 θ: $I^p x \cdot I^{\sim p} x \cdot Sx$
4 A: $I^p x \cdot I^{\sim p} y \cdot Sz$
5 θ°: $I^{\sim p} y \cdot Sz$

Exercise set 8.4

Redo Exercise set 8.3, assuming plural individual actors.

Example: A: $I^p x \cdot Sx$

Answer: The claimant attributes interest x to the personal actors and to society.

Exercise set 8.5

Redo Exercise set 8.3, problems 1 and 2, assuming reflexivity.

Exercise set 8.6

Redo Exercise set 8.3, problems 3 and 4, assuming reflexivity with respect to the personal actor.

Exercise set 8.7

Redo Exercise set 8.3, problems 3 and 4, assuming plural parties, plural individual actors, and reflexivity with respect to the non-personal actor.

9 Theorems and proofs

In this chapter, a technique is introduced for stating more systematically the relationships among agents.

9.1 Inventory of agents

We have now examined all of the agents required for the model. Their relationships are as follows:

Agent postulates

Ps(ψ) $\psi \subset \theta, \alpha$ Ps(θ) $\theta \subset A, Z$

Ps(α) $\alpha \subset I, S$ Ps(I) $I \subset I^{p}, I^{\neg p}$

(Weakly) exclusive symbol		*Inclusive symbol*	
ψ	'Some agent'	(ψ°)	('All agents')
θ	'Some party'	θ°	'Both (all) parties'
α	'Some actor'	α°	'All actors'
I	'Some individual actor'	I°	'All individual actors'

Figure 9.1

Our technique for distinguishing between the weakly exclusive symbol θ and the inclusive symbol θ° can be applied equally to the symbols ψ, α and I, as shown in Figure 9.1. For example, we can note that some party attributes the same interest *i* to all of the individual actors by writing

θ: I°*i*. We can note that both parties attribute interest *j* to some actor by writing θ°: αj. We can note that the respondent attributes interest *k* to all actors by writing Z: α°*k*. (The symbol ψ° appears in parentheses, as it is a purely theoretical construct. It cannot appear in any θ position, as θ positions are so structured to admit only an agent symbol representing a party to appear before the colon, and only an agent symbol representing an actor to appear after the colon. The weakly exclusive ψ would rarely be useful, even if it can appear unproblematically in θ positions. For any formula θ: ψi, it is already stipulated that ψ must be some α. And for any formula ψ: αi, it is already stipulated that ψ must be some θ. Any formula ψ: ψi takes the value θ: αi. The more abstract formulations employing the weakly exclusive ψ are no more than trivially informative.)

9.2 Rapport

The variable I would only be subject to an absolute rule of non-reflexivity *if* it were the case that θ = Z and I = I^p. However, barring any contrary context, it can just as easily be the case that I = $I^{\sim p}$. Similarly, α is subject to absolute non-reflexivity only if θ = Z and α = I^p. However, barring any contrary context, it can just as easily be the case that α = $I^{\sim p}$ or S. Hence:

> **Rule of Rapport (Party and Individual Actor)**: Unless context or usage dictate otherwise, non-reflexivity is assumed between any party and I.

> **Rule of Rapport (Party and Actor)**: Unless context or usage dictate otherwise, non-reflexivity is assumed between any party and α.

Since I° represents all individual actors, and α° represents all actors, it would seem that non-reflexivity would be required if either of these appeared in a Z position. However, just like θ°, these too allow 'disaggregated' translations. For a respondent like Mr Kreisky, although he is a non-personal actor, the formula Z: α°*i* can certainly be translated non-reflexively: 'The respondent attributes interest *i* to all actors.' However, a partially reflexive translation is equally possible, by breaking down α° into its components: 'The respondent attributes interest *i* to himself and to all other actors.' The consolidated statement of the Rule of Rapport as set forth in Section 8.4 therefore remains unchanged:

> **Rule of Rapport (Party and Actor)**: Unless context or usage permit otherwise, non-reflexivity is assumed between any party and any actor. Except, non-reflexivity *must* be assumed between Z and I^p.

Exercise set 9.1

Translate.

Example: The claimant attributes interest x to all actors.

Answer: A: $\alpha^{\circ}x$

1 Both parties attribute interest a to some individual actor.
2 Some party attributes interest a to some actor.
3 All parties attribute interest a to some agent.
4 The respondent attributes interest b to both personal actors.
5 All parties attribute interest a to all actors.
6 Some party attributes interest b to all individual actors.
7 Some agent attributes interest a to some agent.

Exercise set 9.2

Translate.

Example: A: $\mathrm{I}^{\circ}a$

Answer: The claimant attributes interest a to all individual actors.

1 Z: $\mathrm{I}^{\circ}b$
2 θ: αc
3 θ°: $\alpha^{\circ}d$
4 A: $\mathrm{I}^{\circ}a \cdot \mathrm{I}^{\mathrm{p}}b$

Exercise set 9.3

Redo Exercise set 9.2, assuming plural agents and agent reflexivity.

Example: A: $\mathrm{I}^{\mathrm{p}}\mathrm{a}$

Answer: The claimants attribute interest a to themselves.

9.3 Theorems

By combining postulates, we can generate more specific values for variables. For example, by combining Ps(α) and Ps(I), we see that a more precise definition can be given for α. The term *theorem* (Th) will be used to denote a *formula that derives a set of values of a symbol from one or more* postulates. Hence,

Th(α) $\alpha \subset I^{p}, I^{\sim p}, S$

That theorem is simple enough to derive mentally, but later on it will help to have a technique for proving theorems – deriving them from postulates.

The technique will be as follows. To the left of each step, we place a number in parentheses, to show which step it is. To the right, we indicate a justification for the step. The final step is called a 'conclusion'. As an example, let's derive Th(α), which can be proved in two steps: one prior step, and one concluding step, as follows,

(1)	$\alpha \subset I, S$	Ps(α)
conclusion	$\alpha \subset I^{p}, I^{\sim p}, S$	Ps(I)

The same result can be achieved regardless of the order in which the postulates are introduced, as follows,

(1)	$I \subset I^{p}, I^{\sim p}$	Ps(I)
conclusion	$\alpha \subset I^{p}, I^{\sim p}, S$	Ps(α)

As a result, answers provided for exercise sets will, in some cases, represent only one approach.

Exercise set 9.4

Derive the following theorems using the agent postulates.

Example: $\psi \subset A, Z, I, S$

(1)	$\psi \subset \theta, \alpha$	Ps(ψ)
(2)	$\psi \subset A, Z, \alpha$	Ps(θ)
conclusion	$\psi \subset A, Z, I, S$	Ps(α)

1 $\psi \subset \theta, I, S$
2 $\psi \subset A, Z, \alpha$
3 $\psi \subset \theta, I^{p}, I^{\sim p}, S$
4 $\psi \subset A, Z, I^{p}, I^{\sim p}, S$

A small number of postulates can generate a considerable number of theorems. For example, Exercise set 9.4 illustrates four different theorems that state values for the variable ψ. If we wanted to preserve all four for future use, we could label them, for example, Th(ψ1), Th(ψ2), Th(ψ3) and Th(ψ4). However, not all theorems are equally useful. A theorem such as Th(α) is beneficial in so far as it displays all of the most specific values of α. By contrast, a theorem such as $\psi \subset \theta$, I, S, as in problem 1, provides only some practice in using postulates, but will not be important as a general matter.

Appendix 2 will provide a record of all postulates, but only of the more useful theorems. Of the problems in Exercise set 9.4, only the theorem derived in problem 4 is of interest, as it displays all of the most specific values of ψ. While that theorem will be added to Appendix 2, it need not be labelled with an accompanying numeral, as none of the others will be added,

Th(ψ) $\psi \subset$ A, Z, I^p, $I^{\neg p}$, S

Theorems can be used just like postulates to justify steps taken in proving other theorems. In the remaining chapters, only theorems appearing in Appendix 2 will be used for proofs. Moreover, as with postulates, theorems can sometimes be introduced in different order, thus allowing for more than one correct answer.

Exercise set 9.5

Redo Exercise set 9.4, problems 3 and 4, using only the agent postulates and Th(α), and using the fewest possible steps.

9.4 Hierarchy and substitution

The agent postulates, and any theorems deriving from them, provide formulaic expressions of relationships which have already been depicted in tree diagrams. The diagram in Exercise set 7.1 illustrates a *hierarchy* of relationships between the symbols. One symbol is *hierarchically inferior* to another (which is *hierarchically superior*) when the inferior symbol represents only one possible value of the superior one. For example, the personal actor (I^p) represents only one kind of individual actor (I). The symbol I^p is therefore hierarchically inferior to I. Similarly, I is hierarchically inferior to α; and α is inferior to ψ. (Of course, those concepts of hierarchical superiority and inferiority refer only to relatively broader and narrower classes of actors, and not to degrees of power or importance.)

A hierarchically superior variable can always *substitute* for any other variable which is inferior to it. For example, the position Z: $I^p v$ would be translated as:

> The respondent attributes interest v to the personal actor.

That position implies the position θ: $I^p v$:

> Some party attributes interest v to the personal actor.

Or the position θ: Iv:

> Some party attributes interest v to some individual actor.

At the highest level of abstraction, it implies ψ: ψv:

> Some agent attributes interest v to some agent.'

Altogether, the position Z: $I^p v$ implies all of the following formulas set forth in Figure 9.2.

Z: $I^p v$	θ: $I^p v$	ψ: $I^p v$
Z: Iv	θ: Iv	ψ: Iv
Z: αv	θ: αv	ψ: αv
Z: ψv	θ: ψv	ψ: ψv

Figure 9.2

Ordinarily, we would prefer to use the formula Z: $I^p v$. Being hierarchically inferior to all of the others, it is the most precise. Nevertheless, as the analysis proceeds, it will at times be useful to write formulas at higher levels of generality. It will sometimes be useful to refer to a party (θ) without specifying its role as claimant or respondent; or to refer to an individual actor (I) without specifying its role as personal actor or non-personal actor; or to refer to an actor (α) without specifying its role as individual actor or society. (The diagram in Exercise set 7.1 illustrates the rough distinction between the more precise character of symbols represented by

Roman letters and the more abstract character of those represented by Greek letters.) The agent represented by *the most hierarchically inferior* value of a variable will always be a constant (A, Z, I^p, $I^{\sim p}$, S) and can be called *specified.* By contrast, *a hierarchically superior* agent will be represented by a variable (ψ, θ, α, I), and will be called *unspecified.*

9.5 Deriving arguments: the presupposition calculus

By using a technique similar to that for deriving theorems, we can derive more abstract arguments from less abstract ones. The first step always requires that the initial argument be stated. We will justify that step by writing the word 'argument given' (or simply, 'given') in the right-hand column. We can then derive a more abstract argument. For example, the following calculation demonstrates that the statement 'The claimant attributes interest *u* to the non-personal actor', implies the statement 'The claimant attributes interest *u* to some individual actor':

From A: $I^{\sim p}u$ derive A: I*u*,

(1)	A: $I^{\sim p}u$	argument given
conclusion	A: I*u*	Ps(I)

As with theorems, there will often be more than one way to derive an argument. Compare the following two derivations of θ: I*u* from A: $I^{\sim p}u$,

From A: $I^{\sim p}u$ derive θ: I*u*,

(1)	A: $I^{\sim p}u$	given
(2)	θ: $I^{\sim p}u$	Ps(θ)
conclusion	θ: I*u*	Ps(I)

From A: $I^{\sim p}u$ derive θ: I*u*,

(1)	A: $I^{\sim p}u$	given
(2)	A: I*u*	Ps(I)
conclusion	θ: I*u*	Ps(θ)

Here too, the answers to the Exercise sets may represent only one approach.

In view of the limited number of agents and the simple relationships among them, recourse to these formalised techniques may appear unnecessary. As additional elements are added to the model, however, we will see that these techniques allow us to ascertain relationships between more complex formulas. In particular, the foregoing technique of deriving arguments illustrated will be called a *presupposition calculus*. However, the techniques for proving theorems and deriving arguments introduced in this chapter are limited to that role of ascertaining relationships between elements in the model. They should not be seen as serving any broader validity-testing function. None of inclusive symbols ($\psi°$, $\theta°$, $\alpha°$, I°) appear, for the same reason they do not appear in the postulates and tree diagrams. Their role is one of convenience, as they form no necessary part of the model. A calculus incorporating them would become complex, and would yield little additional insight into liberal rights discourse.

Exercise set 9.6

1 Derive A: Ia from A: I^{p}a.
2 Derive θ: αb from Z: I^{p}b, using only postulates.
3 Derive θ: αc from A: I$^{\sim p}c$, using the fewest possible steps.
4 Derive θ: αb from θ: Sb.

9.6 Valid and invalid inference

The process of deriving arguments moves in the opposite direction from the process of proving theorems. To prove a theorem, we move down the ladder of generality in order to ascertain a set of more specific values of a variable. To derive an argument, we move up the ladder, substituting hierarchically superior variables for inferior ones, in order to ascertain a more general statement of the original position.

It is important not to confuse the two processes. The following derivation would be fallacious, as it is impossible to derive an argument by moving down the ladder. It is impossible to derive a specific argument from a more general one,

From θ: Iu derive A: I$^{\sim p}u$,

(1)	θ: Iu	given
(2)	A: Iu	Ps(θ)
conclusion	A: I$^{\sim p}u$	Ps(I)

That calculation contains two errors. In step (2), the value A is inferred from the variable θ. That inference is invalid, however, since A is only one possible value of θ. Similarly, in the concluding step, the value I$^{\sim p}$ is erroneously inferred from the variable I, as I$^{\sim p}$ represents only one possible value of I. Of course, in this example, those two steps may not at first seem particularly jarring, since the resulting formula A: I$^{\sim p}u$ does, after all, represent one possible value of the more general formula θ: I*u*. However, in order to see more clearly the kind of error which could result if such steps were allowed, consider the following derivation,

From A: $I^{\sim p}u$ derive Z: $I^{\sim p}u$,

(1)	A: $I^{\sim p}u$	given
(2)	θ: $I^{\sim p}u$	Ps(θ)
conclusion	Z: $I^{\sim p}u$	Ps(θ)

It is true that A and Z *might* agree on something, but it hardly follows as a matter of course. Similarly, just as deriving arguments cannot move down the ladder of generality, proving theorems cannot move up it. For example, it is permissible to move down the ladder by saying that any value of α or θ represents a value of ψ. However, we cannot move up the ladder by allowing ψ to represent a value of α or θ. In the following proof, each step is fallacious,

Prove the theorem: I ⊂ θ

(1)	I ⊂ α	Ps(α)
(2)	I ⊂ ψ	Ps(ψ)
conclusion	I ⊂ θ	Ps(ψ)

9.7 Binarism

In Section 3.5, we considered one means by which a theory might reject liberal rights altogether – by rejecting the exclusively binary system of parties [θ ⊂ A, Z]. We now have a second approach. The schema of actors represented by the variable α is binary in structure: individuals (I) and society (S) represent the primary distinction [α ⊂ I, S]. Personal and non-personal actors represent only more precisely specified individual actors, and that subordinate relationship to the I variable is itself binary [I ⊂ I^p, $I^{\sim p}$]. Those configurations make no room for the possibility of actors whose composition is intermediary between individual actors and society as a whole, such as social, economic, racial, ethnic, religious, sexual or linguistic groupings, for example in the form of group rights or entitlements.[1] Although the interests of social, political or economic groupings may indeed be adduced in liberal rights discourse, they can be formulated only as individual interests (I) or as interests of society as a whole (S).

The case of *Jersild v. Denmark*[2] provides an illustration. It concerned a weekly television documentary program (*Søndagsavisen*), aired by the Danish Broadcasting Corporation, which had broadcast an interview with members of an extreme right-wing racist group. The group members voiced racist views at length, using gross invective.[3] Shortly thereafter, the Public Prosecutor brought criminal charges against the interviewing journalist, Jersild, under a national law prohibiting the dissemination of communications which are 'threatening, insulting or degrading [to] a group of persons on account of their race, colour, national or ethnic origin or belief'.[4] Following his conviction, Jersild brought a complaint to the European Court.

The measures taken by the government against the radio broadcast were motivated largely by an interest in protecting minority groups.[5] Denmark did not, however, formulate that interest as a right held by an ascertainable group as distinct from interests of individual members of such a group or of society as a whole. Defended by Denmark under the public morals clause of article 10(2), the restriction was justified as an interest v of society as a whole in preventing racist expression [Z: Sv],[6] from which the government's desire to extend protection to individual members of minority groups could be inferred [Z: $I^{\sim p}v$].[7] Liberal rights discourse thus reduces both the quantity and the variety of collective interests to two sets of abstractions: individuals (I^p, $I^{\sim p}$) and society as a whole (S). In the same way, liberal rights discourse can, as a formal matter, only portray the men in *Laskey* as individual agents acting upon each other (I^p, $I^{\sim p}$), without any interpersonal or collective identity being attributable to them. Our present task is not to enter any of the quarrels about the advantages or limitations which follow from that structure, but only to record it – to pinpoint how a disagreement about rights can only become a disagreement *between* parties who are in a binary relationship $[\theta \subset A, Z]$ *about* actors in binary relationships $[\alpha \subset I, S]$, $[I \subset I^p, I^{\sim p}]$.

Review these terms

1 theorem
2 hierarchy
3 substitution

10 Implication and implicature

We have now examined three actors: the personal actor, the non-personal actor and society. Yet arguments made about them are not always distinct. In some cases, a party's view about the interests of an actor must be inferred from an argument made about some other actor. In this chapter, we examine concepts of *implied interests* and *implied actors*.

10.1 Strict and broad implication

Consider the following scenario. Last week, the rumour mill had it that Barbie would graduate from university with a physics degree only if she passed her course in advanced calculus. In other words, if she were to receive her physics degree, then it would be the case that she had passed advanced calculus. This week, the rumour mill has it that Barbie has graduated from university with a physics degree. If the rumour mill is correct, we can deduce that Barbie has passed her course in advanced calculus:

(1) If Barbie has received her physics degree, then Barbie has passed advanced calculus.
(2) Barbie has received her physics degree.
∴ Barbie has passed advanced calculus.

In a sense, that reasoning is flawless. In another sense, however, it is deficient. Let's assume nothing outrageous: Barbie is not living in some weird other world. She lives in our more-or-less familiar world. One feature of our world is that physics degrees are ordinarily awarded upon completion of an entire curriculum of courses. That curriculum may vary from one institution to the next, but every institution will have some specified regimen of courses. Certainly, there will be exceptional cases: some students may be allowed to skip otherwise required courses; or to transfer coursework completed at other institutions. For the most part, however, whatever customary or idiosyncratic requirements Barbie's institution may set, she will ordinarily have to have completed more than just one course in order to receive a physics degree.

Ordinarily, then, we reason within a broader context of assumptions. Consider again the rumour that Barbie would graduate from university with a physics degree only if she passed her course in advanced calculus. Upon hearing that statement, we might reason that Barbie, although universally known as a genius, was also universally known for her 'maths anxiety'; or that it was already known that she had passed her other exams, and advanced calculus was the only exam left for her to sit; or that she had failed advanced calculus once before (not having failed anything else), and, under university regulations, was allowed only one opportunity to resit the advanced calculus exam. In other words, whatever we might conclude, we would not ordinarily take the reasoning in the foregoing syllogism at face value, as a full account of the circumstances surrounding Barbie's receipt of her degree. We would not ordinarily assume (nor does the syllogism strictly imply) that advanced calculus was the *only* subject that Barbie had to pass in order to receive her degree. We would ordinarily assume that, since advanced calculus was only one of several courses that she had to pass, it was being singled out by the rumour mill for some other reason.

Within this familiar, real-world context, a more accurate rendering of the first premise would be, 'If Barbie has received her physics degree, then Barbie has passed the requisite courses, including advanced calculus'; or, more simply, 'If Barbie has received her physics degree, then Barbie has passed the requisite courses'. Yet neither of those more accurate renderings can be derived from the first premise as it stands. Indeed, from those revised versions, we could reach the further conclusion, 'Barbie has passed the requisite courses including advanced calculus', or, more simply, 'Barbie has passed the requisite courses' – yet those conclusions, too, are unattainable from the first and second premises as they stand.

We must distinguish, then, between conclusions strictly implied by the premises, and conclusions which, albeit not strictly implied by the premises, may nevertheless be accurately inferred from them within a generally accepted context. Following Paul Grice, we can distinguish between two kinds of inferences, using the term 'implicature' to denote the latter, broad type of implication.[1] That concept of implicature more closely resembles ordinary, non-technical uses of terms like 'implication', also often denoted by words like 'suggestion' or 'intimation', where an implication is drawn not merely from the letter of the statements, but also from their overall context. By contrast, recall the concept of strict, logical implication, whereby conclusions are valid only in so far as they follow from stated premises.[2]

The point is not that one sense of the concept of implication is superior to the other. Each serves its own purpose. The advantage of the concept of implicature is that it more accurately describes ordinary language and reasoning. Its disadvantage is that agreed contexts and assumptions are not always obvious or undisputed, making it difficult in some cases to distinguish reliable from unreliable reasoning. By contrast, the disadvantage of strict, logical implication is that, as in Barbie's case, it operates within such a narrow band that it can fail to reflect sheer common sense. Its advantage, however, is that, within that narrow band, we can more easily reason without committing fallacies: the reasoning in the foregoing syllogism may be less than fully informative, but, as far as it goes, it is impeccable.

For our purposes, both concepts of implication will be useful, as long as we do not confuse them. In the remainder of the analysis, the concept of implication will be limited to strict logical implication only when applied to arguments expressed in symbolic form, e.g. for proving theorems or deriving arguments according to the method introduced in Chapter 8. Otherwise, where we are considering legal argument more generally, outside of a fully formalised procedure, we will allow the broader concept, as long as the context is clearly stated. That will enable us to construe arguments in the light of the ordinary, non-controversial assumptions that would govern a system of rights like the European Convention. The purpose of this chapter is to consider the broader inferences that can be drawn from assertions made in legal disputes.

10.2 Redundancy

In Section 8.1, we identified the concept of society as an actor by comparing *Handyside* to *Lingens*. In *Lingens*, a restriction on a right is justified with reference to the interests of an identified individual; in *Handyside*, it is justified with reference to a general public interest. Yet that difference is not absolute.

In *Lingens*, the government defends the application of its defamation law not only by referring to the particular grievances of the former Chancellor [Z: $I^{\sim p}b$, F 6.2], but, more generally, with reference to a broader public interest *t* in promoting a climate of amicable public exchanges of views [Z: S*t*].[3] Indeed, *any* restriction on a right justified by the interests of an ascertainable individual can equally be justified with reference to a broader public interest – that is a feature of the generality of legal rules. Thus, at one point, commenting on the substance of Mr Lingens's arguments, the Court notes that '[w]hat was at issue was . . . his right to impart ideas'.[4] By substituting the word 'his' with the word 'one's', we readily see how this observation can be seen to concern not some interest exclusive to Mr Lingens, but rather an interest of all members of society. In that example, an interest is expressly attributed to the personal actor, but broadly implies an interest of society generally. Had the Court used the word 'one's', our inference would run in the opposite direction: we would infer an interest of the personal actor from an interest attributed to society.

Those alternative formulations of the statement represent different ways of making the same argument. It may be a matter of sheer style, or happenstance, or linguistic peculiarity,[5] whether the lawyers or judges in a given case formulate their views in terms of the interests of specified individuals, or in terms of broader interests of society. In other words, there is *redundancy* between the two formulations. Either one makes the same point. That is not a problem, as redundancy does not in itself result in errors of reasoning, and has the advantage of allowing rhetorical flexibility. It does, however, mean that some arguments must be inferred from others.

That redundant relationship between symbols has two consequences. First, it gives rise to *broadly implied interests*, such that some interests which are expressly attributed to one actor will be attributable to another. Second, it gives rise to *broadly implied actors*, such that interests expressly attributed to identified actors become implicitly attributable to unidentified actors. The importance of these two types of broad implication should not be overestimated, since, most of the time, we can arrive at these implied elements intuitively. Nevertheless, some typical examples can be sketched in brief and general terms.

10.3 Implied interests

We are already familiar with one kind of implied interest. To assume identity of interest between two or more actors is to assume that an interest attributable to any one of them is attributable to the others. We have assumed identity of interest only among actors of the same type. However, implied interests can also obtain among different types of actors, namely *between I actors and S actors; and between different kinds of I actors*.

Implication between I and S actors

Interests attributable to society can be inferred from interests attributed to individual actors. In *Lingens*, any argument that the former Chancellor has an interest *r* in protecting his reputation [θ: $I^{\sim p}r$] broadly implies that society as a whole has that interest with respect to its individual members [θ: S*r*]. Any argument that the journalist has an interest *t* in free expression [θ: $I^{p}t$] broadly implies that society as a whole has that interest with respect to its press corps, or indeed with respect to its individual members generally [θ: S*t*]. Again, these observations follow merely from the generality of legal rules.

In *Laskey*, the Commission opinion, adopting the government's view, states that '[t]he types of injuries that were or could be caused by the applicants' activities were of a significant nature and degree'.[6] The Commission attributes to the individual actors an interest *u* in being prevented from committing the acts [Z: $I^{\circ}u$]. That is, it attributes to the men *as personal actors* an interest *u* in being prevented from inflicting such acts upon others or having such acts inflicted on themselves [Z: $I^{p}u$]; and, *as non-personal actors*, an interest *u* in being prevented from having such acts inflicted *by* other such personal actors [Z: $I^{\sim p}u$]. By substituting the phrase 'the applicants' activities' with the phrase 'such activities', we see that the argument refers to those activities regardless of who engages in them. They would be 'of a significant nature and degree' if committed by any similarly situated members of society. The Commission thus by implication attributes to the state the same interest *u* in preventing members of society generally from committing the acts [Z: S*u*].

Conversely, *interests attributable to individual actors can be inferred from interests attributed to society*. The Commission in *Laskey* states that 'respect for the health and rights of others may justify a State in prohibiting activities which cause or risk causing death or serious injury or in imposing certain protective measures'.[7] By attributing that interest *v* to society [Z: S*v*], it implies a corresponding interest of the individual actors concerned in the case [Z: $I^{\circ}v$]. In *Lingens*, the Court, siding with the claimant, states that 'freedom of political debate is at the very core of the concept of a democratic society'.[8] Attributing an interest *w* in such freedom to all of society [Z: S*w*], the Court by implication attributes that interest to Mr Lingens [Z: $I^{p}w$].

Implication between different kinds of I actors

Interests attributable to non-personal actors can be inferred from interests attributed to personal actors. In *Laskey*, an argument that a given personal actor has an interest *x* in inflicting or receiving injuries [θ: $I^{p}x$] broadly implies some reciprocal interest *y* on the part of a non-personal actor [θ: $I^{\sim p}y$]: the claimant would not argue that the personal actor has a right to inflict an injury which some non-personal actor has no right to receive, or that the personal actor has a right to receive an injury which no non-personal actor has the right to inflict. In *Lingens*, an argument that the journalist does or does not have an interest *x* in publishing his articles [θ: $I^{p}x$] broadly implies some reciprocal interest *y* on the part of the former Chancellor [θ: $I^{\sim p}y$]. In arguing that he has an interest *x* in publishing statements about the Chancellor, Lingens by implication attributes to the former Chancellor an insufficient interest *y* in restricting the publication of those statements.

The same process of implication can proceed in the opposite direction. Accordingly, *interests attributable to personal actors can be inferred from interests attributed to non-personal actors*. In *Laskey*, an argument that a given non-personal actor has an interest *x* in inflicting or receiving injuries [θ: $I^{\sim p}x$] broadly implies a reciprocal interest *y* on the part of the personal actor [θ: $I^{p}y$]. In *Lingens*, an argument that the former Chancellor does or does not have an interest *x* in preventing or sanctioning the publication of the articles [θ: $I^{\sim p}x$] broadly implies a reciprocal, insufficient or sufficient (respectively), interest *y* on the part of the journalist in publishing them [θ: $I^{p}y$].

10.4 Implied actors

Interests attributable to implied individual actors can be inferred from interests attributable to society. In *Handyside*, the difficulty of empirically demonstrating or confuting the existence of a moral risk *x* to a specific child would not make it difficult to refer to such a child. For the British government, the assertion that there is a risk *x* to society [Z: S*x*] broadly implies that there is such a risk to at least one individual child [Z: $I^{\sim p}x$], even if that child cannot be identified. The assertion of risk to society as a whole broadly implies risk to some *hypothetical*, i.e. implied, non-personal actor. In response, Mr Handyside denies that there is any such risk to society, attributing some contrary interest *y* to society [A: S*y*] and thus to any such child [Z: $I^{\sim p}y$].

Interests attributable to implied individual actors can be inferred from interests attributed to identified individual actors. This principle extends the concept of identity of interest to include unidentified actors: it attributes to all similarly situated actors the interests attributed to identified individuals. That concept of 'similarly situated actors' is formal, providing a basis for substantive disagreement, as there can be substantive disagreements about who counts as 'similarly situated' in any given case. In *Lingens*, assertions about the interests of the individual journalist and the former Chancellor broadly imply similar interests attributable to any similarly situated journalist or politician in consequence of the generality of legal rules. In *Laskey*, assertions about the interests of the identified individual participants imply similar interests attributable to any similarly situated individuals.

We need not be concerned about drawing precise lines between identified and implied actors – for example, where an argument alludes to an actor imprecisely. The whole purpose of a theory of broad implication is to allow for the attribution of interests to actors without having to determine conclusively whether an actor can or cannot be said to have been clearly identified.

Review these terms

1 strict implication
2 broad implication
3 implicature
4 redundancy
5 implied interest
6 implied actor

Part II

Harm

11 Two harm axioms

In this chapter, we turn to the kinds of interests which are attributed to actors, beginning with the concept of harm. The goal is to identify purely formal concepts underlying assertions about the existence, character or gravity of harm caused by the exercise of a right, or by a restriction upon a right.

11.1 The axioms

The set of possible harms in rights discourse is subject to age-old controversies. Should 'harm' include only material injury? Or also offence to moral interests? Who is to determine the existence, quality or degree of harm? Legislators? Judges? Lawyers? Experts? Communities? As long as there have been legal disputes, there have been disagreements about the concept of harm.[1]

The rest of this book will proceed on the principle that any dispute about a liberal right is a dispute about the existence, character, degree or relevance of some harm. The crucial components of that principle will be stated in the form of two *Harm Axioms*, which will be called the *Claimant Harm Axiom* (HA_A) and the *Respondent Harm Axiom* (HA_Z). The point will be that those axioms express purely formal elements of liberal rights argument that are fixed and determinate. They represent the very possibility for substantive disagreements about the harm caused *by* the personal actor in the exercise of an asserted right, or about the harm caused *to* the personal actor by a restriction. As they contain several components, they cannot easily be discussed as a whole. We will start with an integral statement of both axioms. Then, for the remainder of the chapter, we will refer back to them as we dissect each component in turn.

> **Claimant Harm Axiom (HA_A)**: In an argument that a restriction violates a right, the claimant position assumes:
>
> (1) *Either* that:
>
> (a) some harm is caused by the personal actor's exercise of the right; *and*

(b) such harm is caused to some actor; *and*
(c) the harm is *either*,
(i) insufficient to justify the restriction; *or*
(ii) irrelevant to the question of whether the restriction is justified;

(2) *or* that:
(a) some harm is caused by the restriction; *and*
(b) such harm is caused to the personal actor; *and*
(c) such harm is sufficient to warrant a finding that the restriction is unjustified.

Respondent Harm Axiom (HA_Z): In an argument that a restriction does not violate a right, the respondent position assumes:

(1) *Either* that:
(a) some harm is caused by the personal actor's exercise of the right; *and*
(b) such harm is caused to some actor; *and*
(c) the harm is sufficient to justify the restriction;

(2) *or* that:
(a) some harm is caused by the restriction; *and*
(b) such harm is caused to the personal actor; *and*
(c) the harm is *either*,
(i) insufficient to warrant a finding that the restriction is unjustified, *or*
(ii) irrelevant to the question of whether the restriction is justified.

11.2 Sufficient and insufficient harm

A concept of 'sufficient harm' appears in HA_A(2)(c) and HA_Z(1)(c). A concept of 'insufficient harm' appears in HA_A(1)(c)(i) and HA_Z(2)(c)(i). Such tedious reference back to the various clauses of the two axioms suggests how much easier things will be once the axioms have been translated into symbolic form. But that will only be possible after we have examined the meanings of the axioms' decisive terms. For the time being, we must bear with the cross-references.

As a formal matter, the adjudication of liberal rights is not concerned with whether there is *harm* or *no harm* caused by the exercise of, or by a restriction, on a right. Adjudication is concerned only with whether there is *sufficient* harm or *insufficient* harm to justify a finding of a violation. The mere assertion that 'harm' is caused says too little, as it leaves that question open. Meanwhile, the mere assertion that 'no harm' is caused says too much, for as long as there is insufficient harm, it is immaterial whether there is 'not enough harm' or 'absolutely no harm'. Indeed, in

Laskey or *Dudgeon*, the claimants could argue that, far from causing harm, the conduct promotes the affirmative benefit of sexual pleasure or emotional well-being. Or Mr Handyside could adduce the affirmative benefit of enlightenment on important social issues. An assertion of affirmative benefit is then a fortiori an assertion of insufficient harm. Similarly, an assertion of 'no harm' may arise in argument (and is occasionally used in this book), and is relevant only in so far as it signifies insufficient harm. Accordingly, the formal concept of harm set forth in the two axioms refers to *any effect of the exercise of a right or of a restriction on an actor.*

Consider some examples. Mr Lingens argues that any harm caused by the publication of his articles [HA_A(1)(a)] to the former Chancellor [HA_A(1)(b)] is insufficient to justify the restriction which arose from a finding of defamation in the national courts [HA_A(1)(c)(i)]. The former Chancellor, and then the Austrian state, assert that the harm caused by the journalist [HA_Z(1)(a)] to the former Chancellor [HA_Z(1)(b)] is sufficient to justify that restriction [HA_Z(1)(c)]. Mr Handyside argues that any harm caused by publication of *The Little Red Book* [HA_A(1)(a)] to individual children who may read the book or to society generally [HA_A(1)(b)] is insufficient to justify the restriction imposed by a prohibition on the book [HA_A(1)(c)(i)].[2] The state asserts that the harm which would be caused by that publication [HA_Z(1)(a)] to children or to society generally [HA_Z(1)(b)] is sufficient to justify that restriction [HA_Z(1)(c)].[3] In *Dudgeon*, The claimant argues that any harm caused by his homosexual acts [HA_A(1)(a)] to vulnerable individuals or to the morals of society generally [HA_A(1)(b)] is insufficient to justify the prohibition [HA_A(1)(c)(i)].[4] The state asserts that any harm caused [HA_Z(1)(a)] to vulnerable individuals or to public morals generally [HA_Z(1)(b)] is sufficient to justify the prohibition [HA_Z(1)(c)].[5]

The most detailed analysis of abortion under the European Convention appears in *Brüggemann and Scheuten v. Germany*[6]. In that case, the European Commission declined to find that restrictions on abortion procedures violated a woman's right to privacy. The German government asserted that abortion entails a harm caused by the woman [HA_Z(1)(a)] to a living individual [HA_Z(1)(b)], which is sufficient to justify state regulation [HA_Z(1)(c)].[7] Of course, such an assertion raises the question as to whether that individual in fact exists. We might say that, on the claimant view, the foetus is not a harmed individual because it is not a human being at all. Accordingly, any harm caused by the women [HA_A(1)(a)] to such a being [HA_A(1)(b)] is insufficient to justify the state restrictions [HA_A(1)(c)(i)]. For those claimants, there *is* no such individual. Therefore, there is by definition no harm – there is insufficient harm – to any such individual.[8] To claim the non-existence of an actor is to claim that there is by definition insufficient harm to such an actor.

Later on, the translation of symbolic variables back into standard English will be easier if approximations to ordinary language are available.

Therefore, an assertion of *sufficient* harm will at times be referred to, interchangeably, as an assertion of *unacceptable* harm; and an assertion of *insufficient* harm will, at times, be referred to as an assertion of *acceptable* harm. These alternative but, for our purposes, synonymous terms are introduced for the simple reason that the terms 'sufficient' and 'insufficient', in colloquial usage, can sound stilted in some sentences.

Exercise set 11.1

Fill in the blanks.

The claimants in *Laskey* argue that any harm caused by them [$HA_A(1)$ ___1___] to themselves, to other individuals, or to society's general interest in health or morals [___2___], is insufficient to justify the restriction on consensual, adult sadomasochism [___3___].[9] The state asserts that any harm caused by the men [$HA_Z(1)$___4___] to themselves, to other individuals, or to society's general interest in health or morals [___5___] is sufficient to justify that restriction [___6___].[10]

In *Mellacher v. Austria*,[11] property owners complained about rent control legislation, which restricted their ability freely to assess rental income for their property, and thus to exercise their right to 'peaceful enjoyment of their possessions', under Protocol 1, article 1 of the European Convention.[12] In their view, any harm caused by that exercise of the right [HA_A___7___] to the individual tenants, or to society generally [___8___] was insufficient to justify the restrictions imposed by the rent control legislation [___9___]. (In particular, they disputed the government's view about the need for rent control in light of other available means of meeting the housing needs of persons with low incomes.[13]) The Court, however, found in favour of the government, which argued that the harm that would be caused by the claimants [___10___] to low-income persons, or to society as a whole, as a result of inadequate housing [___11___] was sufficient to justify State interference in the form of rent control [___12___].[14]

All of the foregoing cases are disputes between the positions in $HA_A(1)$ and $HA_Z(1)$. What about disputes between $HA_A(2)$ and $HA_Z(2)$? Of course, there is a more important question as to what it is that distinguishes these two sets of disputes. That question is addressed in the next chapter. For now, our only concern is with the meaning of references to 'sufficient' and 'insufficient' harm. We will make do with some examples, without worrying now about how they differ from the foregoing cases. In *Ireland v. United Kingdom*,[15] the Republic of Ireland brought a complaint arising from hostilities in Northern Ireland during the early 1970s. The complaint included allegations of widespread torture or inhuman or degrading treatment committed in British interrogation centres, in violation of ECHR article 3.[16] While the Court did not find that the practices amounted to torture, it did find that some of them constituted inhuman or degrading treatment. The Irish government claimed that the acts in question had caused harm [HA_A(2)(a)] to the detainees [HA_A(2)(b)] at a level sufficient to warrant a finding that those acts constituted unjustified restrictions on the detainees' rights [HA_A(2)(c)].[17] As to those accusations which the British government contested,[18] it responded that any harm caused by such acts [HA_Z(2)(a)] to the detainees [HA_Z(2)(b)] was insufficient to warrant that finding [HA_Z(2)(c)(i)].

The question was whether any acts committed by the British authorities were sufficiently harmful to warrant a finding that article 3 was violated. The Court noted:

> [I]ll-treatment must attain a minimum level of severity if it is to fall within the scope of Article 3. The assessment of this minimum is, in the nature of things, relative; it depends on all the circumstances of the case, such as the duration of the treatment, its physical or mental effects and, in some cases, the sex, age and state of health of the victim.[19]

Accordingly, in cases concerning allegations of torture or inhuman or degrading treatment, a question for the Court is whether the particular treatment surpasses that 'minimum level of severity'.

That doctrine has been further developed in subsequent cases. In *Tyrer v. United Kingdom*,[20] the Court was confronted with the practice of 'birching' of a juvenile offender. In 1972, the claimant, aged 15, had pleaded guilty before the local juvenile court to unlawful assault occasioning actual bodily harm to another pupil at his school. He was sentenced to three strokes of the birch, administered as follows:

> [Tyrer's] father and a doctor were present. [Tyrer] was made to take down his trousers and underpants and bend over a table; he was held by two policemen whilst a third administered the punishment, pieces of the birch breaking at the first stroke. [Tyrer's] father lost his self-control and after the third stroke 'went for' one of the policemen and had to be restrained.
>
> The birching raised, but did not cut, the claimant's skin and he was sore for about a week and a half afterwards.[21]

The British government responded that any harm caused by the birching [HA_Z(2)(a)] to Mr Tyrer [HA_Z(2)(b)] was insufficient to warrant a finding that the treatment constituted an unjustified infringement on the right [HA_Z(2)(c)(i)].[22] The Court, however, agreed with the claimant, who asserted that the punishment had caused harm [HA_A(2)(a)] to Mr Tyrer [HA_A(2)(b)] at a level sufficient to warrant such a finding [HA_A(2)(c)].[23]

Similarly, *Costello-Roberts v. United Kingdom*[24] concerned a complaint brought on behalf of a schoolchild, aged seven, who had been disciplined by means of three 'whacks' of a slipper on his clothed buttocks. The claimant argued that the beating caused sufficient emotional harm [HA_Z(2)(a)] to such a young boy [HA_A(2)(b)] to warrant a finding that it constituted an unjustified infringement on the right [HA_A(2)(c)].[25] However, the Court agreed with the British government, which responded that any harm caused by the beating [HA_Z(2)(a)] to Costello-Roberts [HA_Z(2)(b)] was insufficient to warrant that finding [HA_Z(2)(c)(i)].[26] The *Tyrer* and *Costello-Roberts* cases (including their dissenting opinions[27]) illustrate how substantive disagreements about the existence, character or degree of harm persist through this fixed, tacitly agreed, formal structure.

In *Tyrer* and *Costello-Roberts*, there was no dispute about the actual acts which took place, but only about whether they rose to the level of inhuman or degrading treatment. By contrast, *Aksoy v. Turkey*[28] presents the common scenario of a state denying outright that the acts in question had been committed. The claimant alleged some of the most severe treatment ever to come before the Court, including aerial suspension ('Palestinian hanging'), electric shock and physical beating.[29] The government largely denied that Mr Aksoy had incurred the injuries as alleged, claiming that any injuries found on Mr Aksoy's body had resulted from an 'accident'.[30] Hence , it was asserted that no harm had been caused [HA_Z(2)(a)] to Mr Aksoy [HA_Z(2)(b)] sufficient to warrant a finding that any unjustified restriction on Mr Aksoy's rights had occurred [HA_Z(2)(c)(i)]. The Court, however, found that a burden remained upon the state to provide a 'plausible explanation' for injuries incurred by prisoners in detention, and that the Turkish authorities had failed to do so. It thus accepted the claimant's assertion that harm had been caused [HA_A(2)(a)] to Mr Aksoy [HA_A(2)(b)] at a level sufficient to warrant a finding that it constituted torture [HA_A(2)(c)].

Exercise set 11.2

Fill in the blanks.

The case of *Soering v. United Kingdom*[31] concerned an individual who was the subject of an extradition request to the British government by the government of the United States. Mr Soering had been indicted in the State of Virginia on several charges of murder, for which the death penalty was a possible punishment. After the request was granted by the British authorities, Mr Soering brought a complaint to the European Court under article 3, asserting that imposition of the death penalty would expose him to the protracted and excessively harsh experience of 'death row phenomenon', which is customarily faced by persons convicted for such crimes. The British government argued that the likelihood of Mr Soering incurring such treatment was small, in view of mitigating circumstances in the case, and in view of assurances made by federal US authorities that the wishes of the United Kingdom opposing imposition of the death penalty would be made to the court during a sentencing procedure.[32] Accordingly, the British government maintained that the likelihood of harm [HA_Z(2)__1__] to Mr Soering [__2__] was insufficient to warrant a finding that such restriction on his article 3 rights was unjustified [__3__]. The European Court, however, accepted Soering's assertion that neither the mitigating circumstances, nor the wishes of the British government represented to the Virginia court at sentencing, could guarantee suspension of a capital sentence. Accordingly, the likelihood of Mr Soering facing torture or cruel or inhuman treatment through 'death row phenomenon' constituted a harm [HA_A(2)__4__] inflicted upon him [__5__] sufficient to warrant a finding that it constituted an unjustified restriction on his article 3 rights [__6__].[33]

11.3 Relativity of harm

A harm may be characterised as insufficient merely in the sense that it is less harmful than the alternative. Indeed, notwithstanding appeals to legal or moral principle, a straightforward utilitarian calculus may be at play, serving to differentiate a greater, and thereby sufficient harm, from a lesser, and thereby insufficient harm. In *Brüggemann and Scheuten*, in addition to arguments about foetal life, the state adduced a paternalist argument that, without restrictions on abortion, physical or psychological harm can be caused by women [HA_Z(1)(a)] to themselves [HA_Z(1)(b)] in electing to undergo an abortion procedure; and that such harm is sufficient to justify government restrictions [HA_Z(1)(c)].[34] On behalf of the claimants, it was asserted, in response, that, if the only two available alternatives are either access or non-access to legal abortion, then the former is less harmful than the latter, as any harms caused to women by abortions are less than those which can be caused through illicit means.[35] Thus, *in comparison* to the greater harm of non-access, any harm which women, by procuring legal abortions, cause [HA_A(1)(a)] to themselves [HA_A(1)(b)] is insufficient to justify the restrictions [HA_A(1)(c)](i)].

The case of *Kjeldsen, Busk Madsen and Pedersen v. Denmark*[36] concerned the requirement in Protocol 1, article 2 of the Convention that education must conform to parents' religious and philosophical convictions.[37]

The complaint was brought by parents protesting on ethical and religious grounds against the compulsory inclusion of sex education within several subject areas of the Danish school curriculum. For the claimants, any harm that would be caused [HA_A(1)(a)] to their children or to society generally [HA_A(1)(b)] by requiring that the government provide primary education without sex education, *in comparison* to the greater evil of sex education, would be insufficient to justify state refusal to permit such exemption [HA_A(1)(c)(i)].[38] The Court, however, found in favour of the government, which adduced a general public interest in social enlightenment on such social issues as reproduction, birth control or sexually-transmitted disease. The government argued that the parents' exercise of the asserted right would result in a diminished level of knowledge about sexuality. Thus, the parents' exercise of the right would result in inadequate sexual education, which would cause harm [HA_Z(1)(a)] to individual children or to society generally [HA_Z(1)(b)], sufficient to justify state intervention through sex education [HA_Z(1)(c)].[39]

The case of *McCann v. United Kingdom*[40] concerned the right to life, protected under article 2 of the Convention.[41] In May 1988, British agents, attempting to foil a car bomb attack by members of the Provisional IRA, shot dead three suspects whom they thought to be about to detonate an explosive device in an automobile. No explosive devices were in fact found in the automobile or on the bodies of the deceased. The claimants argued on behalf of the deceased suspects that the British agents had taken inadequate precautions to avoid recourse to deadly force: the agents had caused harm [HA_A(2)(a)] to the suspects [HA_A(2)(b)] at a level sufficient to warrant a finding that such action constituted an unjustified infringement of the right to life [HA_A(2)(c)].[42] Indeed, death, being the ultimate harm, must by definition be a sufficient harm? Not necessarily. The government invoked a concept of relative harm. Even the harm of death was insufficient in view of the dangerous acts envisaged by the suspects and the urgency of the circumstances under which those acts were committed: *in comparison* to the greater evil of inadequate crime prevention, the harm caused by the British agents [HA_Z(2)(a)] to the suspects [HA_Z(2)(b)] was insufficient to warrant a finding that the killing constituted an unjustified infringement of the right to life [HA_Z(2)(c)(i)].[43] The Court nevertheless accepted the claimants' view.[44]

Exercise set 11.3

Fill in the blanks.

The cases of *Kruslin v. France*[45] and *Huvig v. France*,[46] concerned police interference with correspondence and telephone wires, on suspicion of criminal activity. The claimants alleged a breach of the

European Convention under article 8(1), which provides that '[e]veryone has the right to respect for his . . . home and his correspondence'. Article 8(2) authorises state 'interference' with that right 'for the prevention of disorder or crime', to the extent that such interference 'is in accordance with the law' (*prévue par la loi*[47]). The question in these cases was whether the domestic law was sufficiently clear about the situations in which tapping is permitted. The government argued that French law provided adequate safeguards against abuse. In its view, any harm caused [HA_Z__1__] to the criminal suspects [__2__] was therefore insufficient to warrant a finding that the intrusions were unjustified [__3__]. However, the Court found in favour of the claimants, who asserted that those safeguards were not sufficiently clear to preclude substantial arbitrariness or abuse. The intrusions thus constituted a harm [HA_A(2)__4__] to the personal actors [__5__] sufficient to warrant a finding that those intrusions were unjustified [__6__].[48]

11.4 Harm as cost

Some claims challenge not active state interference, but rather the omission of the state to undertake an affirmative duty.[49] When a state asserts that it has declined to give effect to a right because of excessive cost, that assertion is a claim of unacceptable harm: a claim of unacceptable cost is a claim of unacceptable harm; cost to the state is harm to the state – sufficient, in its view, to justify its interference with, or failure to give effect to, the right.

In such cases, the cost is asserted by the state to be too great to be required for purposes of respecting the right. In *Rees* and *Cossey*, the British government argued that the changes in official practice which would be required to issue documents in accordance with the wishes of post-operative transsexuals would create an unacceptable administrative burden. Three dissenting judges in *Rees*,[50] in an opinion reiterated in *Cossey*,[51] rejected that reasoning, finding that some of the measures requested would not create an excessive burden. In those cases, the restriction on the asserted right takes the form of refusal of the state to grant full recognition of the change in civil status. The cost is asserted by the state to be a harm caused [HA_Z(1)(a)] to society [HA_Z(1)(b)] of a level sufficient to justify the government's refusal to effectuate the requested administrative changes [HA_Z(1)(c)]. For the claimants, any harm caused [HA_A(1)(a)] by imposing that cost upon society [HA_A(1)(b)] is insufficient to justify that refusal [HA_A(1)(c)(i)].

The transition from *Cossey* to *B v. France*, the latter decided barely a year after the former, again illustrates the way in which disagreements about substantive harm work their way through fixed formal concepts. Part of the Court's reasoning in *Rees* and *Cossey* was that British practice in recording civil status does not take the form of a comprehensive, unified national identity registration scheme, as found in other European states. While not allowing changes to all documents, British practice does allow changes to some.[52] The cost to the state of making the residual changes sought by the claimant is deemed by the Court to be too great, given that the transsexuals' change of civil status already enjoys partial recognition. Yet in *B v. France*, decided barely a year after *Cossey*, the fact that the far more integrated French system allowed no partial changes diminished the government's claim of excessive administrative burden by increasing the gravity of the individual claimant's predicament.[53]

Exercise set 11.4

Fill in the blanks.

The case of *Airey v. Ireland*[54] concerned a woman of low income who sought to obtain a legal separation from her husband, but was unable to do so due to lack of legal aid. She brought a complaint under article 6(1),[55] arguing that the state's failure to provide aid effectively barred her from obtaining a remedy to which she was entitled in law. In the government's view, the costs to Mrs Airey were not tantamount to a 'positive obstacle',[56] and 'the Convention should not be interpreted so as to achieve social and economic developments in a Contracting State; such developments can only be progressive'.[57] To construe the right to a hearing so as to include an entitlement to legal aid would impose a cost [__1__] upon society [__2__] sufficient to justify the government's refusal to provide that assistance [__3__]. The Court, however, accepted Mrs. Airey's view that such a construction of the right would impose a cost [__4__] upon society [__5__] which was insufficient to justify the failure to provide legal aid [__6__].

11.5 Acts and omissions

Rees, *Cossey* or *Airey* show how harm arises from omissions as well as affirmative acts. The claimants' assertions that a cost may justifiably be imposed upon society for purposes of protecting a right becomes an assertion that the state's refusal to incur that cost can constitute a violation of the right. However, claims that an omission constitutes a violation of a right also arise in contexts where the respondent does not adduce cost as a justification.

Recall *X and Y v. The Netherlands*, concerning a young woman who, living in a privately-run home for mentally handicapped children, had been the victim of a sexual assault. Her father, on her behalf, accused the state of failing to provide redress in law. The government argued that harsher legal sanctions in the realm of sexual activity for a woman aged 16 would diminish her level of sexual independence: to add that greater level of protection would have the effect of causing harm [HA_Z(1)(a)] to the girl [HA_Z(1)(b)] by limiting her sexual autonomy to a degree which the lack of further protection justifiably avoids [HA_Z(1)(c)]. The claimant replied that any harm caused by exercising a privacy right, which includes greater legal protection [HA_A(1)(a)] to the detriment of one's sexual autonomy [HA_A(1)(b)], is insufficient to justify the absence of that protection [HA_A(1)(c)(i)].[58]

11.6 Irrelevant harm

A concept of 'irrelevant harm' appears in HA_A(1)(c)(ii) and HA_Z(2)(c)(ii). In some arguments, the specific existence, character or level of harm is neither affirmed nor denied. Rather, it is asserted that any inquiry into harm is irrelevant to the disposition of the dispute; that the case must be resolved a certain way *regardless* of the existence, character or level of harm.

In *Laskey*, an alternative to the claimants' HA_A(1)(c)(i) argument is an argument of the form HA_A(1)(c)(ii). Their HA_A(1)(c)(i) argument is, after all, not without difficulties, as the selfsame acts inflicted upon non-consenting persons would readily be characterised as sufficiently harmful to constitute criminal[59] or tortious[60] batteries; and the sheer act of consent does not alter the physical characteristics of the acts. As an alternative argument, the claimants assert that, as long as the participants have given valid consent, any harm caused [HA_A(1)(a)] to themselves, to other individuals or to society generally [HA_A(1)(b)] is irrelevant to the question of whether state interference is justified [HA_A(1)(c)(ii)].[61] The state response by definition remains the same: the assertion that any harm caused by the men is sufficient to justify a legal prohibition [HA_Z(1)(c)] is *ipso facto* an assertion that such harm is relevant, regardless of whether consent is given.[62]

Indeed, we will see that all assertions of irrelevant harm depend upon assertions of consent. Therefore, for the sake of completeness, occasional reference will be made to the concept of irrelevant harm in the next few chapters. However, we will not analyse those assertions in detail until we have reached the chapters about consent. For the time being, we will focus primarily on disputes about sufficient and insufficient harm.

Review these terms

1 sufficient harm
2 insufficient harm
3 relative harm
4 cost
5 irrelevant harm

12 Causation

This chapter continues the examination of the Claimant and Respondent Harm axioms, with attention to their concepts of causation.

12.1 Two concepts of causation

The axioms contain two concepts of causation. One of those concepts refers to harm caused by the personal actor in exercising the right [$HA_A(1)(a)$, $HA_Z(1)(a)$], and will be called a concept of *right-based harm*. The second refers to harm caused by the restriction [$HA_A(2)(a)$, $HA_Z(2)(a)$], and will be called a concept of *restriction-based harm*.

The distinction can be described very roughly now, and will be examined in greater detail throughout this chapter. A right-based harm correlates to *the way in which the personal actor seeks to exercise the right*, such as by publishing a controversial book or article, or by engaging in prohibited sexual relations. An argument using that concept of harm effectively asks a court to scrutinise that means of exercising the right, and the concomitant effects (harms) caused thereby, in order to decide whether the activity falls within the scope of the right's protection. By contrast, a restriction-based harm concerns *the manner in which the restriction is exercised*: What kind of restriction is inflicted? Under what circumstances? How severe is it?

The difference between these two concepts of causation is not always clear-cut. In principle, either concept could be made to fit any claim. No mistake would be made by using one instead of the other. Indeed, at the end of the chapter, we will examine some arguments which can be analysed effectively under either concept. Nevertheless, the distinction will be maintained to allow greater accuracy in recording arguments. We will see that, if we were to use only one of these causation models, cases would arise which, while theoretically amenable to it, would produce awkward or less precise analyses. A number of examples will be introduced to make that point. In most cases, it will be clear enough which model of causation is appropriate. For borderline cases, facility in identifying the more suitable model may require trial and error.

12.2 Right-based harm

There are many ways of seeking to exercise the freedom of speech and expression – through messages on various subject matters, expressed through various media, under various socio-political circumstances, to various kinds of audiences. Similarly, there are many ways of seeking to exercise the right to protection of private life – say, through different kinds of family relationships or intimate relationships, or through any number of solitary activities. Attempts to exercise such rights in new and different ways continue to prompt controversy, requiring courts in each case to evaluate the scope of the right.

In such cases, the respondent justifies the restriction by asserting that the particular means by which the personal actor desires to exercise the right falls outside the scope of that right. In *Lingens* and *Handyside*, the respondent asserts that the restriction on expression is justified because of characteristics of the specific work which the personal actor seeks the freedom to publish. In *Laskey*, *Dudgeon*, *Rees*, *Cossey* or *B v. France*, the respondent asserts that the restriction on privacy is justified because of the harmful or costly nature of the protections which the personal actors seek. In all of these cases, the respondent argues that some harm is *caused by the personal actors through their exercise of the asserted right* [HA_Z(1)(a)], be it harm to themselves, harm to other individuals or harm or cost to society [HA_Z(1)(b)]. The claimant agrees that the personal actor causes that harm [HA_A(1)(a)] to those actors [HA_A(1)(b)], but only in so far as the harm is insufficient to justify the restriction [HA_A(1)(c)(i)], or irrelevant to the question of whether the restriction is justified [HA_A(1)(c)(ii)].

Consider some other rights. Some individuals have complained of violations of the right to life, or the right to protection from inhuman or degrading treatment, by having been denied adequate health care, housing or other social benefits. The denial of such benefits is commonly justified by the respondent state as being a valid restriction on the particular way in which the personal actor seeks to exercise that right, namely, through procurement of a social benefit, on the view that the right cannot be construed so broadly as to impose such a degree of positive obligation.[1] The assertion that such a positive obligation would be too great is an assertion of excessive cost to the state and thus to society: some harm – excessive cost – would be caused by the personal actor in the exercise of the right [HA_Z(1)(a)]; that cost would be inflicted upon society [HA_Z(1)(b)]; and that cost is of a degree that is sufficient to justify the denial of the benefit [HA_Z(1)(c)]. The claimant agrees that the cost would be created by the personal actor in that exercise of the right [HA_A(1)(a)]; and that such cost would be inflicted upon society [HA_A(1)(b)]; but argues that that cost is either insufficient to justify the denial of the benefit [HA_A(1)(c)(i)], or is irrelevant to the question of whether the benefit should be provided [HA_A(1)(c)(ii)].

The case of *Ahmed v. Austria*[2] concerned a government decision to return a refugee, who had been convicted of attempted robbery in Austria, to Somalia. Mr Ahmed complained of an article 3 violation, asserting that he would be a target of torture or inhuman or degrading treatment by being deported to Somalia. Here, too, there is a particular means by which the personal actor seeks to exercise the article 3 right – avoiding deportation. The state asserted that the risk of harm posed by the claimant, through possible criminal recidivism [HA_Z(1)(a)] to individuals or to society generally [HA_Z(1)(b)] was sufficient to justify any interference with his right to evade torture or inhuman or degrading treatment which might arise through deportation [HA_Z(1)(c)].[3] The Court, however, found that the risk of recidivism posed by the claimant was not sufficiently grave: any risk of harm posed by him [HA_A(1)(a)] to other individuals or to society generally [HA_A(1)(b)] was insufficient to justify the risk of his being subjected to torture or inhuman or degrading treatment [HA_A(1)(c)(i)].[4]

Exercise set 12.1

Fill in the blanks.

In *Kjeldsen*, the state defended the compulsory inclusion of sex education in the curriculum, adducing a public interest in enlightenment on issues of sexuality. The government argued that the parents, in exercising their asserted right to determine the content of their children's education, would cause harm [__1__] to those children and to that broader public interest [__2__] sufficient to justify state interference [__3__]. The parents argued that any harm that would be caused [__4__] to their children or to the broader public interest [__5__] by requiring that primary education be provided without compulsory sex education would be insufficient to justify the government's refusal to do so [__6__].

In *X and Y v. The Netherlands* the claimant asserted that no adequate remedy existed in law: the right to privacy should be construed more capaciously so as to extend protection to the victim. The government argued that to exercise the privacy right with a greater level of protection would cause harm [__7__] to that woman [__8__] by unacceptably limiting her sexual autonomy [__9__]. The claimant maintained that any such harm [__10__] to the woman's sexual autonomy [__11__] was insufficient to justify the absence of legal protection [__12__].

12.3 Restriction-based harm

Imagine the following scenario. A state intelligence agency discovers that one of its chief officials, Croft, is receiving money for passing vital national security information to a foreign government. One day, as police officers attempt to apprehend Croft, she resists arrest, brandishing a knife, and then begins to flee, at which point the police officers kill her. On Croft's behalf, a claim is brought against the government, alleging a violation of Croft's right to life. We will assume that the right to life is the only right asserted by the claimant. The claimant argues that recourse to deadly force was unnecessary under the circumstances. For the time being, assume no other relevant facts.

Under the analysis used in the last section, the claimant's argument might run as follows: the risk of harm posed by Croft [HA_A(1)(a)] to the police officers [HA_A(1)(b)] was insufficient to justify the killing [HA_A(1)(c)(i)]. In response, the state asserts that the risk of harm posed by Croft [HA_Z(1)(a)] to the police officers [HA_Z(1)(b)] was sufficient to justify the killing [HA_Z(1)(c)]. These are plausible positions, but do they provide the most precise analysis of the dispute? Under HA_Z(1)(a), the respondent's argument concerns harm which is caused by the personal actor in the exercise *of the asserted right*. Even if we concede that Croft, in brandishing a knife, posed a risk of harm to the police, it seems inaccurate to say that, in brandishing the knife, she was engaging in an exercise of her right to life. That assumption would be plausible only if she had brandished the knife in self-defence, already believing that the police were trying to kill or hurt her *at the time* she brandished it. That additional fact is by no means self-evident, however, and we will not assume it. We will assume that the police originally intended only to apprehend her, and that that intent was fully apparent to her at the time she brandished the knife: she brandished the knife only in order to escape apprehension, and not to protect her life – not in the exercise of her right to life.

Accordingly, it would be strained to say that the claim brought on Croft's behalf seeks judicial recognition of some particular means by which Croft had sought to exercise her right to life. It is more plausible to say that the claimant complains about the way in which the *restriction* was exercised. The claimant argues that the police could have apprehended Croft successfully without recourse to deadly force. That formulation of the argument does not render the use of the knife irrelevant. Rather, it 'factors' the use of the knife into the determination about whether deadly force – *the means of exercising the restriction* – was justified, by citing it as part of the totality of the circumstances under which deadly force was used.

Consider another scenario. Assume that the police did not kill Croft. Rather, they successfully apprehended her, then beat her in order to obtain information about her spying activity. (Do not think that these violent scenarios are invoked fortuitously. We will see that it is precisely in these kinds of cases that parties commonly invoke arguments using concepts of restriction-based harm.) Now, on her own behalf, Croft brings a complaint of torture or inhuman or degrading treatment. Once again, under the analysis used in the last section, her argument might run as follows: any risk of harm posed by any of her actual or alleged espionage [HA_A(1)(a)] to society's national security interests [HA_A(1)(b)] was insufficient to justify the beating [HA_A(1)(c)(i)]. The state might respond that the risk of harm posed by her activities [HA_Z(1)(a)] to society's national security interests [HA_Z(1)(b)] had been sufficient to justify the beating [HA_Z(1)(c)].

Yet, assuming no additional facts, but assuming that Croft did indeed commit breaches of national security, it is awkward to say that she committed those breaches in the exercise of her right [HA_A(1)(a)] not to be tortured or mistreated. Depending on the arguments used, her espionage may or may not be relevant to – 'factored into' – the question of whether the restriction on that right, in the form of the beating, was justified. However, there is no sense in which her espionage was undertaken *in the exercise* of that right.

In these hypothetical cases, we are continuing to balance rights against restrictions. But it is awkward to do so with the same vocabulary that was used for right-based harms in the last section. In the last section, it was plausible to express the balance in terms of harm alleged to be caused by the exercise of the right. However, if we are to achieve a plausible reflection of the ordinary terms of argument, concepts must also be found which refer to the harm alleged to be caused by the *restriction*. That is the language which appears in HA_A(2) and HA_Z(2). We can say that arguments in the foregoing two scenarios take the following form: the claimant asserts that the harm caused by the restriction [HA_A(2)(a)] to the personal actor [HA_A(2)(b)] is sufficient to warrant a finding that the restriction is unjustified [HA_A(2)(c)]. In both scenarios, the respondent agrees that harm is caused by the restriction [HA_Z(2)(a)] to the personal actor [HA_Z(2)(b)], but asserts that the harm is either insufficient to warrant a finding that the restriction was unjustified [HA_Z(2)(c)(i)] or irrelevant [HA_Z(2)(c)(ii)]. Similarly, in *Ireland v. UK*, Ireland claims that British agents inflicted treatment [HA_A(2)(a)] upon the detainees [HA_A(2)(b)], which was sufficient to warrant a finding that such treatment was unjustified [HA_A(2)(c)]. As to the contested acts, the government agrees that harm was caused by the treatment [HA_Z(2)(a)] to the detainees [HA_Z(2)(b)], but only in so far as, under the circumstances, the harm was insufficient to warrant a finding that the treatment was unjustified [HA_Z(2)(c)(i)].

As no attention need be paid to the particular means by which personal actors seek to exercise the right in such cases, judicial scrutiny instead turns to the restriction – to the character and magnitude of the harm, as in *Tyrer* and *Costello-Roberts*, or indeed to the very existence of harm caused by the accused agents, as in *Aksoy*. The claimants in *Tyrer* and *Costello-Roberts* argue that the treatment inflicted [HA_A(2)(a)] upon the personal actors [HA_A(2)(b)] was sufficient to warrant a finding that it constituted an unjustified restriction on those individuals' article 3 rights [HA_A(2)(c)]. The state responds that any harm caused by the treatment [HA_Z(2)(a)] to those individuals [HA_Z(2)(b)] is insufficient to warrant a finding that such restriction was unjustified [HA_Z(2)(c)(i)]. The claimant in *Aksoy* argues that the treatment inflicted [HA_A(2)(a)] on Mr Aksoy [HA_A(2)(b)] was sufficient to warrant a finding that he had been tortured [HA_A(2)(c)]. The state asserts that its officials caused no harm to Mr Aksoy, i.e. that any harm caused by its officials [HA_Z(2)(a)] to Mr Aksoy [HA_Z(2)(b)] was insufficient to warrant a finding that any unjustified restriction on his article 3 rights had occurred [HA_Z(2)(c)(i)].

Consider again the scenario in which Croft is killed by police officers trying to apprehend her. The claimant asserts that the killing [HA_A(2)(a)] of Croft [HA_A(2)(b)] constituted a harm sufficient to warrant a finding that the killing was unjustified [HA_A(2)(c)]. Assuming no dispute on the facts, the respondent agrees that the harm of killing was inflicted [HA_Z(2)(a)] upon the personal actor [HA_Z(2)(b)], but asserts that, under the circumstances, such harm was insufficient to warrant a finding that the restriction was unjustified [HA_Z(2)(c)(i)]. In *McCann*, the claimants assert that the use of deadly force [HA_A(2)(a)] on the suspected terrorists [HA_A(2)(b)] constituted a harm sufficient to warrant a finding that such action was unjustified [HA_A(2)(c)]. The British government agreed that the killings constituted acts of harm [HA_Z(2)(a)] to the suspects [HA_Z(2)(b)], but asserted that, under the circumstances, even recourse to deadly force could not be deemed sufficiently harmful to warrant a finding that the killings were unjustified [HA_Z(2)(c)(i)].

The cases of *Lawless v. United Kingdom*,[5] *Brogan v. United Kingdom*[6] and *Brannigan v. United Kingdom*[7] were brought under article 5 of the European Convention. The claimants alleged *inter alia* that they had been detained without reasonable suspicion of their having committed criminal offences;[8] that they had been detained for periods of several days without hearing or trial[9]; or that they had been denied the opportunity to have the lawfulness of their detention judicially reviewed (*habeas corpus*) [10]. They thus argued that the detention procedures caused harm [HA_A(2)(a)] to them [HA_A(2)(b)] sufficient to warrant a finding that those procedures constituted unjustified restrictions on the article 5 protections [HA_A(2)(c)]. The government responded that any harm caused by the procedures [HA_Z(2)(a)] to the detainees [HA_Z(2)(b)] was insufficient to warrant such a finding [HA_Z(2)(c)(i)]. Later on, we will examine differences between these cases arising from the application of the article 15 derogation prerogative.

Exercise set 12.2

Fill in the blanks.

The British case of *R v. Christou and Wright*[11] concerned the admissibility in a criminal trial of evidence alleged to have been obtained by trick. Undercover police officers operated a jewellery shop, holding themselves out as willing to trade in stolen goods. In an effort to have evidence of their transactions with the undercover officers excluded from the trial, the claimants invoked section 78 of the Police and Criminal Evidence Act 1984, which provides that a court may refuse to allow evidence which would adversely affect the fairness of proceedings. They asserted that the deceptive tactics caused harm [HA_A(2)__1__] to them [__2__] sufficient to warrant a finding that those tactics were unfair within the meaning of article 78 [__3__].[12] However, the Court of Appeal agreed with the prosecution that the tactics were not such as to be coercive; that the accused had thus acted of their own volition. Any harm caused by those tactics [__4__] to the accused [__5__] was insufficient to warrant a finding of adverse effect on the fairness of the proceedings [__6__].[13]

12.4 Scope of agents

The Claimant and Respondent Harm Axioms differ with respect to assertions about the agents *to whom harm is caused*, and with respect to the agents *who cause* harm.

Persons or entities who cause harm

Assertions about right-based harm assume that it is the personal actor who causes the harm [HA_A(1)(a), HA_Z(1)(a)]. By contrast, assertions about restriction-based harm are made without reference to any agent who causes the harm [HA_A(1)(a), HA_Z(1)(a)]. That discrepancy might seem arbitrary. After all, the gravity or validity of a restriction may depend on the status of the entity who causes it, such as, for example, whether that entity is a private agent or a state agent.

Consider an example. We have already examined some cases, such as *Ireland v. UK*, *Tyrer*, *Costello-Roberts* and *McCann*, which involve the infliction of harm by government agents. But the same kinds of harm can be caused by private agents. The case of *Osman v. United Kingdom*[14] concerned the killing of the claimant's husband by her son's schoolteacher. Over a period of two years, a number of individuals, including school officials and the local police, became aware of the teacher's apparently sexual obsession with the claimant's son. A series of increasingly alarming events culminated in an incident in which the teacher, with a firearm, wounded the claimant's son and killed her husband. Under the European Convention, she complained that local authorities had been amply advised of the dangers posed to her family by the teacher, such that their failure to provide adequate protection amounted to a violation of her husband's right to life. The state was thus accused not of actively killing, but of omitting to undertake greater steps to prevent a killing by a private individual.[15]

The Court found that the state's conduct did not amount to a violation of article 2. That result contrasts with the Court's finding of a violation in *McCann*. Of course, those who question the validity of a public–private divide, arguing that rights should enjoy the same degree of protection regardless of the public or private status of those who infringe them, will have no quarrel with a notation form which does not distinguish between different kinds of actors who cause restriction-based harm. However, not all scholars are willing to abolish the distinction; and, in any event, it remains commonplace in legal arguments and judicial decisions. States routinely argue that their responsibilities to protect individuals from harm caused by private agents cannot be placed at the same level as their responsibilities to protect individuals from harm caused by state agents.[16]

We must therefore take account of the ways in which arguments distinguish between the different kinds of agents who cause harm. The different kinds of persons or entities who cause restriction-based harm affect rights discourse not through the element of *agents*, but through the element of *harm*. In *Osman*, the Court accepts that article 2 entails positive obligations on states to protect individuals' right to life not only vis-à-vis the state but also vis-à-vis private agents:

> Article 2 § 1 enjoins the State not only to refrain from the intentional and unlawful taking of life, but also to take appropriate steps to safeguard the lives of those within its jurisdiction [. . .] by putting in place effective criminal law provisions to deter the commission of offences against the person backed up by law-enforcement machinery.[17]

It then goes on to note that the positive obligation upon the state to prevent killings by private agents are not unlimited:

> [B]earing in mind the difficulties involved in policing modern societies, the unpredictability of human conduct and the operational choices which must be made in terms of priorities and resources, such an obligation must be interpreted in a way which does not impose an impossible or disproportionate burden on the authorities. Accordingly, not every claimed risk to life can entail for the authorities a Convention requirement to take operational measures to prevent that risk from materialising.[18]

The Court thus treats the public–private divide as a question of burden or cost to the state: the state's duty to control the conduct of private individuals cannot be as great as its duty to control its own agents.

Accordingly, an element which might have been treated in terms of different kinds of *agents* is instead treated in terms of different levels of *burden or cost*. And, as we have seen, different levels of burden or cost simply denote different levels at which harm is asserted to be sufficient or insufficient. Thus differences between the kinds of agents who cause restriction-based harm are indeed taken into account – not *as* agents, but rather *as factors in the depiction of the character or degree of the harm.* In *Osman*, the government cites the non-state conduct of the murderer in order to characterise *the harm* for which the state was responsible as having been insufficient to warrant a finding that its conduct amounted to a violation of the right [HA_Z(2)(c)(i)]. By contrast, the claimant situates the non-official conduct of the murderer within the context of adequate notice having been given to police, who, having ignored the warnings, caused unjustifiable harm to the personal actors [HA_A(2)(c)].

Persons or entities to whom harm is caused

The difference between right-based and restriction-based harms entails a further consequence. Assertions about actors incurring right-based harm [HA_A(1)(b), HA_Z(1)(b)] can be made with reference to any of the actors we have examined (I^p, $I^{\neg p}$, S). By contrast, only the personal actor is indicated as the actor who incurs a restriction-based harm [HA_A(2)(a), HA_Z(2)(a)]. Therefore, once the components of the Claimant and Respondent Harm Axioms have been translated into symbolic form, we will be able to record restriction-based arguments only through the form θ: $I^p i$, unlike right-based arguments, which we will be able to record through the forms θ: $I^p i$, θ: $I^{\neg p} i$ and θ: Si.

That discrepancy, too, might seem arbitrary. After all, no less than right-based harms, restriction-based harms may involve the interests of actors other than the personal actor. Why would those actors disappear from arguments about restriction-based harm? In fact, they do not disappear. However, rather than retaining the status of *agents*, they, too, become factored into arguments about *harm*.

Suppose that police officer Eve kills private individual Cain in order to prevent Cain from killing a private individual, Abel. (Suppose also that Cain's attempt to kill Abel has no exculpatory motive, such as self-defence or defence of some other individual.) In an action brought by Adam on Cain's behalf, complaining of a violation of Cain's right to life, it might at first seem that Abel counts as a non-personal actor. On closer inspection, however, we see that this it not the case. Abel is indeed an individual who is affected by Cain's actions. However, he is not an individual affected by some particular way in which Cain exercises *his right to life*. The fact that Cain was about to kill Abel is thus factored into arguments about the character or degree of harm inflicted on Cain by Eve, under the circumstances. Yet that fact does not make Abel a non-personal actor affected by Cain's exercise of his right to life. Nor is Eve a non-personal actor: she is indeed affected by Cain's actions, which prompt her to kill him; but the acts committed by Cain which cause Eve to kill him are not undertaken by Cain as an exercise of his right to life. By extension, it is precisely in that totality-of-the-circumstances sense that the effects of alleged terrorist activity upon other individuals, or upon society as a whole, is factored into arguments about restriction-based harm in cases like *McCann*, *Ireland v. UK*, *Lawless*, *Brogan* or *Brannigan*.

Synthesis

The foregoing comparisons reveal the differences between right-based and restriction-based harms:

- Right-based harm is caused *by* the personal actor. It can be caused *to* any actor. Accordingly, in the exercise of their rights, personal actors can be said to cause harm to themselves as personal actors; to themselves as non-personal actors; to other individuals as non-personal actors; or to society.
- Restriction-based harm is caused only *to* the personal actor. The interests of any other agent are relevant only in so far as they are factored into the assessment of harm.

Those observations will affect the notation forms. The non-personal actor and society will be relevant only in so far as they *incur* harms (i.e. only in so far as they incur right-based harms). By contrast, the personal actor can both cause and incur harms (i.e. can cause or incur right-based harms; and can incur restriction-based harms). Later on, we will see that the question of who *causes* harm will be represented by means of markers attached to the harm variables. Accordingly – and this is the important point – we will see that actor variables, including the I^p variable, *will represent actors only in so far as those actors* incur *a harm.*

12.5 Choice of causation model

Recall *Leander*, concerning a privacy claim by an individual who was refused employment on the basis of classified information compiled about him by government authorities. That claim can, with equal plausibility, be treated as right-based or restriction-based. Treating the claim as right-based, we can attribute to the state the following argument: an exercise of the privacy right which would compel the state to disclose classified information would cause harm [$HA_Z(1)(a)$] to society's interest in state security [$HA_Z(1)(b)$] sufficient to justify the government's refusal to disclose it [$HA_Z(1)(c)$]. By contrast, the claimant argues that any such harm [$HA_A(1)(a)$] to society [$HA_A(1)(b)$] is insufficient to justify that refusal [$HA_A(1)(c)(i)$]. Treating the claim as restriction-based, we can say that, for the claimant, the refusal constitutes a harm [$HA_A(2)(a)$] to him [$HA_A(2)(b)$] which is sufficient to warrant a finding that it is unjustified [$HA_A(2)(c)$]; while, for the state, any harm caused [$HA_Z(2)(a)$] to him [$HA_Z(2)(b)$] is insufficient to warrant a finding that the refusal is unjustified [$HA_Z(2)(c)(i)$].

Osman is similar. Treating it as right-based, we can say that the state asserts that an exercise of the right to life which would require greater police protection would place an excessive burden on the state in terms of cost or resources, excessive cost being a form of harm [$HA_Z(1)(a)$] to society [$HA_Z(1)(b)$] which is sufficient to justify the government failure to provide greater protection [$HA_Z(1)(c)$]. For the claimant, any such harm [$HA_A(1)(a)$] to society [$HA_A(1)(b)$] is insufficient to justify that failure [$HA_A(1)(c)(i)$]. But treating the claim as restriction-based, we can say that, for the claimant, the state's failure to provide greater protection constitutes a harm [$HA_A(2)(a)$] to the deceased [$HA_A(2)(b)$] which is sufficient to warrant a finding that such failure was unjustified [$HA_A(2)(c)$]; while, for the state, any harm caused [$HA_Z(2)(a)$] to the deceased [$HA_Z(2)(b)$] is insufficient to warrant a finding that such failure was unjustified [$HA_Z(2)(c)(i)$].

How, then, should we treat these two cases? If either model of causation produces equally accurate renderings of the arguments, then it makes no difference which is used. It is only where one model produces a more accurate rendering that it is to be preferred. Consider some other cases which we have been treating as right-based. We could say that, for Mr Handyside, the censorship causes harm [$HA_A(2)(a)$] to him [$HA_A(2)(b)$] which is sufficient to warrant a finding that the ban is unjustified [$HA_A(2)(c)$]. We could say that the state agrees that the ban causes harm [$HA_Z(2)(a)$] to Mr Handyside [$HA_Z(2)(b)$], but that it is insufficient, in view of the potential harm to society to individual children, to warrant a finding that it is unjustified [$HA_Z(2)(c)(i)$]. That is a valid rendering of the dispute, but less precise, because the effects of the book on individual children or on society in general are simply factored into an argument about relative harm to Mr Handyside: the harm caused by the ban to Mr Handyside is either sufficient [$HA_A(2)(c)$] or insufficient [$HA_Z(2)(c)(i)$] to warrant a finding that it is unjustified.

Similarly, we could say that, for Mr Lingens, the defamation action causes harm [$HA_A(2)(a)$] to him [$HA_A(2)(b)$] which is sufficient to warrant a finding that it is unjustified [$HA_A(2)(c)$]. We could say that the state agrees that the action causes harm [$HA_Z(2)(a)$] to Mr Lingens [$HA_Z(2)(b)$], but that it is insufficient, in view of the potential harm to the former Chancellor, to warrant a finding that it is unjustified [$HA_Z(2)(c)(i)$]. There again, we lose the former Chancellor as a distinct actor.

Even in a sheer harm-as-cost argument, the loss of society as a distinct actor produces a less precise result. We could say that, for Mr Rees or Ms Cossey, the state's refusal to issue them adequate documentation causes harm [HA_A(2)(a)] to them [HA_A(2)(b)] which is sufficient to warrant a finding that it is unjustified [HA_A(2)(c)]. We could say that the state agrees that the action causes harm [HA_Z(2)(a)] to them [HA_Z(2)(b)], but that it is insufficient, in view of the administrative burden to the state, to warrant a finding that it is unjustified [HA_Z(2)(c)(i)]. There again, society's interests are simply factored into arguments about harm to the personal actor.

But if the loss of distinct actors is such a sacrifice, why ever use a restriction-based theory at all? In some cases, it becomes superfluous to refer to other actors – the factoring of their interests into arguments about the personal actor is all that is required. In *Lawless*, *Ireland v. UK*, *Brogan* or *Brannigan*, we could certainly say that, for the state, allowing the detainees to exercise their rights by according them more favourable treatment would, under the circumstances, jeopardise and thus harm [HA_Z(1)(a)] society's ability to maintain public order [HA_Z(1)(b)]; and that such harm would reach a level sufficient to justify the treatment of the detainees [HA_Z(1)(c)]. The claimants could be said to argue that any such harm [HA_A(1)(a)] to society [HA_A(1)(b)] is insufficient to justify that treatment [HA_A(1)(c)(i)]. That rendering, however, places more focus on society's interests than is required to make the point. Society's interest in maintaining public order having largely been accepted, the decisive question in these cases has to do with the way in which that interest should be factored into an assessment of the treatment inflicted on the personal actor.

In *Aksoy*, we could certainly say that, from the respondent's perspective, the government had allowed Aksoy to exercise his rights by treating him more mildly than he had claimed, such that deeming that treatment to be too harsh would harm [HA_Z(1)(a)] society's ability to maintain prison discipline [HA_Z(1)(b)]; and that such harm would reach a level sufficient to justify the regime now in place [HA_Z(1)(c)]. The claimant could be said to argue that any such harm [HA_A(1)(a)] to society [HA_A(1)(b)] is insufficient to justify the treatment that was inflicted [HA_A(1)(c)(i)]. But this is a somewhat awkward way of putting the matter. Society's overall interest in maintaining prison discipline being, in itself, undisputed, the decisive issue has to do with the way in which that interest should be factored into the nature and intensity of the treatment inflicted on Aksoy. Similar observations could be made about society's interest in preventing crime, for example in *Tyrer*, *McCann*, *Kruslin* or *Huvig*; or in maintaining school discipline, for example in *Costello-Roberts*.

Review these terms

1. causation
2. right-based harm
3. restriction-based harm
4. scope of agents

13 The basic harm symbols

In this chapter, we begin the task of translating components of the Claimant and Respondent Harm Axioms into symbolic form and combining them with agent symbols.

13.1 General harm postulates

Assertions of sufficient harm will be denoted by the variable H. Assertions of insufficient harm will be denoted by the variable ~H.[1] The symbols H and ~H must *not* be read, respectively, as 'harm' and 'no harm'. They must be read as 'sufficient harm' or 'unacceptable harm' (H), and 'insufficient harm' or 'acceptable harm' (~H). Where it is useful to speak only of the relevance of harm, without specifying it either as sufficient (H) or insufficient (~H), the variable γ (gamma) will be used. Assertions that inquiry into harm is irrelevant will be denoted by negating γ, hence the variable $\sim\gamma$.[2] Where it is useful merely to indicate the element of harm, without indicating whether the issue of harm is asserted to be relevant (γ) or irrelevant ($\sim\gamma$), the variable η (eta) will be used. Note the use of the numeral '1' in the labels Ps(η1) and Ps(γ1). That specification is used because, in the next chapter, further postulates setting forth the values of the variables η and γ will be introduced,

Harm postulates

Ps(η1) $\quad \eta \subset \gamma, \sim\gamma$

Ps(γ1) $\quad \gamma \subset$ H, ~H

Hence, on the basis of Ps(η1) and Ps(γ1),

Th(η) $\quad \eta \subset$ H, ~H, $\sim\gamma$

The relationships between η symbols are illustrated in Figure 13.1.

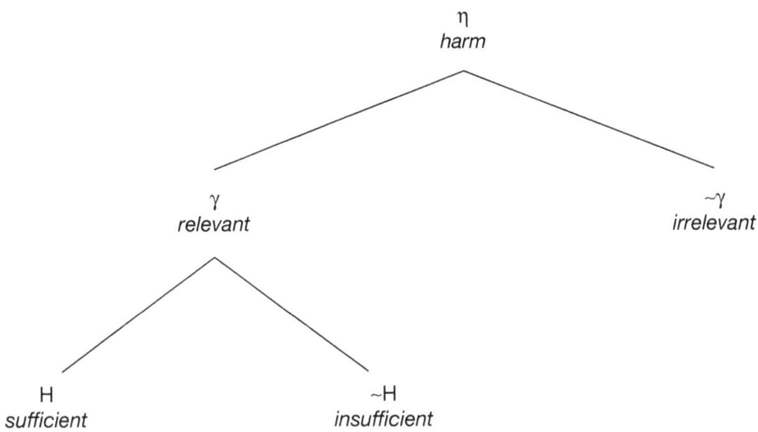

Figure 13.1

13.2 Harm attribution

The next task is to record the attribution of harm to actors:

> **Harm Attribution Corollary to the Claimant and Respondent Harm Axioms**: All θ positions attribute some harm to some actor. That is, for any position θ: α, there is some value of η, such that θ: αη.

Note the use of the word 'some'. The rule does not mean that *any* value of η can be freely correlated to *any* value of α in *any* θ position. That possibility is precluded by the Claimant and Respondent Harm Axioms (which, in turn, presuppose the Claimant and Respondent Corollaries to the Axioms of Recognition and Restriction). For example, the claimant in *Handyside* would not assert that *The Little Red Book* causes unacceptable harm to children or to society in general [A: SH]. Rather, the respondent makes that argument,

F 13.1 Z: SH

Here we see how (unlike traditional or deontic logic, or Hohfeldian analysis) the question whether a formula is admissible or inadmissible depends in part on the person or entity who makes the assertion, i.e. on whether that agent is a claimant or a respondent. That feature follows from the Claimant and Respondent Corollaries to the Axioms of Recognition and Restrictions. At higher levels of abstraction, we could say, for example, that the government assumes the question of harm to society to be relevant [Z: Sγ]; or the question of harm to some actor to be relevant [Z: αγ];

or that the government attributes some kind of harm to society [Z: $S\eta$] or to some actor [Z: $\alpha\eta$]; or indeed that some party attributes some kind of harm to some actor [θ: $\alpha\eta$].

Mr Handyside argues that the book inflicts upon society a level of harm which is *in*sufficient to justify the prohibition,

F 13.2 A: S~H

More abstractly, we could say, for example, that both the claimant and the respondent assume the question of harm to society to be relevant [θ°: $S\gamma$] or the question of harm to some actor to be relevant [θ°: $\alpha\gamma$]; or that both parties attribute some kind of harm to society [θ°: $S\eta$]; or that both parties attribute some kind of harm to some actor [θ°: $\alpha\eta$].

The rule of harm attribution can apply not only to identified actors, but also to the kinds of broadly implied actors that were examined in Section 10.4. As noted earlier, Mr Handyside's assertion of insufficient harm to society [A: S~H] implies an assertion of insufficient harm to any individual child,

F 13.3 A: $I^{\neg p}$~H

The British government's opposing argument about society [Z: SH] implies that there is a risk of sufficient harm to some individual child,

F 13.4 Z: $I^{\neg p}H$

In the case of abortion (*Brüggemann*), the assertion by government (θ = Z) that the woman causes unacceptable harm (η = H) to herself ($\alpha = I^p$) through failure to appreciate relevant physiological, psychological or moral consequences of the procedure, would take the form,

F 13.5 Z: I^pH

It might also be asserted that the woman causes unacceptable harm (η = H) to the interests of two non-personal actors, who are distinct enough to warrant suspension of the assumption of identity of interest. One is the foetus ($\alpha = I^{\neg p}{}_1$),

F 13.6 Z: $I^{\neg p}{}_1H$

Another non-personal actor, in some cases, might be a further interested party, such as a non-consenting father ($I^{\neg p}{}_2$),

F 13.7 Z: $I^{\neg p}{}_2H$

The assertion that abortion would cause unacceptable harm (η = H) to society's overall interest in promoting the value of unborn life (α = S) would take the form,

F 13.8 Z: SH

Formulas F 13.5–F 13.8 generate a compound Z position,

F 13.9 Z: $I^pH \cdot I^{\sim p}{}_1H \cdot I^{\sim p}{}_2H \cdot SH$

As we have seen, a rebuttal (θ = A) could take the form of an assertion of insufficient harm (η = ~H) caused to these actors (α = I^p, $I^{\sim p}{}_1$, $I^{\sim p}{}_2$, S),

F 13.10 A: $I^p{\sim}H \cdot I^{\sim p}{}_1{\sim}H \cdot I^{\sim p}{}_2{\sim}H \cdot S{\sim}H$

Alternative rebuttals are possible, using the concept of irrelevant harm. Again, we will simply consider one example in passing now, examining that option more closely when we reach the chapters on consent. An alternative rebuttal to the position Z: I^pH [F 13.5] could take the form of an assertion that the woman's free consent to run any risk of harm to herself renders irrelevant any inquiry into the acceptably or unacceptably harmful character (η = ~γ) of the act,

F 13.11 A: $I^p{\sim}\gamma$

13.3 Relevant and irrelevant harm

A tilde (~) is now being attached not to a marker, but to the principal symbol (~γ,~H). When attached to H, it performs a straightforward negating function. Say that the formula Z: $I^{\sim p}H$ translates as:

> The respondent asserts that the non-personal actor is sufficiently harmed. (*Adduced to support the restriction.*)

The argument A: $I^{\sim p}{\sim}H$ then provides a rebuttal in the form of a negation:

> The claimant asserts that the non-personal actor is *in*sufficiently harmed. (*Adduced to defeat the restriction.*)

Indeed, suppose that it is *that* claimant's argument [A: $I^{\sim p}{\sim}H$] which is the first to be adduced. We could then say that the respondent's rebuttal is generated through a negation of *that* assertion about harm. We could record that relationship by means of a double negative, e.g. Z: $I^{\sim p}{\sim}{\sim}H$, which would literally translate as:

> The respondent asserts that the non-personal actor is *not in*sufficiently harmed. (*Adduced to support the restriction.*)

Hence, the identical formula Z: $I^{\sim p}H$:

> The respondent asserts that the non-personal actor is sufficiently harmed.

The same principle applies for γ, but with an important caveat. Consider the following problem. The variable γ can take the values H or ~H. At first glance, it might seem that the values H or ~H could freely be plugged in to ~γ, which would then have the effect of negating those two values, turning them, respectively, into their opposites: ~H and ~~H, hence ~H and H. However, ~γ represents an assertion of *irrelevant* harm, i.e. an assertion that *it makes no difference* whether the harm is sufficient or insufficient. How can that same variable generate assertions of sufficient or insufficient harm, while asserting harm to be relevant? The symbol γ is not an empty vessel serving merely to hold H and ~H. It is more determinate: it expresses a point of agreement between those otherwise contradictory terms, namely, that the question as to whether the harm is sufficient or insufficient *is relevant*. That shared assumption can be stated as follows:

> H: There is sufficient harm, and the question of whether the harm is sufficient or insufficient *is relevant.*
>
> ~H: There is insufficient harm, and the question of whether the harm is sufficient or insufficient *is relevant.*

The symbol ~γ cannot straightforwardly negate a given value of γ because ~γ is being used solely to negate the assertion that the question of whether the harm is sufficient or insufficient *is relevant.*

13.4 The strongly exclusive harm variable

The hierarchical relationships between harm variables are not configured entirely the same way as the hierarchical relationships between agent symbols.[3] In θ: *p*, assertion *p* is attributed to *some* party, with nothing implied about whether the other party also asserts, or could assert, *p*. Therefore, if θ = A, then it is the case that A: *p*, but it may also be the case that Z: *p*. In θ: α*i*, interest *i* is attributed to *some* actor, with nothing implied about whether the party attributes, or could attribute, that interest to any other actor. Therefore, if α = S, then it is the case that θ: S*i*, but it may also be the case that θ: $I^{p}i$ or that θ: $I^{\sim p}i$. And, in θ: I*i*, an interest is attributed to *some* individual actor, with nothing implied about whether the party attributes, or could attribute, that interest to any other individual actor. Therefore, if I = $I^{\sim p}$, then it is the case that θ: $I^{\sim p}i$, but it may also be the case that θ: $I^{p}i$.

Consider, however, the formula θ: $\alpha\eta$ ('Some party claims that some harm is caused to some actor'). Assume that the harm turns out to be a sufficient harm (η = H). In that case, it would be wrong to interpret the formula θ: $\alpha\eta$ as meaning 'Some party claims that some harm is caused to some actor', *with nothing implied* about any other harm which might be caused to that actor. Quite the contrary. For any θ: $\alpha\eta$, if, for example, η takes the value H, then all other possible values of η are implied:

(a) It is implied that η takes the value γ.
(b) It is implied that η does not take the values ~H or ~γ.

Accordingly, if η = H, then it is the case that θ: αH, and therefore:

(a′) It is also the case that θ: $\alpha\gamma$.
(b′) It is not the case that θ: α~H or θ: α~γ.

In Section 4.1, a principal distinction was drawn between inclusive symbols (ψ°, θ°, α°, I°) and weakly exclusive ones (ψ, θ, α, I). How do those concepts apply to the harm variables? First, we can see that inclusive harm symbols (e.g. η°, γ°) would be meaningless. A party cannot assert θ: $\alpha\gamma^\circ$, as it cannot simultaneously assert θ: αH *and* θ: α~H. A fortiori it cannot assert θ: $\alpha\eta^\circ$, as it cannot simultaneously assert θ: αH, θ: α~H and θ: α~γ. Second, a weakly exclusive symbol – despite its central role for agents – is also useless: again, a party cannot assert that some harm is caused to some actor, *with nothing implied* regarding the other kinds of harm. Accordingly, we need a strongly exclusive harm variable: e.g. for θ: $\alpha\eta$, if η = H, then $\eta \neq$ ~γ, ~H. Note that 'strongly' exclusive here does not mean absolutely exclusive of all other possible values of η. The case of η = H still allows, indeed logically implies, $\eta = \gamma$. The only point is that there are certain values of η which become positively excluded once the variable η takes a more precise value. As harm variables can only be strongly exclusive in that sense, we need not adopt additional symbols to represent inclusive or weakly inclusive meanings. Rather, *harm variables are always strongly exclusive*, according to the following values,[4]

Harm variable postulates

Ps($\eta = \gamma$): $\eta \neq \sim\gamma$	Ps(γ = H): $\gamma \neq$ ~H
Ps($\eta = \sim\gamma$): $\eta \neq \gamma$	Ps(γ = ~H): $\gamma \neq$ H
Ps(η = H): $\eta \neq \sim\gamma$, ~H	
Ps(η = ~H): $\eta \neq \sim\gamma$, H	

13.5 Reverse translation

Most combinations of actor and harm variables are straightforward. Again, the formula Z: $I^{\sim p}H$ can be translated as:

> The respondent asserts that the non-personal actor is sufficiently harmed.

Alternatively:

> The respondent asserts that the non-personal actor is unacceptably harmed.

The rebuttal A: $I^{\sim p}{\sim}H$, might be translated in any number of ways:

> The claimant asserts that the non-personal actor is not sufficiently harmed.
>
> The claimant asserts that the non-personal actor is not unacceptably harmed.
>
> The claimant asserts that the non-personal actor is insufficiently harmed.

Strictly speaking, a translation along the following lines would also be correct:

> The claimant asserts that the non-personal actor is acceptably harmed.

In ordinary speech, however, the phrase ‘acceptably harmed’ sounds odd, and can be avoided by using one of the other translations.

Although we are not yet stressing arguments about irrelevant harm, they can be noted in passing – in this case, as the alternative rebuttal A: $I^{\sim p}{\sim}\gamma$:

> The claimant asserts that harm to the non-personal actor is irrelevant.

Arguments about the interests of society would be treated in the same way. For example, the formula Z: SH can translate as:

> The respondent asserts that society is sufficiently harmed.

And the rebuttal A: S~H:

> The claimant asserts that society is insufficiently harmed.

Or the rebuttal A: S~γ:

> The claimant asserts that harm to society is irrelevant.

In some contexts, the formula Z: SH can translate as:

> The respondent asserts that the state is sufficiently harmed.

Hence the rebuttal A: S~H:

> The claimant asserts that the state is insufficiently harmed.

Or the rebuttal A: S~γ:

> The claimant asserts that harm to the state is irrelevant.

As noted in the next chapter, the role of personal actor is slightly more complex. In the remainder of this chapter, the focus will be on arguments about the non-personal actor and society.

Arguments can also be made at higher levels of abstraction. Consider the position θ: $I^{\sim p}\gamma$:

> Some party asserts that the harm to the non-personal actor is relevant.

Such a position would be used purely for analytical purposes, and does not in itself entail an argument supporting either side of the dispute. Similarly, consider the position θ: $I^{\sim p}\eta$:

> Some party attributes some harm to the non-personal actor.

That argument expresses the element of harm at the highest level of abstraction [η]. It entails no assertion as to whether that harm is relevant or irrelevant, or, if relevant, whether sufficient or insufficient to justify the restriction. Still higher levels of abstraction can be achieved, e.g. θ: Iγ, θ: $I^{\circ}\gamma$, θ: αγ, θ: $\alpha^{\circ}\gamma$, θ: Iη, θ: $I^{\circ}\eta$, θ: αη, θ: $\alpha^{\circ}\eta$. As these may encompass interests of the personal actor, we will examine them more closely in the next chapter.

Exercise set 13.1

Translate. Assume that reflexive arguments are made *only with reference to the non-personal actor or to society.*

Example: The respondent asserts that a non-personal actor is sufficiently harmed.

Answer: Z: $I^{\sim p}H$

1 The respondent states that a non-personal actor is unacceptably harmed.
2 The claimants had pointed out that the non-personal actors are not unacceptably harmed.
3 Some party ought to insist that society is insufficiently harmed.
4 The respondent rather surprisingly argued that the state is unacceptably harmed.
5 The claimants patiently reminded the court that they believed themselves to be insufficiently harmed.
6 The claimant might have believed that she was not unacceptably harmed.
7 The respondent argued with utmost conviction that he is unacceptably harmed.
8 Counsel for the respondent government truly believed that the state is unacceptably harmed.
9 The respondent state endlessly repeated that it would have to incur an unacceptable cost.
10 Some party should have noted that the harm to society is irrelevant.
11 The claimant would attribute some harm to the non-personal actor.
12 The Court adopted the arguments proffered by the respondent state, that the non-personal actor and society are unacceptably harmed.
13 The parties agreed that the question of harm to the non-personal actor and to society is relevant.
14 The claimants urged the court to agree that any harm to the non-personal actor and to society is irrelevant.
15 Both parties attributed some harm to the non-personal actor.

13.6 Deriving arguments

H and ~H are hierarchically inferior to γ, which is hierarchically inferior to η. The variable η can always substitute for γ, which can always substitute for H and ~H. For example, the assertion that a non-personal actor is sufficiently harmed (θ: $I^{\sim p}H$) presupposes that the harm caused is relevant (θ: $I^{\sim p}\gamma$). *That* assertion, in turn, presupposes that *some* harm is attributable to that actor (θ: $I^{\sim p}\eta$), hence:

From θ: $I^{\sim p}H$ derive θ: $I^{\sim p}\eta$,

(1)	θ: $I^{\sim p}H$	given
(2)	θ: $I^{\sim p}\gamma$	Ps(γ1)
conclusion	θ: $I^{\sim p}\eta$	Ps(η1)

From θ: $I^{\sim p}H$ derive θ: $I^{\sim p}\eta$,

(1)	θ: $I^{\sim p}H$	given
conclusion	θ: $I^{\sim p}\eta$	Th(η)

Exercise set 13.2

1 Derive θ: Sγ from θ: S~H.
2 Derive θ: Sη from θ: S~γ.
3 Derive θ: $I^{\sim p}\eta$ from θ: $I^{\sim p}$~H, using only postulates.
4 Derive θ: $I^{\sim p}\eta$ from θ: $I^{\sim p}H$, using the fewest possible steps.

13.7 Proving theorems

The Harm Attribution Corollary to the Claimant and Respondent Harm Axioms can be introduced into proofs as a justifying step, allowing us to ascertain values for combinations of α and η variables. We will do that by writing 'η attr' in the right-hand column:

Prove the theorem: Sγ $\subset$ SH, S~H

(1)	$\gamma \subset$ H, ~H	Ps(γ1)
conclusion	Sγ $\subset$ SH, S~H	η attr

But that rule is subject to a further rule, which will be introduced in Section 14.4.

Exercise set 13.3

Prove the following theorems.

1 $I^{\sim p}\gamma \subset I^{\sim p}H, I^{\sim p}{\sim}H$
2 $I^{\sim p}\eta \subset I^{\sim p}\gamma, I^{\sim p}{\sim}\gamma$
3 $S\eta \subset SH, S{\sim}H, S{\sim}\gamma$

Exercise set 13.4

Fill in the blanks.

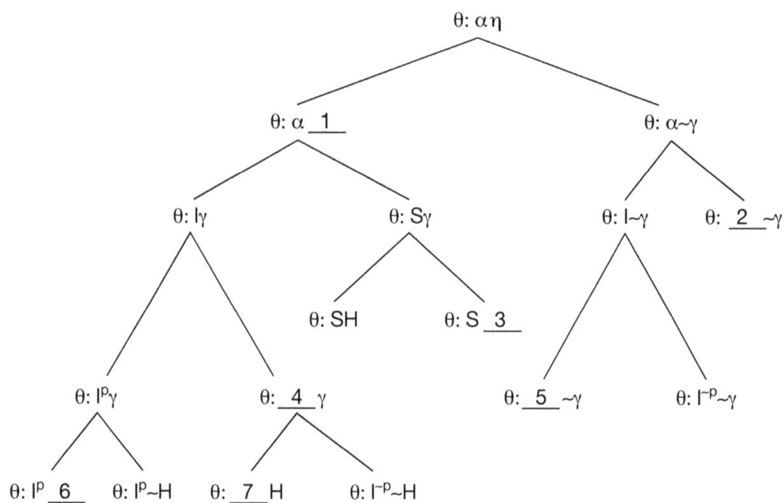

13.8 Presupposition

We can now make a further observation about the meta-theoretical role of the model. Recall the dispute about whether Hamlet ought to have killed Claudius. That dispute could be meaningfully conducted only in so far as all participants agreed with the prior assumption that the killing can be evaluated in ethical terms. One participant in that discussion might, for example, introduce an argument, which we can call argument *t*: 'Claudius himself admitted to the evil of having murdered Hamlet's father.'[5] Argument *t* can easily fit into the terms of the disagreement; it is consistent with the possibility of evaluating an act of vengeance by Hamlet in ethical terms.

Another participant might introduce argument *r*: 'Hamlet and Claudius are only fictional constructs. Their "actions" are not part of a social context sufficiently determinate to warrant plausible ethical evaluation.' Recall that argument *r* does not fit into the disagreement as initially defined. It supports neither the view that Hamlet ought to have killed Claudius, nor the view that Hamlet ought *not* to have killed Claudius. It contradicts the prior assumption that such a killing can be subjected to ethical judgement. Argument *r* can form the basis of some *other* disagreement, such as, for example, a disagreement about whether the actions of fictional persons can be subjected to ethical evaluation. However, it cannot fit within the terms of the disagreement as posed, which already assumes a response to that question.

To that degree, the question whether an argument can meaningfully be introduced into a dispute can be answered with reference to the dispute's prior assumptions. An argument not presupposing them may form part of some other, perhaps directly related, dispute, but cannot meaningfully be adduced within *that* dispute. Hence:

> **Presupposition Corollary to the Axiom of Contentious Character**: A dispute is a dispute about the adjudication of a liberal right only in so far as it is a dispute – between a claimant's position and a respondent's position – about the values to be ascribed to the variables comprising some mutually presupposed θ position.

For example, a dispute between the positions A: $I^{\sim p}\sim H$ and Z: $I^{\sim p}H$ is a dispute between the claimant and the respondent about the value to be ascribed to γ in the mutually presupposed position θ: $I^{\sim p}\gamma$. A dispute between the positions A: $I^{\sim p}\sim\gamma$ and Z: $I^{\sim p}H$ is a dispute about the value to be ascribed to η in θ: $I^{\sim p}\eta$, and so on.

That stipulation provides a framework for distinguishing among theories about rights. A detailed examination would require a separate study, but an outline can be sketched as follows. An initial distinction can be drawn between, on the one hand, theories which reject liberal rights discourse altogether and, on the other hand, theories which accept liberal rights discourse, but which disagree about the balance to be struck between rights and restrictions in specific instances. Theories which reject rights discourse can be defined as rejecting at least one element of the structure of θ positions. We have seen that one element of θ positions is the ascription of only two possible values, A and Z, to the θ variable. One approach for a theory which is hostile to liberal rights regimes would be to reject that bipolar structure of adjudication. By contrast, a set of theories can be said to accept rights discourse to the extent that they at least tacitly accept or assume that bipolar distribution of θ variables, even if they disagree on the range of persons or entities who should be able to qualify as parties. Further elements include the limitation of α to the three values I^p, $I^{\sim p}$ and S, or the limitations to the values of the harm and consent variables which we will be examining. A thoroughgoing critic of liberal rights would be inclined to reject a discourse which so readily reduces human interests to questions of harm and consent. By contrast, an adherent of liberal rights might disagree with applications of those concepts in particular cases, but expressly or implicitly accepts the overall harm–consent structure of liberal rights discourse.[6]

14 Causation markers

In this chapter, we refine the notation form for harm symbols by distinguishing between right-based and restriction-based harms.

14.1 Notation

We have seen that the non-personal actor and society appear only as actors incurring right-based harms [$HA_A(1)(b)$, $HA_Z(1)(b)$]. The personal actor, too, appears in that role, but also appears as the only actor who incurs restriction-based harms [$HA_A(2)(b)$, $HA_Z(2)(b)$]. Confusion could arise, then, from writing a position merely as θ: I^pH. If that harm is right-based, then the personal actor both causes and incurs the alleged harm, as in *Laskey* or *Brüggemann*. If the harm is restriction-based, then the personal actor incurs a harm which is not caused by his or her exercise of the right, as in *McCann*, *Ireland v. UK*, *Tyrer*, *Costello-Roberts* or *Aksoy*. Therefore, assertions about right-based harm will be denoted by the marker 'r' affixed to the η variable (η^r). As any given argument is only either right-based or restriction-based (i.e. even if an argument taking one form can be translated into the other, the two remain formally distinct), we can choose a marker for restriction-based harm which comports mutual exclusion vis-à-vis right-based harm. Accordingly, the marker '~r' will be used to denote an assertion of restriction-based harm ($\eta^{\sim r}$),

Causation postulates

Ps(η2) $\eta \subset \eta^r, \eta^{\sim r}$	Ps(η^r) $\eta^r \subset \gamma^r, \sim\gamma^r$	Ps($\eta^{\sim r}$) $\eta^{\sim r} \subset \gamma^{\sim r}, \sim\gamma^{\sim r}$
Ps(γ2) $\gamma \subset \gamma^r, \gamma^{\sim r}$	Ps(γ^r) $\gamma^r \subset H^r, \sim H^r$	Ps($\gamma^{\sim r}$) $\gamma^{\sim r} \subset H^{\sim r}, \sim H^{\sim r}$
Ps($\sim\gamma$) $\sim\gamma \subset \sim\gamma^r, \sim\gamma^{\sim r}$	Ps(H) $H \subset H^r, H^{\sim r}$	Ps($\sim$H) $\sim H \subset \sim H^r, H^{\sim r}$

14.2 Applications

In *Laskey* or *Brüggemann*, the governments' positions include the argument that the personal actors could unacceptably harm themselves and each other in their exercise of the asserted right [Z: $I^{\circ}H^{r}$]. The claimants respond that they would not unacceptably harm themselves or each other [A: $I^{\circ}{\sim}H^{r}$]. At higher levels of abstraction, we can say, for example, that both parties assume the question of right-based harm to all individual actors to be relevant [θ°: $I^{\circ}\gamma^{r}$], or the question of right-based harm to some actor to be relevant [θ°: $\alpha\gamma^{r}$]. At still higher levels, we can say that both parties attribute some right-based harm to some individual actor [θ°: $I\eta^{r}$] or to some actor [θ°: $\alpha\eta^{r}$]. The highest level of abstraction of any utility is θ: $\alpha\eta$. Any higher level is an empty and generally useless construct [e.g. ψ: $\psi\eta$].

In *Ireland v. UK*, *Tyrer*, *Costello-Roberts* or *Aksoy*, the governments argue that the personal actors are not unacceptably harmed by the acts of state officials [Z: $I^{p}{\sim}H^{\sim r}$]. The claimants respond that they *are* unacceptably harmed by such acts [A: $I^{p}H^{\sim r}$]. Here too, we can say that both parties assume the question of restriction-based harm to the personal actor to be relevant [θ°: $I^{p}\gamma^{\sim r}$]; or of restriction-based harm to some individual actor [θ°: $I\gamma^{\sim r}$] or to some actor [θ°: $\alpha\gamma^{\sim r}$] to be relevant; or that both parties attribute some restriction-based harm to the personal actor [θ°: $I^{p}\eta^{\sim r}$] or to some individual actor [θ°: $I\eta^{\sim r}$] or to some actor [θ°: $\alpha\eta^{\sim r}$].

In principle, marked harm symbols would be unnecessary where the actor incurring the harm is the non-personal actor or society. Those actors are relevant only in so far as they can incur right-based harm. However, for purposes of uniformity, we will also used marked harm symbols in arguments about those actors. For example, in *Laskey* and *Brüggemann*, the governments argue that non-personal actors, and indeed the broader public's interests in health or morals, are unacceptably harmed by the personal actors' exercise of the right [Z: $I^{\sim p}H^{r} \cdot SH^{r}$]. The claimants respond that those actors are not unacceptably harmed [A: $I^{\sim p}{\sim}H^{r} \cdot S{\sim}H^{r}$].

14.3 Theorems

The causation postulates can be introduced as steps to prove theorems:

Prove the theorem: $\gamma \subset H^{r}, {\sim}H^{r}, H^{\sim r}, {\sim}H^{\sim r}$

(1)	$\gamma \subset \gamma^{r}, \gamma^{\sim r}$	Ps(γ2)
(2)	$\gamma \subset H^{r}, {\sim}H^{r}, \gamma^{\sim r}$	Ps(γ^{r})
conclusion	$\gamma \subset H^{r}, {\sim}H^{r}, H^{\sim r}, {\sim}H^{\sim r}$	Ps($\gamma^{\sim r}$)

14.4 Actor limitation

The Harm Attribution Corollary to the Claimant and Respondent Harm Axioms allows harm symbols to combine with agent symbols, but, as we have seen, not entirely freely. Some combinations are precluded by the Claimant and Respondent Harm Axioms, which, in turn, presuppose the Claimant and Respondent Corollaries to the Axioms of Recognition and Restriction. The Claimant and Respondent Harm Axioms provide arguments about the non-personal actor and society only with respect to right-based harm. The rule of harm attribution must therefore be used in conjunction with a rule that prohibits impermissible combinations of actor and harm symbols:

> **Actor Limitation Corollary to the Claimant and Respondent Harm Axioms**: Restriction-based harms are incurred only by the personal actor.

That principle is compulsory. It must be included in any proof in which introduction of the Harm Attribution Corollary would generate any combination of a restriction-based harm with the non-personal actor or society (any $\eta^{\sim r}$ with $I^{\sim p}$ or S). We can include it by writing 'α lim' as a justifying step in the right-hand column:

Prove the theorem: $I^{\sim p}\gamma \subset I^{\sim p}H^{r}, I^{\sim p}{\sim}H^{r}$

(1)	$\gamma \subset \gamma^{r}, \gamma^{\sim r}$	Ps(γ2)
(2)	$\gamma \subset H^{r}, {\sim}H^{r}, \gamma^{\sim r}$	Ps(γ^{r})
(3)	$\gamma \subset H^{r}, {\sim}H^{r}, H^{\sim r}, {\sim}H^{\sim r}$	Ps($\gamma^{\sim r}$)
(4)	$I^{\sim p}\gamma \subset I^{\sim p}H^{r}, I^{\sim p}{\sim}H^{r}, I^{\sim p}H^{\sim r}, I^{\sim p}{\sim}H^{\sim r}$	η attr
conclusion	$I^{\sim p}\gamma \subset I^{\sim p}H^{r}, I^{\sim p}{\sim}H^{r}$	α lim

Compare that proof with the following one, in which the attribution of harm to a personal actor means that no actor limitation is required:

Prove the theorem: $I^{p}\gamma \subset I^{p}H^{r}, I^{p}{\sim}H^{r}, I^{p}H^{\sim r}, I^{p}{\sim}H^{\sim r}$

(1)	$\gamma \subset \gamma^{r}, \gamma^{\sim r}$	Ps(γ2)
(2)	$\gamma \subset H^{r}, {\sim}H^{r}, \gamma^{\sim r}$	Ps(γ^{r})
(3)	$\gamma \subset H^{r}, {\sim}H^{r}, H^{\sim r}, {\sim}H^{\sim r}$	Ps($\gamma^{\sim r}$)
conclusion	$I^{p}\gamma \subset I^{p}H^{r}, I^{p}{\sim}H^{r}, I^{p}H^{\sim r}, I^{p}{\sim}H^{\sim r}$	η attr

The following proof is admissible, as α *can* take the value I^p:

Prove the theorem: $\alpha\gamma \subset \alpha H^r, \alpha{\sim}H^r, \alpha H^{\sim r}, \alpha{\sim}H^{\sim r}$

(1)	$\gamma \subset \gamma^r, \gamma^{\sim r}$	Ps(γ2)
(2)	$\gamma \subset H^r, {\sim}H^r, \gamma^{\sim r}$	Ps(γ^r)
(3)	$\gamma \subset H^r, {\sim}H^r, H^{\sim r}, {\sim}H^{\sim r}$	Ps($\gamma^{\sim r}$)
conclusion	$\alpha\gamma \subset \alpha H^r, \alpha{\sim}H^r, \alpha H^{\sim r}, \alpha{\sim}H^{\sim r}$	η attr

However, once the value of α is expressly specified, the rule of actor limitation must be introduced:

Prove the theorem: $\alpha\gamma \subset I^pH^r, I^{\sim p}H^r, SH^r, I^p{\sim}H^r, I^{\sim p}{\sim}H^r, S{\sim}H^r, I^pH^{\sim r}, I^p{\sim}H^{\sim r}$

(1)	$\gamma \subset \gamma^r, \gamma^{\sim r}$	Ps(γ2)
(2)	$\gamma \subset H^r, {\sim}H^r, \gamma^{\sim r}$	Ps(γ^r)
(3)	$\gamma \subset H^r, {\sim}H^r, H^{\sim r}, {\sim}H^{\sim r}$	Ps($\gamma^{\sim r}$)
(4)	$\alpha\gamma \subset \alpha H^r, \alpha{\sim}H^r, \alpha H^{\sim r}, \alpha{\sim}H^{\sim r}$	η attr
(5)	$\alpha\gamma \subset I^pH^r, I^{\sim p}H^r, SH^r, I^p{\sim}H^r, I^{\sim p}{\sim}H^r, S{\sim}H^r, I^pH^{\sim r}, I^{\sim p}H^{\sim r}, SH^{\sim r}, I^p{\sim}H^{\sim r}, I^{\sim p}{\sim}H^{\sim r}, S{\sim}H^{\sim r}$	Th(α)
conclusion	$\alpha\gamma \subset I^pH^r, I^{\sim p}H^r, SH^r, I^p{\sim}H^r, I^{\sim p}{\sim}H^r, S{\sim}H^r, I^pH^{\sim r}, I^p{\sim}H^{\sim r}$	α lim

Exercise set 14.1

Prove the following theorems.

1 $\eta \subset \gamma^r, {\sim}\gamma^r, \gamma^{\sim r}, {\sim}\gamma^{\sim r}$
2 $I^p{\sim}\gamma \subset I^p{\sim}\gamma^r, I^p{\sim}\gamma^{\sim r}$
3 $I\gamma \subset I^pH^r, I^{\sim p}H^r, I^p{\sim}H^r, I^{\sim p}{\sim}H^r, I^pH^{\sim r}, I^p{\sim}H^{\sim r}$
4 $I\eta \subset IH^r, I{\sim}H^r, I{\sim}\gamma^r, IH^{\sim r}, I{\sim}H^{\sim r}, I{\sim}\gamma^{\sim r}$
5 $\alpha\eta \subset I^pH^r, I^{\sim p}H^r, SH^r, I^p{\sim}H^r, I^{\sim p}{\sim}H^r, S{\sim}H^r, I^p{\sim}\gamma^r, I^{\sim p}{\sim}\gamma^r, S{\sim}\gamma^r, I^pH^{\sim r}, I^p{\sim}H^{\sim r}, I^p{\sim}\gamma^{\sim r}$

14.5 Harm constants

In unmarked form, the symbols H, ~H and ~γ are variables, as each can represent more than one inferior value, as set forth, respectively, in Ps(H), Ps(~H) and Ps(~γ). We can now derive a precise statement of the set of harm constants:

(1)	$\eta \subset \eta^{r}, \eta^{\sim r}$	Ps(η2)
(2)	$\eta \subset \gamma^{r}, \sim\gamma^{r}, \eta^{\sim r}$	Ps(η^{r})
(3)	$\eta \subset \gamma^{r}, \sim\gamma^{r}, \gamma^{\sim r}, \sim\gamma^{\sim r}$	Ps($\eta^{\sim r}$)
(4)	$\eta \subset H^{r}, \sim H^{r}, \sim\gamma^{r}, \gamma^{\sim r}, \sim\gamma^{\sim r}$	Ps(γ^{r})
conclusion	$\eta \subset H^{r}, \sim H^{r}, \sim\gamma^{r}, H^{\sim r}, \sim H^{\sim r}, \sim\gamma^{\sim r}$	Ps($\gamma^{\sim r}$)

Exercise set 14.2

Fill in the blanks.

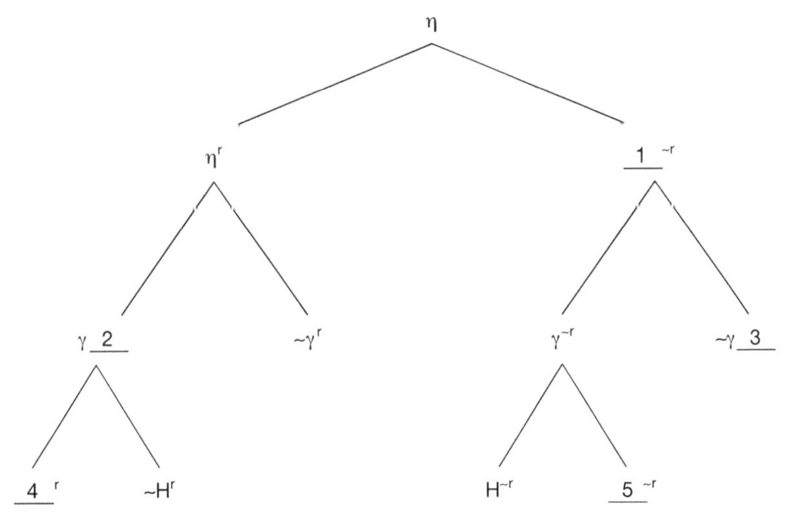

14.6 Deriving arguments

The causation postulates can also be introduced as steps in deriving arguments:

From Z: SH^r derive θ: αη,

(1)	Z: SH^r	given
(2)	θ: SH^r	Ps(θ)
(3)	θ: αH^r	Ps(α)
(4)	θ: αH	Ps(H)
conclusion	θ: αη	Th(η)

Exercise set 14.3

1 Derive θ: Iγ from A: $I^p{\sim}H^r$.
2 Derive θ: Iη from Z: $I^p{\sim}H^{\sim r}$.
3 Derive θ: αγ from A: $I^pH^{\sim r}$.
4 Derive Z: Iη from Z: $I^p{\sim}\gamma^{\sim r}$.
5 Derive θ: αη from A: $I^pH^{\sim r}$.
6 Derive θ: αη from Z: I^pH^r.

15 Right-based harm

In this chapter and the next, we turn back to the case law to examine more closely the relationship between our notation forms, and standard judicial discourse. This chapter focuses on arguments about right-based harms.

15.1 Applications

A study of right-based harm means a study of arguments taking the form $\theta: \alpha\eta^{r}$. We will continue for now to analyse only arguments about sufficient and insufficient harm. In *Handyside*, the state asserts that, by publishing the book, Mr Handyside would cause unacceptable harm to public morals [$Z: SH^{r}$], and, by implication, to individual children [$Z: I^{\sim p}H^{r}$],

F 15.1 $Z: I^{\sim p}H^{r} \cdot SH^{r}$

Mr Handyside asserts that he would cause no unacceptable harm to public morals [$A: S{\sim}H^{r}$] or, by implication, to any individual children [$A: I^{\sim p}{\sim}H^{r}$],

F 15.2 $A: I^{\sim p}{\sim}H^{r} \cdot S{\sim}H^{r}$

Handyside has become famous for the way in which it sought to resolve this controversy, through an approach to balancing rights against restrictions known as the 'margin of appreciation' doctrine.[1] The Court conceded states' prerogatives to reach their own determinations about societies' moral interests:

> [I]t is not possible to find in the domestic law of the various Contracting States a uniform European conception of morals. The view taken by their respective laws of the requirements of morals varies from time to time and from place to place, especially in our era which is characterised by a rapid and far-reaching evolution of opinions on the subject. By reason of their direct and continuous contact with the vital forces of their countries, State authorities are in principle in a better

> position than the international judge to give an opinion on the exact content of these requirements. . . .
>
> Consequently, Article 10 para. 2 leaves to the Contracting States a margin of appreciation. This margin is given both to the domestic legislator . . . and to the bodies, judicial amongst others, that are called upon to interpret and apply the laws in force.[2]

At the same time, the Court affirmed its authority to override that exercise of State prerogative,

> Nevertheless, Article 10 para. 2 does not give the Contracting States an unlimited power of appreciation. The Court, which . . . is responsible for ensuring the observance of those States' engagements (Article 19), is empowered to give the final ruling on whether a 'restriction' or 'penalty' is reconcilable with freedom of expression as protected by Article 10. The domestic margin of appreciation thus goes hand in hand with a European supervision.[3]

The conflict of rights and restrictions thus becomes a conflict between judicial authority and state prerogative. On what grounds, then, is that latter conflict to be resolved? The Court names further criteria:

> Such supervision concerns both the aim of the measure challenged and its 'necessity'. [. . .] The Court's supervisory functions oblige it to pay the utmost attention to the 'principles characterising a democratic society'. [. . .] This means, amongst other things, that every . . . 'restriction' or 'penalty' imposed . . . must be proportionate to the legitimate aim pursued.[4]

Such a formulation leaves several issues to be hashed out. What are the characteristics of 'necessity'? Or of a 'democratic society'? What kinds of aims are 'legitimate'? What level of infringement of a right is 'proportionate' to those aims?

From our perspective, disagreements on those issues are just so many ways of arguing about harm. In *Handyside*, the respondent state asserts the 'necessity' of the restriction by arguing that, without it, individuals or society will incur some unacceptable moral harm, such as a decline in values. The claimant's view that the restriction is unnecessary is a view that, without the restriction, individuals or society will *not* incur any unacceptable moral harm. The respondent's view that the restriction is justified by 'principles characterising a democratic society' is a view that the restriction can be seen to prevent some unacceptable harms to those principles. The claimant's view that a restriction cannot be justified by 'principles characterising a democratic society' is a view that those principles, or that society, would not be so harmed. The respondent's view that the restriction is 'proportionate to a legitimate aim' is a view that, the aim of promoting children's morals being legitimate, less restrictive measures would not adequately accomplish those aims. The claimant's view that the restriction is not proportionate to a legitimate aim is a view that – even assuming the aim of promoting children's morals to be legitimate – the insufficiently harmful character of the book renders the restriction disproportionate to that aim.

A judicial finding that a restriction falls within the state's margin of appreciation is a finding in favour of the respondent's assessment of harm – it is a finding in favour of the value that Z assigns to η (F 15.1). To find that a restriction falls outside of the state's margin of appreciation is to say that it agrees with some possible claimant's assessment – with some value that A can assign to η (F 15.2). What the parties by definition agree on – the background concept which makes the disagreement coherent – is that there is some η, the value of which must decide the case. To subsume such judicial concepts as 'margin of appreciation' or 'legitimacy' or 'proportionality', along with the age-old and ubiquitous 'reasonableness' standards, within this purely formal concept of harm is not to dismiss or to collapse them, as that purely formal concept presupposes no substantive content.

In *Dudgeon*, the respondent asserts that unacceptable harm is caused to public morals [Z: SH^r], and, by implication, to the morals or welfare of individuals who might engage in homosexual conduct, notably those who might bc 'vulncrablc' [Z: $I^{\sim p}H^r$],

F 15.3 Z: $I^{\sim p}H^r \cdot SH^r$

As to vulnerable individuals, the Court accepts the claimant's view that they can receive the same protections in law which are applied to heterosexual acts.[5] Homosexual conduct poses no greater risk of harm to individuals than does heterosexual conduct [A: $I^{\sim p}{\sim}H^r$]. As to public morals, the Court again takes the opportunity to examine the margin of appreciation doctrine in some detail, this time emphasising two further factors. One such factor has come to be known as a principle of 'dynamic interpretation', according to which the Convention was to be construed as a 'living instrument', subject to changes in scientific knowledge or social attitudes.[6] The Court noted changing views towards homosexuality within the broader society as relevant to questions about the effects of legalisation on public morals.[7] A second is the related principle of 'evolving European consensus', whereby the Convention could be interpreted with a view towards the degree of uniformity in the relevant national laws of states' parties. In this case, the Court found that a great majority of European states had, in recent years, abolished absolute proscriptions on homosexual conduct.[8]

Those two factors are of interest, in so far as reference to scientific data, to public opinion or to national legislation appear to have a more overtly empirical or objective quality, distinguishing them from the seemingly subjective quality of assessments about 'legitimacy' or 'proportionality' or indeed 'reasonableness'. Of course, doubt remains as to whether such factors can genuinely lay claim to objectivity, as questions about the certainty or neutrality of appeals to scientific data or to public opinion are far from settled. Yet, even assuming *arguendo* that those factors can lay claim to objectivity, that does not alter their role in arguments about rights. Like 'legitimacy', 'proportionality' or 'reasonableness' standards, both serve as means for characterising the harm caused by the act as acceptably or unacceptably harmful. In *Dudgeon*, both parties lay claim to scientific evidence, and to public opinion, in support of their views. An argument that some scientists continue to raise doubts about the normality of homosexuality, or that, despite changes in many states' laws, a substantial body of public opinion condemns it, is an argument that it does or can cause unacceptable harm to individuals or to the public [Z: $I^{\sim p}H^{r} \cdot SH^{r}$]. An argument that homosexuality is no longer viewed by the scientific establishment or by much of the public to be pathological, or has been legalised by a great majority of states, is an argument that legalisation would cause no unacceptable harm to other individuals or to the public [A: $I^{\sim p}{\sim}H^{r} \cdot S{\sim}H^{r}$].

The concepts of sufficient and insufficient harm are utterly determinate in so far as they are purely formal. They remain fixed and constant despite the malleability or indeterminacy of substantive concepts of harm. Compare *Jersild*, where the Court found a television programme containing explicit and extended racist invective to be protected by article 10, with a case decided just four days earlier, *Otto-Preminger-Institut v. Austria.*[9] In 1985 Innsbruck's Otto-Preminger-Institut planned several showings of a film, *Das Liebeskonzil*, based on an 1894 play by Oskar Panizza. Panizza had been convicted of blasphemy for the play, which ridicules Roman Catholicism through disparaging caricatures of God, Jesus Christ, the Virgin Mary and the papacy. After receiving complaints about the Institut's plans to show the film, local government authorities prohibited the showings. The European Court upheld the restrictions. It found the content of the film sufficiently offensive to prevailing religious sentiments to warrant regulation on grounds of public morals under article 10(2).

Conventional casuistry would distinguish the *Jersild* and *Otto-Preminger-Institut* cases by noting that the *Søndagsavisen* emission involves an attempt at neutral and objective exposition of ideas of public concern. Any harm caused by the television broadcast to members of racial minorities, or to society's broader interest in combating racism was, on this view, insufficient to justify the restriction effectuated by a criminal prosecution [A: $I^{\sim p}{\sim}H^{r} \cdot S{\sim}H^{r}$].[10] By contrast, *Das Liebeskonzil* deliberately debases religion, causing harm to individual Roman Catholics, or to society's broader interest in combating religious hostility, of a kind or a degree sufficient to justify that restriction [Z: $I^{\sim p}H^{r} \cdot SH^{r}$].[11]

Yet dissenting opinions in both cases adduced plausible contrary arguments. It was argued that *Das Liebeskonzil* could be seen as a work of iconoclastic social commentary (indeed, nowhere does the Court offer any distinction between the comparative roles of artistic satire and journalistic commentary which would qualify *Das Liebeskonzil* as 'uncritical' and the *Søndagsavisen* program as 'critical'), which was aimed not at a vulnerable minority group, but at the country's dominant religion. It had been shown only to a small audience within the context of an art house cinema, the very function of which was to show provocative or experimental work.[12] It could therefore be argued that any harm caused by a showing of *Das Liebeskonzil* to society's interest in combating religious hostility was insufficient to justify the restriction imposed by the ban on the film [A: $I^{\sim p}{\sim}H^{r} \cdot S{\sim}H^{r}$]. Meanwhile, dissenting views in *Jersild* argued that the *Søndagsavisen* program had failed to provide sufficiently critical context, conveying the racist utterances with a degree of prurience in excess of what was necessary to make its point, thus amounting to racist expression,[13] causing sufficient harm to members of racial minorities, or to society in general in its broader aim of combating racism to justify that restriction [Z: $I^{\sim p}H^{r} \cdot SH^{r}$].

Substantive disagreement about harm in these cases, far from undermining, only underscores the formal determinacy which keeps the underlying harm concept intelligible. The formal concepts of harm underlying the substantive arguments in these cases remain identical, utterly unchanged, and equally coherent, even if the substantive holdings in *Otto-Preminger* and *Jersild* are reversed. Formally, rights discourse is indifferent to substantive arguments about whether the harms caused in these cases were *in fact* sufficient or insufficient. Its only concern is that those harms, as a formal matter, can always be *characterised* either as sufficient or insufficient. The formal concepts persist immutably in the face of perennial and ubiquitous arguments about whether given restrictions on rights are 'reasonable' or 'unreasonable', or are 'proportionate' or 'disproportionate' to given aims; or about whether those aims are 'legitimate' or 'illegitimate'; or whether such restrictions fall within or outside of states' 'margin of appreciation'.[14] Those conventional constructs are perfectly determinate in so far, but only in so far, as they express the formally determinate concepts of rights discourse, such as concepts of formally sufficient or insufficient harm.

In *Laskey*, the claimants assert that their sadomasochistic acts cause insufficient harm to themselves as personal actors [A: $I^{p}{\sim}H^{r}$], to each other as non-personal actors [A: $I^{\sim p}{\sim}H^{r}$], and to the health and morals of society as a whole [A: $S{\sim}H^{r}$],

F 15.4 A: $I^{p}{\sim}H^{r} \cdot I^{\sim p}{\sim}H^{r} \cdot S{\sim}H^{r}$

Hence,

F 15.5 A: $\alpha^{\circ}{\sim}H^{r}$

Simply put: 'The conduct does not unacceptably harm anyone.' The government claims the contrary, asserting that the injuries inflicted, even if not permanent, were grave enough to qualify as unacceptable with respect to all the personal or non-personal actors, as well as to any implied individuals – i.e. members of society who *would* inflict the same kinds or levels of injuries upon each other [Z: $I^{\circ}H^{r}$]. To legalise the conduct would be to pose an unacceptable risk of harm to public health and morals [Z: SH^{r}]. These two positions provide a comprehensive statement by the respondent,

F 15.6 Z: $\alpha^{\circ}H^{r}$

Exercise set 15.1

Fill in the blanks.

Mr Lingens argues that any harm caused by his articles to the former Chancellor is insufficient to justify the restriction imposed by the national courts through a finding of defamation [A: $I^{\sim p}$___1___^{r}]. The state asserts that the harm caused by the articles to the former Chancellor is sufficient to justify that restriction [Z:___2___H^{r}].

In *Brüggemann*, the German government asserts that abortion entails a harm caused by the woman to a living individual [___3___: $I^{\sim p}$ H___4___]. The claimants argue that the foetus is not a harmed individual, and that any harm caused to such a being is thus insufficient to justify the restrictions [___5___: $I^{\sim p}$___6___^{r}].

In *Mellacher*, the property owners complain that national rent control legislation restricts their ability to assess a rate of rental income, and thus to exercise their right to peaceful enjoyment of their possessions. Any harm caused by that exercise of the right to other individuals, or to society generally is, in their view, insufficient to justify the restrictions imposed by the legislation [A: $I^{\sim p}{\sim}$___7___^{r} · S___8___]. The government argues that the harm is sufficient to justify the legislation [Z: $I^{\sim p}$___9___ · ___10___].

In *Ahmed*, the state asserts that the risk of harm posed by the claimant, through recidivism, to other individuals or to society generally is sufficient to justify any interference with that right which might arise through deportation [Z:__11__· __12__]. The claimant asserts that the risk of harm to those actors was insufficient in view of the risks which he would face by being deported to Somalia [A:__13__ · __14__].

In *X and Y v. The Netherlands,* the government argues that to allow the woman to exercise the privacy right with a greater level of protection would cause harm to her by unjustifiably limiting her sexual autonomy [Z: I__15__H__16__]. The claimant replies that any such harm to the woman's sexual autonomy is insufficient to justify the absence of legal protection [A:__17__].

The claimant in *Airey* argues that the state's failure to provide legal aid prevents her from obtaining a decree of legal separation from her husband. In the government's view, to construe the right to a hearing so as to include an entitlement to legal aid would impose a cost upon society sufficient to justify the government's refusal to provide that assistance [__18__]. The Court, however, accepts the claimant's view that such a construction of the right would impose a cost upon society which is insufficient to justify the failure to provide legal aid [__19__].

15.2 Rapport (actor–causation)

In earlier chapters, a number of exercise sets required translation from symbolic forms into natural language, as a means of acquiring facility with the basic structure of arguments. Special attention was paid to rapport as an illustration of the symbolic rendering of features of natural language. Recall, however, that the point of a symbolic system is to provide an economical notation form for arguments which, in natural language, cannot be expressed so concisely. That role becomes more important as additional elements – and thus the possibility of recording more complex arguments – are added to the system. Therefore, this chapter and the next one will be the last to include exercise sets requiring translation, and then only from natural language into symbolic form. Afterwards, the formulas will become too complex to allow straightforward natural language translations. The additional observations about rapport in this and the next chapter are intended merely to complete the analysis of reflexive and non-reflexive character in θ positions. Some new rules are introduced in this section, and then integrated so as to revise the consolidated statement.

Again, the α variable designates the person or entity who *incurs* a harm. As to the person or entity who *causes* right-based harm, it is the 'r' marker which contains that information: an assertion of right-based harm is an assertion of a harm which is caused by the personal actor in the exercise of the right. Thus in positions taking the form A: $I^p\eta^r$, the personal actor both causes and incurs the harm. For example, formulas F 15.4 and F 15.5 represent the claimants' assertion in *Laskey* that no unacceptable harm is caused to anyone. One component of that argument concerns harm caused by the personal actors to themselves as personal actors [A: $I^p{\sim}H^r$]. We have already recognised such a position as reflexive between the *party* and the *actor*: the claimants (A) assert that insufficient harm is caused to them as personal actors (I^p). That argument is reflexive 'across the colon'. A second reflexivity now arises between elements lying only to the right of the colon: the argument characterises the harm as being caused *by* the personal actors in their exercise of the right (${\sim}H^r$), *and* as being caused *to themselves* (I^p), i.e. as personal actors (I^p), as distinguished from being caused *to each other* as non-personal actors [A: $I^{\neg p}{\sim}H^r$].

The term *actor–causation reflexivity* will be used where the person or entity who causes a right-based harm and the actor who incurs it are the same. That relationship can arise only in positions taking the form θ: $I^p\eta^r$. That form of argument must always be actor–causation reflexive, as it is only the personal actor who can seek to exercise the right. Hence:

> **Rule of Rapport (Personal Actor and Right-based Harm)**: Reflexivity must be assumed between the personal actor and the person or entity causing right-based harm.

In other words, the personal actor and the person or entity causing right-based harm are the same person or entity. Had *Laskey* been brought on behalf of the men by someone who had not participated in the sado-masochistic acts, party–actor reflexivity would be absent, but actor–causation reflexivity would remain: 'The claimant (A) asserts that the men caused no unacceptable harm (${\sim}H^r$) *to themselves* (I^p).' By contrast, a position of the form θ: $I^{\neg p}\eta^r$ cannot be actor–causation reflexive. In *Laskey*, for example, it would denote only harms caused by the men to each other, and not to themselves. Similarly, θ: $S\eta^r$ cannot be actor–causation non-reflexive:

> **Rule of Rapport (Non-personal Actor and Right-based Harm)**: Non-reflexivity must be assumed between the non-personal actor and the person or entity causing right-based harm.

> **Rule of Rapport (Society and Right-based Harm)**: Non-reflexivity must be assumed between society and the person or entity causing right-based harm.

From those rules, we can extrapolate rules for I, α, I° and α°. If I represents the personal actor, then reflexivity must be assumed. If it represents the non-personal actor, then non-reflexivity must be assumed. Accordingly, since a non-reflexive rendering of a reflexive position is never factually false, we will adopt a contingent assumption of non-reflexivity:

> **Rule of Rapport (I and Right-based Harm)**: Unless context or usage dictate otherwise, non-reflexivity is assumed between I and the person or entity causing right-based harm.

Therefore, barring contrary circumstances, a correct translation of θ: Iη^r would be, 'Some party attributes some harm to some individual actor.' Only if it is known that θ = A and I = I ^{p} would a reflexive translation be admissible. Similarly, a correct translation of A: Iγ^r would be, 'The claimant attributes some relevant harm to some individual actor.' A correct translation of Z: IH^r would be, 'The respondent attributes sufficient harm to some individual actor.'

The variable α will be treated in a similar way. If it represents the personal actor, then reflexivity must be assumed. If it represents the non-personal actor or society, then non-reflexivity must be assumed. Hence:

> **Rule of Rapport (α and Right-based Harm)**: Unless context or usage dictate otherwise, non-reflexivity is assumed between α and right-based harm.

Therefore, barring contrary circumstances, a correct translation of θ: $\alpha\eta^r$ would be, 'Some party attributes some harm to some actor.' A correct translation of A: α~γ^r would be, 'The claimant attributes some irrelevant harm to some actor.' A correct translation of θ: α~H^r would be, 'Some party attributes insufficient harm to some individual actor.'

As to I°, it represents all individual actors. In *Laskey*, for example, the formula A: I°η^r must be disaggregated ('The claimants attribute some harm to themselves and to each other') or must be left non-reflexive ('The claimants attribute some harm to the individual actors'). Hence:

> **Rule of Rapport (I° and Right-based Harm)**: Unless context or usage dictate otherwise, non-reflexivity is assumed between I° and the person or entity causing right-based harm.

Similarly, α° represents all actors. In *Laskey*, the formula A: α°η^r must either be disaggregated ('The claimants attribute some harm to themselves, to each other, and to society.') or must be left non-reflexive ('The claimants attribute some harm to all actors.'). Hence:

> **Rule of Rapport (α° and Right-based Harm)**: Unless context or usage dictate otherwise, non-reflexivity is assumed between α° and the person or entity causing right-based harm.

The consolidated statement can be further refined,

> **Rule of Rapport**: Unless context or usage dictate otherwise, non-reflexivity is assumed between any party and any actor. Except,
>
> (1) non-reflexivity *must* be assumed between,
>   (a) Z and I^p;
>   (b) $I^{\neg p}$ or S, and the person or entity causing a right-based harm;
>
> (2) reflexivity must be assumed between I^p and the person or entity causing a right-based harm.

15.3 Rapport (party–causation)

Mr Handyside asserts that he would cause no unacceptable harm to public morals or, by broad implication, to any individual children [A: $I^{\neg p}{\sim}H^r \cdot S{\sim}H^r$, F 15.2]. That position contains neither party–actor reflexivity nor actor–causation reflexivity. But it does contain another kind, detectable when we say 'Mr Handyside asserts that *he* would cause . . .'. Another kind of reflexivity arises across the colon, from Mr Handyside's role as claimant (A) and as the person whose exercise of the right would cause the harm ($\sim H^r$). Of course, we can also imagine that the case could have been brought by someone else on Mr Handyside's behalf. Hence:

> **Rule of Rapport (Claimant and Right-based Harm)**: Unless context or usage dictate otherwise, non-reflexivity is assumed between the claimant and the person or entity causing right-based harm.

Note that, in *Laskey*, the argument A: $I^p{\sim}H^r$ contains all three forms of reflexivity: party–actor, actor–causation and party–causation.

There is no value of η for which an argument of the form Z: $\alpha\eta^r$ could be reflexive. By definition, the respondent does not speak on behalf of the person or entity who causes the harm. Hence:

> **Rule of Rapport (Respondent and Right-based Harm)**: Non-reflexivity must be assumed between the respondent and the person or entity causing right-based harm.

By extension, any formula using the weakly exclusive variables I or α will be contingently non-reflexive, since it is always possible that $I = I^{\neg p}$ or that $\alpha = I^{\neg p}$ or S. And any formula using $\theta°$, I° or $\alpha°$ will be contingently non-reflexive, as it will allow disaggregated translations.

Hence:

Rule of Rapport: Unless context or usage dictate otherwise, non-reflexivity is assumed between any party and any actor. Except,

(1) non-reflexivity *must* be assumed between,
   (a) Z and I^p;
   (b) $I^{\neg p}$, S or Z, and the person or entity causing a right-based harm.

(2) reflexivity must be assumed between I^p and the person or entity causing a right-based harm.

Exercise set 15.2

Translate.

Example: The respondent asserts that a non-personal actor is unacceptably harmed by the personal actor's exercise of the right.

Answer: Z: $I^{\neg p}H^r$

1 The claimant indicated that the personal actor, in exercising the right, causes insufficient harm to herself.
2 The claimants could have indicated that, in exercising the right, they caused no unacceptable harm to themselves.
3 Minnie's attorney fumbled his way through the argument that Minnie incurred no unacceptable harm through her exercise of the right.
4 The claimant fervently insisted that, in exercising the right, he caused no unacceptable harm to any of his employees.
5 Some party noted that some harm would be caused to Ronald through Donald's exercise of the right.
6 The claimant also insisted that, in exercising the right, the question of harm caused by him to his employees was irrelevant.
7 The respondent hotly retorted that the question of harm caused to the employees by their employer's exercise of the right was relevant.
8 And yet the claimant passionately felt that, in exercising the right, he caused no unacceptable harm to any individual.
9 The claimants might have palmed off the view that no unacceptable harm was caused to any actor through their exercise of the right.
10 Some party attributed some harm to some actor.
11 Some party attributed some right-based harm to some individual actor.

12 Some party attributed some risk of harm to some actor.
13 Some party attributed some risk of some relevant harm to some actor.
14 Some party attributed some risk of an acceptable harm to some actor.
15 Some party noted that any risk of harm caused to any actor through Mickey's exercise of the right was irrelevant.
16 The respondent state steadfastly objected to the costs it would have to pay for allowing the company to exercise its asserted right.
17 Both parties later agreed that the costs to the state caused by Minnie's exercise of the right would be minimal.
18 The respondent state noted that some individual actor would be unacceptably harmed by Minnie's exercise of the right.
19 The respondents felt that all individual actors would run an unacceptable risk of harm through Minnie's exercise of the right.
20 The claimants responded that no individual actors would run any unacceptable risk of harm through Minnie's exercise of the right.
21 The claimants responded that Minnie's exercise of the right posed an unacceptable risk neither to herself nor to society.

Exercise set 15.3

Fill in the blanks.

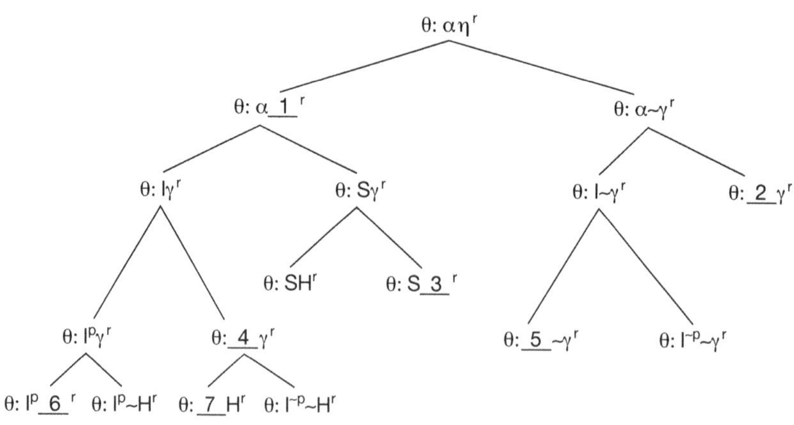

Review these terms

1 actor–causation reflexivity
2 party–causation reflexivity

16 Restriction-based harm

This chapter completes our examination of harm in isolation from consent. Recall that, under the Actor Limitation Corollary to the Claimant and Respondent Harm Axioms, only a personal actor incurs a restriction-based harm. Due to that more limited scope of actors, arguments about restriction-based harm are fewer and structurally simpler than arguments about right-based harm.

16.1 General forms

Although an argument about restriction-based harm may take more general forms, such as θ: $\alpha\eta^{\sim r}$ or θ: $I\gamma^{\sim r}$, it is always the case, respectively, that $\alpha = I^p$ or $I = I^p$. Our attention in this chapter will again remain predominantly focused on arguments about sufficient and insufficient harm, in which the claimant asserts that the restriction causes unacceptable harm to the personal actor,

F 16.1 A: $I^pH^{\sim r}$

And the respondent argues that the harm is insufficient to constitute a violation,

F 16.2 Z: $I^p{\sim}H^{\sim r}$

16.2 Applications

As with right-based arguments, the correlative positions in F 16.1 and F 16.2 reflect the decisive points in adjudication. In addition to claims under article 3, the claimant in *Ireland v. UK* also asserted that persons had been placed in detention contrary to the conditions set forth in article 5. Under article 15, article 5 rights, unlike article 3 rights, may be suspended during states of emergency, as the British government had done during the period in question. However, the conditions under which states may validly derogate from their Convention obligations during states of emergency are themselves subject to scrutiny by the Court. The application of article 5 thus required an interpretation of the crucial terms of article 15, which provides that a state party 'may take measures derogating from its obligations under [the] Convention' in so far as there is a 'public emergency threatening the life of the nation' and to the extent that those measures are 'strictly required by the exigencies of the situation'.

The Irish government claimed that Britain's recourse to special police powers exceeded the exigencies of the situation, thus inflicting an unacceptable harm upon the detainees [A: $I^{p}H^{\sim r}$]. Once again, the Court invoked the margin of appreciation doctrine:

> It falls in the first place to each Contracting State, with its responsibility for 'the life of [its] nation', to determine whether that life is threatened by a 'public emergency' and, if so, how far it is necessary to go in attempting to overcome that emergency. By reason of their direct and continuing contact with the pressing needs of the moment, the national authorities are in principle in a better position than the international judge to decide both on the presence of such an emergency and on the nature and scope of derogations necessary to avert it. In this matter, Article 15(1) leaves those authorities a wide margin of appreciation.
>
> Nevertheless, the States do not enjoy unlimited power in this respect. The Court . . . is responsible for ensuring the observance of the States' engagements [. . .]. The domestic margin of appreciation is thus accompanied by a European supervision.[1]

From our perspective, the Court's application of the doctrine in favour of the British government amounted to a finding that, under the circumstances, the British authorities had not acted in excess of the exigencies of the situation, and thus had not inflicted upon the detainees a level of harm sufficient to justify a finding of a violation of article 5 taken together with article 15 [Z: $I^{p}\sim H^{\sim r}$].

Brogan provides an interesting contrast, as it involved claims of violation of article 5 committed after the state of emergency had been lifted. The claimants complained about having been detained for several days without opportunities for hearing, trial or pleadings of *habeas corpus*. Britain's inability to invoke article 15 might appear *prima facie* to have required different kinds of arguments than those invoked in *Ireland v. UK*. However, the Court stated at the outset of its judgement that circumstances of urgency were not irrelevant in cases where no formally declared state of emergency was in effect:

> The government has adverted extensively to the existence of particularly difficult circumstances in Northern Ireland, notably the threat posed by organised terrorism.

> The Court, having taken notice of the growth of terrorism in modern society, has already recognised the need, inherent in the Convention system, for a *proper balance* between the defence of the institutions of democracy, in the common interest and the protection of individual rights. [. . .]
>
> [T]here is no call in the present proceedings to consider whether any derogation from the United Kingdom's obligations under the Convention might be permissible under Article 15 by reason of a terrorist campaign in Northern Ireland. Examination of the case must proceed on the basis that the Articles of the Convention in respect of which complaints have been made are fully applicable. This does not, however, preclude proper account being taken of the *background circumstances* of the case. In the context of Article 5, it is for the Court to determine the significance to be attached to those circumstances.[2]

That acknowledgement of the relevance of a situation of urgency outside the context of a declared state of emergency sparked controversy among the judges. While the Court did not expressly invoke the margin of appreciation doctrine, judges on both sides of the dispute appeared to see little difference between the application of that doctrine to article 15 and the Court's reference to 'proper balance' and 'background circumstances' in the interpretation of article 5. Dissenting from the Court's rejection of the article 5(1)(c) claim, Judges Walsh and Carrillo Salcedo argued that article 5:

> does not afford to the State any margin of appreciation. If the concept of a margin of appreciation were to be read into Article 5, it would change the whole nature of this all-important provision which would then become subject to executive policy.[3]

That rejection of a broad interpretative scope would favour the claimants' assertion that the state's detention procedures inflicted unacceptable harm upon the detainees [A: $I^{p}H^{\sim r}$].

By contrast, Judge Evans, dissenting from the Court's finding in favour of the claimants on the article 5(3) complaint, embraced the Court's general approach with all the more candour about the similarity of judicial standards applied in these cases, regardless of the existence of a declared state of emergency: '[T]he Court has consistently recognised that States must, in assessing the compatibility of their laws and practices with the requirements of the Convention, be permitted a "margin of appreciation"'.[4] He favoured the British assertion that the circumstances of urgency were sufficient to justify a finding that the detention procedures had inflicted no unacceptable harm [Z: $I^{p}{\sim}H^{\sim r}$].

Whether or not there is a difference between the judicial standards applicable in the two kinds of cases remains a speculative question. The decision in *Brannigan* suggests that there may be some difference, as the British government's resumption of a state of emergency appears, in that case, to have allowed it to prevail on the same kind of article 5(3) claim which it had lost in *Brogan*. What unites all three cases is the purely formal result that doctrines favouring deference to state determinations of urgency translate into findings that no unacceptable harm was inflicted upon the detainees [Z: $I^{p}{\sim}H^{\sim r}$], while doctrines opposing such deference translate into findings that the harm inflicted upon the detainees was unacceptable [A: $I^{p}H^{\sim r}$].

The observation that no categorical distinction can be drawn between the margin of appreciation doctrine and more customary balancing concepts such as 'reasonableness' or 'background circumstances', or indeed 'legitimacy', 'proportionality' or 'evolving standards', or among these latter *inter se*, is confirmed in other cases argued as restriction-based claims. As was the case with right-based claims, it is only the difference between sufficient or insufficient harm (and, as we will see in the following chapters, relevant and irrelevant harm) that defines a necessary – because purely formal – distinction between the opposing positions in such disputes. In *McCann*, the claimants assert that the use of deadly force constituted unacceptable harm [A: $I^{p}H^{\sim r}$]. The British government asserts that, under the circumstances, even the use of deadly force could not be deemed unacceptably harmful [Z: $I^{p}{\sim}H^{\sim r}$]. In *Tyrer* and *Costello-Roberts*, the claimants argue that even less extreme forms of physical punishment caused unacceptable harm [A: $I^{p}H^{\sim r}$]; the state responds that those forms of punishment were not unacceptably harmful [Z: $I^{p}{\sim}H^{\sim r}$].

Recall that the role of the personal actor as the person or agent said to cause right-based harm is 'built into' the meaning of the 'r' marker. Similarly, the role of the person or entity said to cause a restriction-based harm (commonly, but not necessarily, the state) is 'built into' the meaning of the '~r' marker. The claimants in *Aksoy* and *Osman* argue that treatments inflicted were unacceptably harmful [A: $I^{p}H^{\sim r}$]. By denying responsibility for the harms, the state asserts that no acts or omissions of *its* officials cause any unacceptable harm [Z: $I^{p}{\sim}H^{\sim r}$].

16.3 Rapport (actor–causation)

Actor–causation reflexivity cannot arise in restriction-based arguments, as the only actor is the personal actor, who is seeking to exercise the right, and not the restriction. Hence:

> **Rule of Rapport (Personal Actor and Restriction-based Harm)**: Non-reflexivity must be assumed between the personal actor and the person or entity causing restriction-based harm.

I and α can only represent the personal actor. For that same reason, translations of I° and α° cannot be disaggregated to include any reflexive relationships. Hence:

> **Rule of Rapport (Actor and Restriction-based Harm)**: Non-reflexivity must be assumed between any actor and the person or entity causing restriction-based harm.

The consolidated statement of the Rule of Rapport is almost complete:

> **Rule of Rapport**: Unless context or usage permit otherwise, non-reflexivity is assumed between a person or entity represented by one symbol and a person or entity represented by another symbol. Except,
>
> (1) non-reflexivity *must* be assumed between,
> (a) Z and I^{p};
> (b) $I^{\sim p}$, S or Z, and the person or entity causing a right-based harm;
> (c) I^{p}, I, I°, α or α° and the person or entity causing restriction-based harm;
>
> (2) reflexivity must be assumed between I^{p} and the person or entity causing a right-based harm.

16.4 Rapport (party–causation)

Party–causation reflexivity will commonly arise in the Z positions, in so far as a great number of cases are brought against governments, and the restriction-based harm at the heart of the complaint is commonly imposed by government. For example, in all of the foregoing cases, it is asserted on behalf of the respondent government that *it* caused insufficient harm to the personal actors [Z: I^{p}~$H^{\sim r}$]. Nevertheless, as that need not always be the case, we will assume contingent non-reflexivity:

> **Rule of Rapport (Respondent and Restriction-based Harm)**: Unless the facts are known or stipulated to be otherwise, non-reflexivity is assumed between the respondent and the person or entity causing restriction-based harm.

By contrast, under the Claimant Corollary to the Axiom of Restrictions, and in so far as the case is genuinely in dispute, the claimant cannot be the person or entity causing restriction-based harm:

> **Rule of Rapport (Claimant and Restriction-based Harm)**: Non-reflexivity must be assumed between the claimant and the person or entity causing restriction-based harm.

θ requires only a contingent rule of non-reflexivity, in so far as it can take the value of A or Z; and $\theta°$ requires only a contingent rule, in so far as translations can be disaggregated. The consolidated statement of the rule can now be set forth in its final form:

> **Rule of Rapport**: Unless context or usage permit otherwise, non-reflexivity is assumed between a person or entity represented by one symbol and a person or entity represented by another symbol. Except,
>
> (1) non-reflexivity *must* be assumed between,
>   (a) Z and I^p;
>   (b) $I^{\neg p}$, S or Z, and the person or entity causing a right-based harm;
>   (c) A, I^p, I, I°, α or $\alpha°$ and the person or entity causing restriction-based harm;
>
> (2) Reflexivity must be assumed between I^p and the person or entity causing a right-based harm.

Exercise set 16.1

Translate.

Example: The claimant asserts that the personal actor is unacceptably harmed by the restriction.

Answer: A: $I^pH^{\neg r}$

1 The claimants could assert that they are unacceptably harmed by the restriction.
2 The respondent should have asserted that the harm caused by the restriction is relevant.
3 Some party asserted that some restriction-based harm is caused.
4 The respondent had asserted that the harm caused by the restriction is irrelevant.

Exercise set 16.2

Fill in the blanks.

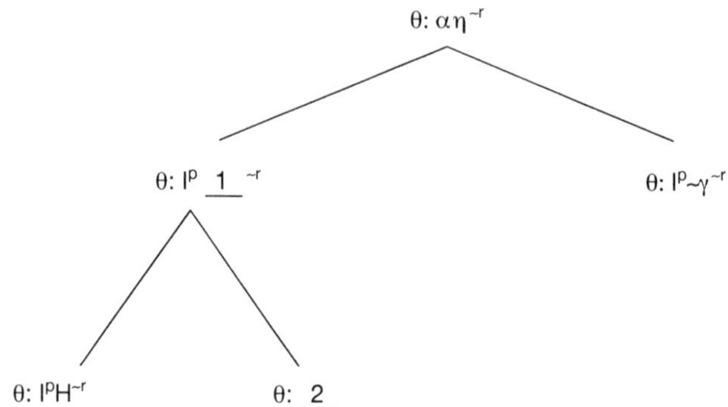

Part III

Consent

17 The concept of consent

Every assertion about harm entails some assertion about consent. Or, more precisely, within a θ position, an assertion about harm entails some assertion about the actor's consent to incur the harm; and, within a θ position, an assertion about consent entails some assertion about the harm. Ordinarily, that thesis would seem counterintuitive. It would seem that consent must be ascertained precisely because it is something distinct from harm. Our task in the next few chapters will be to explore that thesis as a cornerstone of the formal structure of liberal rights discourse. Before linking the two concepts, however, we will first consider what is meant by 'consent'.

17.1 Consent in fact and in law

Arguments about consent often involve the familiar *in fact/in law* distinction. In a given case, a dispute may arise as to whether an actor consented to incur a harm *in fact*. If it is agreed that consent was given in fact, a further dispute may arise as to whether that consent is valid *in law*. Or, if it is not agreed that consent was given in fact, a dispute may arise as to whether consent should be supplied in law. As an initial matter, those factors generate four kinds of assertions:

1 *Consent given in fact is valid in law.* This is an assertion that consent given in fact to incur a harm should be deemed legally valid; that factual consent suffices to constitute legal consent. Such an argument is commonly made where the competence of the party to give consent, vis-à-vis age, mental health and other such factors, has already been asserted, or is not in dispute. Assume, for example, that a party has asserted, or has not disputed, that a patient is competent to consent to receive or deny medical treatment.[1] That assertion can then be used to argue that consent has been given in fact and should therefore be deemed valid in law. Similarly, valid consent in fact keeps boxing from becoming battery, or sexual intercourse from becoming rape.

2 *Consent given in fact is invalid in law.* Here we have an assertion that, in the dispute at hand, factual consent does not suffice to constitute legal consent; that consent given in fact should be deemed invalid in law. For example, consent given in fact by a young child to engage in sexual relations may be asserted by the state to be invalid.[2] Similarly, duelling, Russian roulette or street brawling do not become legal merely because otherwise competent adults have consented to participate in them.

3 *Consent is not given in fact, but there is valid consent in law.* This is an assertion that, in the dispute at hand, valid consent should be construed in law despite the absence of consent in fact. For example, it can be argued that consent to receive, or to refuse, medical treatment can be recognised in law (by 'proxy' or by a court order) even where it is absent in fact, as in the case of young children, or of persons deemed unconscious or mentally impaired.[3]

4 *Consent is not given in fact, and there is therefore no valid consent in law.* Finally, we have an assertion that, in the dispute at hand, valid consent not having been given in fact, no valid consent should be construed in law. For example, under traditional principles of criminal or tort law, it would commonly be argued that a battery was committed in so far as no consent in fact was given to incur the touching by a person who is deemed otherwise competent to give consent.[4]

This configuration of arguments may appear to ignore the ambiguous or fluid quality of consent in some contexts. For example, legal recognition of consent by children, as to certain important decisions, is often construed along a continuum which matures throughout childhood. That continuum accords less deference at younger ages, but progressively greater deference as childhood advances, suggesting that no fixed concept of consent can be applied to children.[5] The point of the foregoing configuration, however, is that even highly complex concepts of consent *in general* can only produce finite sets of arguments in any given case. Keeping with this example, the criteria which distinguish younger children from older children, or children from adults, or competent persons from incompetent, is not *whether* the four arguments apply to them, but rather *which* arguments apply under which circumstances.

17.2 Basic symbols

Using the symbol C to denote an assertion of *valid consent in law*, we find that arguments (1) and (3) amount to assertions that *consent should be recognised in law* (C): either on the basis of consent in fact (1), or regardless of non-consent in fact (3). Using the symbol ~C to denote *no valid consent in law*, we find that arguments (2) and (4) amount to assertions that *no consent should be recognised in law* (~C): either on the

	Consent in fact	Non-consent in fact
Assertion of valid consent in law (C = 'valid consent')	(1)	(3)
Assertion of no valid consent in law (~C = 'invalid consent')	(2)	(4)

Figure 17.1

basis of non-consent in fact (4), or regardless of consent in fact (2). Those correlations are set forth in Figure 17.1. The terms 'valid consent' or 'invalid consent' ('invalid consent' meaning 'no valid consent') must always, respectively, accompany any construction of the symbols C and ~C. To read them, respectively, as 'consent' and 'non-consent' would be unsatisfactory, as a simple assertion that consent is given or withheld in fact only raises the further question as to any assertion about its status in law. Where it is useful to speak only of the relevance of consent, without specifying it either as valid (C) or invalid (~C), the variable χ (chi) will be used.

There are additional kinds of assertions about consent. In the next chapter, we will see how a party can argue that the very question of consent is irrelevant to the disposition of the case. That party would argue that the case must be resolved in a particular way *regardless* of which of the foregoing four scenarios might otherwise apply. An assertion of irrelevant consent can be represented by negating χ, hence $\sim\chi$. The variable κ (kappa) will thus represent assertions as to the relevance of consent. Note the use of the numeral '1' in the labels Ps(κ1) and Ps(χ1). Later on, further postulates defining the values of κ and χ will be introduced:

Consent postulates

Ps(κ1) $\kappa \subset \chi, \sim\chi$ Ps(χ1) $\chi \subset C, \sim C$

Hence,

$$\text{Th}(\kappa) \quad \kappa \subset C, \sim C, \sim\chi$$

The relationships among those κ variables are illustrated in Figure 17.2.

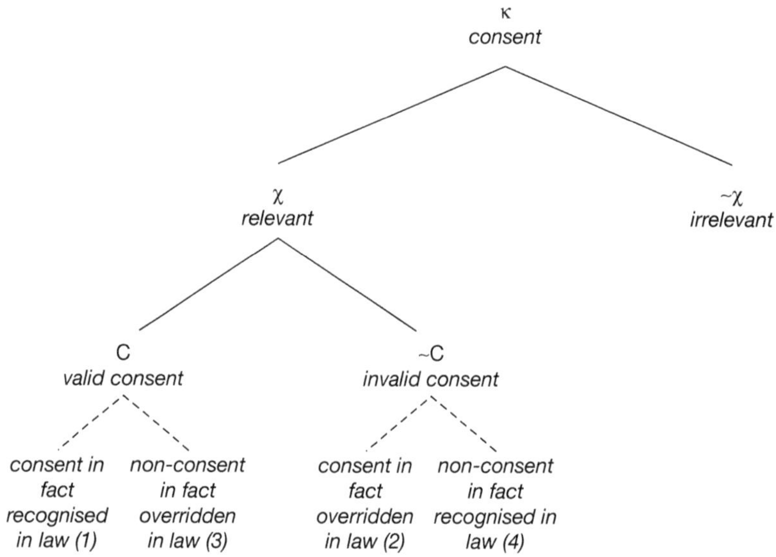

Figure 17.2

Those relationships will have the following consequences:

- The term *consent* will refer merely to the element of consent (κ), which may be relevant (χ) or irrelevant (~χ), and, if relevant, valid (C) or invalid (~C).
- The terms *consent in fact* and *non-consent in fact* will refer to the presence or absence of some act of consent, which may or may not be given effect in law.
- The term *valid consent* (C) will refer not only to consent in fact which is recognised in law, but also to non-consent in fact which is overridden in law. That latter meaning deviates in some cases from ordinary usage, but signifies an effective equivalence with the former meaning.
- The term *invalid consent* (~C) will refer not only to consent in fact which is not given effect in law, but also to non-consent in fact which is given effect in law. Again, that latter meaning departs in some cases from common usage, but signifies an effective equivalence with the former meaning.

> ***Exercise set 17.1***
>
> Derive Th(κ).

17.3 Consent attribution

We are construing the concept of consent as the disposition of an actor to incur a harm. The following rule will allow us to do that by symbolic means:

> **Consent Attribution Corollary to the Claimant and Respondent Harm Axioms**: All θ positions attribute to some actor some disposition to incur some harm. That is, for any position θ: αη, there is some value of κ, such that θ: αηκ.

The term 'corollary' may seem particularly questionable here, as the Claimant and Respondent Harm Axioms contain no language which would appear to imply anything about consent, even when taken in conjunction with other previously adopted axioms. In the next chapter, however, the link drawn between harm and consent will provide a justification for accepting that, within a θ position, an assertion about harm implies some assertion about consent.

We can introduce the corollary into proofs in a way similar to the technique adopted for the Harm Attribution Corollary. For example, recall how harm variables were introduced in the last step of the second proof in Section 14.4. In the same way, we can introduce consent attribution by writing 'κ attr' as a justifying step:

Prove the theorem: $I^p\gamma\kappa \subset I^pH^r\kappa, I^p{\sim}H^r\kappa, I^pH^{\sim r}\kappa, I^p{\sim}H^{\sim r}\kappa$

(1)	$\gamma \subset \gamma^r, \gamma^{\sim r}$	Ps(γ2)
(2)	$\gamma \subset H^r, {\sim}H^r, \gamma^{\sim r}$	$Ps(\gamma^r)$
(3)	$\gamma \subset H^r, {\sim}H^r, H^{\sim r}, {\sim}H^{\sim r}$	$Ps(\gamma^{\sim r})$
(4)	$I^p\gamma \subset I^pH^r, I^p{\sim}H^r, I^pH^{\sim r}, I^p{\sim}H^{\sim r}$	η attr
conclusion	$I^p\gamma\kappa \subset I^pH^r\kappa, I^p{\sim}H^r\kappa, I^pH^{\sim r}\kappa,$ $I^p{\sim}H^{\sim r}\kappa$	κ attr

Of course, that proof only raises the question as to the precise values for κ in each formula. As with harm attribution, consent attribution does not permit unfettered combination of any consent symbol with any harm symbol. Indeed, in the next chapter, we will see that there are important limitations on the possible combinations. The κ variable is therefore left unspecified in the following exercises.

Exercise set 17.2

Prove the following theorems.

1 $\alpha\eta^{r}\kappa \subset \alpha\gamma^{r}\kappa, \alpha{\sim}\gamma^{r}\kappa$

2 $I{\sim}\gamma\kappa \subset I^{p}{\sim}\gamma^{r}\kappa, I^{\sim p}{\sim}\gamma^{r}\kappa, I^{p}{\sim}\gamma^{\sim r}\kappa$

3 $I\gamma\kappa \subset I^{p}H^{r}\kappa, I^{\sim p}H^{r}\kappa, I^{p}{\sim}H^{r}\kappa, I^{\sim p}{\sim}H^{r}\kappa, I^{p}H^{\sim r}\kappa, I^{p}{\sim}H^{\sim r}\kappa$

17.4 General formula for θ positions

The variables α, η and κ represent the three core components of liberal rights arguments. We will see that every argument represents some set of values attributed to the variables of a more general formula. In the remainder of this book, notations representing the general form of θ positions will be recorded as *general formulas* (GF),

$$GF(\theta) \quad \theta\text{: } \alpha\eta\kappa$$

In accordance with the Presupposition Corollary of the Axiom of Contentious Character, a dispute is a dispute about the adjudication of a liberal right only in so far as it is a dispute, between a claimant position and a respondent position, about the values to be ascribed to the variables comprising GF(θ).

17.5 Consent attributed to society

The general formula θ: $\alpha\eta\kappa$ suggests the possibility of attributing some form of consent to society as a whole, where $\alpha = S$. Yet one might hesitate to use the same concepts of consent to speak about particular individuals and whole societies. Certainly, we are familiar with notions of popular will (*volonté générale*) or the will of the majority, but we tend to use those phrases metaphorically, without assuming the objective existence of a collective mind. Nevertheless, for our model, we will adopt formal concepts of consent which allow the κ variables to be applied to society as well as to individuals. For the purposes of this discussion, it will simplify matters to speak only of valid consent and non-consent. The idea of attributing relevant and irrelevant consent to society as a whole will be examined in subsequent chapters. Recall that arguments about restriction-based harm concern only the personal actor [θ: $I^{p}\eta^{\sim r}\kappa$]. Accordingly, the concept of consent attributable to society relates only to arguments about right-based harm [θ: $S\eta^{r}\kappa$].

Consent in fact applied to society ('public opinion')

One way to defend a restriction on a right is to say that the restriction enjoys public support. Of course, such arguments are not always persuasive. Short of a formally binding referendum, the means of ascertaining the existence or degree of public support, such as through public opinion polls or expert opinion, may not be universally accepted. Nevertheless, arguments about the nature or degree of public opinion on an issue are common. Typically, the respondent asserts that (some sufficiently representative part of) the public does not want – *does not consent* – to incur the harm caused by the individual's exercise of the right [Z: $SH^{r}{\sim}C$]. In other words, the respondent asserts that the public do not consent to that exercise of the asserted right which is in dispute, and such absence of consent should be given effect in law. That configuration corresponds to Figure 17.1 and 17.2: '*Public* consent is not given in fact, and therefore no valid public consent should be given effect in law.'

The claimant can challenge the restriction by asserting that (some sufficiently representative part of) the public does support the exercise of the right – does consent to incur any harm caused thereby [A: $S\eta^{r}C$] (for the time being, we will leave the value of η in the A positions undefined – that is the topic of the next chapter). In other words, the claimant asserts that the public consent in fact to incur any effects of that particular exercise of the asserted right, and such consent should be recognised in law. That configuration corresponds to scenario (1) (see Figures 17.1 and 17.2): '*Public* consent is given in fact, and should be given effect in law.'

The Court in *Dudgeon*, considering whether the outright prohibition of homosexual conduct could be deemed 'necessary' in the sense required by article 8(2) of the Convention, undertook a detailed examination of the actual state of public opinion in Northern Ireland. Public opinion appeared split, with strong opinions on both sides, but no strong majority in support of or in opposition to the prohibition.[6] One might have surmised that this division would have a cancelling-out effect, with neither the claimant nor the respondent able to speak for the wishes of society. But just the opposite occurred. Although neither side could claim the support of a clear majority, both sides claimed to represent the views attributable to society by claiming to speak for some 'substantial' portion of the population.[7] Thus the problem with finding consent in fact, or non-consent in fact, attributable to society as a whole does not lie with the difficulty of ascertaining a numerical consensus. In *Dudgeon*, the A and Z positions 'solve' that problem in so far as they *both* claim public support for their arguments. The Z position claims that (some sufficiently representative part of) society as a whole does not support – does not consent – to incur the moral harm which would be caused by legalising homosexual conduct [Z: $SH^{r}{\sim}C$]. The A position claims that (some sufficiently representative part of) society as a whole *does* consent to incur any such harm [A: $S\eta^{r}C$].

Consent in law applied to society ('public interest')

Unlike *Dudgeon*, many disputes, albeit invoking questions of public *interest*, include no detailed reference to public *opinion*. Problems of public interest are ubiquitous in law, owing to the generality of legal rules. The adjudication of a dispute involving particular persons or entities will commonly have broader consequences for other persons or entities in society. Yet, in the context of adjudication, arguments about public interest do not perforce refer to public support. In *Dudgeon*, a government commission had been specially charged to investigate public opinion on the law in question. That practice, however, is more the exception than the rule.

Recall that a liberal rights dispute is being understood in this study as arising within an at least nominally parliamentary democracy. Within that parliamentary-democratic context, an argument by government which asserts a public interest without empirical reference to public opinion is an argument that valid or invalid consent attributable to the public can be given effect in law *regardless* of the character or degree of public consent or non-consent in fact. In its laws and actions, government asserts, or assumes, its legitimacy in determining the will – the valid consent or non-consent – of the people to incur actual or putative harms. Of course, for a critically-minded political science, which would take into account the panoply of forces motivating government officials (party politics, private contributions, individual career advancement) it may appear to be at best conceptually murky, at worst dangerous demagogy, for government categorically to assume its actions to be the will of the people. Within the context of liberal rights argument, however, it is precisely the legitimacy – or if you prefer, some rhetoric of legitimacy – for its actions which government must put forth. In courtroom testimony or appellate argument, government never officially adopts the position that it has restricted a right in order to secure future party contributions from one constituency or to win votes from another, even if everyone knows that to be the case. Rather, government categorically asserts, as a matter of sheer democratic legitimacy, that its actions properly represent the will of the people. It can, then, assert that its determination that an unacceptable harm would be caused to society is *ipso facto* a determination that society cannot *validly* consent to incur that harm [Z: $SH^{r}{\sim}C$]. (The margin of appreciation doctrine expresses a *prima facie* acceptance of that legitimacy: 'State authorities are in principle in a better position than the international judge to give an opinion [on the requirements of morals in their States].'[8] *Handyside* and *Dudgeon* concern above all the legitimacy of state determinations of the public will, however firmly or weakly rooted it may be in actual public sentiment.) A claimant challenging that government determination of public interest thereby challenges the attribution of consent or non-consent to society made by government. In so doing, it asserts that some other attribution of consent or non-consent must be made.

In *Handyside*, the government determination that unacceptable harm would be caused to children is *ipso facto* a government determination that society cannot *validly* consent to expose itself to that harm [Z: SH^r~C]. In *Jersild* or *Otto-Preminger-Institut*, the government determination that unacceptable harm would be caused to society by permitting racist or anti-religious expression is *ipso facto* a government determination that society cannot *validly* consent to incur the effects of the publication, broadcast or dissemination of such works. In *Laskey*, the government determination that unacceptable harm would be caused through the legalisation of sado-masochism is *ipso facto* a government determination that society cannot *validly* consent to expose itself to that harm. Indeed, in *Dudgeon*, the respondent government can put to one side its arguments about actual levels of public support, and can argue that the government determination that homosexuality is immoral represents *ipso facto* a government determination that society cannot validly consent to expose itself to that moral harm. The government position in each of these cases corresponds to scenario 2 (see Figures 17.1 and 17.2): 'No public consent should be recognised in law, regardless of any public consent in fact' [Z: SH^r~C]. The claimants' response in these cases would correspond to scenario (3) (see Figures 17.1 and 17.2): 'Public consent should be recognised in law regardless of any non-consent in fact' [A: $S\eta^r C$].

We might go so far as to define much of governing as nothing but a process of attributing κ values to α actors on the basis of determinations about η values. We will not explore that idea, as we are examining only the structure of individual rights disputes, and not the entire process of governing. Yet it is worthwhile to consider the broad significance of arguments taking the form Z: SH^r~C. That Z position merely represents a formalised version of the idea that *some* public interest – however reasonable or preposterous, however great or small may be the public support it actually enjoys – can always be adduced to justify a restriction. A law might be passed, for example, that would prohibit any publications which disparage newborn kittens. The state might defend the law by arguing that it is intended to prevent offence to cat lovers, or to protect a burgeoning market in kittens. The state can thereby assert an interest in determining that society as a whole (S) cannot validly consent (~C) to incur the harm caused by any individual who, in the exercise of the right of free speech, would cause unacceptable harm (H^r) to society's interest in protecting the feelings of cat lovers or the market in kittens [Z: SH^r~C]. Substantively, the argument may be ridiculous. Formally, it does not differ from any other argument of the type Z: SH^r~C.

The hallmark of a sham liberal regime is the bogus application of that Z position. The hallmark of a more democratically accountable regime is the good faith application of that formula. Phrases like 'sham' and 'good faith' are, of course, by no means self-evident. My good faith may be your sham. Nevertheless, in so far as there is agreement that a regime is a sham liberal regime, there will be agreement that the position Z: $SH^{r}{\sim}C$ is routinely and successfully applied in willy-nilly fashion. In so far as there is agreement that a regime is democratically responsible, there will be agreement that Z: $SH^{r}{\sim}C$ is invoked more-or-less conscientiously, and not always successfully. Of course, sham regimes can exploit some other Z positions, such as the paternalist[9] view Z: $I^{p}H^{r}{\sim}C$, or can concoct harms to other identified individuals,[10] e.g. through bogus defamation suits via the position Z: $I^{\sim p}H^{r}{\sim}C$. Indeed, those positions commonly suggest the more specified and detailed determination of harm affecting an ascertainable individual. Still, the easier and more common route is merely to adduce some general harm to some generalised population.

Given the formula Z: $SH^{r}{\sim}C$ as a general form of argument supporting a restriction on a right, one response by a claimant would be to adduce empirical evidence of public support (public opinion), as was done in *Dudgeon*. However, in view of the practical difficulties of that strategy – indeed, in view of the purported mission of human rights to protect individuals from the power of the majority – the claimant can instead, or in addition, argue that no unacceptable harm is caused by the exercise of the right, thus undermining the respondent's premise. The former argument (public opinion) would take the form A: $S\eta^{r}C$. The latter would take the form A: $S{\sim}H^{r}\kappa$. What are the values of the variables η and κ, respectively, in these two formulas? That question is the subject of the next chapter.

17.6 The strongly exclusive consent variable

The hierarchical relationships between consent variables resemble those between harm variables.[11] For θ: $\alpha\eta\kappa$ ('Some party claims that some harm and some consent are attributable to some actor'), assume that the element of consent turns out to be valid consent ($\kappa = C$). All other possible values of κ are implied as follows:

(a) It is implied that κ takes the value χ.
(b) It is implied that κ does not take the values ${\sim}\chi$ or ${\sim}C$.

Accordingly, if $\kappa = C$, then it is the case that θ: $\alpha\eta C$, hence:

(a′) It is also the case that θ: $\alpha\eta\chi$.
(b′) It is not the case that θ: $\alpha\eta{\sim}\chi$ or θ: $\alpha\eta{\sim}C$.

Like an inclusive harm symbol (η°, γ°), an inclusive consent symbol (κ°, χ°) would be meaningless. For example, a party cannot assert θ: $\alpha\eta\chi^{\circ}$, as it cannot simultaneously assert θ: $\alpha\eta C$ and θ: $\alpha\eta{\sim}C$. A weakly exclusive symbol is also meaningless. A party cannot attribute consent to an actor, while implying nothing about the kinds of consent. Accordingly, we need a strongly exclusive consent variable: for θ: $\alpha\eta\kappa$, if $\kappa = C$, then

$\kappa \neq {\sim}\chi, {\sim}C$. ‘Strongly’ exclusive does not mean absolutely exclusive of all other possible values of κ. The case of $\kappa = C$ implies $\kappa = \chi$. The point is that there are certain values of κ which become positively excluded once the variable κ takes a more precise value. As consent variables can only be strongly exclusive in that sense, we need not adopt additional symbols to represent inclusive or weakly inclusive meanings. Rather, *consent variables are always strongly exclusive*, according to the following values:[12]

Consent variable postulates

$Ps(\kappa = \chi): \kappa \neq {\sim}\chi$	$Ps(\chi = C): \chi \neq {\sim}C$
$Ps(\kappa = {\sim}\chi): \kappa \neq \chi$	$Ps(\chi = {\sim}C): \chi \neq C$
$Ps(\kappa = C): \kappa \neq {\sim}\chi, {\sim}C$	
$Ps(\kappa = {\sim}C): \kappa \neq {\sim}\chi, C$	

Exercise set 17.3

Derive θ: $IH^r\chi$ from Z: $I^pH^r{\sim}C$.
Derive θ: $I\eta\kappa$ from A: $I^pH^{\sim r}{\sim}C$.

Review these terms

1 valid consent
2 invalid consent
3 relevant consent
4 irrelevant consent
5 public opinion
6 public interest

18 Harm and consent

Again, harm and consent are ordinarily understood to be utterly distinct things. For example, the question as to the harm caused by euthanasia – death – differs from the question as to whether the individual validly consented to incur that harm. The evidence required to show that death had occurred (data about physical condition) is distinct from the evidence required to show that one had consented to die (data concerning mental state and acts of will). However, that difference between actual harm and consent to incur the harm does not mean that there is no relationship between the two concepts. In this chapter, we examine the hypothesis that every assertion about harm implies some assertion about consent, and that every assertion about consent implies some assertion about harm.

18.1 Sufficient Harm Axiom (θ: αH~C)

In $HA_Z(1)$(b) and (c), the argument that interference with a right is justified translates as an assertion of sufficient harm to some actor [Z: αH^r]. How can that argument be deployed to rebut an A assertion that the actor gave valid consent to incur the harm [A: $\alpha\eta^r C$]? The terms 'valid' and 'consent' provide Z with two possibilities. Z can *either* dispute A's factual claim, by asserting that consent was *not* given, or can concede that consent was given, but assert that it was not valid in law. Accordingly, Z can assert either (1) that there is invalid consent in law through lack of consent in fact; or (2) that there is invalid consent in law regardless of consent in fact. In either case, Z asserts that there is invalid consent. (Recall that valid non-consent is being treated as identical to invalid consent. Both occupy quadrant (1) in Figure 17.1.)

Those alternatives are more than mere possibilities. One or the other assertion is implied by the assertion that sufficient harm is caused to α [Z: αH^r]. Compare the meaning of H with that of ~H. An assertion that the harm caused by an act is *in*sufficient (~H) is an assertion that there is nothing to consent to, that it does not matter whether or not valid consent to incur it is given. Consent given to something which, through its insufficiently harmful character, requires no consent, is not meaningful consent. If my failure to greet a neighbour (to whom I bear no other duty or relationship, such as that of an employee) is a harm insufficient to constitute a legal wrongdoing, then that neighbour's failure to give valid consent to my conduct is of no relevance to the disposition of a legal action brought against me for, so to speak, lack of neighbourliness. In a word, the consent is irrelevant ($\sim\chi$). By contrast, it is precisely where a harm is otherwise unacceptable, as asserted by Z, that it matters whether or not there is consent to incur it, i.e. where consent is relevant (χ). At the very least, then, Z cannot argue that consent is irrelevant [Z: $\alpha H^r\sim\chi$], but rather argues that it is relevant [Z: $\alpha H^r\chi$].

The question then arises as to which value Z adopts for χ. Under the Claimant and Respondent Corollaries to the Axioms of Recognition and Restriction, Z cannot and indeed would not want to assert valid consent (C), which would defeat Z's whole effort to uphold the restriction. It would be contradictory for Z to maintain both that the restriction on the conduct is legitimate *and* that consent is validly given to incur the effects of the conduct [Z: αH^rC]. An otherwise legal restriction serves precisely to render invalid any consent given to incur the effects of that act. To seek a restriction on a right is to argue that no consent to incur the effects of the right should be deemed valid. Accordingly, the only remaining value for χ is ~C. For Z to assert sufficient harm means that Z asserts invalid consent, hence Z: $\alpha H^r\sim C$. In short, an assertion of sufficient harm (H) implies an assertion of invalid consent (~C) to incur that harm – i.e. either no consent was given in fact, or no consent should be recognised as valid in law – hence the position θ: $\alpha H^r\sim C$.

Similarly, an assertion of invalid consent (~C) implies an assertion of sufficient harm (H). It is only in so far as the giving or withholding of valid consent could make some difference to the resolution of the case that it matters that valid consent is not given. The withholding of valid consent[1] would be meaningless if it did not matter what the harm was ($\sim\gamma$), i.e. if it did not matter whether the harm was the kind of harm for which consent can be meaningfully withheld. At the very least, it can only be meaningfully asserted that consent is invalid where the quality or level of harm is relevant [θ: $\alpha\gamma\sim C$]. And, again, the value of γ cannot be ~H, since an assertion of insufficient harm means there is nothing to consent to, that it does not matter whether or not consent is given. Accordingly, an assertion of invalid consent to incur a harm (~C) can only meaningfully imply an assertion that the harm is unacceptable [θ: $\alpha H^r\sim C$]. In criminal or tort law, it is in so far as no valid consent is given (~C), that a physical touching of one human being by another can be deemed to be a harm sufficient (H) to constitute a battery.[2]

> **Sufficient Harm Axiom** (θ: $\alpha H\sim C$): An assertion of sufficient harm (H) implies an assertion of invalid consent (~C); and an assertion of invalid consent (~C) implies an assertion of sufficient harm (H). For all θ: $\alpha\eta\kappa$, if η = H, then κ = ~C; and if κ = ~C, then η = H.

That principle can be represented by two postulates [Ps(ηκ)]:

Postulates for Sufficient Harm Axiom

Ps(Hκ) $\alpha H\kappa \subset \alpha H{\sim}C$ Ps(η~C) $\alpha\eta{\sim}C \subset \alpha H{\sim}C$

In *Lingens*, the argument that the former Chancellor is unacceptably harmed implies his not having given valid consent to incur the harm [Z: $I^{\sim p}H^{r}{\sim}C$]. The argument in *Dudgeon* that homosexuality unacceptably harms public morals is asserted with reference to actual public opinion – public refusal to consent to incur the social or moral effects of legalisation [Z: $SH^{r}{\sim}C$]. By contrast, the argument in *Handyside* that *The Little Red Book* would unacceptably harm children's moral interests is an assertion of a state determination that society, and, by broad implication, individual children, cannot validly consent to incur that harm [Z: $I^{\sim p}H^{r}{\sim}C \cdot SH^{r}{\sim}C$].

Now consider the Sufficient Harm Axiom in terms of restriction-based harm. In $HA_A(2)$(b) and (c) the argument that interference with a right is unjustified translates as an assertion of sufficient harm to some personal actor [A: $I^{p}H^{\sim r}$]. How would that argument be deployed to rebut a Z assertion that the personal actor gives valid consent to incur the harm? Once again there are two possibilities. The A position can dispute Z's factual claim, by asserting that consent was *not* given. In most cases, notably where the state is respondent, that A position is so obvious that it need not be stated expressly. In *Ireland v. UK*, *Lawless*, *Brogan*, *Brannigan*, *Tyrer*, *Costello-Roberts* or *Aksoy* it is readily assumed that the personal actors did not consent to incur the treatment at issue. Alternatively, even if some kind of consent could be found in a case such as these (say, an expression of willingness to incur physical punishment in exchange for a some benefit, such as reduced period of detention), the claimant would concede that consent was given, but assert that it was not valid. The point is that one could not maintain the position A: $I^{p}H^{\sim r}$ while conceding *valid* consent on the part of the personal actor [A: $I^{p}H^{\sim r}C$], hence A: $I^{p}H^{\sim r}{\sim}C$.

In some cases, the Sufficient Harm Axiom follows from legal doctrine as a matter of course, namely, where harm is itself defined by consent. For example, a legal distinction between lawful sexual intercourse and rape depends on the presence or absence of valid consent.[3] An assertion of non-consent in fact or invalid consent in law is then *ipso facto* an assertion of sufficient harm [Z: $I^{\sim p}H^{r}{\sim}C$]. Assuming fulfilment of the *actus reus,* A cannot rebut that Z position by conceding invalid consent (~C) while denying sufficient harm: A cannot assert A: $I^{\sim p}{\sim}H^{r}{\sim}C$. A can only argue ${\sim}H^{r}$ by denying fulfilment of the *actus reus*, i.e. by denying the commission of any act to which the absence of valid consent would be relevant. Similarly, in the case of sexual intercourse with a young child, consent is commonly invalid by definition.[4] Once the requisite *actus reus* is fulfilled, the correlative harm is by definition a sufficient harm – any other construction of the harm variable η would conflict with the meaning of the prohibition. Despite the possible absence of violence or coercion, the statutory proscription of specified sexual acts means that the commission of any such act is by definition harmful to the individual who is deemed, as a matter of law, unable to give valid consent.

Even where the harm is not expressly defined with reference to consent, this axiom applies. In *Dudgeon*, the state's position Z: $SH^r{\sim}C$ does not assume that the sufficient harm follows from the collective non-consent, but rather that the collective non-consent follows from the sufficient harm, i.e. from the putative immorality of homosexuality. Similarly, in *Handyside*, *Jersild* or *Otto-Preminger-Institut*, the state determination of public moral interests serves as an assertion of public non-consent on the basis of the unacceptable quality or magnitude of the offence that might be provoked by the impugned works.

18.2 Irrelevant Harm Axiom (θ: $\alpha{\sim}\gamma C$)

Consider again the question, how can the argument Z: αH^r be deployed to rebut an A assertion that α gave valid consent to incur the harm [A: $\alpha\eta^r C$]? We saw that Z's assertion of sufficient harm to an α actor implies that no valid consent is given by that α actor to incur the harm [Z: $\alpha H^r{\sim}C$]. But which A position does that Z position rebut? In the formula A: $\alpha\eta^r C$, what is the value of η^r? What kind of assertion about harm is assumed by A's assertion of valid consent?

Since the Z position is meant to rebut A's assertion of valid consent, it might seem that we need simply start with that Z position, replacing ~C in the Z position with C in the A position, and leaving the α and η values the same [A: $\alpha H^r C$]. However, that conclusion would be wrong. The A position cannot simultaneously claim that harm caused by the exercise of the right is validly consented to (C) *and* that such harm is sufficient to justify government interference (H^r). The claimant's whole purpose is to have the government action found *un*justified. Another solution would be to negate both the harm and the consent symbols in the Z position [A: $\alpha{\sim}H^r C$]. Yet that solution, too, would be incorrect. As we have seen, the assertion that a harm is insufficient means that it cannot matter whether valid consent is given to incur it. Even if no consent is given in fact by the affected actor, it can make no difference, if the harm is asserted to be insufficient.

An assertion of valid consent (C) is, then, incompatible with an assertion of sufficient harm (H) or with an assertion of insufficient harm (~H). The assertion that valid consent is given is an assertion that there can be no meaningful inquiry into the sufficiently or insufficiently harmful character of the act.[5] In other words, an assertion of valid consent is an assertion of irrelevant harm (~γ). For that same reason, an assertion of irrelevant harm is an assertion of valid consent. To assert that harm is irrelevant is to assert that it is valid consent which renders the harm irrelevant. Irrelevant harm cannot imply irrelevant consent, as that would mean that nothing is relevant, which would amount to no argument at all. And, as we saw in the last section, irrelevant harm is incompatible with invalid consent: invalid consent means that the harm must be relevant, since it means that the harm must be sufficient to make it matter that no valid consent is given. Thus, in HA_A(1)(b) and (c)(ii), the A position that harm is irrelevant to the question of whether interference with the right is justified is based on the assertion that valid consent is given by the relevant α actor. Similarly, in HA_Z(2)(b) and (c)(ii), the Z position that harm is irrelevant is based on the assertion that valid consent is given by the relevant personal actor. Hence:

> **Irrelevant Harm Axiom** (θ: $\alpha{\sim}\gamma C$): An assertion of valid consent (C) implies an assertion of irrelevant harm (${\sim}\gamma$); and an assertion of irrelevant harm (${\sim}\gamma$) implies an assertion of valid consent (C). For all θ: $\alpha\eta\kappa$, if $\eta = {\sim}\gamma$, then $\kappa = C$; and if $\kappa = C$, then $\eta = {\sim}\gamma$.

Postulates for Irrelevant Harm Axiom

$Ps({\sim}\gamma\kappa)$ $\alpha{\sim}\gamma\kappa \subset \alpha{\sim}\gamma C$ $Ps(\eta C)$ $\alpha\eta C \subset \alpha{\sim}\gamma C$

For example, an assertion of valid individual consent to engage in sexual relations is itself an assertion that there can be no meaningful inquiry into the sufficiency of harm. An assertion of valid consent obviously cannot imply unacceptable harm (H). Nor, however, can it imply insufficient harm (~H), as has already been seen: an assertion of insufficient harm means there is nothing for which the giving or withholding of consent would matter. The harm can therefore only be irrelevant (${\sim}\gamma$). The position Z: $I^{\sim p}H^{r}{\sim}C$ is rebutted not by an assertion that valid consent renders the harm insufficient – again, to call a harm insufficient is to say that there is nothing to consent *to* – but rather that it renders the question of harm irrelevant [A: $I^{\sim p}{\sim}\gamma^{r}C$]. One of the arguments made in *Dudgeon* is that two adults who are otherwise able to give valid consent are also able to consent to have sexual relations, rendering irrelevant any inquiry into any harm caused to them merely by virtue of their homosexuality [A: $I^{\circ}{\sim}\gamma^{r}C$].[6] That argument is also made by the claimants in *Laskey*, but without success. Once it had been argued by the state that substantial levels of physical injury had been inflicted, it became difficult for the claimants to sustain the view that the question of harm is irrelevant, and easier for the state to argue that the conduct causes an unacceptable harm to which consent cannot validly be given [Z: $I^{\circ}H^{r}{\sim}C$]. In *Dudgeon*, the absence of any such evidence with respect to homosexuality in general meant that the state had to rely more strongly on an assertion of public disapproval [Z: $SH^{r}{\sim}C$]. As we have seen, the claimant pointed to contrary views, citing a significant body of favourable public opinion [A: $S{\sim}\gamma^{r}C$].

In *Jersild* and *Otto-Preminger-Institut*, one can imagine a libertarian perspective[7] from which any identified or implied non-personal actors, or society as a whole, might argue that they were willing to incur any harms of hate speech, on the view that free speech is always the greater value [A: $I^{p}{\sim}\gamma^{r}C \cdot S{\sim}\gamma^{r}C$][8] – a view not argued or examined in those cases. That view renders irrelevant the content or gravity of the hate speech. As we have seen, in cases like *Ireland v. UK*, *Lawless*, *Brogan*, *Brannigan*, *Tyrer*, *Costello-Roberts* or *Aksoy*, one can imagine an argument that the personal actor consented to incur the harm, perhaps to procure a benefit [Z: $I^{p}{\sim}\gamma^{\sim r}C$]. However, such arguments are still rare. The more common Z position in such cases is examined in the next section.

18.3 Insufficient Harm Axiom (θ: $\alpha{\sim}H{\sim}\chi$)

The Sufficient Harm Axiom paired H with ~C. The Irrelevant Harm Axiom paired ~γ with C. How is ~H to be paired off? We have seen that an assertion of insufficient harm (~H) implies an assertion of irrelevant consent (~χ). Similarly, an assertion of irrelevant consent (~χ) implies an assertion of insufficient harm (~H): consent can only be irrelevant when the harm is insufficient for it to matter whether or not consent is validly given. Hence:

> **Insufficient Harm Axiom** (θ: $\alpha{\sim}H{\sim}\chi$): An assertion of insufficient harm (~H) implies an assertion of irrelevant consent (~χ); and an assertion of irrelevant consent (~χ) implies an assertion of insufficient harm (~H). For all θ: $\alpha\eta\kappa$, if $\eta = {\sim}H$, then $\kappa = {\sim}\chi$; and if $\kappa = {\sim}\chi$, then $\eta = {\sim}H$.

Postulates for Insufficient Harm Axiom

Ps(~Hκ) $\alpha{\sim}H\kappa \subset \alpha{\sim}H{\sim}\chi$ Ps($\eta{\sim}\chi$) $\alpha\eta{\sim}\chi \subset \alpha{\sim}H{\sim}\chi$

An alternative argument by the claimants in *Laskey* was that the conduct was insufficiently harmful, as it did not result in serious or permanent injuries [A: $I^{\circ}{\sim}H^{r}{\sim}\chi$]. That argument, too, failed to overcome the position Z: $I^{\circ}H^{r}{\sim}C$. Similarly, its implied position that insufficient harm is caused to society's interest in health and morals A: $S{\sim}H^{r}{\sim}\chi$ failed to overcome the state's position Z: $SH^{r}{\sim}C$. In *Dudgeon*, the state's failure to identify any unacceptable harm to individuals meant that it had to rely more strongly on public disapproval Z: $SH^{r}{\sim}C$. In addition to its own empirical reference to public opinion, however, the claimant could also respond that the lack of any unacceptable harm to society meant that public approval or disapproval was irrelevant [A: $S{\sim}H^{r}{\sim}\chi$]. We saw in the last section that the claimants in *Jersild* and *Otto-Preminger-Institut* do not attempt, nor does the Court entertain, an American-style libertarian argument. That approach would have little success in most European jurisdictions, where it is widely accepted that some hate speech constitutes an affirmative harm, which therefore cannot be irrelevant. The claimants must then acknowledge the relevance of the harm, arguing however that it is not of an unacceptable nature or degree [A: $\alpha^{\circ}{\sim}H^{r}{\sim}\chi$].

In *Tyrer*, *Costello-Roberts* and *Aksoy*, the respondent states reply to the argument A: $I^{p}H^{\sim r}{\sim}C$ by asserting that they had not inflicted unacceptable levels of harm, thus rendering the question of consent irrelevant [Z: $I^{p}{\sim}H^{\sim r}{\sim}\chi$]. In *Ireland v. UK*, *Lawless*, *Brogan* and *Brannigan*, the British government responds to the argument A: $I^{p}H^{\sim r}{\sim}C$ by claiming that it had not acted in excess of the exigencies of the situation, and thus had not inflicted upon the detainees a level of harm sufficient to justify a finding of a violation of article 5, again rendering the question of consent irrelevant [Z: $I^{p}{\sim}H^{\sim r}{\sim}\chi$]. This pairing completes all possible pairings of κ and η variables. (Again, the η and κ variables cannot simultaneously be asserted to be irrelevant [θ: $\alpha{\sim}\gamma{\sim}\chi$], as such a position claims that everything is irrelevant, which amounts to no argument at all.)

In view of those three sets of pairings of harm and consent elements, it is important to consider a likely objection. There are many cases – *Laskey*, *Handyside*, *Dudgeon*, *Jersild* or *Otto-Preminger* – in which a party would want to assert both that a harm was insufficient *and* that valid consent was given to incur it [A: $I^{\circ}{\sim}H^{r}C$]. Such an argument seems not only persuasive, but indeed seems to be the strongest argument a claimant could adduce, as it expressly precludes both unacceptable harm and invalid consent. Indeed, such an argument is casually made from time to time. On the foregoing analysis, however, it emerges not as a single, coherent argument at all. It merges two distinct arguments, submitted, however knowingly or unknowingly, in the alternative [A: $I^{\circ}{\sim}H^{r}{\sim}\chi \cdot I^{\circ}{\sim}\gamma^{r}C$].

As was noted in Section 5.4, some arguments recorded as conjunctive in this study might more accurately be recorded as disjunctive. A disjunctive notation might appear particularly preferable for arguments submitted in the alternative, where it is uncertain whether two or more arguments are, or are intended by the party to be, compatible, hence A: $I^{\circ}{\sim}H^{r}{\sim}\chi \vee I^{\circ}{\sim}\gamma^{r}C$. In legal practice, arguments in the alternative are not always submitted either in unequivocally conjunctive or disjunctive form. The choice may be more strategic than substantive, as illustrated by *Laskey*. Ideally, the claimants want to maintain both A: $I^{\circ}{\sim}H^{r}{\sim}\chi$ and A: $I^{\circ}{\sim}\gamma^{r}C$: 'In fact the harm is acceptable, but, in any event, it is irrelevant, through valid consent.' At the same time, they will happily sacrifice one if they can prevail on the other. As a validity calculus is not being developed, we will maintain the convention of using only conjunctions, in accordance with the Axiom of Compound Positions, solely for the sake of simplicity.

Exercise set 18.1

Rewrite each argument, supplying a value for the κ or η, and stating which postulate provides that value.

Example: Z: $I^{\sim p}H^{r}\kappa$

Answer: Z: $I^{\sim p}H^{r}{\sim}C$ [Ps(Hκ)]

1 Z: $I^{\circ}H^{r}\kappa$
2 A: $I^{p}{\sim}H^{r}\kappa$
3 A: $I\eta^{r}C$
4 A: $I^{p}\eta^{\sim r}{\sim}C$
5 A: $S{\sim}\gamma^{r}\kappa$
6 θ: $S\eta^{r}{\sim}\chi$

Exercise set 18.2

1 Derive θ: $I^{p}\gamma\chi$ from A: $I^{p}H^{\sim r}{\sim}C$.
2 Derive θ: $\alpha\gamma^{r}{\sim}\chi$ from A: $I{\sim}H^{r}{\sim}\chi$.
3 Derive Z: $I\eta\chi$ from Z: $I^{p}H^{r}{\sim}C$.

Exercise set 18.3

Fill in the blanks.

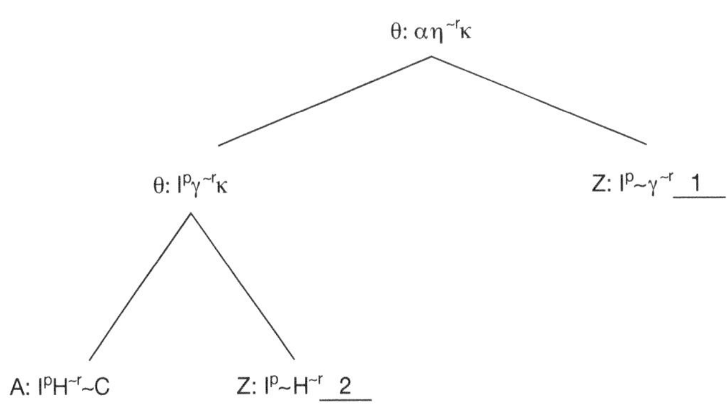

Exercise set 18.4

Fill in the blanks.

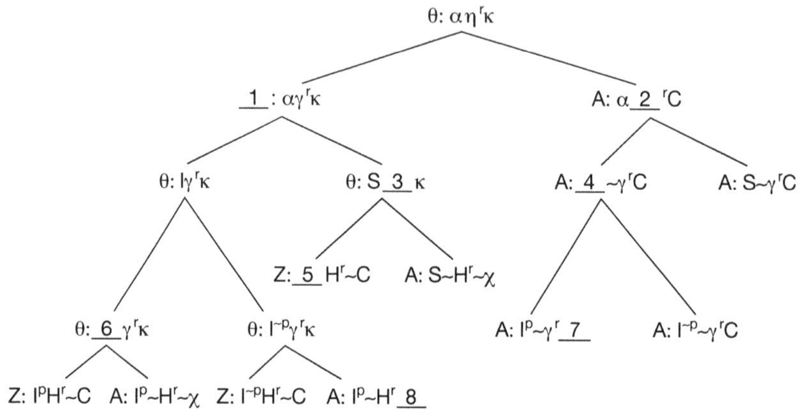

18.4 Theorems

It is now possible to prove theorems taking into account more specific values of κ. For example, compare the proof in Section 17.3 with the following one:

Prove the theorem: $I^p\gamma\kappa \subset I^pH^r\sim C,\ I^p\sim H^r\sim\chi,$
$I^pH^{\sim r}\sim C,\ I^p\sim H^{\sim r}\sim\chi$

(1)	$\gamma \subset \gamma^r,\ \gamma^{\sim r}$	Ps(γ2)
(2)	$\gamma \subset H^r,\ \sim H^r,\ \gamma^{\sim r}$	Ps(γ^r)
(3)	$\gamma \subset H^r,\ \sim H^r,\ H^{\sim r},\ \sim H^{\sim r}$	Ps($\gamma^{\sim r}$)
(4)	$I^p\gamma \subset I^pH^r,\ I^p\sim H^r,\ I^pH^{\sim r},\ I^p\sim H^{\sim r}$	η attr
(5)	$I^p\gamma\kappa \subset I^pH^r\kappa,\ I^p\sim H^r\kappa,\ I^pH^{\sim r}\kappa,\ I^p\sim H^{\sim r}\kappa$	κ attr
(6)	$I^p\gamma\kappa \subset I^pH^r\sim C,\ I^p\sim H^r\kappa,\ I^pH^{\sim r}\sim C,\ I^p\sim H^{\sim r}\kappa$	Ps(Hκ)
conclusion	$I^p\gamma\kappa \subset I^pH^r\sim C,\ I^p\sim H^r\sim\chi,\ I^pH^{\sim r}\sim C,\ I^p\sim H^{\sim r}\sim\chi$	Ps(~Hκ)

Recall that the rule of actor limitation restricts the number of possible formulas that can be generated from α and η combinations. The postulates introduced in this chapter can play a similar kind of limiting role:

Prove the theorem: $I^{p}\eta{\sim}C \subset I^{p}H^{r}{\sim}C, I^{p}H^{\sim r}{\sim}C$

(1)	$\eta \subset H, {\sim}H, {\sim}\gamma$	Th(η)
(2)	$I^{p}\eta \subset I^{p}H, I^{p}{\sim}H, I^{p}{\sim}\gamma$	η attr
(3)	$I^{p}\eta\kappa \subset I^{p}H\kappa, I^{p}{\sim}H\kappa, I^{p}{\sim}\gamma\kappa$	κ attr
(4)	$I^{p}\eta{\sim}C \subset I^{p}H{\sim}C$	Ps($\eta{\sim}C$)
conclusion	$I^{p}\eta{\sim}C \subset I^{p}H^{r}{\sim}C, I^{p}H^{\sim r}{\sim}C$	Ps(H)

Exercise set 18.5

Prove the following theorems.

1 $I\eta^{r}{\sim}C \subset I^{p}H^{r}{\sim}C, I^{\sim p}H^{r}{\sim}C$
2 $\alpha{\sim}\gamma\kappa \subset I^{p}{\sim}\gamma^{r}C, I^{\sim p}{\sim}\gamma^{r}C, S{\sim}\gamma^{r}C, I^{p}{\sim}\gamma^{\sim r}C$
3 $I^{p}\eta{\sim}\chi \subset I^{p}{\sim}H^{r}{\sim}\chi, I^{p}{\sim}H^{\sim r}{\sim}\chi$
4 $I{\sim}H\kappa \subset I^{p}{\sim}H^{r}{\sim}\chi, I^{\sim p}{\sim}H^{r}{\sim}\chi, I^{p}{\sim}H^{\sim r}{\sim}\chi$
5 $I\gamma\kappa \subset I^{p}H^{r}{\sim}C, I^{\sim p}H^{r}{\sim}C, I^{p}{\sim}H^{r}{\sim}\chi, I^{\sim p}{\sim}H^{r}{\sim}\chi, I^{p}H^{\sim r}{\sim}C, I^{p}{\sim}H^{\sim r}{\sim}\chi$
6 $\alpha\eta C \subset I^{p}{\sim}\gamma^{r}C, I^{\sim p}{\sim}\gamma^{r}C, S{\sim}\gamma^{r}C, I^{p}{\sim}\gamma^{\sim r}C$
7 $I^{p}\gamma{\sim}C \subset I^{p}H^{r}{\sim}C, I^{p}H^{\sim r}{\sim}C$

19 Volition

In this chapter, we return to the distinction between consent in fact and in law in order to refine the notation forms.

19.1 Notation

In Figure 17.1, C and ~C were correlated to four types of arguments about consent, with reference to the distinction between consent in fact and consent in law. It was possible to overlook that distinction in the last chapter, for the purpose of generating axioms based solely on the values of C, ~C and $\sim\chi$. But it would be unsatisfactory to keep the distinction suspended.

With the use of markers, we can record whether an argument about consent is adduced *on the basis of* consent in fact, or *in spite of* consent in fact. Consent asserted to be valid or invalid *because* it is, respectively, given or withheld in fact – because it purportedly represents the will of the actor – will be called *volitional*, and represented by the marker 'v'. Consent asserted to be valid or invalid regardless of whether it was given or withheld in fact – regardless of the will of the actor – will be called 'non-volitional', and represented by the marker '~v'. The schemas for representing consent can thus be revised as illustrated in Figure 19.1 and Figure 19.2. Hence the following *volition postulates* (cf. Figure 19.2):

Volition postulates

Ps(κ2) $\kappa \subset \kappa^{v}, \kappa^{\sim v}$ Ps(κ^{v}) $\kappa^{v} \subset \chi^{v}, \sim\chi^{v}$ Ps($\kappa^{\sim v}$) $\kappa^{\sim v} \subset \chi^{\sim v}, \sim\chi^{\sim v}$

Ps(χ2) $\chi \subset \chi^{v}, \chi^{\sim v}$ Ps(χ^{v}) $\chi^{v} \subset C^{v}, \sim C^{v}$ Ps($\chi^{\sim v}$) $\chi^{\sim v} \subset C^{\sim v}, \sim C^{\sim v}$

Ps(C) $C \subset C^{v}, C^{\sim v}$ Ps(~C) $\sim C \subset \sim C^{v}, \sim C^{\sim v}$

	C	~C
Volitional	C^{v} (1)	$\sim C^{v}$ (4)
Non-volitional	$C^{\sim v}$ (3)	$\sim C^{\sim v}$ (2)

Figure 19.1

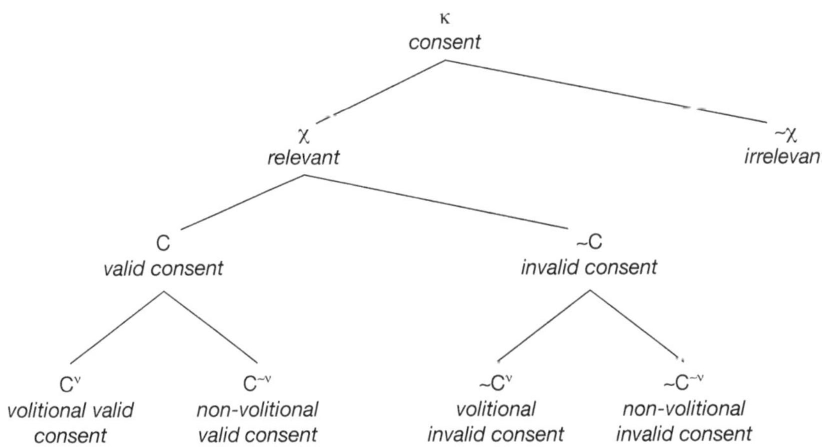

Figure 19.2

19.2 Consent to incur right-based harm

The state in *Laskey* argues that the participants caused unacceptable harm to themselves [Z: $I^{p}H^{r}$] and to each other [Z: $I^{\sim p}H^{r}$]. Applying the Sufficient Harm Axiom, Z attributes to those actors invalid consent to incur that harm, Z: $I^{\circ}H^{r}{\sim}C$. The claimants respond with an assertion of insufficient harm [A: $I^{\circ}{\sim}H^{r}$], hence, under the Insufficient Harm Axiom, an assertion of irrelevant consent [A: $I^{\circ}{\sim}H^{r}{\sim}\chi$]. We have seen that the claimants cannot rely entirely on this latter argument, as some of the physical injuries at issue, in the absence of valid consent, would constitute serious batteries. Alternatively, the claimants assert valid consent in fact *and thus* in law [A: $I^{\circ}\eta^{r}C^{v}$], hence, under the Irrelevant Harm Axiom, irrelevant harm

[A: $I^{\circ}{\sim}\gamma^{r}C^{v}$]. As no evidence was adduced of failure to give consent in fact, the state is restricted to conceding valid consent in fact, but claiming invalid consent in law [Z: $I^{\circ}H^{r}{\sim}C^{\sim v}$], in the view that the state may legitimately determine that individuals cannot validly consent to incur such harms. Here again, we see that the claimants' assertions of valid consent and insufficient harm are not one argument, but in fact two distinct arguments submitted in the alternative.[1]

Had the government adduced evidence about the involvement of individuals who had not consented to incur the harms, it could then have alleged a failure of valid consent in fact [Z: $I^{\sim p}H^{r}{\sim}C^{v}$], without having to adduce invalid consent in law [Z: $I^{\sim p}H^{r}{\sim}C^{\sim v}$]. That argument would have been so evident as to have the case summarily resolved: if the respondent can argue Z: $I^{\sim p}H^{r}{\sim}C^{v}$ with no challenge on the facts (i.e. no assertion that there *was* valid individual consent), then the case involves a straightforward rape, battery or assault. However, once A asserts valid consent to incur any harm inflicted, with no challenges on factual grounds, the only remaining state rebuttal on point is that such consent is non-volitionally invalid [Z: $I^{\circ}H^{r}{\sim}C^{\sim v}$].

In *Dudgeon*, the state noted the interests of 'vulnerable' persons, such as young people, who might be harmed if homosexual conduct were legal [Z: $I^{\sim p}H^{r}{\sim}C^{\sim v}$]. However, the claimant does not dispute the need for protection of persons lacking legal competence, seeking only a right for competent adults [A: $I^{\circ}{\sim}\gamma^{r}C^{v}$]. It is difficult for Z, in response, to maintain the position Z: $I^{\circ}H^{r}{\sim}C^{\sim v}$ with regard to competent adults, where H^{r} can represent only a moral harm. Instead, under article 8(2), the Z position points to public objections to homosexuality in order to justify its appeal to public morals [Z: $SH^{r}{\sim}C^{v}$]. Meanwhile, as we have seen, the A position points to changes in public attitudes, which have grown more supportive of legalisation [A: $S{\sim}\gamma^{r}C^{v}$]. Of course, by claiming that permissiveness would unacceptably harm public morals, the Z position can argue that government may construe such harm to be sufficient to preclude the possibility of valid public consent, regardless of the actual state of public opinion [Z: $SH^{r}{\sim}C^{\sim v}$]. The only other argument open to A is to argue that the harm to public morals is insufficient, thus rendering irrelevant any question of consent [A: $S{\sim}H^{r}{\sim}\chi$].

In cases such as *Jersild* or *Otto-Preminger-Institut*, little empirical reference is made to public opinion, leaving the Z position relying on a harm argument: government may construe the harm to be sufficient to preclude the possibility of valid public consent [Z: $SH^{r}{\sim}C^{\sim v}$]. Again, in the absence of empirical evidence of public support for the claimants' position, the only rebuttal is to argue that the harm to public morals is not unacceptable [A: $S{\sim}H^{r}{\sim}\chi$], which may include the argument that the works are positively beneficial. Of course, the absence of empirical reference to specifically harmed individuals does not preclude implied reference to hypothetical individuals who might be offended by the works in question [Z: $I^{\sim p}H^{r}{\sim}C^{v}$], which follows by broad implication from Z: $SH^{r}{\sim}C^{v}$. Alternatively, Z's implicit assertion of unacceptable harm to other individuals need not reflect those individuals' actual consent or non-consent in fact. Rather, Z can assert a state prerogative to determine as a matter of law that those individuals cannot validly consent to incur such harm: it is against the individuals' own interest to be exposed to such works, even if they consent in fact to do so [Z: $I^{\sim p}H^{r}{\sim}C^{\sim v}$]. The claimant can rebut those positions either by arguing that legal effect should be given to the choice of competent adults to be exposed to the works [A: $I^{\sim p}{\sim}\gamma^{r}C^{v}$]; or that the works are insufficiently harmful to those individuals [A: $I^{\sim p}{\sim}H^{r}{\sim}\chi$].

In *Brüggemann*, Z's assertion that the foetus is an affected individual ($I^{\sim p}$) entails an assertion of non-voluntary invalid consent by that actor to incur an unacceptable harm [Z: $I^{\sim p}H^{r}{\sim}C^{\sim v}$]. A's claim that there is no unacceptable harm to another individual means that there is nothing to consent to, thus negating the element of consent [A: $I^{\sim p}{\sim}H^{r}{\sim}\chi$]. That A position might appear strange, as abortion advocates recognise the foetus not as an entity whose consent is irrelevant, but rather as an entity which is not an individual actor at all. From our perspective, however, those are just two ways of saying the same thing. For ascertaining the violation or non-violation of a right, liberal rights discourse accords the same status to the statement '*Consent is irrelevant*' regardless of whether that statement means that there *is no* actor who *could* give or withhold consent, or rather that there *is* such an actor, whose consent, however, is irrelevant.

19.3 Consent to incur restriction-based harm

The very fact of bringing a case which does not challenge a restriction-based harm assumes the view that the personal actor does not validly consent to incur that harm [A: $I^{p}H^{\sim r}{\sim}C$]. Yet individual non-consent to incur restriction-based harm also raises a question as to its volitional or non-volitional character, as has been mentioned in the case of benefit restrictions. A legally competent person might, for example, without ostensible coercion, consent to sign confessions, to forgo legal counsel, or to submit to castration, sterilisation or medical experimentation, in order to procure some benefit from the state, such as a reduced period of detention. If that individual were subsequently to challenge the treatment, the state might then assert that the individual was in no way compelled to make the choice, having been free to accept a longer prison term, and therefore had validly consented [Z: $I^{p}{\sim}\gamma^{\sim r}C^{v}$]. The claimant would respond that, notwithstanding the absence of immediate coercion or the nominally voluntary circumstances governing the choice, the unacceptable nature of the harm rendered such consent non-volitionally invalid [A: $I^{p}H^{\sim r}{\sim}C^{\sim v}$].

Similar scenarios arise in the case of consent to undergo medical treatment, where medical authorities act pursuant to laws governing patients' consent (even if the medical establishment or practitioner is private).

In 1988, the French Conseil d'État, in the *Camara* case,[2] rendered an opinion on a 1976 law[3] concerning the removal of internal organs from the corpses of deceased persons. The law authorised the removal of organs unless, while still alive, the individuals had expressed a specific objection. It thus created a presumption of valid consent. The question before the Conseil d'État was whether such a presumption applies to minors, in particular, whether the removal of the internal organs of a deceased child, for purposes of performing an autopsy, required express consent of the parents or legal guardians.

Of particular significance were the family's Islamic beliefs, which required that a deceased body remain intact in order to assure an afterlife. The law was challenged for permitting excessive intrusion on the right to bodily integrity.[4] In opposition to the law, it was argued that consent cannot be presumed – that non-consent should be presumed in law, hence a presumption of non-volitional non-consent [A: $I^pH^{\sim r}{\sim}C^{\sim v}$]. Upholding the law, however, the Conseil d'État ruled that express consent was required only for organ donation. For autopsy alone, a presumption of consent could be applied to minors, hence a presumption of valid, albeit non-volitional, consent [Z: $I^p{\sim}\gamma^{\sim r}C^{\sim v}$].

Where a respondent cannot argue, or cannot argue solely, that a personal actor validly consented in fact to incur a restriction-based harm [Z: $I^p{\sim}\gamma^{\sim r}C^v$], the only remaining option is to argue that no unacceptable harm has been inflicted, thus rendering irrelevant the question of individual consent [Z: $I^p{\sim}H^{\sim r}{\sim}\chi$]. Where there is no question of A asserting non-volitionally invalid consent [A: $I^pH^{\sim r}{\sim}C^{\sim v}$], then the A position always assumes that the personal actor resists the state action *in fact*, i.e. withholds volitionally valid consent [A: $I^pH^{\sim r}{\sim}C^v$]. For, if the personal actor gives volitionally valid consent, then there is no dispute. Again, in the many cases, like *McCann*, *Aksoy* or *Costello-Roberts*, where there is no question of individual consent to incur the restriction-based harm, and thus no question of the validity of such consent, invalid volitional consent is presupposed by the very bringing of the claim.

19.4 Public opinion (θ: $S\eta^r\chi^v$) and public interest (Z: $SH^r{\sim}C^{\sim v}$, A: $S{\sim}H^r{\sim}\chi$)

We can now add some precision to the distinction drawn earlier between the concepts of *public opinion* and *public interest.* A party makes an argument about *public opinion* by asserting that certain views are sufficiently prevalent among the public to be attributable to society as a whole [θ: $S\eta^r\chi^v$]. An assertion about public opinion is an assertion about what the public want or do not want, support or do not support, *in fact*. A party thus makes an argument about public opinion by asserting that certain views are attributable to society as a volitional matter [θ: $S\eta^r\chi^v$], either in favour of the restriction [Z: $SH^r{\sim}C^v$] or in favour of the right [A: $S{\sim}\gamma^rC^v$].

In *Dudgeon*, the government argued that a representative body of public opinion supported the ban [Z: $SH^{r}{\sim}C^{v}$], while the claimant argued that a representative body of public opinion opposed it [A: $S{\sim}\gamma^{r}C^{v}$]. In *Handyside*, the government argued that newspaper campaigns, which included publication of letters from members of the public, expressed 'the genuine emotion felt by citizens faithful to traditional moral values'.[5] [Z: $SH^{r}{\sim}C^{v}$] Mr Handyside referred to these initiatives as 'ultra-conservative hysteria' which could not be taken to represent the views of society as a whole. Citing *The Little Red Book*'s wide circulation throughout many European states, he surmised that public opinion was, on the whole, favourable [A: $S{\sim}\gamma^{r}C^{v}$].[6]

Other arguments about the public interest are not based on public opinion. In *Handyside*, as well as *Laskey*, *Jersild* or *Otto-Preminger*, questions about actual levels of public support, although their relevance is recognised, were not predominant. More commonly, in cases like these, the respondent argues that the unacceptable character of the harm is such as to justify a government determination that society cannot consent to incur it [Z: $SH^{r}{\sim}C^{\sim v}$]. The claimant commonly replies that public opinion is irrelevant, by arguing that no unacceptable harm is caused to society (thus there is nothing to consent to) [A: $S{\sim}H^{r}{\sim}\chi$].

19.5 Theorems

The volition postulates can be introduced into proofs:

Prove the theorem: $I^{p}{\sim}\gamma\kappa \subset I^{p}{\sim}\gamma^{r}C^{v}, I^{p}{\sim}\gamma^{r}C^{\sim v}, I^{p}{\sim}\gamma^{\sim r}C^{v}, I^{p}{\sim}\gamma^{\sim r}C^{\sim v}$

(1)	${\sim}\gamma \subset {\sim}\gamma^{r}, {\sim}\gamma^{\sim r}$	Ps(~γ)
(2)	$I^{p}{\sim}\gamma \subset I^{p}{\sim}\gamma^{r}, I^{p}{\sim}\gamma^{\sim r}$	η attr
(3)	$I^{p}{\sim}\gamma\kappa \subset I^{p}{\sim}\gamma^{r}\kappa, I^{p}{\sim}\gamma^{\sim r}\kappa$	κ attr
(4)	$I^{p}{\sim}\gamma\kappa \subset I^{p}{\sim}\gamma^{r}C, I^{p}{\sim}\gamma^{\sim r}C$	Ps(~γκ)
conclusion	$I^{p}{\sim}\gamma\kappa \subset I^{p}{\sim}\gamma^{r}C^{v}, I^{p}{\sim}\gamma^{r}C^{\sim v}, I^{p}{\sim}\gamma^{\sim r}C^{v}, I^{p}{\sim}\gamma^{\sim r}C^{\sim v}$	Ps(C)

19.6 Improbable and impossible arguments

If rigorously applied, the volition postulates will occasionally yield arguments which, albeit conceivable in theory, are difficult to imagine in practice. Consider the following proof:

Prove the theorem: $S\eta C \subset S{\sim}\gamma^{r}C^{v}, S{\sim}\gamma^{r}C^{\sim v}$

(1)	$\eta \subset \gamma, {\sim}\gamma$	Ps(η1)
(2)	$S\eta \subset S\gamma, S{\sim}\gamma$	η attr

(3)	$S\eta\kappa \subset S\gamma\kappa, S{\sim}\gamma\kappa$	κ attr
(4)	$S\eta C \subset S{\sim}\gamma C$	$Ps(\eta C)$
(5)	$S\eta C \subset S{\sim}\gamma^{r}C, S{\sim}\gamma^{\sim r}C$	$Ps({\sim}\gamma)$
(6)	$S\eta C \subset S{\sim}\gamma^{r}C$	α lim
conclusion	$S\eta C \subset S{\sim}\gamma^{r}C^{v}, S{\sim}\gamma^{r}C^{\sim v}$	$Ps(\eta\kappa 2)$

As we have seen, the first of the theorem's possible values, although not among the most common arguments, does sometimes appear as an argument by the claimant that public opinion favours the right [A: $S{\sim}\gamma^{r}C^{v}$]. However, the second possible value is difficult to imagine in practice. It would appear to represent an argument, made by a claimant [A: $S{\sim}\gamma^{r}C^{\sim v}$], that society *should* be construed to consent to the exercise of the right, regardless of actual public opinion (hence $C^{\sim v}$), and regardless of any harm that might be caused (hence ${\sim}\gamma^{r}$). In practice, it seems more likely that the claimant in such a case would simply assert insufficient harm to society, hence irrelevant consent [A: $S{\sim}H^{r}{\sim}\chi$]. Nevertheless, as there is no reason to exclude the possibility of such an argument in principle, the proof is admissible.

By contrast, some arguments are precluded in principle. For example, it would be erroneous to suppose a postulate which would ascribe volition or non-volition to irrelevant consent [${\sim}\chi \subset {\sim}\chi^{v}, {\sim}\chi^{\sim v}$]. The argument that consent is irrelevant means that its volitional or non-volitional character is also irrelevant, thus obviating any need for providing such specification. Accordingly, no such postulate has been included among the volition postulates.

Exercise set 19.1

Prove the following theorems.

1 $\kappa \subset \chi^{v}, {\sim}\chi^{v}, \chi^{\sim v}, {\sim}\chi^{\sim v}$

2 $\kappa \subset C^{v}, {\sim}C^{v}, {\sim}\chi^{v}, C^{\sim v}, {\sim}C^{\sim v}, {\sim}\chi^{\sim v}$

3 $I^{\sim p}\gamma\kappa \subset I^{\sim p}H^{r}{\sim}C^{v}, I^{\sim p}H^{r}{\sim}C^{\sim v}, I^{\sim p}{\sim}H^{r}{\sim}\chi$

4 $S\eta\kappa \subset SH^{r}{\sim}C^{v}, SH^{r}{\sim}C^{\sim v}, S{\sim}H^{r}{\sim}\chi, S{\sim}\gamma^{r}C^{v}, S{\sim}\gamma^{r}C^{\sim v}$

5 $I\eta C \subset I^{p}{\sim}\gamma^{r}C^{v}, I^{p}{\sim}\gamma^{r}C^{\sim v}, I^{\sim p}{\sim}\gamma^{r}C^{v}, I^{\sim p}{\sim}\gamma^{r}C^{\sim v}, I^{p}{\sim}\gamma^{\sim r}C^{v}, I^{p}{\sim}\gamma^{\sim r}C^{\sim v}$

Exercise set 19.2

1 Derive θ: $I^{p}\gamma\chi^{\sim v}$ from A: $I^{p}H^{\sim r}{\sim}C^{\sim v}$.
2 Derive Z: $I\eta\chi^{v}$ from Z: $I^{p}H^{r}{\sim}C^{v}$.
3 Derive A: $\alpha\eta^{r}\kappa^{\sim v}$ from A: $I{\sim}\gamma^{r}C^{\sim v}$.

19.7 Determinacy and indeterminacy

We have now completed our analysis of the core elements of arguments. In the rest of the book, they will be used to ascertain the background theories. We will say that a rights argument is formally determinate in so far as it assumes some instance of the general formula θ: $\alpha\eta\kappa$, and to the extent of that formula's specificity. Assume, for *Laskey*, that the respondent's position Z: $I^{\circ}H^{r}{\sim}C^{\sim v}$ is countered by the claimants' positions A: $I^{\circ}{\sim}H^{r}{\sim}\chi$ and A: $I^{\circ}{\sim}\gamma^{r}C^{v}$. The most specific level of agreement necessarily presupposed by this disagreement can be ascertained by identifying the formula common to all three positions at the lowest level of abstraction. While all three positions obviously agree that there is some disagreement about the combined values of θ: $\alpha\eta\kappa$, their disagreement can be identified at a more precise level. We can say that the claimant and respondent agree on the proposition θ: $I^{\circ}\eta^{r}\kappa$, which defines the extent and limits of formal determinacy to their underlying agreement. Their disagreement is then about the values which should be attributed to the variables η^{r} and κ. (As noted in Section 9.5, we are relying on intuition to abstract from, or to, positions containing the inclusive symbols θ°, I° and α°. We can then avoid the complexities that a formal calculus incorporating them would require.)

Now assume that the claimant abandons the argument that valid consent renders the level of harm irrelevant [A: $I^{\circ}{\sim}\gamma^{r}C^{v}$], retaining only the argument that the level of harm is insufficient to justify the restriction [A: $I^{\circ}{\sim}H^{r}{\sim}\chi$]. The underlying agreement between A and Z can now be expressed with further determinacy, as a dispute about the values to be attributed to the γ^{r} and κ variables of the formula θ: $I^{\circ}\gamma^{r}\kappa$. In other words, both parties now additionally agree that the question of the acceptable or unacceptable character of the right-based harm is *relevant* (γ^{r}). Their disagreement is now formally determinate to the following extent – and *only* to this extent: (1) the disagreement about the value of γ^{r} is a disagreement between Z's assertion $\gamma^{r} = H^{r}$ and A's assertion $\gamma^{r} = {\sim}H^{r}$; and, concomitantly, (2) the disagreement about the value of κ is a disagreement between Z's assertion $\kappa = {\sim}C^{\sim v}$ and A's assertion $\kappa = {\sim}\chi$. Under the axioms introduced in Chapter 18, these are just two ways of saying the same thing.

For purposes of adjudication, the question is how to choose between those values. That is a question of substantive determinacy. The respondent explains why the harm is unacceptable, why $\gamma^r = H^r$, by arguing, for example, that the acts cause bad health, or involve brutality. The claimant explains why the harm is acceptable, why $\gamma^r = \sim H^r$, by arguing, for example, that the injuries are not severe or permanent, or are outweighed by feelings of sexual or psychological well-being. We can say that a dispute is *substantively determinate* in so far as there is certainty or agreement about the material values to be ascribed to the variables of a θ position; and, by extension, is *substantively indeterminate* in so far as no such values can be found. Similar questions arise for any dispute.

By what criteria is substantive determinacy ascertained? That is where our purely formal analysis stops and the standard questions of jurisprudence and legal theory begin – which is the reason why the substantive debates waged by exponents of, for example, liberalism, communitarianism, law and economics, natural law, or critical legal studies are of interest to, but remain distinct from, a formal analysis. In accordance with the Presupposition Corollary to the Axiom of Contentious Character, we can say that a controversy about liberal rights is a controversy about which formal values are to be assigned to the variables contained by some presupposed θ position, which, in turn, is a dispute about which material values should be assigned to those formal values.

A proponent of liberal rights accepts that a dispute can be accurately represented by *some* set of θ positions; and, moreover, would say that the values attributable to the variables of θ positions in a given dispute can be made substantively determinate – determinate enough to provide fair outcomes. By contrast, an exponent of critical legal studies would presumably say *either* that the limitation of θ positions to formal elements of harm and consent preclude attention to factors – for example, human compassion or social inclusion – which should decide disputes; *or* that θ positions do indeed accurately characterise disputes, but that law's determinacy begins and ends with formal determinacy, such that the process of attributing substantive values to the variables of θ positions can never be made sufficiently determinate to assure fair outcomes. Our task is not to resolve those controversies, but only to observe how they arise within a fixed, formal structure.

Part IV

Forms of argument

20 Breach

The θ positions examined thus far do not yet constitute complete arguments about the violation or non-violation of rights. In this chapter, we examine how θ positions generate such arguments.

20.1 θ positions and syllogistic form

One contention in *Handyside* is that the claimant has caused no harm to any actor sufficient to justify government interference with his right of free expression [A: $\alpha^{\circ}\sim H^{r}\sim\chi$]. But that contention does not tell the claimant's whole story. It is part of a larger argument, which can be stated in classic syllogistic form:

A's first premise	*If* the personal actor, in exercising the right, causes to no actor any harm sufficient to justify the restriction, *then* the restriction violates the right.
A's second premise	The personal actor, in exercising the right, causes to no actor any harm sufficient to justify the restriction.
A's conclusion	The restriction violates the right.

That syllogistic matrix suggests that θ positions, as developed thus far, represent only the second premise. How can they be refined so as to represent the entire argument?

To begin, note that A's second premise recapitulates the 'if ' clause of the first premise. We'll illustrate that identity by replacing both statements with the letter *p*:

A's first premise	*If p*, *then* the restriction violates the right.
A's second premise	*p*
A's conclusion	The restriction violates the right.

Next, note that A’s conclusion recapitulates the ‘then’ clause of the first premise. We’ll illustrate that identity by replacing both statements with the letter *q*:

A’s first premise	*If p then q*
A’s second premise	*p*
A’s conclusion	*q*

In that configuration, the first premise asserts only a contingent relationship: it is the case that *q if* it is the case that *p*. The second premise then proceeds to assert that this contingency is fulfilled: it *is* the case that *p*.

What, then, are the values of *p* and *q* asserted by A? We have seen that A’s second premise takes the form $\alpha^{\circ}{\sim}H^{r}{\sim}\chi$:

A’s first premise	*If p, then q*
A’s second premise	$\alpha^{\circ}{\sim}H^{r}{\sim}\chi$
A’s conclusion	*q*

We have thus assigned to *p* the value of $\alpha^{\circ}{\sim}H^{r}{\sim}\chi$ in the second premise. Accepting the equivalence $p = p$, we can assign to it the same value in the first premise:

A’s first premise	*If* $\alpha^{\circ}{\sim}H^{r}{\sim}\chi$, *then q*
A’s second premise	$\alpha^{\circ}{\sim}H^{r}{\sim}\chi$
A’s conclusion	*q*

The goal of A’s argument is to demonstrate that a right has been violated. We will represent the claim of violation (‘breach’) of a right with the symbol ‘B’. That claim represents A’s *conclusion*:

A’s first premise	*If* $\alpha^{\circ}{\sim}H^{r}{\sim}\chi$, *then q*
A’s second premise	$\alpha^{\circ}{\sim}H^{r}{\sim}\chi$
A’s conclusion	B

We have thus assigned to *q* the value of B in the conclusion. Assuming the equivalence $q = q$, we can assign to *q* the same value in the first premise:

A’s first premise	*If* $\alpha^{\circ}{\sim}H^{r}{\sim}\chi$, *then* B
A’s second premise	$\alpha^{\circ}{\sim}H^{r}{\sim}\chi$
A’s conclusion	B

Of course, for both B and ~B, the Axiom of Generality plays a role in ascertaining the right of which breach or non-breach is predicated.

20.2 Horizontal representation

Economy of expression can be further enhanced if we can replace the conditional locution 'If . . . then . . .' with symbols serving to arrange the expressions in a way which will more concisely illustrate that conditional relationship. We already know something about how to deal with the problem of representing a relationship between two different propositions. In order to assert a relationship of conjunction ('*p* and *q*'), we have used the dot. This time, it is not a conjunctive relationship between two propositions that we wish to represent, but a conditional one ('If *p*, then *q*'). The conditional relationship asserts that one proposition is true *if* another is true. That relationship is commonly denoted with an operator known as an 'arrow' (→)[1] placed between the two propositions, hence $p \rightarrow q$. A's first premise thus asserts that there is a violation (B) *if* it is the case that $\alpha^{\circ}{\sim}H^{r}{\sim}\chi$, hence $\alpha^{\circ}{\sim}H^{r}{\sim}\chi \rightarrow B$:

A's first premise	$\alpha^{\circ}{\sim}H^{r}{\sim}\chi \rightarrow B$
A's second premise	$\alpha^{\circ}{\sim}H^{r}{\sim}\chi$
A's conclusion	B

In the conditional statement $p \rightarrow q$, the proposition p is commonly called the *antecedent*,[2] and the proposition q is commonly called the *consequent*.[3] In the second premise, A further asserts that the antecedent condition required by the first premise is fulfilled: it *is* the case that $\alpha^{\circ}{\sim}H^{r}{\sim}\chi$. These two simple premises can be expressed as one compound premise by use of parentheses (just to keep the grouping of symbols clear) and a dot:

A's premise	$(\alpha^{\circ}{\sim}H^{r}{\sim}\chi \rightarrow B) \cdot \alpha^{\circ}{\sim}H^{r}{\sim}\chi$
A's conclusion	B

The argument is now sufficiently formalised to allow us to forego vertical representation. It can be reduced to linear form if we represent the distinction between the premise and the conclusion by means of an operator. The double arrow (⇒) will be used for that purpose:

F 20.1 A: $[(\alpha^{\circ}{\sim}H^{r}{\sim}\chi \rightarrow B) \cdot \alpha^{\circ}{\sim}H^{r}{\sim}\chi] \Rightarrow B$

In this construction, the terms preceding the double arrow constitute the argument's premise or premises; and terms following the double arrow constitute the argument's conclusion.

How would we formulate an opposing Z position? One rebuttal to the claimant's second premise [A: $\alpha{\sim}H^{r}{\sim}\chi$] is the respondent's argument Z: $\alpha H^{r}{\sim}C^{\sim v}$:

Z's first premise	*If* $\alpha H^{r}{\sim}C^{\sim v}$, *then* q
Z's second premise	$\alpha H^{r}{\sim}C^{\sim v}$
Z's conclusion	q

Just as A positions claim a *violation* (B) of a right, Z positions claim *no violation* of the right (~B):

Z's first premise	$\alpha H^{r}{\sim}C^{\sim v} \rightarrow {\sim}B$
Z's second premise	$\alpha H^{r}{\sim}C^{\sim v}$
Z's conclusion	~B

Hence, the Z position in linear form:

F 20.2 Z: $[(\alpha H^{r}{\sim}C^{\sim v} \rightarrow B) \cdot \alpha H^{r}{\sim}C^{\sim v}] \Rightarrow {\sim}B$

20.3 General formulas for θ positions

All A and Z positions, then, can be represented by means of the following general formulas,

GF(B) A: $[(\alpha\eta\kappa \rightarrow B) \cdot \alpha\eta\kappa] \Rightarrow B$

GF(~B) Z: $[(\alpha\eta\kappa \rightarrow {\sim}B) \cdot \alpha\eta\kappa] \Rightarrow {\sim}B$

Where it is useful to speak of a B or ~B conclusion generally, the variable β (beta) will be used,

Ps(β) $\beta \subset B, {\sim}B$

Hence, a general form for all arguments in liberal rights disputes,

GF(β) θ: $[(\alpha\eta\kappa \rightarrow \beta) \cdot \alpha\eta\kappa] \Rightarrow \beta$

20.4 Shorthand notation

The notation form for GF(β) has a redundant quality in so far as the second premise merely confirms that the condition set forth in the first premise (αηκ) is fulfilled. Moreover, any A position will always take a β value of B, and any Z position will always take a β value of ~B. There is therefore some redundancy in repeating that value both as conclusion to the entire argument (B) and as consequent to the conditional in the first premise (αηκ → B).

In another departure from traditional logic, a shorthand notation form will be adopted which will preserve the essential elements of the formula, while shortening it for ease of use. As with the Axiom of Compound Positions, such a departure is warranted only in so far as our principal concern is with ascertaining the formal structure of arguments, rather than testing validity by means of a rigorous calculus. An underlined double arrow will therefore be used ($\underline{\Rightarrow}$) to signify that *the second premise alone is being used to represent the conjunction of the first and second premises,*

GF(β) θ: αηκ $\underline{\Rightarrow}$ β

Hence, for all A and Z positions, respectively,

GF(B) A: αηκ $\underline{\Rightarrow}$ B

GF(~B) Z: αηκ $\underline{\Rightarrow}$ ~B

Thus, for example, F 20.1 would be written,

F 20.3 A: $\alpha^{\circ}\sim H^{r}\sim\chi$ $\underline{\Rightarrow}$ B

And F 20.2 would be written,

F 20.4 Z: $\alpha H^{r}\sim C^{\sim v}$ $\underline{\Rightarrow}$ ~B

Since all A positions take B conclusions, and all Z positions take ~B conclusions, we could further economise by eliminating β values entirely, thus eliminating the $\underline{\Rightarrow}$ symbol. That would leave us with θ positions looking exactly as they did at the beginning of the chapter [θ: αηκ]. Certainly, it makes sense to economise on redundant notation forms. However, β states the conclusion – the whole point of the argument – and is therefore important enough to include. In fact, the term 'β position' will sometimes be used to emphasise that a θ position includes a conclusion of breach or non-breach.

Exercise set 20.1

Write both complete and simplified β positions for the following arguments, supplying the most specific values of κ or η variables.

Example: A: $I^{p}{\sim}H^{r}\kappa$

Answer: A: $[(I^{p}{\sim}H^{r}{\sim}\chi \rightarrow B) \cdot I^{p}{\sim}H^{r}{\sim}\chi] \Rightarrow B$
A: $I^{p}{\sim}H^{r}{\sim}\chi \underline{\Rightarrow} B$

1 Z: $I^{\sim p}\eta^{r}{\sim}C^{\sim v}$
2 A: $I^{p}H^{\sim r}\kappa^{\sim v}$
3 A: $\alpha\eta^{r}C^{v}$
4 A: $S{\sim}\gamma^{r}\kappa^{\sim v}$
5 Z: $IH^{r}\kappa^{\sim v}$
6 A: $I^{p}{\sim}H^{\sim r}\kappa$

21 The *Urtheorie*

Grammatically, the propositions 'There is a violation of right x' and 'There is no violation of right x' contain no normative content. They employ no modal or conditional locutions such as 'must,' 'should' or 'ought'. Of course, we do not read such propositions purely grammatically. Every β position assumes some background theory that the rights at issue *ought* to be ordered in a particular way. In this chapter, we turn to that body of *Urtheorie* that represents the background theories necessarily presupposed by rights arguments.

21.1 Postulating a background theory

One of the claimants' arguments in *Laskey* is that the individual participants had a right to engage in sadomasochism in so far as they had competently consented to do so [A: $I^{\circ}{\sim}\gamma^{r}C^{v} \rightarrow B$]. From what broader theory of rights does that argument arise? We might call it 'liberal' or 'libertarian'. But what do those terms mean? We could no doubt concoct *some* theory of liberalism or libertarianism to explain the argument, but can we identify only that background theory which it strictly presupposes?

Let's not give A's background theory a name just yet. For the time being, we'll just call it τ (tau). In this chapter and the next, the existence of the background theories will simply be hypothesised. A few further structural elements must be put in place in order for the set of possible background theories – the set of possible values of τ – to be ascertained. We will say that the A position presupposes some background theory τ. That background theory might, for example, run as follows: 'There is some set of activities which competent adults have a right to undertake if they wish to do so.' Having adopted that theory, the claimant must then proceed to argue that the participants are competent adults and that they wish to engage in activities included within that set of activities. In accordance with the Axiom of Truth Value, adopting theory τ will be understood to mean accepting, for the purposes of resolving the dispute, that τ is *true*. For A, if τ is true, then the rest of its argument must be true,

F 21.1 $\quad$ A: $\tau \rightarrow (I^{\circ}{\sim}\gamma^{r}C^{v} \rightarrow B)$

We could read this formula as follows: '*If* it is the case that τ, *and if* it is the case that $I^{\circ}{\sim}\gamma^{r}C^{v}$, *then* the right has been violated.' More generally, for all θ positions,

F 21.2 $\theta: \tau \rightarrow (\alpha\eta\kappa \rightarrow \beta)$

That is, '*If* it is the case that τ, *and if* it is the case that $\alpha\eta\kappa$, *then* it is the case that β.' What, then, are the components of τ? What kind of background theory τ produces the argument $I^{\circ}{\sim}\gamma^{r}C^{v} \rightarrow B$, and what kinds of background theories produce other arguments? Our task in the reminder of the book will be to find values for τ. (It will become clear that τ, too, functions as a strongly exclusive variable, so a symbol τ° would be meaningless. Its most specific values exclude all of the others.)

21.2 Reasoning to the result

How does a θ position reason from a background theory to a conclusion that a right has or has not been breached? In *Laskey*, the A position begins by assuming A: $\tau \rightarrow (I^{\circ}{\sim}\gamma^{r}C^{v} \rightarrow B)$. Yet that position contains only conditional propositions. Thus, in a second premise, A must *affirm* τ, even if not expressly:

(1)	$\tau \rightarrow (I^{\circ}{\sim}\gamma^{r}C^{v} \rightarrow B)$
(2)	τ
conclusion	$I^{\circ}{\sim}\gamma^{r}C^{v} \rightarrow B$

That conclusion is still only conditional. In a further step, A must affirm $I^{\circ}{\sim}\gamma^{r}C^{v}$:

conclusion from last argument	$I^{\circ}{\sim}\gamma^{r}C^{v} \rightarrow B$
(3)	$I^{\circ}{\sim}\gamma^{r}C^{v}$
conclusion	B

Taken together, A has adopted three premises in order to reach the conclusion that a right has been breached:

(1)	$\tau \rightarrow (I^{\circ}{\sim}\gamma^{r}C^{v} \rightarrow B)$
(2)	τ
(3)	$I^{\circ}{\sim}\gamma^{r}C^{v}$
conclusion	B

More generally, a structure for all θ positions is as follows:

(1)	$\tau \rightarrow (\alpha\eta\kappa \rightarrow \beta)$
(2)	τ
(3)	$\alpha\eta\kappa$
conclusion	β

In linear form, the configuration appears as follows:

F 21.3 θ: $\{[\tau \rightarrow (\alpha\eta\kappa \rightarrow \beta)] \cdot \tau \cdot \alpha\eta\kappa\} \Rightarrow \beta$

21.3 Shorthand notation

The notation form for F 21.3 is cumbersome. It has a redundant quality in so far as the second and third premises merely confirm that the conditions set forth in the first premise (τ and $\alpha\eta\kappa$) are fulfilled. Again departing from traditional logic, a shorthand notation form will be adopted which will preserve the essential elements of the formula, while considerably shortening it. Here, too, such a departure is warranted only in so far as our concern is with ascertaining the formal structure of arguments, rather than with comprehensive validity testing. A crab symbol ($\propto$) will be used so that *the conjunction of the second and third premises will serve to represent the conjunction of the first, second and third premises*. We will designate as *background formulas* (BF) those *formulas which express general forms for the background theories*,

BF(τ) θ: $(\tau \cdot \alpha\eta\kappa) \propto \beta$

That formula expresses the background theory at the most general level of abstraction, and will be called a 'τ position'. It is the general formula, the *Urtheorie* from which more specific background theories will derive. In *Laskey*, A adopts some background theory τ, which entails $I^{\circ}{\sim}\gamma^{r}C^{v} \rightarrow B$, and then reasons to a final conclusion by affirming $I^{\circ}{\sim}\gamma^{r}C^{v}$,

F 21.4 A: $\{[\tau \rightarrow (I^{\circ}{\sim}\gamma^{r}C^{v} \rightarrow B)] \cdot \tau \cdot I^{\circ}{\sim}\gamma^{r}C^{v}\} \Rightarrow B$

Hence the shorthand form,

F 21.5 A: $(\tau \cdot I^{\circ}{\sim}\gamma^{r}C^{v}) \propto B$

In response, Z adopts some other background theory (some other value of τ) which entails the position Z: $I^{\circ}H^{r}{\sim}C^{\sim v} \rightarrow {\sim}B$, and then reasons to a final conclusion by affirming $I^{\circ}H^{r}{\sim}C^{\sim v}$,

F 21.6 Z: $\{[\tau \rightarrow (I^{\circ}H^{r}{\sim}C^{\sim v} \rightarrow {\sim}B)] \cdot \tau \cdot I^{\circ}H^{r}{\sim}C^{\sim v}\} \Rightarrow {\sim}B$

Hence,

F 21.7 $Z: (\tau \cdot I^{o}H^{r}{\sim}C^{\sim v}) \propto {\sim}B$

Exercise set 21.1

Derive τ positions from the following arguments in vertical form, supplying the most specific values of κ or η variables.

Example: $A: I^{p}{\sim}H^{r}\kappa$

(1)	$\tau \rightarrow (I^{p}{\sim}H^{r}{\sim}\chi \rightarrow B)$
(2)	τ
(3)	$I^{p}{\sim}H^{r}{\sim}\chi$
conclusion	B

1 $Z: I^{\sim p}H^{r}\kappa^{\sim v}$
2 $A: I^{p}\eta^{\sim r}{\sim}C^{\sim v}$
3 $A: S\eta^{r}C^{v}$
4 $Z: IH^{r}\kappa^{\sim v}$
5 $Z: I^{p}\eta^{\sim r}{\sim}\chi$

Exercise set 21.2

Write both complete and simplified horizontal τ positions for the arguments in Exercise set 21.1.

Example: $A: I^{p}{\sim}H^{r}\kappa$

Answer: $A: \{[\tau \rightarrow (I^{p}{\sim}H^{r}{\sim}\chi \rightarrow B)] \cdot \tau \cdot I^{p}{\sim}H^{r}{\sim}\chi\} \Rightarrow B$
$A: (\tau \cdot I^{p}{\sim}H^{r}{\sim}\chi) \propto B$

22 Individualism and collectivism

In order to identify the more specific background theories, we will first distinguish between theories about individual interests and theories about the interests of society. The word *individualist* will be used to characterise *any background theory about some individual interest.* The word *collectivist* will be used to characterise *any background theory about the interests of society as a whole.* Like τ, these theories will still have a placeholder quality, as they are not yet the most specific background theories. But they provide the last step towards identifying the full set of background theories.

22.1 Individualism

The term *individualist* is to be understood neutrally. It will not always mean *pro*-individual – that the argument in question *favours* the individual rights claim. It means only that the argument is framed in terms of the interests of some I actor. The variable ι (iota) will be used to characterise individualist positions: for all individualist assertions, the variable τ takes the value ι. That is, for all τ positions, if $\alpha = \mathrm{I}$, then $\tau = \iota$,

BF(ι) $\theta: (\iota \cdot \mathrm{I}\eta\kappa) \propto \beta$

In A positions, this form of argument does indeed attribute interests to the individual actor in order to favour an individual rights claim,

F 22.1 $\mathrm{A}: (\iota \cdot \mathrm{I}\eta\kappa) \propto \mathrm{B}$

By contrast, in Z positions this form of argument attributes interests to the individual actor in order to oppose an individual rights claim,

F 22.2 $\mathrm{Z}: (\iota \cdot \mathrm{I}\eta\kappa) \propto \sim\mathrm{B}$

In *Laskey*, the A position comports two individualist arguments. One of them emphasises the consensual nature of the acts,

F 22.3 $\quad$ A: $(\iota \cdot I^{\circ}{\sim}\gamma^{r}C^{v}) \propto B$

The other emphasises the acts' insufficiently harmful character,

F 22.4 $\quad$ A: $(\iota \cdot I^{\circ}{\sim}H^{r}{\sim}\chi) \propto B$

The respondent rebuts both positions by asserting that the acts are sufficiently harmful to invalidate any consent in fact,

F 22.5 $\quad$ Z: $(\iota \cdot I^{\circ}H^{r}{\sim}C^{\sim v}) \propto {\sim}B$

In the following chapter, we will further refine our understanding of the background theories in order to find values for ι in these kinds of arguments.

Exercise set 22.1

Derive ι positions from the following arguments in vertical form, supplying the most specific values of κ or η variables.

Example: A: $I^{p}{\sim}H^{r}\kappa$

(1)	$\iota \rightarrow (I^{p}{\sim}H^{r}{\sim}\chi \rightarrow B)$
(2)	ι
(3)	$I^{p}{\sim}H^{r}{\sim}\chi$
conclusion	B

1 A: $I^{p}H^{\sim r}\kappa^{\sim v}$
2 Z: $I^{p}{\sim}H^{\sim r}\kappa$
3 A: $I{\sim}\gamma^{r}\kappa^{v}$
4 Z: $I^{\sim p}\eta^{r}{\sim}C^{\sim v}$
5 Z: $IH^{r}\kappa^{v}$

Exercise set 22.2

Write complete and simplified horizontal ι positions for the arguments in Exercise set 22.1, supplying the most specific values of κ or η variables.

Example: A: $I^{p}{\sim}H^{r}\kappa$

Answer: A: $\{[\iota \rightarrow (I^{p}{\sim}H^{r}{\sim}\chi \rightarrow B)] \cdot \iota \cdot I^{p}{\sim}H^{r}{\sim}\chi\} \Rightarrow B$
A: $(\iota \cdot I^{p}{\sim}H^{r}{\sim}\chi) \propto B$

22.2 Collectivism

As with the term 'individualist', the term *collectivist* will not necessarily mean *pro*-collectivist. It means only that the argument is framed in terms of the interests of the S actor. The variable δ (delta) will be used to characterise collectivist positions: for all collectivist assertions, the variable τ takes the value δ. In other words, for all θ positions, if $\alpha = S$, then $\tau = \delta$,

F 22.6 $\theta\colon (\delta \cdot S\eta^{r}\kappa) \propto \beta$

Recall, moreover, that assertions about society as a whole appear only in arguments about right-based harms,

BF(δ) $\theta\colon (\delta \cdot S\eta\kappa) \propto \beta$

In the Z position, this form of argument characterises the harm as unacceptable, and as lacking valid public consent, thus favouring some collective interest over the individual rights claim,

F 22.7 $Z\colon (\delta \cdot SH^{r}{\sim}C) \propto {\sim}B$

For example, citing empirical research or even a referendum, Z can argue that the public do not support the individual right – that the public volitionally withholds consent to incur any harm caused by the individual exercise of the right,

F 22.8 $Z\colon (\delta \cdot SH^{r}{\sim}C^{v}) \propto {\sim}B$

Alternatively, Z can argue that government may itself determine the public interest, regardless of actual levels of public support – that government may legitimately deem the harm caused by the exercise of the right to be unacceptable, and thus maintains the prerogative to determine that the public cannot validly consent to incur the harm,

F 22.9 $Z\colon (\delta \cdot SH^{r}{\sim}C^{\sim v}) \propto {\sim}B$

In *Jersild*, for example, no detailed reference was made to actual public opinion. Rather, the government asserted its prerogative (indeed, its duty, under international law) to determine that the public cannot validly consent to incur harms caused by racist expression.

In response, the A position can deny that the harm to society as a whole is unacceptable,

F 22.10 $A\colon (\delta \cdot S{\sim}H^{r}{\sim}\chi) \propto B$

Alternatively, the A position could try, as was done in *Dudgeon*, to adduce evidence of public support,

F 22.11 A: $(\delta \cdot S{\sim}\gamma^{r}C^{v}) \propto B$

When we begin the search for values of δ, we will examine these various kinds of arguments in greater detail. (As with τ, it will become clear that ι and δ also function as strongly exclusive variables, so the symbols ι° and δ° would be meaningless. Their most specific values exclude all of the others.)

Exercise set 22.3

Derive δ positions from the following arguments in vertical form, supplying the most specific values of κ or η variables.

Example: A: $S{\sim}H^{r}\kappa$

(1)	$\delta \rightarrow (S{\sim}H^{r}{\sim}\chi \rightarrow B)$
(2)	δ
(3)	$S{\sim}H^{r}{\sim}\chi$
conclusion	B

1 Z: $SH^{r}\kappa^{\sim v}$ 2 A: $S{\sim}\gamma^{r}\kappa^{v}$ 3 Z: $S\eta^{r}{\sim}C^{v}$

Exercise set 22.4

Write complete and simplified horizontal δ positions for the arguments in Exercise set 22–3, supplying the most specific values of κ or η variables.

Example: A: $S{\sim}H^{r}\kappa$

Answer: A: $\{[\delta \rightarrow (S{\sim}H^{r}{\sim}\chi \rightarrow B)] \cdot \delta \cdot S{\sim}H^{r}{\sim}\chi\} \Rightarrow B$
A: $(\delta \cdot S{\sim}H^{r}{\sim}\chi) \propto B$

22.3 Schema of individualist and collectivist theories

We have thus far identified two values for τ,

Ps(τ) $\tau \subset \iota, \delta$

> ***Exercise set 22-5***
>
> Draw a tree diagram of τ values and a tree diagram of α values, connecting their corresponding variables with dotted lines.

In the remainder of the book, we will examine more precise values for ι and δ. We will first examine three distinct values for ι, i.e. three 'individualist' background theories. Two of them will be called *liberal*, and will be designated with the variable 'L'. The third will be *anti-liberal* and will be designated with the symbol ~L,

Ps(ι) $\iota \subset$ L, ~L

We will then examine three values for δ, i.e. three 'collectivist' background theories. Two of them will be called *democratic*, and will be designated with the variable 'D'. The third will be *anti-democratic* and will be designated with the symbol ~D,

Ps(δ) $\delta \subset$ D, ~D

> ***Exercise set 22.6***
>
> Draw a tree diagram of all τ values introduced thus far.

> ***Exercise set 22.7***
>
> Derive the following theorems, using only postulates.
>
> *Example:* $\tau \subset$ L, ~L, δ
>
> | *Answer:* | (1) | $\tau \subset \iota, \delta$ | Ps(τ) |
> |---|---|---|---|
> | | conclusion | $\tau \subset$ L, ~L , δ | Ps(ι) |
>
> 1 $\tau \subset \iota$, D, ~D
> 2 $\tau \subset$ L, ~L, D, ~D

Part V

The background theories

23 Volitional liberalism

In this chapter, we examine one of the individualist theories identified as *liberal*. The second appears in the next chapter. All of the background theories are compiled in Appendix 1.

23.1 Volition [θ: ($L^{\kappa} \cdot I\eta\chi^{v}$) $\propto$ β]

In *Laskey*, one A position asserts valid, individual volitional consent as a basis for claiming that the right to privacy has been breached [A: ($\iota \cdot I^{\circ}{\sim}\gamma^{r}C^{v}$) $\propto$ B]. The κ value (C^{v}) becomes decisive in that argument, as it renders the existence, nature or level of harm irrelevant. The claimants assert that it is the free will of the individual actors – their volitional consent – which should decide the case. Recall that, had the state adduced evidence of volitional non-consent (${\sim}C^{v}$) by some non-personal actor ($I^{\sim p}$), it could have made a straightforward claim of assault, battery or rape [Z: ($\iota \cdot I^{\sim p}H^{r}{\sim}C^{v}$) $\propto$ ~B]. That Z position asserts the relevance of both harm and consent, valid non-consent providing the very basis for sufficient harm. What that Z position crucially shares with the A position is the element of volition (κ^{v}) – the attribution to the actor of ${\sim}C^{v}$ or C^{v}, respectively.

The term *liberal* (L) will be used to denote that theory as *an individualist background theory which adduces volitional consent or non-consent (χ^{v}) as a basis for a finding that a right has or has not been violated*. That is, we will denominate as liberal (L) any β position which attributes a χ^{v} value to any I actor,

F 23.1 $\quad \theta: \{[L \rightarrow (I\eta\chi^{v} \rightarrow \beta)] \cdot L \cdot I\eta\chi^{v}\} \Rightarrow \beta$

F 23.2 $\quad \theta: (L \cdot I\eta\chi^{v}) \propto \beta$

In the next chapter, we will examine an alternative liberal position, not based on consent. To distinguish the two, we will attach a superscript κ to this value of L so as to label it as consent-based. We will call this background theory a *theory of volitional liberalism* ($\iota = L^{\kappa}$):

Theory of Volitional Liberalism (L^{κ}): A θ position attributing χ^{v} to an I actor is a volitional liberal position (L^{κ}),

F 23.3 θ: $\{[L^{\kappa} \rightarrow (I\eta\chi^{v} \rightarrow \beta)] \cdot L^{\kappa} \cdot I\eta\chi^{v}\} \Rightarrow \beta$

BF(L^{κ}) θ: $(L^{\kappa} \cdot I\eta\chi^{v}) \propto \beta$

L^{κ} is only our first background theory. In order to examine it more closely, we face the predicament of having to compare it with others, which can only be taken up one at a time. Therefore, any other individualist theories will simply appear with the variable ι, and collectivist theories will appear with the variable δ. Although L^{κ} has been introduced first, it by no means represents the most common type of argument. Arguments expressly focused on individual consent appear in a fairly small number of disputes. In some cases, as we will see, that is because their principles are so widely accepted as to provide little room for controversy, the dispute then shifting to questions of harm. In other cases, it is because they are so controversial as to arise only where no better arguments are available.

23.2 Individual volitional consent to incur right-based harm [A: $(L^{\kappa} \cdot I{\sim}\gamma^{r}C^{v}) \propto B$]

The position A: $(L^{\kappa} \cdot I{\sim}\gamma^{r}C^{v}) \propto B$ is distinctly libertarian. It asserts that individual actors have the right to incur a harm *because* they validly consent to incur it. A paradigm case would be the claim, even of a healthy individual, of a right to commit suicide. Death, the ultimate harm, would be claimed to be irrelevant, as long as it is competently chosen. Somewhat less dramatically, in *Laskey*, the participants' right to engage in sado-masochism, which, at least with regard to 'heavier' practices, cannot easily rely on assertions of insufficient harm, relies on a theory of volitional consent, aiming to render the question of harm irrelevant. In *Dudgeon*, one of the claimants' tactics is to oppose the sodomy law by challenging the state's characterisation of the law as necessary to protect vulnerable individuals: the right is sought only with respect to competent adults giving volitional consent.

Libertarian arguments readily arise in opposition to health and safety regulations. In a case[1] brought under article 2(1) of the German *Grundgesetz*[2] (hereinafter the *Easy Rider* case), the Bundesverfassungsgericht rejected the claimant's assertion of a right to ride a motorcycle without wearing a helmet. When confronted with the safety rationale underlying the requirement, the claimant asserted the right to reach an individual decision about the risk involved in riding without a helmet. He argued that an individual assessment of risk, once made, must be respected by government without any further inquiry into harm: the only criterion should be volitional consent[3] [A: $(L^{\kappa} \cdot I^{p}{\sim}\gamma^{r}C^{v}) \propto B$]. There will be more to say about this case in the following chapters.

In many cases, libertarian views, while not the focus of the dispute, do hover in the background. In *Jersild*, Denmark asserts an interest in protecting society generally from racist speech [Z: $(\delta \cdot SH^{r}{\sim}C^{\sim v}) \propto {\sim}B$]. That interest comports an express or implied interest in protecting individual members of racial minorities from the offence caused by such speech [Z: $(\iota \cdot I^{\sim p}H^{r}{\sim}C^{\sim v}) \propto {\sim}B$]. In theory, the journalist might well have argued that some members of such minorities may not desire such protective legislation, as they may place a higher value on the right of free expression, on the old maxim 'I disapprove of what you say, but I will defend to the death your right to say it',[4] thus consenting to incur the offence caused by racist speech [A: $(L^{\kappa} \cdot I^{\sim p}{\sim}\gamma^{r}C^{v}) \propto B$]. However, that argument did not figure prominently in the case. Rather than cast the dispute in terms of consent on the part of members of minority groups, the Court characterised the harm as insufficient, relative to the greater good of unrestrained journalism on matters of public interest [A: $(\iota \cdot I^{\sim p}{\sim}H^{r}{\sim}\chi) \propto B$]. In *Otto-Preminger-Institut*, the claimant opposes the state's assertion of harm to *individual* viewers of the film by noting the volitional character of viewing the work in a special art house cinema, and of the spectators having received notice about the content of the work in promotional materials. Those who do not wish to view it need not do so, and thus are not harmed [A: $(\iota \cdot I^{\sim p}{\sim}H^{r}{\sim}\chi) \propto B$]. Those who do wish to view it do so by free consent [A: $(L^{\kappa} \cdot I^{\sim p}{\sim}\gamma^{r}C^{v}) \propto B$].

In *Kokkinakis*, the statute banning proselytism defined the act as follows:

> By 'proselytism' is meant, in particular, any direct or indirect attempt to intrude on the religious beliefs of a person of a different religious persuasion . . . with the aim of undermining those beliefs, either by any kind of inducement or promise of an inducement or moral support . . ., or by fraudulent means or by taking advantage of his inexperience, trust, need, low intellect or naïvety.[5]

Mr Kokkinakis had been imprisoned for having attempted to convince a woman to embrace the beliefs of the Jehovah's Witnesses by having taken advantage of her 'inexperience . . . low intellect and naïvety'.[6] Kokkinakis argued that he had used no coercive or fraudulent means; that the woman, who was the wife of an Orthodox church cantor, was not inexperienced in matters of religion; and that she had not been shown to be of low intellect or naïve. She had freely allowed him into her home, where he then spoke with her for no more than 15 minutes, and, moreover, had not succeeded in changing her beliefs.[7] On that view, she had freely and competently consented to engage in the conversation [A: $(L^{\kappa} \cdot I^{\sim p}{\sim}\gamma^{r}C^{v}) \propto B$].

23.3 Individual volitional non-consent to incur right-based harm [Z: $(L^{\kappa} \cdot I^{\sim p}H^{r}{\sim}C^{v}) \propto {\sim}B$]

The 'arch-rebuttal' to an argument of the form A: $I{\sim}\gamma^{r}C^{v} \propto B$ is an argument asserting that there is *no* violation of a right where the exercise of that right would unacceptably harm a party validly *not* consenting to incur that harm. That is the very formula for classical concepts of criminal or civil liability, that is, for concepts of harm based on the non-consent of parties who are otherwise competent to consent. The respondent asserts that the right can be restricted in the interest of preventing harm to a person validly not consenting to incur that harm [Z: $(L^{\kappa} \cdot I^{\sim p}H^{r}{\sim}C^{v}) \propto {\sim}B$]. That argument applies only to the non-personal actor, as there is no situation in which the respondent would attribute valid *volitional* non-consent to a personal actor who is challenging the restriction on the right – that is, there is no dispute in which Z would assert Z: $(L^{\kappa} \cdot I^{p}H^{r}{\sim}C^{v}) \propto {\sim}B$. Presumably, a personal actor who does not want to incur that right-based harm will not seek to exercise the right, and no claim will arise.

In *Dudgeon* or *Laskey*, the claimants presumably accept the argument that there would be no violation of the right to privacy if valid individual consent were not given to engage in the acts [Z: $(L^{\kappa} \cdot I^{\sim p}H^{r}{\sim}C^{v}) \propto {\sim}B$]. The claimants assert that the relevant individual actors are those who give valid consent [A: $(L^{\kappa} \cdot I^{\circ}{\sim}\gamma^{r}C^{v}) \propto B$]. Similarly, one of the standard rights debates is whether sheer speech or expression can suffice to constitute unacceptable harm. The very existence of defamation law [Z: $(L^{\kappa} \cdot I^{\sim p}H^{r}{\sim}C^{v}) \propto {\sim}B$] suggests an affirmative answer, although, as in *Lingens*, disputes continue to arise with respect to specific works. The issue of harmful speech or expression is particularly controversial with regard to racial, ethnic or religious invective. In *Jersild* or *Otto-Preminger*, the Z positions did refer *inter alia* to individuals who had specifically complained about the offensive content of the works in question.[8] [Z: $(L^{\kappa} \cdot I^{\sim p}H^{r}{\sim}C^{v}) \propto {\sim}B$]. *Mellacher* illustrates a very different kind of dispute, yet employing the same form of argument: individuals entitled to low-rent accommodations would not have consented to forego that entitlement [Z: $(L^{\kappa} \cdot I^{\sim p}H^{r}{\sim}C^{v}) \propto {\sim}B$].[9] In *Lingens*, *Jersild*, *Otto-Preminger* or *Mellacher*, the claimant cannot reply with an assertion of valid consent given by the affected non-personal actors [A: $(L^{\kappa} \cdot I^{\sim p}{\sim}\gamma^{r}C^{v}) \propto B$], and responds instead with an assertion that those actors are insufficiently harmed, as we will see in the next chapter.

23.4 Individual volitional consent to incur restriction-based harm [Z: $(L^{\kappa} \cdot I^{p}{\sim}\gamma^{\sim r}C^{v}) \propto {\sim}B$]

With respect to its policing function, an ideal of the liberal state might be stated, in simplified form, as follows. The state is prohibited from impeding that conduct which is otherwise lawful, even if it is disliked by the majority or is inconvenient to the state. It is precisely that exclusion from the domain of lawful conduct which then justifies a policing function to prevent and punish unlawful conduct, indeed by such coercive means as police forces and prisons. Accordingly, within liberal rights discourse, disagreements arise with regard to the *means* of coercive control – the competence or incompetence, the moderation or excess with which it is exerted – but not with regard to the very legitimacy of a coercive policing function. The Z position that such means have not been deployed in violation of a right is an argument that they have been deployed either without sufficient harm to the individual (we examine that position later) or with the individual's valid consent. As to the latter argument, the state might, as a benefit-restriction, give some convicted criminals a choice between remaining in prison, or being released on condition of submitting, say, to castration or to electronic tagging. An otherwise competent prisoner choosing such an option might then be deemed by Z to have validly consented to it [Z: $(L^{\kappa} \cdot I^{p}{\sim}\gamma^{\sim r}C^{v}) \propto {\sim}B$]. We will soon see that one response open to the claimant is to argue that such consent cannot be deemed valid.

That Z position has not yet become very common, as most restriction-based arguments arise in disputes, as in the cases concerning torture or inhuman or degrading treatment, where there is no serious contention on the part of the respondent that the personal actor had given consent to incur the treatment at issue. The disputes in those cases tend to focus more on the existence, character or degree of the harm, and not on the giving or withholding of valid consent to incur that harm. The position may become more frequent, with the increased use of alternative forms of punishment for criminal offences, or with advances in medical technology.

23.5 Individual volitional non-consent to incur restriction-based harm [A: $(L^{\kappa} \cdot I^{p}H^{\sim r}{\sim}C^{v}) \propto B$]

Many complaints about restriction-based harms assume the non-consent of the personal actor in a way which is not contested by the respondent, and thus may not be expressly stated, or emphasised, in adjudication. *Ireland v. UK*, *Lawless*, *Brogan* and *Brannigan* included complaints that individuals had been detained for excessive periods of time without having been brought before a magistrate or having been charged with any offences. In such cases, there is rarely any suggestion that the detainees had willingly submitted to such conditions. Any attempt by the state to adduce evidence of volitional individual consent [Z: $(L^{\kappa} \cdot I^{p}{\sim}\gamma^{\sim r}C^{v}) \propto {\sim}B$] would raise not only questions about whether consent was given in fact [A: $(L^{\kappa} \cdot I^{p}H^{\sim r}{\sim}C^{v}) \propto B$], but also – even if it is given in fact – about the validity of such consent, for example where the state's means involve coercion, or where the personal actor is a minor [A: $(\iota \cdot I^{p}H^{\sim r}{\sim}C^{\sim v}) \propto B$]. In most other cases, where personal actors are assumed to be competent, the claimant asserts or simply assumes that that personal actor has not given valid consent to incur the treatment at issue.

Recall that, in *Aksoy*, one means by which the state rebutted allegations of torture or inhuman or degrading treatment was to assert that an insufficient causal link had been drawn between the injuries suffered and the conduct of state officials [Z: $(\iota \cdot I^{p}{\sim}H^{\sim r}{\sim}\chi) \propto {\sim}B$]. The Court rejected that argument, stating that 'where an individual is taken into police custody in good health but is found to be injured at the time of release, it is incumbent on the State to provide a plausible explanation as to the causing of the injury, failing which a clear issue arises under Article 3 of the Convention'.[10] The Court's view entailed a *prima facie* presumption of sufficient harm. There was no suggestion that consent had been given (or indeed *could* be given in such circumstances), and indeed volitional non-consent could readily be assumed [A: $(L^{\kappa} \cdot I^{p}H^{\sim r}{\sim}C^{v}) \propto B$]. A fortiori, in *McCann*, an individual who was killed would be presumed not to have given volitional consent. Moreover, in such cases, the claimant argues or indeed assumes that valid consent *could not* be given to incur such harms [A: $(\iota \cdot I^{p}H^{\sim r}{\sim}C^{\sim v}) \propto B$].

Sometimes the state acts secretly against the individual, with the intention that the individual should not know what the state is doing, precluding any possibility of volitional consent or non-consent. In *Kruslin* and *Huvig*, concerning police interference with correspondence and telephone wires, the claimants alleged a breach of ECHR article 8. In such cases, the A position assumes volitional non-consent as part of the very characterisation of the intrusive act [A: $(L^{\kappa} \cdot I^{p}H^{\sim r}{\sim}C^{v}) \propto B$]: the state's whole purpose is that such intrusions should occur without the knowledge of the individual who is under surveillance. Here again, that A position can be complemented by an argument that no valid consent *could* be given [A: $(\iota \cdot I^{p}H^{\sim r}{\sim}C^{\sim v}) \propto B$].

In a case from 1987 (hereinafter the *Small Town Blues* case),[11] the Dutch High Court examined a privacy claim by a woman living in the city of Edam, whose social benefits were terminated on the basis of information disclosed to the authorities about her living arrangements. The complainant was divorced and living with three minor children. She had been receiving a level of benefits conferred only upon persons who are not married and not living in a relationship which would qualify as economically integrated (*een economische eenheid*). As luck would have it, a social services employee was also a neighbour, and submitted to the department memoranda about her relationship with a man, which included references to, or inferences about, their sexual life. One memorandum concluded that the relationship resembled a familial bond qualifying as economically integrated, and recommended a reduction in benefits. The claimant discovered these memoranda upon subsequent inspection of her file. As in cases involving intrusions into correspondence or telephone conversations, she does not specifically adduce her own non-consent; that is assumed by the sheer bringing of the complaint. The point is that she never gave consent to have details of her private life used for purposes of gathering information about her financial circumstances. Non-consent on her part could be assumed under a volitional liberal theory [A: $(L^{\kappa} \cdot I^{p}H^{\sim r}{\sim}C^{v}) \propto B$] as well as a non-volitional theory [A: $(\iota \cdot I^{p}H^{\sim r}{\sim}C^{\sim v}) \propto B$].

At this point it is easier to draw a comparison to a private-law dispute. Recall the hypothetical dispute introduced earlier between baker Bernard, who has agreed to purchase perishable cream, and farmer Fatima, who has agreed to deliver it. Bernard, claiming to have duly rescinded the contract, subsequently refuses to accept delivery, and Fatima is unable to sell the cream elsewhere. Bernard's attempted rescission can be understood as a restriction on Fatima's asserted right to enforce the contract. The dispute then concerns the legality of that restriction. Fatima might, for example, argue that the attempted rescission was improperly communicated, or not otherwise agreed to by her, thus causing her an unacceptable economic harm [A: $(L^{\kappa} \cdot I^{p}H^{\sim r}{\sim}C^{v}) \propto B$]. Baker Bernard could counter that the rescission was communicated and agreed in a way which rendered acceptable any harm incurred by Fatima [A: $(L^{\kappa} \cdot I^{p}{\sim}\gamma^{\sim r}C^{v}) \propto B$]. That analysis certainly elicits elements of the dispute which are of particular concern to liberal society: the way in which the law construes acts of will between private parties. Yet it also suggests the limits of the analysis for private law. The central question of when and how a rescission would be lawful in such a case will commonly entail factual issues which cannot be illuminated by the background theories. Many examples could be found for which the background theories would have no real relevance at all. Others could be found where, as in *Fatima v. Bernard*, they illuminate the case, but only to limited degree. Accordingly, the background theories do not warrant drawing a clear line between 'liberal' and 'ordinary' rights disputes, but do provide a paradigm for disputes specifically concerning civil rights and liberties.

Exercise set 23.1

Write complete and simplified horizontal L^{κ} positions for the following arguments, supplying the most specific values of η or κ variables.

Example: A: $I^{\sim p}\eta^{r}C^{v}$

Answer: A: $\{[L^{\kappa} \rightarrow (I^{\sim p}{\sim}\gamma^{r}C^{v} \rightarrow B)] \cdot L^{\kappa} \cdot I^{\sim p}{\sim}\gamma^{r}C^{v}\} \Rightarrow B$
A: $(L^{\kappa} \cdot I^{\sim p}{\sim}\gamma^{r}C^{v}) \propto B$

1 A: $I^{\sim p}{\sim}\gamma^{r}\kappa^{v}$
2 A: $I^{\circ}\eta^{r}C^{v}$
3 Z: $I^{p}\eta^{\sim r}C^{v}$
4 Z: $I^{p}{\sim}\gamma^{\sim r}\kappa^{v}$

24 Non-consensual liberalism

In this chapter, we examine a second theory which can be called *liberal*, but on the basis of a principle of harm rather than consent.

24.1 Insufficient harm to the individual actor [θ: ($L^{\eta} \cdot I{\sim}H{\sim}\chi$) $\propto$ β]

We have seen that the A positions in *Jersild* or *Otto-Preminger* do not refer primarily to the volitional consent of non-personal actors [A: $(\iota \cdot I^{\sim p}{\sim}\gamma^{r}C^{v}) \propto B$]. In so far as the interests of any given individual are concerned, the more prominent A position asserts that, relative to the value of free expression, the works are not sufficiently harmful to justify the restrictions, rendering irrelevant questions of individual consent [A: $(\iota \cdot I^{\sim p}{\sim}H^{r}{\sim}\chi) \propto B$]. In that position, it is the assertion of insufficient harm ($\sim H^{r}$) which, rendering consent irrelevant ($\sim\chi$), structures the argument. That argument, too, can be called liberal: individuals should be free to do that which causes no unacceptable harm; not *because* any affected individual actors may consent, but rather regardless of their consent. In this context, we can say that the term *liberal* denotes *an individualist background theory which adduces insufficient harm* ($\sim$H), hence *irrelevant consent* ($\sim\chi$), *as a basis for a finding that a right had or had not been violated.* In order to distinguish this liberal theory as a theory which is harm-based rather than consent-based, we will use a superscript η marker (L^{η}):

> **Theory of Non-consensual Liberalism** (L^{η}): A θ position attributing $\sim\chi$ to an I actor is a non-consensual liberal position (L^{η}),
>
> F 24.1 $\quad \theta: [(L^{\eta} \cdot I{\sim}H{\sim}\chi) \rightarrow \beta) \cdot L^{\eta} \cdot I{\sim}H{\sim}\chi] \Rightarrow \beta$
>
> BF(L^{η}) $\quad \theta: (L^{\eta} \cdot I{\sim}H{\sim}\chi) \propto \beta$

The wording could substitute ~H for $\sim\chi$ with no material change in meaning, since ~H implies $\sim\chi$, just as $\sim\chi$ implies ~H. Accordingly, it is unnecessary to refer to both elements. The choice in favour of the consent symbol provides consistency, and thus easier comparison, with the theories for which consent is decisive, such as the Theory of Volitional Liberalism.

24.2 Insufficient right-based harm [A: $(L^{\eta} \cdot I{\sim}H^{r}{\sim}\chi) \propto B$]

In so far as the respondent asserts an unacceptable, right-based harm [Z: $(\iota \cdot IH^{r}{\sim}C) \propto {\sim}B$], the claimant can attempt to portray the harm as acceptable. In *Laskey*, it was argued that the physical injuries, even some of the more severe ones, had caused no lasting health problems, and thus should not be considered unacceptable [A: $(L^{\eta} \cdot I^{\circ}{\sim}H^{r}{\sim}\chi) \propto B$]. Another argument of this same formal structure was alluded to, but not emphasised. The claimants noted that the sadomasochistic conduct was pursued in the course of *sexual* activity. In other words, as a matter of relative harm, the pleasure gained through sexual sadomasochism exceeds the harm incurred, hence, relatively speaking, no harm at all – i.e. pleasure, rather than harm – and therefore no unacceptable harm. The Court, however, was unwilling to place that, so to speak, 'subjective' claim of pleasure over the state's, so to speak, 'objective' claim of unacceptable physical harm [Z: $(\iota \cdot I^{\circ}H^{r}{\sim}C^{\sim v}) \propto {\sim}B$].

The claimants' positions in *Lingens*, *Handyside*, *Jersild* and *Otto-Preminger-Institut*, to the extent that they concern harm to identified or implied individual actors, include similar concepts of insufficient harm. In each case, the claimant argues that the harm is insufficient relative to the expressive value of the work. In *Kjeldsen*, the parents, seeking to exercise rights over their children's education, claim that their parental choices in matters of sexuality and morals would cause less harm to their children than would be caused if the children were exposed to compulsory sex education in school [A: $(L^{\eta} \cdot I^{\sim p}{\sim}H^{r}{\sim}\chi) \propto B$]. In *Kokkinakis*, the state seeks to depict the woman concerned as being inexperienced, of low intellect and naïve. The Court, however, finding no convincing evidence to that effect, rejects that position, in favour of the claimant's argument that the proselytism had not caused her unacceptable harm [A: $(L^{\eta} \cdot I^{\sim p}{\sim}H^{r}{\sim}\chi) \propto B$]. In *Brüggemann*, denial of the personhood of the foetus (if only at the earlier stages of pregnancy) is a denial of harm to that $I^{\sim p}$ actor. The claimants also deny that unacceptable harm is caused to the individual woman, particularly in view of the relatively greater harm of penalising abortion [A: $(L^{\eta} \cdot I^{\circ}{\sim}H^{r}{\sim}\chi) \propto B$].

Disputes concerning the free exercise of private property rights are also illustrative. For the claimant in *Mellacher* to take an extreme libertarian position – 'It's my property to do with as I like' [A: $(L^{\kappa} \cdot \alpha{\sim}\gamma^{r}C^{v}) \propto B$] – would be difficult to maintain in a contemporary *Sozialstaat*, raising the further question as to harms suffered by tenants having to pay high rents. The fuller claimants' position thus included harm-based arguments. It was argued that a sustained period of economic growth in Austria after 1967, along with an increase in moderately priced housing, had eliminated the need for the more intrusive measures authorised under the disputed legislation. The landowners asserted, albeit unsuccessfully, that insufficient harm would be caused to the tenants [A: $(L^{\eta} \cdot I^{\sim p}{\sim}H^{r}{\sim}\chi) \propto B$] through the landlords' exercise of their property rights.

In the *Easy Rider* case, the Bundesverfassungsgericht examines an interesting A response to Z's claim that riding without a helmet increases the risk of injury. As in *Laskey*, the A position provides a theory of harm complementary to – indeed, simply another version of – its consent-based, libertarian theory: 'The responsible citizen should able to *evaluate the risk personally* and to act accordingly.'[1] In other words, the degree of risk should be a matter of subjective assessment. If the otherwise competent individual rider finds the risk to be acceptable, then it should be regarded as such $[A: (L^{\eta} \cdot I^{p}{\sim}H^{r}{\sim}\chi) \propto B]$. Of course, in that case, the argument is utterly derivative of a volitional-liberal argument: to say that determinations of harm should be left to the individual is to say that they are purely matters of individual consent. Ultimately, then, it is the libertarian argument which dominates the claimants' position in that case $[A: (L^{\kappa} \cdot I^{p}{\sim}\gamma^{r}C^{v}) \propto B]$.

F v. Switzerland[2] concerned a man who had been twice divorced. The third time he married a woman six weeks after meeting her, and filed for divorce barely two weeks thereafter. Having found the grounds for divorce to be adultery, the divorce court, pursuant to national law, prohibited the man from marrying for a period of three years. The man asserted a violation of the right to marry,[3] prevailing only by a 9–8 vote. The state defended its temporary prohibition as a measure intended 'to protect . . . the rights of others and even the person affected by the prohibition'.[4] By 'the rights of others', the state meant not only future spouses, but also any children who might be born of the remarriage.[5] The state also argued that the prohibition served the man's own interests by creating a temporary cooling off period 'to take time for reflection . . . to protect him from himself'.[6]

As to his own interests (I^{p}), the man might have argued, under a theory of volitional liberalism, that his valid consent to remarry obviates inquiry into harm caused to himself $[A: (L^{\kappa} \cdot I^{p}{\sim}\gamma^{r}C^{v}) \propto B]$. Yet the Court, albeit unwilling to dismiss the relevance of harm, did deem the harm to be insufficient. It found that the man would cause no unacceptable harm to himself in exercising the marriage right,[7] thus obviating inquiry into the validity of his consent $[A: (L^{\eta} \cdot I^{p}{\sim}H^{r}{\sim}\chi) \propto B]$. Of course, the complaint is brought precisely because the man does claim to give valid consent to exercise the right in this case.

As to the interests of a potential spouse ($I^{\neg p}$), the claimant might have adduced a classically liberal position that it would be the responsibility of a future spouse to 'know what she's getting into' before consenting to marry him. Such consent would obviate any inquiry into harm $[A: (L^{\kappa} \cdot I^{\neg p}{\sim}\gamma^{r}C^{v}) \propto B]$. However, that was not the Court's approach. The Court noted the measure's punitive effect upon a future spouse who might want to exercise her own article 12 right to marry, and whose interests are not necessarily better protected during the intervening period before the applicant is again permitted to wed, thus forcing her either to leave the man or to remain with him, but without the legal securities of marriage.[8] However great the harm caused by the personal actor's exercise of the article 12 right, it was less than the harm caused by the state's abridgement of the right, and thereby became an insufficient harm to justify interference with the right [A: $(L^{\eta} \cdot I^{\sim p}{\sim}H^{r}{\sim}\chi) \propto B$]. Similarly, as to the interests of future children, the Court found that the harm caused by the abridgement of the right, namely the prospect that they might be born out of wedlock, was greater than that caused by the applicant's exercise of the marriage right.[9]

An alternative argument of the same form might be read into *Dudgeon*, whereby the claimant adduces insufficient harm, hence irrelevant consent. After all, if homosexual acts are no more dangerous than heterosexual acts, what harm can come of them? Yet, as we have seen, even as to heterosexual acts, there is insufficient harm only in so far as valid consent is given. The claimant's stronger position therefore falls under the theory of volitional liberalism.

24.3 Insufficient restriction-based harm [Z: $(L^{\eta} \cdot I^{p}{\sim}H^{\sim r}{\sim}\chi) \propto {\sim}B$]

We have seen that Z positions can defend restriction-based harms by alleging valid consent on the part of the individual [Z: $(L^{\kappa} \cdot I^{p}{\sim}\gamma^{\sim r}C^{v}) \propto {\sim}B$]; but that – even if the individual has indeed consented in fact – such arguments only raise further questions about the validity of such consent in law [A: $(\iota \cdot I^{p}H^{\sim r}{\sim}C^{\sim v}) \propto B$]. An alternative for the respondent is to argue that individual consent is irrelevant, by arguing that the harm is not unacceptable [Z: $(L^{\eta} \cdot I^{p}{\sim}H^{\sim r}{\sim}\chi) \propto {\sim}B$]. In *Costello-Roberts*, the Court accepted Z's assertion that any physical or psychological harm caused by a slipper on the bare buttocks within a disciplinary context was insufficient to amount to inhuman or degrading treatment. The same Z position was adduced, albeit unsuccessfully, in *Tyrer*, where the government argued that factors such as the limited number of strokes with the birch, and the presence of a physician, overcame any suggestion that the harm to the individual was excessive. In *McCann*, we have seen that the assertion of insufficient harm relies on a relative harm. In the government's view, the use of deadly force was not unacceptable, in view of the risk of greater harm which might be caused by the suspects under the circumstances.

Cases such as *Tyrer* and *Costello-Roberts* reflect the Court's attempt to use some kind of 'minimum level of severity' test in examining complaints under article 3. The result is that, the more severe the apparent injuries, the more difficult it is for the state to characterise them as insufficient to justify a finding of breach. Where it is the state which is accused of inflicting the harm, another argument which the state, as respondent, may attempt is to assert that the harm is not the result of state action, and thus insufficient harm is caused *by the state*, as in *Aksoy*.

Of course, the concept of government-caused harm extends beyond the infliction of physical or psychological injuries. The harms alleged in *Brogan* and *Brannigan* do not concern ill-treatment in detention, but rather the legality of the detention itself. Having been detained without being brought before a magistrate or being informed of charges against them, the applicants claim that the duration of the detention was unacceptably long, and in that sense sufficiently harmful [A: $(L^{\kappa} \cdot I^{p}H^{\sim r}{\sim}C^{v}) \propto B$].

As we have seen, the state responses in these two cases are very different. *Brannigan* illustrates how a dispute is argued when a government has suspended legal protections of civil rights and liberties pursuant to a declared state of emergency. For the claimants, the level of conflict at the time was not grave enough to warrant a suspension of rights so broad in scope as to justify their periods of detention. That argument, in turn, entails an assertion of relative harm: any harm to the interests of the state due to the conflict in Northern Ireland was insufficient to justify reliance upon article 15. Accordingly, the government-caused harms relevant to the article 5 claim were sufficient to constitute a violation [A: $(L^{\kappa} \cdot I^{p}H^{\sim r}{\sim}C^{v}) \propto B$]. Nevertheless, the Court accepted the state's opposite view, namely, that the conflict in Northern Ireland was grave enough to justify the state's suspension of article 5 rights under article 15, and thus to warrant a finding that the harm caused to the detainees was insufficient [Z: $(L^{\eta} \cdot I^{p}{\sim}H^{\sim r}{\sim}\chi) \propto {\sim}B$]. In *Brogan*, decided five years earlier, no state of emergency under article 15 had been in effect. As we have seen, the Court might nevertheless have accepted the prevailing conflict as grounds for viewing the detentions as insufficiently harmful [Z: $(L^{\eta} \cdot I^{p}{\sim}H^{\sim r}{\sim}\chi) \propto {\sim}B$]. But it did not. The claimants prevailed [A: $(L^{\kappa} \cdot I^{p}H^{\sim r}{\sim}C^{v}) \propto B$]. In response to its defeat in *Brogan*, the government proclaimed the state of emergency which was then applied, successfully, to similar circumstances, in *Brannigan*.[10]

In *Kruslin* and *Huvig*, the state does not justify interference with correspondence or with telephone communications in absolute terms, but only as means of combating criminal acts, as authorised by article 8(2). For the Court, the question of sufficient or insufficient harm is then determined with reference to such factors as whether the circumstances under which such intrusions are authorised are prescribed with sufficient clarity in law[11] [Z: $(L^{\eta} \cdot I^{p}{\sim}H^{\sim r}{\sim}\chi) \propto {\sim}B$; A: $(L^{\kappa} \cdot I^{p}H^{\sim r}{\sim}C^{v}) \propto B$]. Similarly, in *Small Town Blues,* the state defends its intrusions on the privacy of the complainant by reference to a relative harm: the benefit of combating fraudulent or improper enjoyment of welfare benefits outweighed the harm caused by the use of the confidentially rendered 'tips', thus rendering the restriction-based harm insufficient to constitute a violation of the right to privacy [Z: $(L^{\eta} \cdot I^{p}{\sim}H^{\sim r}{\sim}\chi) \propto {\sim}B$; A: $(L^{\kappa} \cdot I^{p}H^{\sim r}{\sim}C^{v}) \propto B$].

Exercise set 24.1

Write complete and simplified horizontal L^{η} positions for the following arguments, supplying the most specific values of κ or η variables.

Example: A: $I^{\sim p}{\sim}H^{r}\kappa$

Answer: A: $\{[L^{\eta} \rightarrow (I^{\sim p}{\sim}H^{r}{\sim}\chi \rightarrow B)] \cdot L^{\eta} \cdot I^{\sim p}{\sim}H^{r}{\sim}\chi\} \Rightarrow B$
A: $(L^{\eta} \cdot I^{\sim p}{\sim}H^{r}{\sim}\chi) \propto B$

1 A: $I^{p}\gamma^{r}{\sim}\chi$
2 A: $I{\sim}H^{r}\kappa$
3 Z: $I^{p}\eta^{\sim r}{\sim}\chi$
4 Z: $I^{p}{\sim}H^{\sim r}\kappa$

24.4 Schema of individualist theories

In this chapter and the last, we have identified two liberal theories (L),

Ps(L) $L \subset L^{\kappa}, L^{\eta}$

In the next chapter, we will identify a non-liberal theory (~L).

Exercise set 24.2

Derive the following theorems, using only postulates.

1 $\iota \subset L^{\kappa}, L^{\eta}, {\sim}L$
2 $\tau \subset L^{\kappa}, L^{\eta}, {\sim}L, \delta$
3 $\tau \subset L^{\kappa}, L^{\eta}, {\sim}L, D, {\sim}D$

The theorem derived in Exercise set 24.2, problem 1 provides a statement of the most specific values of ι,

Th(ι) $\iota \subset L^{\kappa}, L^{\eta}, {\sim}L$

Exercise set 24.3

Redo Exercise set 24.2, problems 2 and 3, using the fewest possible steps.

Exercise set 24.4

Draw a tree diagram of all τ values introduced thus far.

25 Paternalism

In this chapter, we examine the third individualist theory. It is non-liberal, indeed anti-liberal, in so far as it attributes to the individual interests which disregard that individual's will.

25.1 Non-volition [θ: ($\sim$L $\cdot$ I$\eta\chi^{\sim v}$) $\propto$ β]

As we have seen, the state in *Laskey* adduced no evidence of coerced, deceived or otherwise unwilling participants – no evidence of volitional non-consent attributable to any non-personal actor [Z: (L^{κ} $\cdot$ $I^{\sim p}H^{r}{\sim}C^{v}$) $\propto$ $\sim$B]. It instead asserts that, the harm caused by the acts being unacceptable, the participants *cannot* validly consent to incur it [Z: (ι $\cdot$ $I^{\circ}H^{r}{\sim}C^{\sim v}$) $\propto$ $\sim$B]. That latter Z position asserts an individual interest not on the basis of, but rather in spite of, individual will: any consent given in fact is asserted to be invalid in law. We will call such a position *anti-liberal* or *paternalist* ($\sim$L):

> **Theory of Paternalism**: A θ position attributing $\chi^{\sim v}$ to an I actor is a paternalist, or anti-liberal, position ($\sim$L),
>
> F 25.1 $\quad\theta$: [($\sim$L $\cdot$ I$\eta\chi^{\sim v}$) $\rightarrow$ β) $\cdot$ $\sim$L $\cdot$ I$\eta\chi^{\sim v}$] $\Rightarrow$ β
>
> BF($\sim$L) $\quad\theta$: ($\sim$L $\cdot$ I$\eta\chi^{\sim v}$) $\propto$ β

25.2 Non-volitional non-consent to incur right-based harm [Z: ($\sim$L $\cdot$ $IH^{r}{\sim}C^{\sim v}$) $\propto$ $\sim$B]

Under the Sufficient Harm Axiom, an assertion of sufficient harm implies an assertion that the actor cannot validly consent to incur it [θ: (τ $\cdot$ αH$\sim$C) $\propto$ β]. In the *Easy Rider* case, the claimant's assertion of insufficient harm on the basis of individual volition [A: (L^{κ} $\cdot$ $I^{p}{\sim}\gamma^{r}C^{v}$) $\propto$ B] meets with the response that safety helmets do serve the purpose of reducing head injuries – which the claimant does not dispute on factual grounds – thus justifying a government determination that an individual driver's consent to incur such harm can be deemed invalid[1] [Z: ($\sim$L $\cdot$ $I^{p}H^{r}{\sim}C^{\sim v}$) $\propto$ $\sim$B].

In *Brüggemann*, the state assertion of interest in unborn life attributes some measure of personhood, and thus of status as an $I^{\sim p}$ actor, to the foetus, who must then be deemed to give non-volitional non-consent to be killed [Z: $(\sim L \cdot I^{\sim p}H^{r}{\sim}C^{\sim v}) \propto \sim B$]. The state assertion of interest in the woman's own welfare consists of a determination that she cannot validly consent to incur certain physiological or psychological risks of the procedure [Z: $(\sim L \cdot I^{p}H^{r}{\sim}C^{\sim v}) \propto \sim B$]. Similarly, laws prohibiting suicide, like laws prohibiting sadomasochism, deem individuals incompetent to consent to incur such harms. In *F v. Switzerland*, the state asserts an interest in protecting a potential spouse, potential children and the applicant himself, from harm caused by his irresponsible attitude towards marriage [Z: $(\sim L \cdot I^{\circ}H^{r}{\sim}C^{\sim v}) \propto \sim B$].

To the claimant's implied assertions of insufficient individual harm in *Handyside* [A: $(L^{\eta} \cdot I^{\sim p}{\sim}H^{r}{\sim}\chi) \propto B$], the state responds that the work can cause an unacceptable harm to children, whom it can deem incompetent to consent to incur that harm [Z: $(\sim L \cdot I^{\sim p}H^{r}{\sim}C^{\sim v}) \propto \sim B$]. In *Kjeldsen*, the government's position is substantively opposed (given the very different policies of the Danish and British states) yet formally identical to that in *Handyside*: exercise of the right to exempt children from sexual education would unacceptably harm the children, by depriving them of vital knowledge about sex. The respondents' positions in *Jersild* and *Otto-Preminger-Institut* include the implied assertion that the works are unacceptably harmful to individual members of the concerned racial or religious groups, who are presumed to withhold consent to incur offence caused by the works to those groups. Although certain specific individuals had objected to the works in both cases, the state position is not an empirical submission that certain such individuals *do not*, in fact, consent to incur the offence. In both cases, there may well have been individual members of the racial and religious groups concerned who would place a higher value on freedom of expression. Rather, the respondent's position consists of a government determination that the harms caused by such works, being unacceptable, *cannot* validly be consented to by such individuals [Z: $(\sim L \cdot I^{\sim p}H^{r}{\sim}C^{\sim v}) \propto \sim B$]. For *Mellacher*, we saw the argument that individuals entitled to low-rent accommodations would not have consented to forgo that entitlement [Z: $(L^{\kappa} \cdot I^{\sim p}H^{r}{\sim}C^{v}) \propto \sim B$]. An alternative, paternalist welfare-state argument would be that the state would or should not recognise their right to place themselves in danger of homelessness [Z: $(\sim L \cdot I^{\sim p}H^{r}{\sim}C^{\sim v}) \propto \sim B$].

The liberal focus on consent raises questions about the volitional nature of consent attributed to deceased persons. In a case which attracted considerable attention in France (hereinafter the *Yves Montand* case), a woman claiming to be the natural daughter of the well-known entertainer brought an action to establish paternity.[2] Montand having died in the course of the litigation, the question was then whether the Court could order exhumation for purposes of extracting genetic material from the deceased. In opposition to that motion, it was argued that the deceased maintained a right to individual bodily integrity, which would be unacceptably harmed by such a procedure. In the absence of the possibility of obtaining actual consent of the deceased, absence of valid consent should thus be presumed $[Z: ({\sim}L \cdot I^{\sim p}H^{r}{\sim}C^{\sim v}) \propto {\sim}B]$. However, finding that greater certainty as to the claimant's paternity rendered any such harm acceptable, the Court issued the order $[A: (L^{\eta} \cdot I^{\sim p}{\sim}H^{r}{\sim}\chi) \propto B]$.

25.3 Non-volitional consent to incur right-based harm $[A: ({\sim}L \cdot I{\sim}\gamma^{r}C^{\sim v}) \propto B]$

State regulatory power sometimes includes the authority to devolve decision-making power upon non-state agents. For example, the state may determine that all persons below the age of 16 must receive education, but may also grant to parents the prerogative to choose between different kinds of schools. Once a parent places a child – certainly a younger child – in a given school, any question about the child's consent to attend the school will ordinarily be resolved in favour of the parent's choice, even if the child does not consent in fact to attend. It is commonly the parents, then, who exercise the right (I^{p}), albeit in a way which affects the child ($I^{\sim p}$). From the child's perspective, a case like *Kjeldsen* pits a paternalism exercised by the state against a paternalism devolved upon the parents: the state argues that children, if enrolled in public school, cannot consent to forgo sex education $[Z: ({\sim}L \cdot I^{\sim p}H^{r}{\sim}C^{\sim v}) \propto {\sim}B]$; the parents argue that, under Protocol 1, article 2, the child's consent to do so must in effect be implied in law $[A: ({\sim}L \cdot I^{\sim p}{\sim}\gamma^{r}C^{\sim v}) \propto B]$.

The fluid nature of consent as applied to children would bring a number of disputes within this sphere of argument. In *X, Y and Z v. United Kingdom*,[3] the Court considered the right of a post-operative transsexual to be recognised, in law, as the father of a child born to his long-term partner by means of artificial insemination. The claimants' evidence indicated an otherwise stable and prosperous family, and the claimant cited a conscious desire on the part of the child to enjoy a parent–child relationship with the father. Due to the child's young age (born in 1992), the national courts declined to accord great weight to the conscious will of a child who, in their view, might not fully appreciate the circumstances. In other words, the courts were not prepared to accept assertions by the claimant of volitional consent on the part of the child to incur possible consequences of the father's condition $[A: (L^{\kappa} \cdot I^{\sim p}{\sim}\gamma^{r}C^{v}) \propto B]$. More plausibly, the claimant's evidence of a durable and prosperous family life served to suggest the legitimacy of implied consent on the child's part $[A: ({\sim}L \cdot I^{\sim p}{\sim}\gamma^{r}C^{\sim v}) \propto B]$. Nevertheless, the British government managed to convince the Court that the consequences of parenting by transsexuals, notably by means of artificial insemination, presented new and unforeseeable problems, which justified state measures to protect the child's interests, through a denial of paternity in this case $[Z: ({\sim}L \cdot I^{\sim p}H^{r}{\sim}C^{\sim v}) \propto {\sim}B]$.

The concept of non-volitional consent to incur right-based harm also provides a way of characterising the interests of personal actors, in particular, those deemed to lack competence to give valid consent. For example, we have seen two possible arguments in defence of a right to commit euthanasia. A non-consensual liberal position can be adduced, but only in so far as it can be asserted that death is an acceptable harm, i.e. relative to the alternative of chronic suffering [A: $(L^{\eta} \cdot I^{p}{\sim}H^{r}{\sim}\chi) \propto B$]. States commonly respond that death cannot be deemed an acceptable harm, particularly in view of the potential for abuse [Z: $({\sim}L \cdot I^{p}H^{r}{\sim}C^{\sim v}) \propto {\sim}B$]. In order to avoid that characterisation of the harm, a claimant might adduce a volitional liberal position, namely, a 'libertarian' right to commit suicide, or, less controversially, to refuse medical treatment; but then only in so far as it is asserted, or assumed, that the personal actor is competent to give valid consent [A: $(L^{\kappa} \cdot I^{p}{\sim}\gamma^{r}C^{v}) \propto B$]. Assuming either of those rights to exist, then, for actors not competent to give consent, a paternalist argument can be introduced, such that consent to incur the harm of death should be implied in law, e.g. on the wishes of family members or on compassionate grounds [A: $({\sim}L \cdot I^{p}{\sim}\gamma^{r}C^{\sim v}) \propto B$].

25.4 Non-volitional non-consent to incur restriction-based harm [A: $({\sim}L \cdot I^{p}H^{\sim r}{\sim}C^{\sim v}) \propto B$]

We have already seen that many complaints about restriction-based harm often assume personal non-consent with little dispute [A: $(L^{\kappa} \cdot I^{p}H^{\sim r}{\sim}C^{v}) \propto B$]. In many such cases, the claimant could argue that non-consent must be assumed even if there is evidence of consent. In disputes resembling *Aksoy* or the Northern Ireland cases, if the state were to argue that some form of consent had been given by the personal actors to incur the harm, the claimant could respond that such consent must be deemed invalid – that the state must assume the paternalist stance of negating individual volition, not in the interest of restricting a right but in the interest of respecting it [A: $({\sim}L \cdot I^{p}H^{\sim r}{\sim}C^{\sim v}) \propto B$].

25.5 Non-volitional consent to incur restriction-based harm [Z: $({\sim}L \cdot I^{p}{\sim}\gamma^{\sim r}C^{\sim v}) \propto {\sim}B$]

In some cases, the state may point to discretion devolved upon a non-state agent in order to assert valid consent. In *Costello-Roberts*, one of the state's arguments consisted in pointing to the voluntary nature of sending one's children to the school. Assuming the child to be too young to make an independent decision about his schooling, the respondent argued that the parent's choice to send the child to the school became a choice, made on behalf of the child, to submit to that school's disciplinary regime[4] [Z: $({\sim}L \cdot I^{p}{\sim}\gamma^{\sim r}C^{\sim v}) \propto {\sim}B$]. The claimant responded that the beating was nevertheless unacceptably harmful to such a young child – who indeed appeared to have resisted in fact [A: $(L^{\kappa} \cdot I^{p}H^{\sim r}{\sim}C^{v}) \propto B$].[5] For the claimant, the child's presence in the school should not be taken to qualify as consent to such treatment [A: $({\sim}L \cdot I^{p}H^{\sim r}{\sim}C^{\sim v}) \propto B$]. In *Camara*, which concerned the consent to be attributed to a deceased child, two paternalist positions clash. The claimants had challenged a legal presumption of consent to the removal of their deceased child's internal organs for purposes of autopsy [A: $({\sim}L \cdot I^{p}H^{\sim r}{\sim}C^{\sim v}) \propto B$], but the Conseil d'État accepted the government's position supporting a presumption of consent [Z: $({\sim}L \cdot I^{p}{\sim}\gamma^{\sim r}C^{\sim v}) \propto {\sim}B$].

Exercise set 25.1

Write complete and simplified horizontal ~L positions for the following arguments, supplying the most specific values of κ or η variables.

Example: Z: $I^{p}\eta^{r}{\sim}C^{\sim v}$

Answer: Z: $\{[{\sim}L \rightarrow (I^{p}H^{r}{\sim}C^{\sim v} \rightarrow {\sim}B)] \cdot {\sim}L \cdot I^{p}H^{r}{\sim}C^{\sim v}\} \Rightarrow {\sim}B$
Z: $({\sim}L \cdot I^{p}H^{r}{\sim}C^{\sim v}) \propto {\sim}B$

1 Z: $I\eta^{r}{\sim}C^{\sim v}$
2 A: $I^{\sim p}\eta^{r}C^{\sim v}$
3 A: $I^{p}\eta^{\sim r}{\sim}C^{\sim v}$

---

26 Democracy

In this chapter, we examine three collectivist theories. Two of them will be identified as theories of *democracy*. The third will be called an *anti-democratic* theory.

26.1 Popular democracy [θ: $(D^v \cdot S\eta^r\chi^v) \propto \beta$]

Arguments about public opinion [θ: $S\eta^r\chi^v$] are not always supported by empirical evidence. Or, if they are, that evidence may be contested, as in *Dudgeon*. Nevertheless, they are put forth as representing the view which should be recognised as most legitimately attributable to society as a whole. In that sense – and not in any sense which would rigorously require reference to some empirically ascertained majority – these will be called *popularly democratic* arguments. While other arguments about public interest specifically disregard public opinion [Z: $SH^r{\sim}C^{\sim v}$, A: $S{\sim}H^r{\sim}\chi$], the position θ: $S\eta^r\chi^v$ expressly refers to it. In that sense, the attribution of volitional non-consent to society as a whole is a background theory of popular democracy. The expressly volitional basis of that theory can be denoted by affixing the 'v' marker not only to the χ variable but also to D. Accordingly, the concept of popular democracy (D^v) denotes a θ position attributing actual consent or non-consent (χ^v) to society as a whole (S) to incur a harm caused by the exercise of a right (η^r):

> **Theory of Popular Democracy (D^v)**: A θ position attributing χ^v to S is a popular-democratic position (D^v),
>
> BF(D^v) θ: $(D^v \cdot S\eta^r\chi^v) \propto \beta$

We have seen that, in *Dudgeon*, reference to popular opinion is made by the claimant [A: $(D^v \cdot S{\sim}\gamma^rC^v) \propto B$] as well as the respondent [Z: $(D^v \cdot SH^r{\sim}C^v) \propto {\sim}B$]. In *Handyside*, a newspaper campaign is adduced by the government as evidence of public opinion [Z: $(D^v \cdot SH^r{\sim}C^v) \propto {\sim}B$]. But, again, it is uncommon for parties to rely heavily on these kinds of arguments.

26.2 Constitutional democracy [Z: $(D^{\sim v} \cdot SH^{r}{\sim}C^{\sim v}) \propto {\sim}B$]

It is rare for courts or lawyers to attach express priority to surveys of public opinion (except, of course, in the form of binding referenda), much less to cite such data as a conclusive basis for resolving a rights dispute. More commonly, the respondent asserts a public interest not on grounds of actual public opinion, but on constitutional grounds. The respondent's reference to the public interest assumes that restrictions on rights (barring their imposition *ultra vires*) as acts of a democratic government are *ipso facto* democratic. In simple terms: 'that's why government and law are there – to make the day-to-day decisions which the public cannot make through any other collectively deliberative process'. The terms *constitutional democracy* and *constitutionally democratic* can be used to characterise arguments invoked by the respondent to restrict rights in the public interest, without express reference to public opinion.

We have seen that, by deeming the exercise of an individual right to be unacceptably harmful to a public interest, the state determines that the public *ipso facto* cannot validly consent to incur that harm. Under a liberal rights regime, that determination can be justified in democratic terms only in so far as the state is assumed to be democratically constituted, i.e. constitutionally democratic, through legislative, executive, judicial or administrative processes assumed to be democratically legitimate. In such a case, any claim to democratic legitimacy is not volitional, as it is not empirically grounded in public opinion (except, of course, in so far as a periodic, popular electoral process is said to legitimate the acts of government institutions). Rather, the claim is non-volitional. It asserts a purely institutional (constitutional) legitimacy, and is, in that sense, *non-popular* ($D^{\sim v}$). The term *constitutional democracy* ($D^{\sim v}$) thus denotes any Z position attributing government-determined, hence non-volitional, non-consent (${\sim}C^{\sim v}$) to society as a whole (S), to incur a harm caused by an individual in the exercise of a right:

> **Theory of Constitutional Democracy ($D^{\sim v}$)**: A Z position attributing ${\sim}C^{\sim v}$ to S is a constitutional-democratic position,
>
> BF($D^{\sim v}$)   Z: $(D^{\sim v} \cdot SH^{r}{\sim}C^{\sim v}) \propto {\sim}B$

Customarily, as a matter of implicature, paternalist Z assertions about individual interests [e.g. Z: $({\sim}L \cdot IH^{r}{\sim}C^{\sim v}) \propto {\sim}B$] broadly imply, or are broadly implied by, constitutional-democratic assertions about the interests of society [Z: $(D^{\sim v} \cdot SH^{r}{\sim}C^{\sim v}) \propto {\sim}B$]. The government's paternalist argument in *Handyside* about sufficient harm to individual children who might read the book reflects its broader argument that the book is harmful to public morals as a whole. In *Mellacher*, state concern about the impact of high rent upon the individuals directly concerned in the case reflects a broader social interest in problems of housing and rent control. In *Kjeldsen*, Z's assertion of risk of unacceptable harm to individual children deprived of compulsory sex education is part of a broader assertion of unacceptable harm to society as a whole from lack of sex education. In cases concerning restrictions on abortion, such as *Brüggemann*, an assertion of harm to unborn life can be linked to broader assertions of public interest in unborn life. In *Kokkinakis*, Z's concerns about undermining individuals' religious beliefs is expressed as part of a broader interest in preserving Eastern Orthodox Christianity, which had become a symbol of Greek identity during several centuries of foreign domination.

In *F v. Switzerland*, the Z position, in addition to I interests, asserts S interests by seeking 'to protect . . . the institution of marriage'.[1] The Z position, albeit not relying on data about public opinion, envisages society's continued approval of fault-based divorce, hence a collective rejection of the harm to society of 'making a mockery of the institution of marriage'.[2] In *Laskey*, the assertion of harm to individuals is expressed in terms of a presumed broader concern with public health. In *Otto-Preminger* and *Jersild*, the Z assertion of presumably unacceptable offence to society, or to certain social groups, entails an assertion of harm to some individuals who may be affected by the works. The Z positions in *Rees* and *Cossey* avoid probing reference to controversial questions of public morals by focusing on administrative costs. The principle of constitutional democracy is thus invoked to support a claim of excessive administrative cost or burden, and thus unacceptable harm, to society as a whole.

As with the other background theories, a theory of constitutional democracy is, in itself, neither progressive or repressive. Libertarians will almost always look askance at it, not only in a case like *Handyside* or *Otto-Preminger*, but even in a case like *Mellacher*. By contrast, social democrats would share that scepticism with respect to *Handyside*, but would applaud the use of the theory in *Mellacher* or *Kjeldsen*. Just as a libertarian will generally reject the theory, the totalitarian will commonly use it. A hallmark of sham liberal democracy is the willy-nilly recourse to a theory of constitutional democracy to abridge a rights claim on the basis of a concocted public interest. A case like *Handyside* arising in such a regime will differ not because of the background theories which could in principle be invoked, but because of the dismissive attitude a decision maker will take in practice towards any competing theory. Although paternalist or popular democratic theories might also occasionally be invoked, the theory of constitutional democracy will be particularly common, invoked in short order, without serious regard to contrary A positions.

That is not to say that the background theories allow a bright line to be drawn between genuine and sham liberal democracies. Abuses of paternalist or constitutional-democratic theories are not unknown in vibrant liberal democracies (as is arguably demonstrated by several of the cases on transsexualism, or by covert government operations which preclude judicial redress for human rights abuses). Similarly, a gradually more robust interplay of background theories may emerge as a sham regime moves towards genuine democracy, as in the transition from apartheid. Nor is a bright line always to be drawn between sham regimes and overtly non-liberal regimes. Even the virulently anti-liberal Nazi government, notoriously conscious of the power of the mass media, adduced justifications – however bogus – for many of its acts along constitutional-democratic lines, while other acts were conducted without formal justification. Similarly, Stalinist dictatorships, guided by expedience, have invoked constitutional-democratic justifications at times, while dispensing with all justification at other times. But those are only thumbnail sketches. More analysis would be required to substantiate such claims.

26.3 Anti-democracy [A: $(\sim D \cdot S{\sim}H^r{\sim}\chi) \propto B$]

The only other argument about society which is available to a claimant is to challenge the very appeal to the public interest as a basis for restricting the right. That argument can be called *anti-democratic*. It does not mean that the claimant's position is hostile to all democracy, but only to a finding in favour of interests attributed to society as a whole to the detriment of the right in question. The more common rebuttal to the position Z: $(D^v \cdot SH^r{\sim}C^v) \propto {\sim}B$ avoids reference to what society 'wants' by shifting the focus away from the κ variable. It does so by means of an argument asserting that the exercise of the right causes insufficient harm to society [A: $S{\sim}H^r{\sim}\chi \propto B$]. That argument complements the non-volitional liberal argument: individuals should be free to do that which causes no unacceptable harm (${\sim}H^r$) to society as a whole (S); not *because* society approves, but rather regardless of whether society approves (${\sim}\chi$):

> **Theory of Anti-democracy (~D)**: An A position attributing ${\sim}\chi$ to S is an anti-democratic position (~D),
>
> BF(~D) A: $(\sim D \cdot S{\sim}H^r{\sim}\chi) \propto B$

Accordingly, in disputes about right-based harms, non-consensual liberal A positions [A: $(L^{\neg} \cdot I{\sim}H^r{\sim}\chi) \propto B$] commonly correlate to broader concerns about public welfare, asserted as interests of society as a whole [A: $({\sim}D \cdot S{\sim}H^r{\sim}\chi) \propto B$]. Mr Handyside's argument about insufficient harm to the interests of individual children who might read the book correlates to a broader argument that the book is insufficiently harmful to the morals of children, and ultimately of society, as a whole. In *Kjeldsen*, A's argument about insufficient harm to the interests of individual children deprived of compulsory sex education correlates to a broader argument that children, or society, is not unacceptably harmed by such a choice. In cases concerning restrictions on abortion, such as *Brüggemann*, the A position, the assertion of insufficient harm to any actual or potential human being, correlates to an assertion of insufficient harm to society's broader interest in preserving life.

In *F v. Switzerland*, one possible rebuttal to Z's claim to be promoting society's interest in the institution of traditional marriage, as in *Dudgeon*, might take the form of an empirical (volitional liberal) submission that the more tolerant views of contemporary society are not faithfully reflected in the state's position [A: $(D^{v} \cdot S{\sim}\gamma^{r}C^{v}) \propto B$]. Indeed, the Court notes the abolition of such waiting periods in other contracting states,[3] and its otherwise brief opinion devotes considerable attention to proposals for law reform in Switzerland.[4] Yet, ever loath to challenge a state's claim to represent society's collective interest, the Court rejects this position.[5] Instead, by resolving the case purely on the basis of the applicant's rebuttals on the I interests [A: $(L^{\eta} \cdot I^{\circ}{\sim}H^{r}{\sim}\chi) \propto B$], A's rebuttal concerning S interests takes the corresponding form: the premise A: $I^{\circ}{\sim}H^{r}{\sim}\chi$ provides, itself, a sufficient basis for finding that insufficient harm to society renders collective non-consent irrelevant [A: $({\sim}D \cdot S{\sim}H^{r}{\sim}\chi) \propto B$].

Similarly, A positions expressly denying sufficient harm to society as a whole nevertheless implicitly assert insufficient harm to individuals. The A position in *Dudgeon* that homosexuality does not unacceptably harm the morals or welfare of society as a whole [A: $({\sim}D \cdot S{\sim}H^{r}{\sim}\chi) \propto B$] implies *ipso facto* that homosexuality does not sufficiently harm the morals or welfare of individuals who practise it [A: $(L^{\eta} \cdot I{\sim}H^{r}{\sim}\chi) \propto B$]. In *Otto-Preminger* and *Jersild*, the A assertion of insufficient offence to society, or to certain social groups, entails an assertion of insufficient harm to any individuals who may be affected by the works.

In *Rees*, *Cossey* or *B v. France*, the A positions adduce insufficient harm to society [A: $({\sim}D \cdot S{\sim}H^{r}{\sim}\chi) \propto B$] by rejecting the Z assertion of excessive cost that would be caused by the revision of administrative practices in order to meet the needs of post-operative transsexuals [Z: $(D^{\sim v} \cdot SH^{r}{\sim}C^{\sim v}) \propto {\sim}B$]. Similarly, in the *Easy Rider* case, the claimant rejects the government's assertion of excessive cost to society through motor vehicle accidents, by arguing that, if such a position were true, the state would also prohibit such activities as dangerous sports, or alcohol and nicotine consumption. Its failure to do so undermines the suggestion that motorcycling without a helmet imposes unacceptable health costs upon society as a whole.[6]

Exercise set 26.1

Write complete and simplified horizontal δ positions for the following arguments, supplying the most specific values of κ or η variables.

Example: Z: $S\eta^{r}{\sim}C^{v}$

Answer: Z: $\{[D^{v} \rightarrow (SH^{r}{\sim}C^{v} \rightarrow {\sim}B)] \cdot D^{v} \cdot SH^{r}{\sim}C^{v}\} \Rightarrow {\sim}B$

Z: $(D^{v} \cdot SH^{r}{\sim}C^{v}) \propto {\sim}B$

1 Z: $S\eta^{r}{\sim}C^{\sim v}$
2 A: $S\eta^{r}{\sim}\chi$
3 A: $S{\sim}\gamma^{r}\kappa^{v}$

26.4 Schema of collectivist theories

In this chapter, we have identified two democratic theories (D),

Ps(D) $D \subset D^{v}, D^{\sim v}$

Hence, a concise statement of the most specific values of δ,

Th(δ) $\delta \subset D^{v}, D^{\sim v}, {\sim}D$

Exercise set 26.2

Derive Th(δ).

Exercise set 26.3

Derive the following theorems, using only postulates.
1 $\tau \subset \iota, D^{v}, D^{\sim v}, {\sim}D$
2 $\tau \subset L^{\kappa}, L^{\eta}, {\sim}L, D^{v}, D^{\sim v}, {\sim}D$

Exercise set 26.4

Draw a tree diagram of all τ values.

The theorem in Exercise set 26.3, problem 2, represents the six most specific values of τ. Hence, the most precise statement of the background theories of liberal rights discourse,

$$\mathrm{Th}(\tau) \quad \tau \subset L^{\kappa}, L^{\eta}, {\sim}L, D^{v}, D^{\sim v}, {\sim}D$$

27 Conclusion

A roomful of scholars

We began by postulating the existence of background concepts P_1, P_2, P_3, . . . P_n. We asked how many they are, why they are that number and what that says about liberal rights discourse.

The response depends on the level of abstraction at which the background theories are cast. At the highest level of abstraction, we could say $n = 1$, since every argument reflects some combination of values of ψ, η, κ, β and τ. Hence the *Urtheorie*,

$$\mathrm{BF}(\tau) \quad \theta\text{: } (\tau \cdot \alpha\eta\kappa) \propto \beta$$

Yet we have identified six more specific values of τ. At a more precise level of abstraction, $n = 6$,

$$\mathrm{Th}(\tau) \quad \tau \subset L^{\kappa}, L^{\eta}, {\sim}L, D^{v}, D^{\sim v}, {\sim}D$$

The number six is also somewhat arbitrary. We have seen that those six values can, themselves, represent more than one combination of variables. In Chapter 23, four distinct versions of L^{κ} emerged: a volitional liberal argument favouring a right [e.g. A: $(L^{\kappa} \cdot I{\sim}\gamma^{r}C^{v}) \propto B$] certainly differs from one which opposes it [e.g. Z: $(L^{\kappa} \cdot I{\sim}\gamma^{r}{\sim}C^{v}) \propto {\sim}B$]. Similarly, a paternalist argument favouring a right [e.g. A: $({\sim}L \cdot I^{p}H^{\sim r}{\sim}C^{\sim v}) \propto B$] differs from one which opposes it [e.g. Z: $(L^{\kappa} \cdot IH^{r}{\sim}C^{\sim v}) \propto {\sim}B$]. In Chapter 24, we examined two versions of L^{η}, and in Chapter 25, four versions of ${\sim}L$. Yet those findings also reveal that such variations are limited. The values represented by τ variables as set forth in $\mathrm{Th}(\tau)$ cannot exceed the total number of combinations of ψ, η and κ variables which can generate β positions.

In Section 1.1, we were promised some link between the concept of liberal rights and a corpus conventionally recognised as such. It is $\mathrm{BF}(\tau)$ which provides that link. In accordance with the Presupposition Corollary to the Axiom of Contentious Character,[1] a dispute is a dispute about the adjudication of a liberal right only in so far as it is a dispute, between a claimant position and a respondent position, about the formal values to be ascribed to the variables comprising some mutually presupposed θ position. Ultimately, that mutually presupposed position is BF(τ), hence, θ: $(\tau \cdot \alpha\eta\kappa) \propto \beta$. In any given case, we may be able to ascertain that the disagreement is more specifically about, say, the value of $\gamma^{\sim r}$ or χ. But every dispute is ultimately a dispute about the formal values to be ascribed to the variable comprising BF(τ). That observation has allowed further conclusions beyond the narrow framework of particular disputes. We have seen that a dispute about BF(τ) also arises in other areas of law, e.g. in ordinary private law disputes, but less centrally, less crucially, than in disputes about civil rights and liberties.

We have seen that disputes about BF(τ) arise just as surely in sham liberal regimes. In a non-liberal regime, arguments about individual interests would not inevitably presuppose τ positions. In sham liberal regimes, by contrast, τ positions will be ascertainable in disputes about rights, but in highly predictable ways. In so far as rights discourse is concerned, a genuine liberal democracy is one in which τ positions arise in multiple, mutating, unpredictable ways, and where no one τ position is certain to prevail in a controversial case. The set of possible β positions represents the limits of formal determinacy in rights discourse. The formal determinacy of rights discourse is represented by the set of values formally attributable to the variables contained in BF(τ). To that extent, rights discourse is determinate. Substantive indeterminacy results from disagreement about the content of those values. Questions about how great that substantive indeterminacy is are questions about the determinacy of that content – about which the formal structure has nothing more to say.

Where does all of this leave our roomful of scholars? What do they agree on? Who is making what kind of argument?

By definition, they are all discussing some feature of BF(τ). They differ only according to their views about it. Some scholars will be willing to accept the terms of liberal rights discourse in principle. The libertarian, for example, embraces a concept of consent such that the presence of volitional consent (C^{v}) by individuals (I) practising sadomasochism renders irrelevant ($\sim\gamma^{r}$) any inquiry into the existence, character or level of harm caused [A: $(L^{\kappa} \cdot I{\sim}\gamma^{r}C^{v}) \propto B$]; or embraces a concept of 'purely moral' harms, such that any harm caused by the right (η^{r}) is insufficient ($\sim H^{r}$) to justify the restriction of the right, either in the interests of the individuals concerned [A: $(L^{\eta} \cdot I{\sim}H^{r}{\sim}\chi) \propto B$] or in the interests of society as a whole [A: $({\sim}D \cdot S{\sim}H^{r}{\sim}\chi) \propto B$]. The Christian conservative disagrees, arguing, for example, that government should deem such practices to be sufficiently harmful to a broader interest in public morals [Z: $(D^{\sim v} \cdot SH^{r}{\sim}C^{\sim v}) \propto {\sim}B$]. Some feminists or race theorists would take that same formal Z position, but by attributing a different substantive value to H^{r} – the harm caused to society being not a harm to Christian values, but the harm caused by perpetuation of an aesthetic of violence, with pernicious consequences for women, or for ethnic minorities, who have had histories of political and social subordination through violent means.

Some practitioners of law and economics, too, might adopt that formal Z position, but by attributing yet a different substantive value to H^r. They might argue that the cost of remedying any injuries caused by sadomasochistic activity would raise public health care costs for persons who are not insured (assuming a society with public health care), thus justifying a view that government may deem the activity to be unduly harmful to society as a whole [Z: $(D^{\sim v} \cdot SH^r{\sim}C^{\sim v}) \propto {\sim}B$]. Yet those same scholars might just as easily take the opposite view, attributing a value of $\sim H^r$ to η^r, by arguing that the cost to public health care would increase if a legal prohibition meant that injuries were left unattended until they had become aggravated to the point of requiring more costly treatment, and that legalised sadomasochism is therefore less costly, ergo less harmful, to society as a relative matter [A: $({\sim}D \cdot S{\sim}H^r{\sim}\chi) \propto B$].

Meanwhile, the black-letter lawyer, distinguishing sexual sadomasochism from lawful sexual activity not involving violence, or from lawful violent activity not involving sex, would either (1) adopt the A position, arguing that those distinctions are irrelevant, thus ascribing the values of ${\sim}\gamma^r C^v$ to the I^p and $I^{\sim p}$ actors, and the value of ${\sim}H^r{\sim}\chi$ to the S actor; or (2) adopt the Z position, arguing that those distinctions are relevant, thus ascribing the values of $H^r{\sim}C^{\sim v}$ to all actors – using, in either case, any arguments a court may accept. A race theorist or feminist of more postmodernist leanings, and, moreover, willing to use the terms of liberal rights discourse, would embrace position (1), but, again for different substantive reasons, arguing that sadomasochism can play an ironically subversive role vis-à-vis oppressive practices.

In short, a scholar may vigorously oppose the particular values ascribed to one or more variables of the general formula by a lawmaker or court in a given case; however, if the reason for such opposition is simply to favour the ascription of some other value – otherwise leaving the general formula intact – then that scholar is, in principle, sympathetic to the principle of liberal rights. Even those theories which periodically come along as 'radical' cannot be said to be undermining the radix if they assume the *Urtheorie*. Those scholars who accept liberal rights agree that their dispute is about the values to be ascribed to the variables of the general formula. Disagreement arises only in so far as different scholars ascribe different values to those variables. In so far as every argument is constrained to express some β position, no argument can be entirely original. Originality is possible only where new ways are devised to attribute substantive values to the variables of one of the existing β positions.

By contrast, some scholars reject liberal rights altogether. Early on, we saw that the binarism of rights discourse may be challenged through a critique of the formal values attributable to θ or α. Scholars hostile to liberal rights may differ among themselves by disagreeing either about which components of θ formulas they reject, or about the reasons why they reject them. The only factor which must necessarily unite all theories opposed to liberal rights is that all of them must, expressly or implicitly, reject at least one component of BF(τ). The cogency of a critique of liberal rights will depend upon the cogency of the critique of that component. Scholars who reject the very terms of a standard liberal-versus-conservative debate on moral harms might do so by rejecting the very inclusion of the η variable in the general formula. What kind of jurisprudence would they propose instead? With what logic assumed as a basis for *its* sheer coherence? Those questions would leave us with much more work. Our only task in this book has been to analyse the fundamental concepts underlying arguments about liberal rights, such as they are. That effort can pinpoint the overall structure of liberal rights discourse, but cannot improve it. Because it is logically coherent, rights discourse is a trap.

Appendix 1

Axioms and background theories

Numbers in parentheses indicate the section where the axiom, corollary or background theory is introduced.

Position axioms

Axiom of Generality (1.1): There is no necessary distinction between a norm in itself and a norm enunciated as part of a broader norm.

Axiom of Recognition (1.1): A right is liberal if it is recognised as such within a corpus conventionally regarded as a body of liberal rights.

> **Claimant Corollary** (3.2): Every claimant position asserts that the right must be recognised.
>
> **Respondent Corollary** (3.2): Every respondent position asserts that the right must not be recognised.
>
> **Party Corollary** (3.2): Every party position asserts either that the right must be recognised, or that the right must not be recognised.

Axiom of Restrictions (1.2): A restriction is any means by which a person or entity impedes the right-seeker (personal actor) in, or penalises the right-seeker (personal actor) for, the exercise of an asserted right.

> **Claimant Corollary** (3.2): Every claimant position opposes some means by which a person or entity impedes the right-seeker in, or penalises the right-seeker for, the exercise of an asserted right.
>
> **Respondent Corollary** (3.2): Every respondent position favours some means by which a person or entity impedes the right-seeker in, or penalises the right-seeker for, the exercise of an asserted right.
>
> **Party Corollary** (3.2): Every party position either opposes or favours some means by which a person or entity impedes the right-seeker in, or penalises the right-seeker for, the exercise of an asserted right.

Axiom of Contentious Character (1.3): A right is liberal only if it can in principle conflict with some ascertainable restriction.

Claimant Corollary (3.2): Every claimant position conflicts with some possible respondent position.

Respondent Corollary (3.2): Every respondent position conflicts with some possible claimant position.

Party Corollary (3.2): Every party position conflicts with some other possible party position.

Rebuttal Corollary (3.2): Every party position can be rebutted by some other party position.

Adjudication Corollary (3.2): A dispute about a liberal right is adjudicated if and only if it adopts either some possible claimant position or some possible respondent position.

Dispute Corollary (3.5): A dispute is about the adjudication of a liberal right only in so far as it is a dispute – between a claimant position and a respondent position – about the formal values to be ascribed to variables representing those respective positions.

Presupposition Corollary (13.8): A dispute is a dispute about the adjudication of a liberal right only in so far as it is a dispute – between a claimant position and a respondent position – about the formal values to be ascribed to the variables comprising some mutually presupposed θ position.

Axiom of Truth Value (3.3): Every assertion in a θ position is assumed to be true or false.

Claimant Corollary (3.3): The claimant assumes some A position to be true, and any contradictory position to be false.

Respondent Corollary (3.3): The respondent assumes some Z position to be true, and any contradictory position to be false.

Axiom of Assertion (3.4): A party is assumed to make an assertion attributed to that party in a θ position, subject to the Axiom of Recognition and the Axiom of Restriction, and their corollaries.

Indicative Tense Corollary (3.4): A party is assumed to make any past, present or future assertion attributed to that party in a θ position, subject to the Axiom of Recognition and the Axiom of Restriction, and their corollaries.

Hypothetical Case Corollary (3.4): A party is assumed to make any assertion attributable to that party in a θ position, subject to the Axiom of Recognition and the Axiom of Restriction, and their corollaries.

Axiom of Compound Positions (5.4): All compound positions are assumed to be conjunctive.

Axiom of Individual Actors (5.5): Every individual actor is either a personal actor or a non-personal actor, and nothing else.

Axiom of Mutual Exclusion of Individual Actors (7.2): For any given argument, an individual actor is either a personal actor or a non-personal actor, but not both.

Harm axioms

Claimant Harm Axiom (HA_A) (11.1): In an argument that a restriction violates a right, the claimant position (A) assumes:

(1) Either that:
  (a) some harm is caused by the personal actor's exercise of the right (η^r); and
  (b) such harm is caused to some actor ($\alpha\eta^r$); and
  (c) the harm is either,
    (i) insufficient ($\eta^r = \sim H^r$) to justify the restriction ($\beta = B$); or
    (ii) irrelevant ($\eta^r = \sim\gamma^r$) to the question of whether the restriction is justified ($\beta = B$);

(2) or that:
  (a) some harm is caused by the restriction ($\eta^{\sim r}$); and,
  (b) such harm is caused to the personal actor ($I^p\eta^{\sim r}$); and,
  (c) such harm is sufficient ($\eta^{\sim r} = H^{\sim r}$) to warrant a finding that the restriction is unjustified ($\beta = B$).

Respondent Harm Axiom (HA_Z) (11.1): In an argument that a restriction does not violate a right, the respondent's position (Z) assumes,

(1) Either that:
  (a) some harm is caused by the personal actor's exercise of the right (η^r); and
  (b) such harm is caused to some actor ($\alpha\eta^r$); and
  (c) the harm is sufficient to justify the restriction ($\eta^r = H^r$);

(2) or that:
  (a) some harm is caused by the restriction ($\eta^{\sim r}$); and
  (b) such harm is caused to the personal actor ($I^p\eta^{\sim r}$); and
  (c) the harm is either,
    (i) insufficient ($\eta^{\sim r} = \sim H^{\sim r}$) to warrant a finding that the restriction is unjustified ($\beta = \sim B$), or
    (ii) irrelevant ($\eta^{\sim r} = \sim\gamma^{\sim r}$) to the question of whether the restriction is justified ($\beta = \sim B$).

Corollaries to the Claimant and Respondent Harm Axioms:

Harm Attribution Corollary (η attr) (13.2): All θ positions attribute some harm to some actor. That is, for any position θ: α, there is some value of η, such that θ: αη.

Actor Limitation Corollary (α lim) (14.4): Restriction-based harms are incurred only by the personal actor.

Consent Attribution Corollary (κ attr) (17.3): All θ positions attribute to some actor some disposition to incur some harm. That is, for any position θ: αη, there is some value of κ, such that θ: αηκ.

Sufficient Harm Axiom (θ: αH~C) (18.1): An assertion of sufficient harm (H) implies an assertion of invalid consent (~C); and an assertion of invalid consent (~C) implies an assertion of sufficient harm (H). For all θ: αηκ, if η = H, then κ = ~C; and if κ = ~C, then η = H.

Irrelevant Harm Axiom (θ: α~γC) (18.2): An assertion of valid consent (C) implies an assertion of irrelevant harm (~γ); and an assertion of irrelevant harm (~γ) implies an assertion of valid consent (C). For all θ: αηκ, if η = ~γ, then κ = C; and if κ = C, then η = ~γ.

Insufficient Consent Axiom (θ: α~H~χ) (18.3): An assertion of insufficient harm (~H) implies an assertion of irrelevant consent (~χ); and an assertion of irrelevant consent (~χ) implies an assertion of insufficient harm (~H). For all θ: αηκ, if η = ~H, then κ = ~χ; and if κ = ~χ, then η = ~H.

Background theories

Theory of Volitional Liberalism (L^κ) (23.1): A θ position attributing χ^v to an I actor is a volitional liberal position.

Theory of Non-consensual Liberalism (L^η) (24.1): A θ position attributing ~χ to an I actor is a non-consensual liberal position.

Theory of Paternalism (~L) (25.1): A θ position attributing $\chi^{\sim v}$ to an I actor is a paternalist, or anti-liberal, position.

Theory of Popular Democracy (D^{v}) (26.1): A θ position attributing χ^{v} to S is a popular-democratic position.

Theory of Constitutional Democracy ($D^{\sim v}$) (26.2): A Z position attributing $\sim C^{\sim v}$ to S is a constitutional-democratic position.

Theory of Anti-democracy (~D) (26.3): An A position attributing $\sim\chi$ to S is an anti-democratic position.

Appendix 2

Symbols and formulas

Numbers in parentheses indicate the section where the symbol is introduced.

Symbols

Basic symbols and operators

:	position (3.1)
$\subset$	set of possible values (2.3)
$\cdot$	conjunction ('dot') (5.4)
$\therefore$	conclusion (Introduction)
$\rightarrow$	sufficient condition ('arrow') (20.2)
$\Rightarrow$	conclusion ('double arrow') (20.2)
$\underline{\Rightarrow}$	conclusion for β positions ('underlined double arrow') (20.4)
$\propto$	conclusion ('crab') (21.3)

Formulas

F	formula (3.1)
Ps	postulate (2.3)
Th	theorem (9.3)
GF	general formula (17.4)
BF	background formula (21.3)

Markers

°	inclusive symbol (4.1)
p	personal (individual actor) (6.1)
~p	non-personal (individual actor) (7.3)
r	right-based (harm) (14.1)
~r	restriction-based (harm) (14.1)
v	volitional (consent) (19.1)
~v	non-volitional (consent) (19.1)

Agent variables

ψ	agent (2.2)
θ	party (2.2)
α	actor (2.2)
A	claimant (3.1)
Z	respondent (3.1)
I	individual actor (5.2)
I^{p}	personal actor (6.1)
$I^{\sim p}$	non-personal actor (7.3)
S	society (8.2)

Position variables

θ:	party position (2.2)
A:	claimant position (3.1)
Z:	respondent position (3.1)
β	conclusion as to breach or non-breach (20.3)
B	breach (20.1)
~B	non-breach (20.1)

Axioms

HA_{A}	claimant harm axiom (11.1)
HA_{Z}	respondent harm axiom (11.1)

Harm variables

η	harm (13.1)
η^{r}	right-based harm (14.1)
$\eta^{\sim r}$	restriction-based harm (14.1)
γ	relevant harm (13.1)
γ^{r}	relevant right-based harm (14.1)
$\gamma^{\sim r}$	relevant restriction-based harm (14.1))
$\sim\gamma$	irrelevant harm (13.1)
$\sim\gamma^{r}$	irrelevant right-based harm (14.1)
$\sim\gamma^{\sim r}$	irrelevant restriction-based harm (14.1)
H	sufficient harm (13.1)
H^{r}	sufficient right-based harm (14.1)
$H^{\sim r}$	sufficient restriction-based harm (14.1)
~H	insufficient harm (13.1)
$\sim H^{r}$	insufficient right-based harm (14.1
$\sim H^{\sim r}$	insufficient restriction-based harm (14.1)

Consent variables

κ	consent (17.2)
κ^{v}	volitional consent (19.1)
$\kappa^{\sim v}$	non-volitional consent (19.1)
χ	relevant consent (17.2)
χ^{v}	relevant volitional consent (19.1)

$\chi^{\sim v}$ relevant non-volitional consent (19.1)
$\sim\chi$ irrelevant consent (17.2)
~C invalid consent (17.2)
C valid consent (17.2)
C^{v} valid volitional consent (19.1)
$\sim C^{v}$ invalid volitional consent (19.1)
$C^{\sim v}$ valid non-volitional consent (19.1)
$\sim C^{\sim v}$ invalid non-volitional consent (19.1)

Background theories

τ background theory (21.1)
ι individualist theory (22.1)
δ democratic theory (22.2)
L liberal theory (22.3)
D democratic theory (22.3)
L^{κ} volitional liberalism (23.1)
L^{η} non-consensual liberalism (24.1)
~L paternalism (25.1)
D^{v} popular democracy (26.1)
$D^{\sim v}$ constitutional democracy (26.2)
~D anti-democracy (26.3)

Formulas

Agents

Postulates

Ps(ψ) $\psi \subset \theta, \alpha$ (2.3)
Ps(θ) $\theta \subset A, Z$ (3.1)
Ps(α) $\alpha \subset I, S$ (8.2)
Ps(I) $I \subset I^{p}, I^{\sim p}$ (7.3)

Theorems

Th(ψ) $\psi \subset A, Z, I^{p}, I^{\sim p}, S$ (9.3)
Th(α) $\alpha \subset I^{p}, I^{\sim p}, S$ (9.3)

Harm

Postulates

Ps(η1) $\eta \subset \gamma, \sim\gamma$ (13.1)
Ps(γ1) $\gamma \subset H, \sim H$ (13.1)

Theorems

Th(η) $\eta \subset H, \sim H, \sim\gamma$ (13.1)

Harm variable postulates

Ps($\eta = \gamma$): $\eta \neq \sim\gamma$ (13.4)
Ps($\eta = \sim\gamma$): $\eta \neq \gamma$ (13.4)
Ps(η = H): $\eta \neq \sim\gamma, \sim H$ (13.4)
Ps(η = ~H): $\eta \neq \sim\gamma$, H (13.4)
Ps(γ = H): $\gamma \neq \sim H$ (13.4)
Ps(γ = ~H): $\gamma \neq H$ (13.4)

Causation

Postulates

Ps(η2)	$\eta \subset \eta^{r}, \eta^{\sim r}$ (14.1)	Ps(H)	$H \subset H^{r}, H^{\sim r}$ (14.1)
Ps(γ2)	$\gamma \subset \gamma^{r}, \gamma^{\sim r}$ (14.1)	Ps($\eta^{\sim r}$)	$\eta^{\sim r} \subset \gamma^{\sim r}, \sim\gamma^{\sim r}$ (14.1)
Ps($\sim\gamma$)	$\sim\gamma \subset \sim\gamma^{r}, \sim\gamma^{\sim r}$ (14.1)	Ps($\gamma^{\sim r}$)	$\gamma^{\sim r} \subset H^{\sim r}, \sim H^{\sim r}$ (14.1)
Ps(η^{r})	$\eta^{r} \subset \gamma^{r}, \sim\gamma^{r}$ (14.1)	Ps($\sim$H)	$\sim H \subset \sim H^{r}, \sim H^{\sim r}$ (14.1)
Ps(γ^{r})	$\gamma^{r} \subset H^{r}, \sim H^{r}$ (14.1)		

Consent

Postulates

Ps(κ1)	$\kappa \subset \chi, \sim\chi$ (17.2)
Ps(χ1)	$\chi \subset C, \sim C$ (17.2)

Theorems

Th(κ)	$\kappa \subset C, \sim C, \sim\chi$ (17.2)

Consent variable postulates

Ps($\kappa = \chi$): $\kappa \neq \sim\chi$ (17.6)
Ps($\kappa = \sim\chi$): $\kappa \neq \chi$ (17.6)
Ps($\kappa = C$): $\kappa \neq \sim\chi, \sim C$ (17.6)
Ps($\kappa = \sim C$): $\kappa \neq \sim\chi, C$ (17.6)
Ps($\chi = C$): $\chi \neq \sim C$ (17.6)
Ps($\chi = \sim C$): $\chi \neq C$ (17.6)

Harm-Consent postulates

Ps(Hκ)	$\alpha H\kappa \subset \alpha H\sim C$ (18.1)	Ps(ηC)	$\alpha\eta C \subset \alpha\sim\gamma C$ (18.2)
Ps($\eta\sim$C)	$\alpha\eta\sim C \subset \alpha H\sim C$ (18.1)	Ps($\sim$Hκ)	$\alpha\sim H\kappa \subset \alpha\sim H\sim\chi$ (18.3)
Ps($\sim\gamma\kappa$)	$\alpha\sim\gamma\kappa \subset \alpha\sim\gamma C$ (18.2)	Ps($\eta\sim\chi$)	$\alpha\eta\sim\chi \subset \alpha\sim H\sim\chi$ (18.3)

Volition postulates

Ps(κ2)	$\kappa \subset \kappa^{v}, \kappa^{\sim v}$ (19.1)	Ps(χ^{v})	$\chi^{v} \subset C^{v}, \sim C^{v}$ (19.1)
Ps(χ2)	$\chi \subset \chi^{v}, \chi^{\sim v}$ (19.1)	Ps($\sim$C)	$\sim C \subset \sim C^{v}, \sim C^{\sim v}$ (19.1)
Ps(C)	$C \subset C^{v}, C^{\sim v}$ (19.1)	Ps($\kappa^{\sim v}$)	$\kappa^{\sim v} \subset \chi^{\sim v}, \sim\chi^{\sim v}$ (19.1)
Ps(κ^{v})	$\kappa^{v} \subset \chi^{v}, \sim\chi^{v}$ (19.1)	Ps($\chi^{\sim v}$)	$\chi^{\sim v} \subset C^{\sim v}, \sim C^{\sim v}$ (19.1)

General formulas

GF(θ)	θ: $\alpha\eta\kappa$ (17.4)	GF(B)	A: $\alpha\eta\kappa \Rightarrow B$ (20.4)
GF(β)	θ: $\alpha\eta\kappa \Rightarrow \beta$ (20.4)	GF($\sim$B)	Z: $\alpha\eta\kappa \Rightarrow \sim B$ (20.4)

Background formulas

BF(τ)	θ: $(\tau \cdot \alpha\eta\kappa) \propto \beta$	general background theory (*Urtheorie*) (21.3)
BF(ι)	θ: $(\iota \cdot I\eta\kappa) \propto \beta$	individualist theory (22.1)
BF(δ)	θ: $(\delta \cdot S\eta^{r}\kappa) \propto \beta$	collectivist theory (22.2)
BF(L^{κ})	θ: $(L^{\kappa} \cdot I\eta\chi^{v}) \propto \beta$	volitional liberalism (23.1)
BF(L^{η})	θ: $(L^{\eta} \cdot I{\sim}H{\sim}\chi) \propto \beta$	non-consensual liberalism (24.1)
BF($\sim$L)	θ: $({\sim}L \cdot I\eta\chi^{\sim v}) \propto \beta$	paternalism (25.1)
BF(D^{v})	θ: $(D^{v} \cdot S\eta^{r}\chi^{v}) \propto \beta$	popular democracy (26.1)
BF($D^{\sim v}$)	Z: $(D^{\sim v} \cdot SH^{r}{\sim}C^{\sim v}) \propto {\sim}B$	constitutional democracy (26.2)
BF($\sim$D)	A: $({\sim}D \cdot S{\sim}H^{r}{\sim}\chi) \propto B$	anti-democracy (26.3)

Ps(τ)	$\tau \subset \iota, \delta$ (22.3)	Ps(D)	$D \subset D^{v}, D^{\sim v}$ (26.4)
Ps(ι)	$\iota \subset L, {\sim}L$ (22.3)	Th(ι)	$\iota \subset L^{\kappa}, L^{\eta}, {\sim}L$ (24.4)
Ps(δ)	$\delta \subset D, {\sim}D$ (22.3)	Th(δ)	$\delta \subset D^{v}, D^{\sim v}, {\sim}D$ (26.4)
Ps(L)	$L \subset L^{\kappa}, L^{\eta}$ (24.4)	Th(τ)	$\tau \subset L^{\kappa}, L^{\eta}, {\sim}L, D^{v}, D^{\sim v}, {\sim}D$ (26.4)

Appendix 3

Reverse translation rules

Numbers in parentheses indicate the section where the rule is introduced.

Rule of Verbal Uniformity (4.2): Unless context or usage permit otherwise, verbs are translated into the present, simple tense and active voice. (Contingent.)

Rule of θ Translation (4.6): Unless context permits, plural translations of θ must not imply agreement between the claimant and respondent positions. (Contingent.)

Rule of Identity of Interest (4.3, 6.2, 7.6, 8.5): Unless context permits otherwise,

1. the arguments of more than one claimant are assumed to be identical (4.3);
2. the arguments of more than one respondent are assumed to be identical (4.3);
3. the interests of more than one personal actor are assumed to be identical (6.2);
4. the interests of more than one non-personal actor are assumed to be identical (7.6);
5. the interests of more than one society are assumed to be identical (8.5). (Contingent.)

Rule of Singular Agents (4.4, 6.3, 7.7, 8.5): Unless context permits otherwise, any agent is assumed to be singular. (Contingent.)

Rule of Singular Locutions for Agents (4.5, 6.4, 7.8, 8.5): Unless context or usage dictate otherwise, choice of singular locution for any agent is free. (Contingent.)

Rule of Rapport (6.5, 7.5, 8.4, 9.2, 15.2, 15.3, 16.3, 16.4): Unless context or usage permit otherwise, non-reflexivity is assumed between a person or entity represented by one symbol and a person or entity represented by another symbol. (Contingent.) Except,

(1) non-reflexivity must be assumed between,
  (a) Z and I^p (6.5);
  (b) $I^{\sim p}$, S or Z, and the person or entity causing a right-based harm (15.2, 15.3);
  (c) A, I^p, I, I°, α or α° and the person or entity causing restriction-based harm (16.3, 16.4). (Absolute.)

(2) reflexivity must be assumed between I^p and the person or entity causing a right-based harm (15.2). (Absolute.)

Appendix 4

European Convention on Human Rights (excerpts)

Convention for the Protection of Human Rights and Fundamental Freedoms, herein as amended by Protocol 11.

[. . .]

Section I – Rights and freedoms

Article 2 – Right to life

1. Everyone's right to life shall be protected by law. No one shall be deprived of his life intentionally save in the execution of a sentence of a court following his conviction of a crime for which this penalty is provided by law.
2. Deprivation of life shall not be regarded as inflicted in contravention of this article when it results from the use of force which is no more than absolutely necessary:
   a. in defence of any person from unlawful violence;
   b. in order to effect a lawful arrest or to prevent the escape of a person lawfully detained;
   c. in action lawfully taken for the purpose of quelling a riot or insurrection.

Article 3 – Prohibition of torture

No one shall be subjected to torture or to inhuman or degrading treatment or punishment.

[. . .]

Article 5 – Right to liberty and security

1. Everyone has the right to liberty and security of person. No one shall be deprived of his liberty save in the following cases and in accordance with a procedure prescribed by law:
   a. the lawful detention of a person after conviction by a competent court; [. . .]
   c. the lawful arrest or detention of a person effected for the purpose of bringing him before the competent legal authority on reasonable suspicion of having committed an offence or when it is reasonably considered necessary to prevent his committing an offence or fleeing after having done so; [. . .]
3. Everyone arrested or detained in accordance with the provisions of paragraph 1(c) of this article shall be brought promptly before a judge or other officer authorised by law to exercise judicial power and shall be entitled to trial within a reasonable time or to release pending trial. Release may be conditioned by guarantees to appear for trial.
4. Everyone who is deprived of his liberty by arrest or detention shall be entitled to take proceedings by which the lawfulness of his detention shall be decided speedily by a court and his release ordered if the detention is not lawful. [. . .]

Article 6 – Right to a fair trial

1. In the determination of his civil rights and obligations or of any criminal charge against him, everyone is entitled to a fair and public hearing within a reasonable time by an independent and impartial tribunal established by law. [. . .]

Article 8 – Right to respect for private and family life

1. Everyone has the right to respect for his private and family life, his home and his correspondence.
2. There shall be no interference by a public authority with the exercise of this right except such as is in accordance with the law and is necessary in a democratic society in the interests of national security, public safety or the economic well-being of the country, for the prevention of disorder or crime, for the protection of health or morals, or for the protection of the rights and freedoms of others.

Article 9 – Freedom of thought, conscience and religion

1. Everyone has the right to freedom of thought, conscience and religion; this right includes freedom to change his religion or belief and freedom, either alone or in community with others and in public or private,

to manifest his religion or belief, in worship, teaching, practice and observance.

2. Freedom to manifest one's religion or beliefs shall be subject only to such limitations as are prescribed by law and are necessary in a democratic society in the interests of public safety, for the protection of public order, health or morals, or for the protection of the rights and freedoms of others.

Article 10 – Freedom of expression

1. Everyone has the right to freedom of expression. This right shall include freedom to hold opinions and to receive and impart information and ideas without interference by public authority and regardless of frontiers. This article shall not prevent States from requiring the licensing of broadcasting, television or cinema enterprises.
2. The exercise of these freedoms, since it carries with it duties and responsibilities, may be subject to such formalities, conditions, restrictions or penalties as are prescribed by law and are necessary in a democratic society, in the interests of national security, territorial integrity or public safety, for the prevention of disorder or crime, for the protection of health or morals, for the protection of the reputation or rights of others, for preventing the disclosure of information received in confidence, or for maintaining the authority and impartiality of the judiciary.

Article 11 – Freedom of assembly and association

1. Everyone has the right to freedom of peaceful assembly and to freedom of association with others, including the right to form and to join trade unions for the protection of his interests.
2. No restrictions shall be placed on the exercise of these rights other than such as are prescribed by law and are necessary in a democratic society in the interests of national security or public safety, for the prevention of disorder or crime, for the protection of health or morals or for the protection of the rights and freedoms of others. This article shall not prevent the imposition of lawful restrictions on the exercise of these rights by members of the armed forces, of the police or of the administration of the State.

Article 12 – Right to marry

Men and women of marriageable age have the right to marry and to found a family, according to the national laws governing the exercise of this right.

[. . .]

Article 15 — Derogation in time of emergency

1. In time of war or other public emergency threatening the life of the nation any High Contracting Party may take measures derogating from its obligations under this Convention to the extent strictly required by the exigencies of the situation, provided that such measures are not inconsistent with its other obligations under international law.
2. No derogation from Article 2, except in respect of deaths resulting from lawful acts of war, or from Articles 3, 4 (paragraph 1) and 7 shall be made under this provision.
3. Any High Contracting Party availing itself of this right of derogation shall keep the Secretary General of the Council of Europe fully informed of the measures which it has taken and the reasons therefor. It shall also inform the Secretary General of the Council of Europe when such measures have ceased to operate and the provisions of the Convention are again being fully executed.

[. . .]

Section II – European Court of Human Rights

[. . .]

Article 33 – Inter-State cases

Any High Contracting Party may refer to the Court any alleged breach of the provisions of the Convention and the protocols thereto by another High Contracting Party.

Article 34 – Individual applications

The Court may receive applications from any person, non-governmental organisation or group of individuals claiming to be the victim of a violation by one of the High Contracting Parties of the rights set forth in the Convention or the protocols thereto. [. . .]

First Protocol (1952)

[. . .]

Article 1 – Protection of Property

Every natural or legal person is entitled to the peaceful enjoyment of his possessions. No one shall be deprived of his possessions except in the public interest. . . .

The preceding provisions shall not, however, in any way impair the right of a State to enforce such laws as it deems necessary to control the use of property in accordance with the general interest. . . .

Article 2 – Right to Education

No person shall be denied the right to education. In the exercise of any functions which it assumes in relation to education and to teaching, the State shall respect the right of parents to ensure such education and teaching in conformity with their own religious and philosophical convictions.

[. . .]

Answers to exercises

Chapter 3

Exercise set 3.1

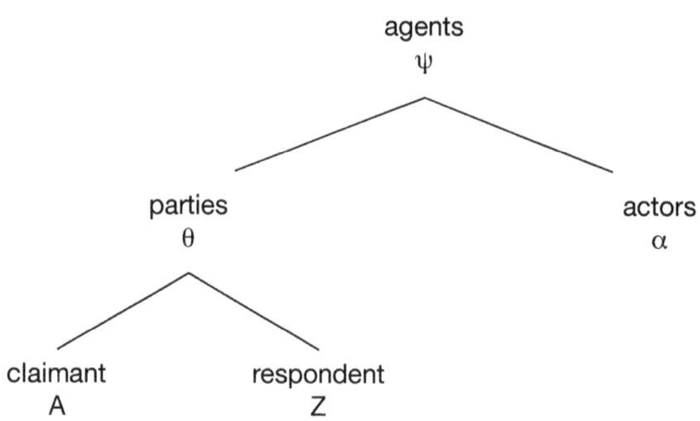

Exercise set 3.2

1 A: *x*
2 Z: *y*
3 A: *p*
4 θ: *p*

Chapter 4

Exercise set 4.1

1 The respondent asserts *p*.
2 Some party asserts *y*.
3 Both parties assert *y*.

Exercise set 4.2

1 The respondents assert *p*.
2 Some parties assert *y*.
3 All parties assert *y*.

Chapter 5

Exercise set 5.1

1 A: Iq	2 Z: Ir	3 θ: Is
4 θ: It	5 Λ: Iv	6 θ°: Iv
7 Z: Iw		

Exercise set 5.2

1 Z: $I_1p \cdot I_2q$	2 θ: $I_1r \cdot I_2r$	3 A: $Is \cdot It \cdot Iu$
4 θ°: $I_1r \cdot I_1s \cdot I_2s$		

Chapter 6

Exercise set 6.1

1 Z: I^pu	2 θ: I^pv	3 A: $I^pa \cdot I^pb \cdot I^pc$
4 θ°: $I^pb \cdot I^pc$		

Exercise set 6.2

1 Z: I^pu	2 θ: I^pv	3 θ°: I^pv
4 A: $I^pa \cdot I^pb \cdot I^pc$		

Exercise set 6.3

1 Z: $I^p{}_1u \cdot I^p{}_2u \cdot \ldots I^p{}_nu$	2 θ: $I^p{}_1v \cdot I^p{}_2v \cdot \ldots I^p{}_nv$
3 θ°: $I^p{}_1v \cdot I^p{}_2v \cdot \ldots I^p{}_nv$	

Exercise set 6.4

1 The respondent attributes interest *t* to the personal actor.
2 Some party attributes interest *k* to the personal actor.
3 The claimant attributes interests *a*, *b* and *c* to the personal actor.

Exercise set 6.5

1 The respondent attributes interest *t* to the personal actors.
2 Some party attributes interest *k* to the personal actors.
3 The claimant attributes interests *a*, *b* and *c* to the personal actors.

Exercise set 6.6

1 The respondents attribute interest *t* to the personal actor.
2 Some parties attribute interest *k* to the personal actor.
3 The claimants attribute interests *a*, *b* and *c* to the personal actor.

Exercise set 6.7

1 The respondents attribute interest *t* to the personal actors.
2 Some parties attribute interest *k* to the personal actors.
3 The claimants attribute interests *a*, *b* and *c* to the personal actors.

Exercise set 6.8

1 The respondent attributes interest *t* to the personal actor. (*Why?*)
2 Some party attributes interest *k* to (her-, him-) itself. *Which party must* θ *be?*)
3 The claimant attributes interests *a*, *b* and *c* to (her-, him-) itself.

Exercise set 6.9

1 The respondents attribute interest *t* to the personal actors.
2 Some parties attribute interest *k* to the personal actors.
3 The claimants attribute interests *a*, *b* and *c* to the personal actors.

Exercise set 6.10

1 The respondents attribute interest *t* to the personal actors.
2 Some parties attribute interest *k* to themselves.
3 The claimants attribute interests *a*, *b* and *c* to themselves.

Chapter 7

Exercise set 7.1

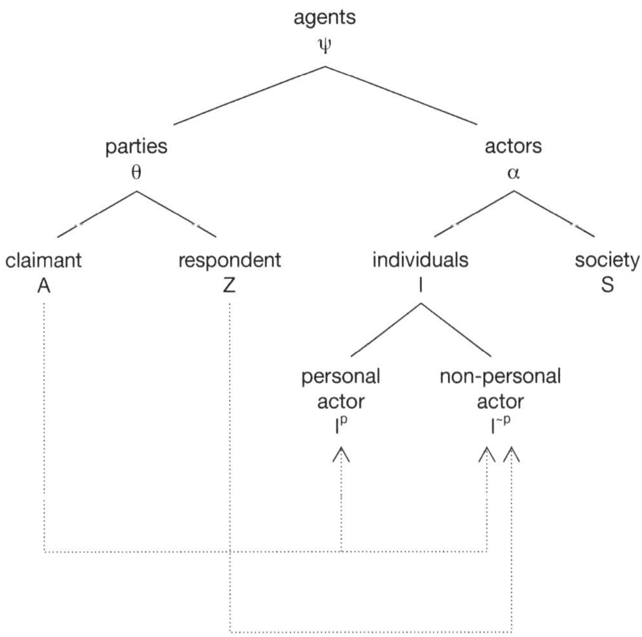

Exercise set 7.2

1 Z: $I^{\sim p}s$
2 θ: $I^{\sim p}m \cdot I^{\sim p}n$
3 θ: $I^{p}m \cdot I^{\sim p}m$
4 θ: $I^{p}m \cdot I^{\sim p}m$
5 A: $I^{p}q$ or A: $I^{\sim p}q$
6 Z: $I^{\sim p}r$
7 θ: $I^{p}s$ or θ: $I^{\sim p}s$

Exercise set 7.3

5 A: $I^{p}q$
6 (no response possible)
7 θ: $I^{p}s$

Exercise set 7.4

1 The claimant attributes interest *y* to the personal actor.
2 Some party attributes interest *s* to the non-personal actor.
3 The respondent attributes interest *x* to the personal actor and interest *y* to the non-personal actor.

4 The respondent attributes interests *x* and *y* to the non-personal actor.
5 The claimant attributes interest *x* to the personal actor and to the non-personal actor.
6 Some party attributes interest *s* to the personal actor and to the non-personal actor.

Exercise set 7.5

1 The claimants attribute interest *y* to the personal actor.
2 Some party attributes interest *s* to the non-personal actor.
3 The respondents attribute interest *x* to the personal actor and interest *y* to the non-personal actor
4 The respondents attribute interests *x* and *y* to the non-personal actor.
5 The claimants attribute interest *x* to the personal actor and to the non-personal actor.
6 Some parties attribute interest *s* to the personal actor and to the non-personal actor.

Exercise set 7.6

1 The claimant attributes interest *y* to the personal actors.
2 Some party attributes interest *s* to the non-personal actor.
3 The respondent attributes interest *x* to the personal actors and interest *y* to the non-personal actor
4 The respondent attributes interests *x* and *y* to the non-personal actor.
5 The claimant attributes interest *x* to the personal actors and to the non-personal actor.
6 Some party attributes interest *s* to the personal actors and to the non-personal actor.

Exercise set 7.7

1 The claimant attributes interest *y* to the personal actor.
2 Some party attributes interest *s* to the non-personal actors.
3 The respondent attributes interest *x* to the personal actor and interest *y* to the non-personal actors
4 The respondent attributes interests *x* and *y* to the non-personal actors.
5 The claimant attributes interest *x* to the personal actor and to the non-personal actors.
6 Some party attributes interest *s* to the personal actor and to the non-personal actors.

Exercise set 7.8

1 The claimant attributes interest *y* to the personal actors.
2 Some party attributes interest *s* to the non-personal actors.
3 The respondent attributes interest *x* to the personal actors and interest *y* to the non-personal actors
4 The respondent attributes interests *x* and *y* to the non-personal actors.
5 The claimant attributes interest *x* to the personal actors and to the non-personal actors.
6 Some party attributes interest *s* to the personal actors and to the non-personal actors.

Exercise set 7.9

1 The claimants attribute interest *y* to the personal actors.
2 Some party attributes interest *s* to the non-personal actors.
3 The respondents attribute interest *x* to the personal actors and interest *y* to the non-personal actors
4 The respondents attribute interests *x* and *y* to the non-personal actors.
5 The claimants attribute interest *x* to the personal actors and to the non-personal actors.
6 Some parties attribute interest *s* to the personal actors and to the non-personal actors.

Exercise set 7.10

1 The claimant attributes interest *y* to (her-, him-) itself.
2 Some party attributes interest *s* to the non-personal actor.
3 The respondent attributes interest *x* to the personal actor and interest *y* to the non-personal actor
4 The respondent attributes interests *x* and *y* to the non-personal actor
5 The claimant attributes interest *x* to (her-, him-) itself and to the non-personal actor.
6 Some party attributes interest *s* to (her-, him-) itself and to the non-personal actor.

Exercise set 7.11

1 The claimant attributes interest *y* to the personal actor.
2 Some party attributes interest *s* to (her-, him-) itself.
3 The respondent attributes interest *x* to the personal actor and interest *y* to (her-, him-) itself
4 The respondent attributes interests *x* and *y* to (her-, him-) itself.
5 The claimant attributes interest *x* to the personal actor and to (her-, him-) itself.
6 Some party attributes interest *s* to the personal actor and to (her-, him-) itself.

Exercise set 7.12

1 The claimants attribute interest *y* to themselves.
2 Some party attributes interest *s* to the non-personal actors.
3 The respondents attribute interest *x* to the personal actors and interest *y* to the non-personal actors
4 The respondents attribute interests *x* and *y* to the non-personal actors.
5 The claimants attribute interest *x* to themselves and to the non-personal actors.
6 Some party attributes interest *s* to (her-, him-) itself and to the non-personal actors.

Exercise set 7.13

1 The claimants attribute interest *y* to the personal actors.
2 Some party attributes interest *s* to (her-, him-) itself
3 The respondents attribute interest *x* to the personal actors and interest *y* to themselves
4 The respondents attribute interest *x* and *y* to themselves.
5 The claimants attribute interest *x* to the personal actors and to themselves.
6 Some party attributes interest *s* to the personal actor and to (her-, him-) itself.

Chapter 8

Exercise set 8.1

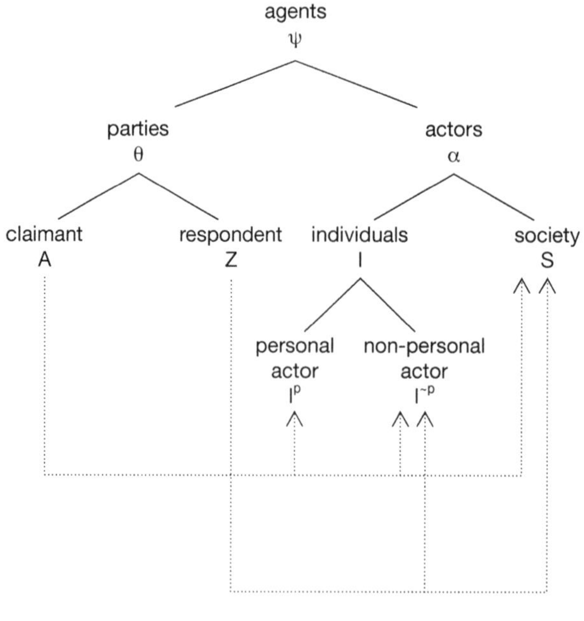

Exercise set 8.2

1	θ: $\mathrm{I}^{\sim p}x \cdot \mathrm{S}y$	2	Z: $\mathrm{I}^{p}x \cdot \mathrm{S}x$	3	Z: $\mathrm{I}^{p}x \cdot \mathrm{S}x$
4	Z: $\mathrm{S}x$	5	A: $\mathrm{S}x \cdot \mathrm{S}y \cdot \mathrm{S}z$	6	θ°: $\mathrm{S}x \cdot \mathrm{S}z$

Exercise set 8.3

1 The respondent attributes interest *p* to society.
2 The respondent attributes interests *a*, *b* and *c* to society.
3 Some party attributes interest *x* to the personal actor, to the non-personal actor and to society.
4 The claimant attributes interest *x* to the personal actor, interest *y* to the non-personal actor, and interest *z* to society.
5 Both parties attribute interest *y* to the non-personal actor and interest *z* to society.

Exercise set 8.4

1 The respondent attributes interest *p* to society.
2 The respondent attributes interests *a*, *b* and *c* to society.
3 Some party attributes interest *x* to the personal actors, to the non-personal actors and to society.
4 The claimant attributes interest *x* to the personal actors, interest *y* to the non-personal actors, and interest *z* to society.
5 Both parties attribute interest *y* to the non-personal actors, and interest *z* to society.

Exercise set 8.5

1 The respondent (state) attributes interest *p* to itself.
2 The respondent (state) attributes interests *a*, *b* and *c* to itself.

Exercise set 8.6

3 Some party attributes interest *x* to (her-, him-) itself, to the non-personal actor and to society.
4 The claimant attributes interest *x* to (her-, him-) itself, interest *y* to the non-personal actor and interest *z* to society.

Exercise set 8.7

3 Some party attributes interest *x* to the personal actors, to itself and to society.
4 The claimants attribute interest *x* to the personal actors, interest *y* to themselves and interest *z* to society.

Chapter 9

Exercise set 9.1

1 $\theta^{\circ}: \mathrm{I}a$
2 $\theta: \alpha a$
3 $\theta^{\circ}: \psi a$
4 $\mathrm{Z}: \mathrm{I}^{p}b$
5 $\theta^{\circ}: \alpha^{\circ}a$
6 $\theta^{\circ}: \mathrm{I}^{\circ}b$
7 $\psi: \psi a$

Exercise set 9.2

1 The respondent attributes interest *b* to all individual actors.
2 Some party attributes interest *c* to some actor.
3 Some party attributes interest *d* to all actors.
4 The claimant attributes interest *a* to all individual actors and interest *b* to the personal actor.

Exercise set 9.3

1 The respondents attribute interest *b* to themselves.
2 Some parties attribute interest *c* to themselves.
3 Both (all) parties attribute interest *d* to all actors.
4 The claimants attribute interest *a* and *b* to themselves.

Exercise set 9.4

1	(1)	$\psi \subset \theta, \alpha$	$\mathrm{Ps}(\psi)$
	conclusion	$\psi \subset \theta, \mathrm{I}, \mathrm{S}$	$\mathrm{Ps}(\alpha)$
2	(1)	$\psi \subset \theta, \alpha$	$\mathrm{Ps}(\psi)$
	conclusion	$\psi \subset \mathrm{A}, \mathrm{Z}, \alpha$	$\mathrm{Ps}(\theta)$
3	(1)	$\psi \subset \theta, \alpha$	$\mathrm{Ps}(\psi)$
	(2)	$\psi \subset \theta, \mathrm{I}, \mathrm{S}$	$\mathrm{Ps}(\alpha)$
	conclusion	$\psi \subset \theta, \mathrm{I}^{p}, \mathrm{I}^{\sim p}, \mathrm{S}$	$\mathrm{Ps}(\mathrm{I})$
4	(1)	$\psi \subset \theta, \alpha$	$\mathrm{Ps}(\psi)$
	(2)	$\psi \subset \mathrm{A}, \mathrm{Z}, \alpha$	$\mathrm{Ps}(\theta)$
	(3)	$\psi \subset \mathrm{A}, \mathrm{Z}, \mathrm{I}, \mathrm{S}$	$\mathrm{Ps}(\alpha)$
	conclusion	$\psi \subset \mathrm{A}, \mathrm{Z}, \mathrm{I}^{p}, \mathrm{I}^{\sim p}, \mathrm{S}$	$\mathrm{Ps}(\mathrm{I})$

Exercise set 9.5

3	(1)	$\psi \subset \theta, \alpha$	$\mathrm{Ps}(\psi)$
	conclusion	$\psi \subset \theta, \mathrm{I}^{p}, \mathrm{I}^{\sim p}, \mathrm{S}$	$\mathrm{Th}(\alpha)$
4	(1)	$\psi \subset \theta, \alpha$	$\mathrm{Ps}(\psi)$
	(2)	$\psi \subset \mathrm{A}, \mathrm{Z}, \alpha$	$\mathrm{Ps}(\theta)$
	conclusion	$\psi \subset \mathrm{A}, \mathrm{Z}, \mathrm{I}^{p}, \mathrm{I}^{\sim p}, \mathrm{S}$	$\mathrm{Th}(\alpha)$

Exercise set 9.6

1	(1)	A: $\mathrm{I}^{p}a$	given
	conclusion	A: $\mathrm{I}a$	Ps(I)
2	(1)	Z: $\mathrm{I}^{p}b$	given
	(2)	θ: $\mathrm{I}^{p}b$	Ps(θ)
	(3)	θ: $\mathrm{I}b$	Ps(I)
	conclusion	θ: αb	Ps(α)
3	(1)	A: $\mathrm{I}^{\sim p}c$	given
	(2)	θ: $\mathrm{I}^{\sim p}c$	Ps(θ)
	conclusion	θ: αc	Th(α)
4	(1)	θ: $\mathrm{S}b$	given
	conclusion	θ: αb	Ps(α)

Chapter 11

Exercise set 11.1

1	(a)	2	$\mathrm{HA_A}$(1)(b)	3	$\mathrm{HA_A}$(1)(c)(i)
4	(a)	5	$\mathrm{HA_Z}$(1)(b)	6	$\mathrm{HA_Z}$(1)(c)
7	(1)(a)	8	$\mathrm{HA_A}$(1)(b)	9	$\mathrm{HA_A}$(1)(c)(i)
10	$\mathrm{HA_Z}$(1)(a)	11	$\mathrm{HA_Z}$(1)(b)	12	$\mathrm{HA_Z}$(1)(c)

Exercise set 11.2

1	(a)	2	$\mathrm{HA_Z}$(2)(b)	3	$\mathrm{HA_Z}$(2)(c)(i)
4	(a)	5	$\mathrm{HA_A}$(2)(b)	6	$\mathrm{HA_A}$(2)(c)

Exercise set 11.3

1	(2)(a)	2	$\mathrm{HA_Z}$(2)(b)	3	$\mathrm{HA_Z}$(2)(c)(i)
4	(a)	5	$\mathrm{HA_A}$(2)(b)	6	$\mathrm{HA_A}$(2)(c)

Exercise set 11.4

1	$\mathrm{HA_Z}$(1)(a)	2	$\mathrm{HA_Z}$(1)(b)	3	$\mathrm{HA_Z}$(1)(c)
4	$\mathrm{HA_A}$(1)(a)	5	$\mathrm{HA_A}$(1)(b)	6	$\mathrm{HA_A}$(1)(c)(i)

Chapter 12

Exercise set 12.1

1	$\mathrm{HA_Z}$(1)(a)	2	$\mathrm{HA_Z}$(1)(b)	3	$\mathrm{HA_Z}$(1)(c)
4	$\mathrm{HA_A}$(1)(a)	5	$\mathrm{HA_A}$(1)(b)	6	$\mathrm{HA_A}$(1)(c)(i)
7	$\mathrm{HA_Z}$(1)(a)	8	$\mathrm{HA_Z}$(1)(b)	9	$\mathrm{HA_Z}$(1)(c)
10	$\mathrm{HA_A}$(1)(a)	11	$\mathrm{HA_A}$(1)(b)	12	$\mathrm{HA_A}$(1)(c)(i)

Exercise set 12.2

1	(a)	2	$HA_A(2)(b)$	3	$HA_A(2)(c)$
4	$HA_Z(2)(a)$	5	$HA_Z(2)(b)$	6	$HA_Z(2)(c)(i)$

Chapter 13

Exercise set 13.1

1	Z: $I^{\sim p}H$	2	A: $I^{\sim p}{\sim}H$	3	θ: $S{\sim}H$
4	Z: SH	5	A: $I^{\sim p}{\sim}H$	6	A: $I^{\sim p}{\sim}H$
7	Z: $I^{\sim p}H$	8	Z: SH	9	Z: SH
10	θ: $S{\sim}\gamma$	11	A: $I^{\sim p}\eta$	12	Z: $I^{\sim p}H \cdot SH$
13	$\theta°$: $I^{\sim p}\gamma \cdot S\gamma$	14	θ: $I^{\sim p}{\sim}\gamma \cdot S{\sim}\gamma$	15	$\theta°$: $I^{\sim p}\eta$

Exercise set 13.2

1	(1)	θ: $S{\sim}H$	given
	conclusion	θ: $S\gamma$	Ps(γ1)
2	(1)	θ: $S{\sim}\gamma$	given
	conclusion	θ: $S\eta$	Ps(η1)
3	(1)	θ: $I^{\sim p}{\sim}H$	given
	(2)	θ: $I^{\sim p}\gamma$	Ps(γ1)
	conclusion	θ: $I^{\sim p}\eta$	Ps(η1)
4	(1)	θ: $I^{\sim p}H$	given
	conclusion	θ: $I^{\sim p}\eta$	Th(η)

Exercise set 13.3

1	(1)	$\gamma \subset H, {\sim}H$	Ps(γ1)
	conclusion	$I^{\sim p}\gamma \subset I^{\sim p}H, I^{\sim p}{\sim}H$	η attr
2	(1)	$\eta \subset \gamma, {\sim}\gamma$	Ps(η1)
	conclusion	$I^{\sim p}\eta \subset I^{\sim p}\gamma, I^{\sim p}{\sim}\gamma$	η attr
3	(1)	$\eta \subset H, {\sim}H, {\sim}\gamma$	Th(η)
	conclusion	$S\eta \subset SH, S{\sim}H, S{\sim}\gamma$	η attr

Exercise set 13.4

1	γ	2	S	3	~H
4	$I^{\sim p}$	5	I^{p}	6	H
7	$I^{\sim p}$				

Chapter 14

Exercise set 14.1

1	(1)	$\eta \subset \eta^{r}, \eta^{\sim r}$	Ps(η2)
	(2)	$\eta \subset \gamma^{r}, \sim\gamma^{r}, \eta^{\sim r}$	Ps(η^{r})
	conclusion	$\eta \subset \gamma^{r}, \sim\gamma^{r}, \gamma^{\sim r}, \sim\gamma^{\sim r}$	Ps($\eta^{\sim r}$)
2	(1)	$\sim\gamma \subset \sim\gamma^{r}, \sim\gamma^{\sim r}$	Ps($\sim\gamma$)
	conclusion	$I^{p}\sim\gamma \subset I^{p}\sim\gamma^{r}, I^{p}\sim\gamma^{\sim r}$	η attr
3	(1)	$\gamma \subset \gamma^{r}, \gamma^{\sim r}$	Ps(γ2)
	(2)	$\gamma \subset H^{r}, \sim H^{r}, \gamma^{\sim r}$	Ps(γ^{r})
	(3)	$\gamma \subset H^{r}, \sim H^{r}, H^{\sim r}, \sim H^{\sim r}$	Ps($\gamma^{\sim r}$)
	(5)	$I\gamma \subset IH^{r}, I\sim H^{r}, IH^{\sim r}, I\sim H^{\sim r}$	η attr
	(6)	$I\gamma \subset I^{p}H^{r}, I^{\sim p}H^{r}, I^{p}\sim H^{r}, I^{\sim p}\sim H^{r}, I^{p}H^{\sim r}, I^{\sim p}H^{\sim r}, I^{p}\sim H^{\sim r}, I^{\sim p}\sim H^{\sim r}$	Ps(I)
	conclusion	$I\gamma \subset I^{p}H^{r}, I^{\sim p}H^{r}, I^{p}\sim H^{r}, I^{\sim p}\sim H^{r}, I^{p}H^{\sim r}, I^{p}\sim H^{\sim r}$	α lim
4	(1)	$\eta \subset \eta^{r}, \eta^{\sim r}$	Ps(η2)
	(2)	$\eta \subset \gamma^{r}, \sim\gamma^{r}, \eta^{\sim r}$	Ps(η^{r})
	(3)	$\eta \subset \gamma^{r}, \sim\gamma^{r}, \gamma^{\sim r}, \sim\gamma^{\sim r}$	Ps($\eta^{\sim r}$)
	(4)	$\eta \subset H^{r}, \sim H^{r}, \sim\gamma^{r}, \gamma^{\sim r}, \sim\gamma^{\sim r}$	Ps(γ^{r})
	(5)	$\eta \subset H^{r}, \sim H^{r}, \sim\gamma^{r}, H^{\sim r}, \sim H^{\sim r}, \sim\gamma^{\sim r}$	Ps($\gamma^{\sim r}$)
	conclusion	$I\eta \subset IH^{r}, I\sim H^{r}, I\sim\gamma^{r}, IH^{\sim r}, I\sim H^{\sim r}, I\sim\gamma^{\sim r}$	η attr
5	(1)	$\eta \subset \eta^{r}, \eta^{\sim r}$	Ps(η2)
	(2)	$\eta \subset \gamma^{r}, \sim\gamma^{r}, \eta^{\sim r}$	Ps(η^{r})
	(3)	$\eta \subset \gamma^{r}, \sim\gamma^{r}, \gamma^{\sim r}, \sim\gamma^{\sim r}$	Ps($\eta^{\sim r}$)
	(4)	$\eta \subset H^{r}, \sim H^{r}, \sim\gamma^{r}, \gamma^{\sim r}, \sim\gamma^{\sim r}$	Ps(γ^{r})
	(5)	$\eta \subset H^{r}, \sim H^{r}, \sim\gamma^{r}, H^{\sim r}, \sim H^{\sim r}, \sim\gamma^{\sim r}$	Ps($\gamma^{\sim r}$)
	(6)	$\alpha\eta \subset \alpha H^{r}, \alpha\sim H^{r}, \alpha\sim\gamma^{r}, \alpha H^{\sim r}, \alpha\sim H^{\sim r}, \alpha\sim\gamma^{\sim r}$	η attr
	(7)	$\alpha\eta \subset I^{p}H^{r}, I^{\sim p}H^{r}, SH^{r}, I^{p}\sim H^{r}, I^{\sim p}\sim H^{r}, S\sim H^{r}, I^{p}\sim\gamma^{r}, I^{\sim p}\sim\gamma^{r}, S\sim\gamma^{r}, I^{p}H^{\sim r}, I^{\sim p}H^{\sim r}, SH^{\sim r}, I^{p}\sim H^{\sim r}, I^{\sim p}\sim H^{\sim r}, S\sim H^{\sim r}, I^{p}\sim\gamma^{\sim r}, I^{\sim p}\sim\gamma^{\sim r}, S\sim\gamma^{\sim r}$	Th(α)
	conclusion	$\alpha\eta \subset I^{p}H^{r}, I^{\sim p}H^{r}, SH^{r}, I^{p}\sim H^{r}, I^{\sim p}\sim H^{r}, S\sim H^{r}, I^{p}\sim\gamma^{r}, I^{\sim p}\sim\gamma^{r}, S\sim\gamma^{r}, I^{p}H^{\sim r}, I^{p}\sim H^{\sim r}, I^{p}\sim\gamma^{\sim r}$	α lim

Exercise set 14.2

1 η
2 r
3 ~r
4 H
5 ~H

Exercise set 14.3

1	(1)	A: $I^{p}{\sim}H^{r}$	given
	(2)	θ: $I^{p}{\sim}H^{r}$	Ps(θ)
	(3)	θ: $I{\sim}H^{r}$	Ps(I)
	(4)	θ: I~H	Ps(~H)
	conclusion	θ: Iγ	Ps(γ1)
2	(1)	Z: $I^{p}{\sim}H^{\sim r}$	given
	(2)	θ: $I^{p}{\sim}H^{\sim r}$	Ps(θ)
	(3)	θ: $I{\sim}H^{\sim r}$	Ps(I)
	(4)	θ: I~H	Ps(~H)
	conclusion	θ: Iη	Th(η)
3	(1)	A: $I^{p}H^{\sim r}$	given
	(2)	θ: $I^{p}H^{\sim r}$	Ps(θ)
	(3)	θ: $IH^{\sim r}$	Ps(I)
	(4)	θ: $\alpha H^{\sim r}$	Ps(α)
	(5)	θ: αH	Ps(H)
	conclusion	θ: αγ	Ps(γ1)
4	(1)	Z: $I^{p}{\sim}\gamma^{\sim r}$	given
	(2)	Z: $I{\sim}\gamma^{\sim r}$	Ps(I)
	(3)	Z: I~γ	Ps(~γ)
	conclusion	Z: Iη	Ps(η1)
5	(1)	A: $I^{p}H^{\sim r}$	given
	(2)	θ: $I^{p}H^{\sim r}$	Ps(θ)
	(3)	θ: $\alpha H^{\sim r}$	Th(α)
	(4)	θ: αH	Ps(H)
	conclusion	θ: αη	Th(η)
6	(1)	Z: $I^{p}H^{r}$	given
	(2)	θ: $I^{p}H^{r}$	Ps(θ)
	(3)	θ: αH^{r}	Th(α)
	(4)	θ: αH	Ps(H)
	conclusion	θ: αη	Th(η)

Chapter 15

Exercise set 15.1

1	~H	2	$I^{\sim p}$	3	Z
4	r	5	A	6	~H
7	H	8	${\sim}H^{r}$	9	H^{r}
10	SH^{r}	11	$I^{\sim p}H^{r}$	12	SH^{r}
13	$I^{\sim p}{\sim}H^{r}$	14	$S{\sim}H^{r}$	15	p
16	r	17	$I^{p}{\sim}H^{r}$	18	Z: SH^{r}
19	A: $S{\sim}H^{r}$				

Exercise set 15.2

1	A: $I^{p}\sim H^{r}$	2	A: $I^{p}\sim H^{r}$	3	A: $I^{p}\sim H^{r}$
4	A: $I^{\sim p}\sim H^{r}$	5	θ: $I^{\sim p}\eta^{r}$	6	A: $I^{\sim p}\sim\gamma^{r}$
7	Z: $I^{\sim p}\gamma^{r}$	8	A: $I^{\circ}\sim H^{r}$	9	A: $\alpha^{\circ}\sim H^{r}$
10	θ: $\alpha\eta$	11	θ: $I\eta^{r}$	12	θ: $\alpha\eta$
13	θ: $\alpha\gamma$	14	θ: $\alpha\sim H$	15	θ: $\alpha^{\circ}\sim\gamma^{r}$
16	Z: SH^{r}	17	θ°: $S\sim H^{r}$	18	Z: IH^{r}
19	Z: $I^{\circ}H^{r}$	20	Z: $I^{\circ}\sim H^{r}$	21	A: $I^{p}\sim H^{r}\cdot S\sim H^{r}$

Exercise set 15.3

1	γ	2	S	3	$\sim H$
4	$I^{\sim p}$	5	I^{p}	6	H
7	$I^{\sim p}$				

Chapter 16

Exercise set 16.1

1	A: $I^{p}H^{\sim r}$	2	Z: $I^{p}\gamma^{\sim r}$	3	θ: $I^{p}\eta^{\sim r}$
4	Z: $I^{p}\sim\gamma^{\sim r}$				

Exercise set 16.2

1	γ	2	$I^{p}\sim H^{\sim r}$

Chapter 17

Exercise set 17.1

(1)	$\kappa \subset \chi, \sim\chi$	Ps(κ1)
conclusion	$\kappa \subset C, \sim C, \sim\chi$	Ps(χ1)

Exercise set 17.2

1	(1)	$\eta^{r} \subset \gamma^{r}, \sim\gamma^{r}$	Ps(η^{r})
	(2)	$\alpha\eta^{r} \subset \alpha\gamma^{r}, \alpha\sim\gamma^{r}$	η attr
	conclusion	$\alpha\eta^{r}\kappa \subset \alpha\gamma^{r}\kappa, \alpha\sim\gamma^{r}\kappa$	κ attr
2	(1)	$\sim\gamma \subset \sim\gamma^{r}, \sim\gamma^{\sim r}$	Ps(~γ)
	(2)	$I\sim\gamma \subset I\sim\gamma^{r}, I\sim\gamma^{\sim r}$	η attr
	(3)	$I\sim\gamma \subset I^{p}\sim\gamma^{r}, I^{\sim p}\sim\gamma^{r}, I^{p}\sim\gamma^{\sim r}, I^{\sim p}\sim\gamma^{\sim r}$	Ps(I)
	(4)	$I\sim\gamma \subset I^{p}\sim\gamma^{r}, I^{\sim p}\sim\gamma^{r}, I^{p}\sim\gamma^{\sim r}$	α lim
	conclusion	$I\sim\gamma\kappa \subset I^{p}\sim\gamma^{r}\kappa, I^{\sim p}\sim\gamma^{r}\kappa, I^{p}\sim\gamma^{\sim r}\kappa$	κ attr

3	(1)	$\gamma \subset \gamma^r, \gamma^{\sim r}$	$Ps(\gamma 2)$
	(2)	$\gamma \subset H^r, {\sim}H^r, \gamma^{\sim r}$	$Ps(\gamma^r)$
	(3)	$\gamma \subset H^r, {\sim}H^r, H^{\sim r}, {\sim}H^{\sim r}$	$Ps(\gamma^{\sim r})$
	(4)	$I\gamma \subset IH^r, I{\sim}H^r, IH^{\sim r}, I{\sim}H^{\sim r}$	η attr
	(5)	$I\gamma \subset I^pH^r, I^{\sim p}H^r, I^p{\sim}H^r, I^{\sim p}{\sim}H^r, I^pH^{\sim r}, I^{\sim p}H^{\sim r}, I^p{\sim}H^{\sim r}, I^{\sim p}{\sim}H^{\sim r}$	$Ps(I)$
	(6)	$I\gamma \subset I^pH^r, I^{\sim p}H^r, I^p{\sim}H^r, I^{\sim p}{\sim}H^r, I^pH^{\sim r}, I^p{\sim}H^{\sim r}$	α lim
	conclusion	$I\gamma\kappa \subset I^pH^r\kappa, I^{\sim p}H^r\kappa, I^p{\sim}H^r\kappa, I^{\sim p}{\sim}H^r\kappa, I^pH^{\sim r}\kappa, I^p{\sim}H^{\sim r}\kappa$	κ attr

Exercise set 17.3

1	(1)	Z: $I^pH^r{\sim}C$	given
	(2)	θ: $I^pH^r{\sim}C$	$Ps(\theta)$
	(3)	θ: $IH^r{\sim}C$	$Ps(I)$
	conclusion	θ: $IH^r\chi$	$Ps(\chi 1)$
2	(1)	A: $I^pH^{\sim r}{\sim}C$	given
	(2)	θ: $I^pH^{\sim r}{\sim}C$	$Ps(\theta)$
	(3)	θ: $IH^{\sim r}{\sim}C$	$Ps(I)$
	(4)	θ: $IH{\sim}C$	$Ps(H)$
	(5)	θ: $I\eta{\sim}C$	$Th(\eta)$
	conclusion	θ: $I\eta\kappa$	$Th(\kappa)$

Chapter 18

Exercise set 18.1

1 Z: $I^{\circ}H^r{\sim}C$ [$Ps(H\kappa)$]

2 A: $I^p{\sim}H^r{\sim}\chi$ [$Ps({\sim}H\kappa)$]

3 A: $I{\sim}\gamma^rC$ [$Ps(\eta C)$]

4 A: $I^pH^{\sim r}{\sim}C$ [$Ps(\eta{\sim}C)$]

5 A: $S{\sim}\gamma^rC$ [$Ps({\sim}\gamma\kappa)$]

6 θ: $S{\sim}H^r{\sim}\chi$ [$Ps(\eta{\sim}\chi)$]

Exercise set 18.2

1	(1)	A: $I^pH^{\sim r}{\sim}C$	given
	(2)	θ: $I^pH^{\sim r}{\sim}C$	$Ps(\theta)$
	(3)	θ: $I^pH{\sim}C$	$Ps(H)$
	(4)	θ: $I^p\gamma{\sim}C$	$Ps(\gamma 1)$
	conclusion	θ: $I^p\gamma\chi$	$Ps(\chi 1)$
2	(1)	A: $I{\sim}H^r{\sim}\chi$	given
	(2)	θ: $I{\sim}H^r{\sim}\chi$	$Ps(\theta)$
	(3)	θ: $\alpha{\sim}H^r{\sim}\chi$	$Ps(\alpha)$
	conclusion	θ: $\alpha\gamma^r{\sim}\chi$	$Ps(\gamma^r)$

3	(1)	Z: $I^{p}H^{r}\sim C$	given
	(2)	Z: $IH^{r}\sim C$	Ps(I)
	(3)	Z: $IH\sim C$	Ps(H)
	(4)	Z: $I\eta\sim C$	Th(η)
	conclusion	Z: $I\eta\chi$	Ps(χ1)

Exercise set 18.3

1	C	2	$\sim\chi$

Exercise set 18.4

1	θ	2	$\sim\gamma$	3	γ^{r}
4	I	5	S	6	I^{p}
7	C	8	$\sim\chi$		

Exercise set 18.5

1	(1)	$\eta^{r} \subset \gamma^{r}, \sim\gamma^{r}$	Ps(η^{r})
	(2)	$\eta^{r} \subset H^{r}, \sim H^{r}, \sim\gamma^{r}$	Ps(γ^{r})
	(3)	$I\eta^{r} \subset IH^{r}, I\sim H^{r}, I\sim\gamma^{r}$	η attr
	(4)	$I\eta^{r} \subset I^{p}H^{r}, I^{\sim p}H^{r}, I^{p}\sim H^{r}, I^{\sim p}\sim H^{r}, I^{p}\sim\gamma^{r}, I^{\sim p}\sim\gamma^{r}$	Ps(I)
	(5)	$I\eta^{r}\kappa \subset I^{p}H^{r}\kappa, I^{\sim p}H^{r}\kappa, I^{p}\sim H^{r}\kappa, I^{\sim p}\sim H^{r}\kappa, I^{p}\sim\gamma^{r}\kappa, I^{\sim p}\sim\gamma^{r}\kappa$	κ attr
	conclusion	$I\eta^{r}\sim C \subset I^{p}H^{r}\sim C, I^{\sim p}H^{r}\sim C$	Ps($\eta\sim C$)
2	(1)	$\sim\gamma \subset \sim\gamma^{r}, \sim\gamma^{\sim r}$	Ps($\sim\gamma$)
	(2)	$\alpha\sim\gamma \subset \alpha\sim\gamma^{r}, \alpha\sim\gamma^{\sim r}$	η attr
	(3)	$\alpha\sim\gamma \subset I^{p}\sim\gamma^{r}, I^{\sim p}\sim\gamma^{r}, S\sim\gamma^{r}, I^{p}\sim\gamma^{\sim r}, I^{\sim p}\sim\gamma^{r}, S\sim\gamma^{r}$	Th(α)
	(4)	$\alpha\sim\gamma \subset I^{p}\sim\gamma^{r}, I^{\sim p}\sim\gamma^{r}, S\sim\gamma^{r}, I^{p}\sim\gamma^{\sim r}$	α lim
	(5)	$\alpha\sim\gamma\kappa \subset I^{p}\sim\gamma^{r}\kappa, I^{\sim p}\sim\gamma^{r}\kappa, S\sim\gamma^{r}\kappa, I^{p}\sim\gamma^{\sim r}\kappa$	κ attr
	conclusion	$\alpha\sim\gamma\kappa \subset I^{p}\sim\gamma^{r}C, I^{\sim p}\sim\gamma^{r}C, S\sim\gamma^{r}C, I^{p}\sim\gamma^{\sim r}C$	Ps($\sim\gamma\kappa$)
3	(1)	$\eta \subset H, \sim H, \sim\gamma$	Th(η)
	(2)	$I^{p}\eta \subset I^{p}H, I^{p}\sim H, I^{p}\sim\gamma$	η attr
	(3)	$I^{p}\eta\kappa \subset I^{p}H\kappa, I^{p}\sim H\kappa, I^{p}\sim\gamma\kappa$	κ attr
	(4)	$I^{p}\eta\sim\chi \subset I^{p}\sim H\sim\chi$	Ps($\eta\sim\chi$)
	conclusion	$I^{p}\eta\sim\chi \subset I^{p}\sim H^{r}\sim\chi, I^{p}\sim H^{\sim r}\sim\chi$	Ps($\sim H$)
4	(1)	$\sim H \subset \sim H^{r}, \sim H^{\sim r}$	Ps($\sim H$)
	(2)	$I\sim H \subset I\sim H^{r}, I\sim H^{\sim r}$	η attr
	(3)	$I\sim H \subset I^{p}\sim H^{r}, I^{\sim p}\sim H^{r}, I^{p}\sim H^{\sim r}, I^{\sim p}\sim H^{\sim r}$	Ps(I)
	(4)	$I\sim H \subset I^{p}\sim H^{r}, I^{\sim p}\sim H^{r}, I^{p}\sim H^{\sim r}$	α lim
	(5)	$I\sim H\kappa \subset I^{p}\sim H^{r}\kappa, I^{\sim p}\sim H^{r}\kappa, I^{p}\sim H^{\sim r}\kappa$	κ attr
	conclusion	$I\sim H\kappa \subset I^{p}\sim H^{r}\sim\chi, I^{\sim p}\sim H^{r}\sim\chi, I^{p}\sim H^{\sim r}\sim\chi$	Ps($\sim H\kappa$)

5	(1)	$\gamma \subset \gamma^{r}, \gamma^{\sim r}$	Ps(γ2)
	(2)	$\gamma \subset H^{r}, {\sim}H^{r}, \gamma^{\sim r}$	Ps(γ^{r})
	(3)	$\gamma \subset H^{r}, {\sim}H^{r}, H^{\sim r}, {\sim}H^{\sim r}$	Ps($\gamma^{\sim r}$)
	(4)	$I\gamma \subset IH^{r}, I{\sim}H^{r}, IH^{\sim r}, I{\sim}H^{\sim r}$	η attr
	(5)	$I\gamma \subset I^{p}H^{r}, I^{\sim p}H^{r}, I^{p}{\sim}H^{r}, I^{\sim p}{\sim}H^{r}, I^{p}H^{\sim r}, I^{\sim p}H^{\sim r}, I^{p}{\sim}H^{\sim r}, I^{\sim p}{\sim}H^{\sim r}$	Ps(I)
	(6)	$I\gamma \subset I^{p}H^{r}, I^{\sim p}H^{r}, I^{p}{\sim}H^{r}, I^{\sim p}{\sim}H^{r}, I^{p}H^{\sim r}, I^{p}{\sim}H^{\sim r}$	α lim
	(7)	$I\gamma\kappa \subset I^{p}H^{r}\kappa, I^{\sim p}H^{r}\kappa, I^{p}{\sim}H^{r}\kappa, I^{\sim p}{\sim}H^{r}\kappa, I^{p}H^{\sim r}\kappa, I^{p}{\sim}H^{\sim r}\kappa$	κ attr
	(8)	$I\gamma\kappa \subset I^{p}H^{r}{\sim}C, I^{\sim p}H^{r}{\sim}C, I^{p}{\sim}H^{r}\kappa, I^{\sim p}{\sim}H^{r}\kappa, I^{p}H^{\sim r}{\sim}C, I^{p}{\sim}H^{\sim r}\kappa$	Ps(Hκ)
	conclusion	$I\gamma\kappa \subset I^{p}H^{r}{\sim}C, I^{\sim p}H^{r}{\sim}C, I^{p}{\sim}H^{r}{\sim}\chi, I^{\sim p}{\sim}H^{r}{\sim}\chi, I^{p}H^{\sim r}{\sim}C, I^{p}{\sim}H^{\sim r}{\sim}\chi$	Ps(~Hκ)
6	(1)	$\eta \subset \gamma, {\sim}\gamma$	Ps(η1)
	(2)	$\alpha\eta \subset \alpha\gamma, \alpha{\sim}\gamma$	η attr
	(3)	$\alpha\eta\kappa \subset \alpha\gamma\kappa, \alpha{\sim}\gamma\kappa$	κ attr
	(4)	$\alpha\eta C \subset \alpha{\sim}\gamma C$	Ps(ηC)
	(5)	$\alpha\eta C \subset \alpha{\sim}\gamma^{r}C, \alpha{\sim}\gamma^{\sim r}C$	Ps(~γ)
	(6)	$\alpha\eta C \subset I^{p}{\sim}\gamma^{r}C, I^{\sim p}{\sim}\gamma^{r}C, S{\sim}\gamma^{r}C, I^{p}{\sim}\gamma^{\sim r}C, I^{\sim p}{\sim}\gamma^{\sim r}C, S{\sim}\gamma^{\sim r}C$	Th(α)
	conclusion	$\alpha\eta C \subset I^{p}{\sim}\gamma^{r}C, I^{\sim p}{\sim}\gamma^{r}C, S{\sim}\gamma^{r}C, I^{p}{\sim}\gamma^{\sim r}C$	α lim
7	(1)	$\gamma \subset H, {\sim}H$	Ps(γ1)
	(2)	$I^{p}\gamma \subset I^{p}H, I^{p}{\sim}H$	η attr
	(3)	$I^{p}\gamma\kappa \subset I^{p}H\kappa, I^{p}{\sim}H\kappa$	κ attr
	(4)	$I^{p}\gamma{\sim}C \subset I^{p}H{\sim}C$	Ps(η~C)
	conclusion	$I^{p}\gamma{\sim}C \subset I^{p}H^{r}{\sim}C, I^{p}H^{\sim r}{\sim}C$	Ps(H)

Chapter 19

Exercise set 19.1

1	(1)	$\kappa \subset \kappa^{v}, \kappa^{\sim v}$	Ps(κ2)
	(2)	$\kappa \subset \chi^{v}, {\sim}\chi^{v}, \kappa^{\sim v}$	Ps(κ^{v})
	conclusion	$\kappa \subset \chi^{v}, {\sim}\chi^{v}, \chi^{\sim v}, {\sim}\chi^{\sim v}$	Ps($\kappa^{\sim v}$)
2	(1)	$\kappa \subset \kappa^{v}, \kappa^{\sim v}$	Ps(κ2)
	(2)	$\kappa \subset \chi^{v}, {\sim}\chi^{v}, \kappa^{\sim v}$	Ps(κ^{v})
	(3)	$\kappa \subset \chi^{v}, {\sim}\chi^{v}, \chi^{\sim v}, {\sim}\chi^{\sim v}$	Ps($\kappa^{\sim v}$)
	(4)	$\kappa \subset C^{v}, {\sim}C^{v}, {\sim}\chi^{v}, \chi^{\sim v}, {\sim}\chi^{\sim v}$	Ps(χ^{v})
	conclusion	$\kappa \subset C^{v}, {\sim}C^{v}, {\sim}\chi^{v}, C^{\sim v}, {\sim}C^{\sim v}, {\sim}\chi^{\sim v}$	Ps($\chi^{\sim v}$)

3	(1)	$\gamma \subset \gamma^{r}, \gamma^{\sim r}$	Ps(γ2)
	(2)	$\gamma \subset H^{r}, {\sim}H^{r}, \gamma^{\sim r}$	Ps(γ^{r})
	(3)	$\gamma \subset H^{r}, {\sim}H^{r}, H^{\sim r}, {\sim}H^{\sim r}$	Ps($\gamma^{\sim r}$)
	(4)	$I^{\sim p}\gamma \subset I^{\sim p}H^{r}, I^{\sim p}{\sim}H^{r}, I^{\sim p}H^{\sim r}, I^{\sim p}{\sim}H^{\sim r}$	η attr
	(5)	$I^{\sim p}\gamma \subset I^{\sim p}H^{r}, I^{\sim p}{\sim}H^{r}$	α lim
	(6)	$I^{\sim p}\gamma\kappa \subset I^{\sim p}H^{r}\kappa, I^{\sim p}{\sim}H^{r}\kappa$	κ attr
	(7)	$I^{\sim p}\gamma\kappa \subset I^{\sim p}H^{r}{\sim}C, I^{\sim p}{\sim}H^{r}\kappa$	Ps(Hκ)
	(8)	$I^{\sim p}\gamma\kappa \subset I^{\sim p}H^{r}{\sim}C, I^{\sim p}{\sim}H^{r}{\sim}\chi$	Ps(~Hκ)
	conclusion	$I^{\sim p}\gamma\kappa \subset I^{\sim p}H^{r}{\sim}C^{v}, I^{\sim p}H^{r}{\sim}C^{\sim v}, I^{\sim p}{\sim}H^{r}{\sim}\chi$	Ps(~C)
4	(1)	$\eta \subset H, {\sim}H, {\sim}\gamma$	Ps(η)
	(2)	$\eta \subset H^{r}, H^{\sim r}, {\sim}H, {\sim}\gamma$	Ps(H)
	(3)	$\eta \subset H^{r}, H^{\sim r}, {\sim}H^{r}, {\sim}H^{\sim r}, {\sim}\gamma$	Ps(~H)
	(4)	$\eta \subset H^{r}, H^{\sim r}, {\sim}H^{r}, {\sim}H^{\sim r}, {\sim}\gamma^{r}, {\sim}\gamma^{\sim r}$	Ps(~γ)
	(5)	$S\eta \subset SH^{r}, SH^{\sim r}, S{\sim}H^{r}, S{\sim}H^{\sim r}, S{\sim}\gamma^{r}, S{\sim}\gamma^{\sim r}$	η attr
	(6)	$S\eta \subset SH^{r}, S{\sim}H^{r}, S{\sim}\gamma^{r}$	α lim
	(7)	$S\eta\kappa \subset SH^{r}\kappa, S{\sim}H^{r}\kappa, S{\sim}\gamma^{r}\kappa$	κ attr
	(8)	$S\eta\kappa \subset SH^{r}{\sim}C, S{\sim}H^{r}\kappa, S{\sim}\gamma^{r}\kappa$	Ps(Hκ)
	(9)	$S\eta\kappa \subset SH^{r}{\sim}C, S{\sim}H^{r}{\sim}\chi, S{\sim}\gamma^{r}\kappa$	Ps(~Hκ)
	(10)	$S\eta\kappa \subset SH^{r}{\sim}C, S{\sim}H^{r}{\sim}\chi, S{\sim}\gamma^{r}C$	Ps(~$\gamma\kappa$)
	(11)	$S\eta\kappa \subset SH^{r}{\sim}C^{v}, SH^{r}{\sim}C^{\sim v}, S{\sim}H^{r}{\sim}\chi, S{\sim}\gamma^{r}C$	Ps(~C)
	conclusion	$S\eta\kappa \subset SH^{r}{\sim}C^{v}, SH^{r}{\sim}C^{\sim v}, S{\sim}H^{r}{\sim}\chi, S{\sim}\gamma^{r}C^{v}, S{\sim}\gamma^{r}C^{\sim v}$	Ps(C)
5	(1)	$\eta \subset \gamma, {\sim}\gamma$	Ps(η1)
	(2)	$I\eta \subset I\gamma, I{\sim}\gamma$	η attr
	(3)	$I\eta\kappa \subset I\gamma\kappa, I{\sim}\gamma\kappa$	κ attr
	(4)	$I\eta C \subset I{\sim}\gamma C$	Ps(ηC)
	(5)	$I\eta C \subset I{\sim}\gamma^{r}C, I{\sim}\gamma^{\sim r}C$	Ps(~γ)
	(6)	$I\eta C \subset I^{p}{\sim}\gamma^{r}C, I^{\sim p}{\sim}\gamma^{r}C, I^{p}{\sim}\gamma^{\sim r}C, I^{\sim p}{\sim}\gamma^{\sim r}C$	Ps(I)
	(7)	$I\eta C \subset I^{p}{\sim}\gamma^{r}C, I^{\sim p}{\sim}\gamma^{r}C, I^{p}{\sim}\gamma^{\sim r}C$	α lim
	conclusion	$I\eta C \subset I^{p}{\sim}\gamma^{r}C^{v}, I^{p}{\sim}\gamma^{r}C^{\sim v}, I^{\sim p}{\sim}\gamma^{r}C^{v}, I^{\sim p}{\sim}\gamma^{r}C^{\sim v}, I^{p}{\sim}\gamma^{\sim r}C^{v}, I^{p}{\sim}\gamma^{\sim r}C^{\sim v}$	Ps(C)

Exercise set 19.2

1	(1)	A: $I^{p}H^{\sim r}{\sim}C^{\sim v}$	given
	(2)	θ: $I^{p}H^{\sim r}{\sim}C^{\sim v}$	Ps(θ)
	(3)	θ: $I^{p}H{\sim}C^{\sim v}$	Ps(H)
	(4)	θ: $I^{p}\gamma{\sim}C^{\sim v}$	Ps(γ)
	conclusion	θ: $I^{p}\gamma\chi^{\sim v}$	Ps($\chi^{\sim v}$)

2	(1)	Z: $I^{p}H^{r}{\sim}C^{v}$	given
	(2)	Z: $IH^{r}{\sim}C^{v}$	Ps(I)
	(3)	Z: $IH{\sim}C^{v}$	Ps(H)
	(4)	Z: $I\eta{\sim}C^{v}$	Th(η)
	conclusion	Z: $I\eta\chi^{v}$	Ps(χ^{v})
3	(1)	A: $I{\sim}\gamma^{r}C^{\sim v}$	given
	(2)	A: $\alpha{\sim}\gamma^{r}C^{\sim v}$	Ps(α)
	(3)	A: $\alpha\eta^{r}C^{\sim v}$	Ps(η^{r})
	(4)	A: $\alpha\eta^{r}\chi^{\sim v}$	Ps($\chi^{\sim v}$)
	conclusion	A: $\alpha\eta^{r}\kappa^{\sim v}$	Th($\kappa^{\sim v}$)

Chapter 20

Exercise set 20.1

1 Z: $[(I^{\sim p}H^{r}{\sim}C^{\sim v} \rightarrow {\sim}B) \cdot I^{\sim p}H^{r}{\sim}C^{\sim v}] \Rightarrow {\sim}B$
Z: $I^{\sim p}H^{r}{\sim}C^{\sim v} \underline{\Rightarrow} {\sim}B$

2 A: $[(I^{p}H^{\sim r}{\sim}C^{\sim v} \rightarrow B) \cdot I^{p}H^{\sim r}{\sim}C^{\sim v}] \Rightarrow B$
A: $I^{p}H^{\sim r}{\sim}C^{\sim v} \underline{\Rightarrow} B$

3 A: $[(\alpha{\sim}\gamma^{r}C^{v} \underline{\Rightarrow} B) \cdot \alpha{\sim}\gamma^{r}C^{v}] \Rightarrow B$
A: $\alpha{\sim}\gamma^{r}C^{v} \propto B$

4 A: $[(S{\sim}\gamma^{r}C^{\sim v} \underline{\Rightarrow} B) \cdot S{\sim}\gamma^{r}C^{\sim v}] \Rightarrow B$
A: $S{\sim}\gamma^{r}C^{\sim v} \propto B$

5 Z: $[(IH^{r}{\sim}C^{\sim v} \underline{\Rightarrow} {\sim}B) \cdot IH^{r}{\sim}C^{\sim v}] \Rightarrow {\sim}B$
Z: $IH^{r}{\sim}C^{\sim v} \propto {\sim}B$

6 A: $[(I^{p}{\sim}H^{\sim r}{\sim}\chi \underline{\Rightarrow} B) \cdot I^{p}{\sim}H^{\sim r}{\sim}\chi] \Rightarrow B$
A: $I^{p}{\sim}H^{\sim r}{\sim}\chi \propto B$

Chapter 21

Exercise set 21.1

1	(1)	$\tau \rightarrow (I^{\sim p}H^{r}{\sim}C^{\sim v} \rightarrow {\sim}B)$
	(2)	τ
	(3)	$I^{\sim p}H^{r}{\sim}C^{\sim v}$
	conclusion	${\sim}B$
2	(1)	$\tau \rightarrow (I^{p}H^{\sim r}{\sim}C^{\sim v} \rightarrow B)$
	(2)	τ
	(3)	$I^{p}H^{\sim r}{\sim}C^{\sim v}$
	conclusion	B

3	(1)	$\tau \rightarrow (S{\sim}\gamma^{r}C^{v} \rightarrow B)$
	(2)	τ
	(3)	$S{\sim}\gamma^{r}C^{v}$
	conclusion	B
4	(1)	$\tau \rightarrow (IH^{r}{\sim}C^{\sim v} \rightarrow {\sim}B)$
	(2)	τ
	(3)	$IH^{r}{\sim}C^{\sim v}$
	conclusion	${\sim}B$
5	(1)	$\tau \rightarrow (I^{p}{\sim}H^{\sim r}{\sim}\chi \rightarrow {\sim}B)$
	(2)	τ
	(3)	$I^{p}{\sim}H^{\sim r}{\sim}\chi$
	conclusion	${\sim}B$

Exercise set 21.2

1 Z: $\{[\tau \rightarrow (I^{\sim p}H^{r}{\sim}C^{\sim v} \rightarrow {\sim}B)] \cdot \tau \cdot I^{\sim p}H^{r}{\sim}C^{\sim v}\} \Rightarrow {\sim}B$
Z: $(\tau \cdot I^{\sim p}H^{r}{\sim}C^{\sim v}) \propto {\sim}B$

2 A: $\{[\tau \rightarrow (I^{p}H^{\sim r}{\sim}C^{\sim v} \rightarrow B)] \cdot \tau \cdot I^{p}H^{\sim r}{\sim}C^{\sim v}\} \Rightarrow B$
A: $(\tau \cdot I^{p}H^{\sim r}{\sim}C^{\sim v}) \propto B$

3 A: $\{[\tau \rightarrow (S{\sim}\gamma^{r}C^{v} \rightarrow B)] \cdot \tau \cdot S{\sim}\gamma^{r}C^{v}\} \Rightarrow B$
A: $(\tau \cdot S{\sim}\gamma^{r}C^{v}) \propto B$

4 Z: $\{[\tau \rightarrow (IH^{r}{\sim}C^{\sim v} \rightarrow {\sim}B)] \cdot \tau \cdot IH^{r}{\sim}C^{\sim v}\} \Rightarrow {\sim}B$
Z: $(\tau \cdot IH^{r}{\sim}C^{\sim v}) \propto {\sim}B$

5 Z: $\{[\tau \rightarrow (I^{p}{\sim}H^{\sim r}{\sim}\chi \rightarrow {\sim}B)] \cdot \tau \cdot I^{p}{\sim}H^{\sim r}{\sim}\chi\} \Rightarrow {\sim}B$
Z: $(\tau \cdot I^{p}{\sim}H^{\sim r}{\sim}\chi) \propto {\sim}B$

Chapter 22

Exercise set 22.1

1	(1)	$\iota \rightarrow (I^{p}H^{\sim r}{\sim}C^{\sim v} \rightarrow B)$
	(2)	ι
	(3)	$I^{p}H^{\sim r}{\sim}C^{\sim v}$
	conclusion	B
2	(1)	$\iota \rightarrow (I^{p}{\sim}H^{\sim r}{\sim}\chi \rightarrow {\sim}B)$
	(2)	ι
	(3)	$I^{p}{\sim}H^{\sim r}{\sim}\chi$
	conclusion	${\sim}B$
3	(1)	$\iota \rightarrow (I{\sim}\gamma^{r}C^{v} \rightarrow B)$
	(2)	ι
	(3)	$I{\sim}\gamma^{r}C^{v}$
	conclusion	B

4 (1) $\iota \rightarrow (I^{\sim p}H^{r}{\sim}C^{\sim v} \rightarrow {\sim}B)$
(2) ι
(3) $I^{\sim p}H^{r}{\sim}C^{\sim v}$
conclusion ${\sim}B$

5 (1) $\iota \rightarrow (IH^{r}{\sim}C^{v} \rightarrow {\sim}B)$
(2) ι
(3) $IH^{r}{\sim}C^{v}$
conclusion ${\sim}B$

Exercise set 22.2

1 A: $\{[\iota \rightarrow (I^{p}H^{\sim r}{\sim}C^{\sim v} \rightarrow B)] \cdot \iota \cdot I^{p}H^{\sim r}{\sim}C^{\sim v}\} \Rightarrow B$
A: $(\iota \cdot I^{p}H^{\sim r}{\sim}C^{\sim v}) \propto B$

2 Z: $\{[\iota \rightarrow I^{p}{\sim}H^{\sim r}{\sim}\chi \rightarrow {\sim}B)] \cdot \iota \cdot I^{p}{\sim}H^{\sim r}{\sim}\chi\} \Rightarrow {\sim}B$
Z: $(\iota \cdot I^{p}{\sim}H^{\sim r}{\sim}\chi) \propto {\sim}B$

3 A: $\{[\iota \rightarrow (I{\sim}\gamma^{r}C^{v} \rightarrow B)] \cdot \iota \cdot I{\sim}\gamma^{r}C^{v}\} \Rightarrow B$
A: $(\iota \cdot I{\sim}\gamma^{r}C^{v}) \propto B$

4 Z: $\{[\iota \rightarrow (I^{\sim p}H^{r}{\sim}C^{\sim v} \rightarrow {\sim}B)] \cdot \iota \cdot I^{\sim p}H^{r}{\sim}C^{\sim v}\} \Rightarrow {\sim}B$
Z: $(\iota \cdot I^{\sim p}H^{r}{\sim}C^{\sim v}) \propto {\sim}B$

5 Z: $\{[\iota \rightarrow (IH^{r}{\sim}C^{v} \rightarrow {\sim}B)] \cdot \iota \cdot IH^{r}{\sim}C^{v}\} \Rightarrow {\sim}B$
Z: $(\iota \cdot IH^{r}{\sim}C^{v}) \propto {\sim}B$

Exercise set 22.3

1 (1) $\delta \rightarrow (SH^{r}{\sim}C^{\sim v} \rightarrow {\sim}B)$
(2) δ
(3) $SH^{r}{\sim}C^{\sim v}$
conclusion ${\sim}B$

2 (1) $\delta \rightarrow (SH^{r}{\sim}C^{v} \rightarrow {\sim}B)$
(2) δ
(3) $SH^{r}{\sim}C^{v}$
conclusion ${\sim}B$

3 (1) $\delta \rightarrow (S{\sim}\gamma^{r}C^{v} \rightarrow B)$
(2) δ
(3) $S{\sim}\gamma^{r}C^{v}$
conclusion B

Exercise set 22.4

1 Z: $\{[\delta \rightarrow (SH^{r}{\sim}C^{\sim v} \rightarrow {\sim}B)] \cdot \delta \cdot SH^{r}{\sim}C^{\sim v}\} \Rightarrow {\sim}B$
Z: $(\delta \cdot SH^{\sim r}{\sim}C^{\sim v}) \propto {\sim}B$

2 Z: $\{[\delta \rightarrow (SH^{r}{\sim}C^{v} \rightarrow {\sim}B)] \cdot \delta \cdot SH^{r}{\sim}C^{v}\} \Rightarrow {\sim}B$
Z: $(\delta \cdot SH^{\sim r}{\sim}C^{v}) \propto {\sim}B$

3 A: $\{[\delta \rightarrow (S{\sim}\gamma^{r}C^{v} \rightarrow B)] \cdot \delta \cdot S{\sim}\gamma^{r}C^{v}\} \Rightarrow B$
A: $(\delta \cdot S{\sim}\gamma^{r}C^{v}) \propto B$

Exercise set 22.5

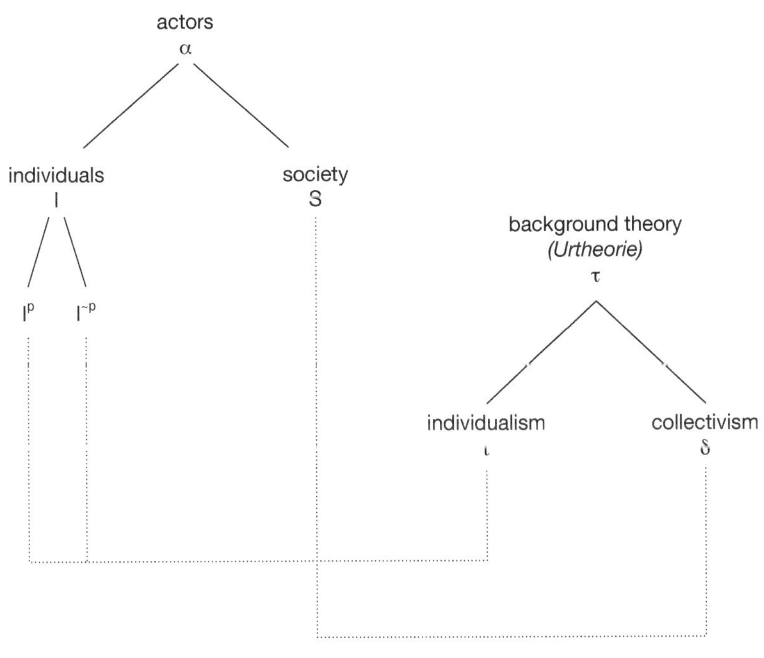

Exercise set 22.6

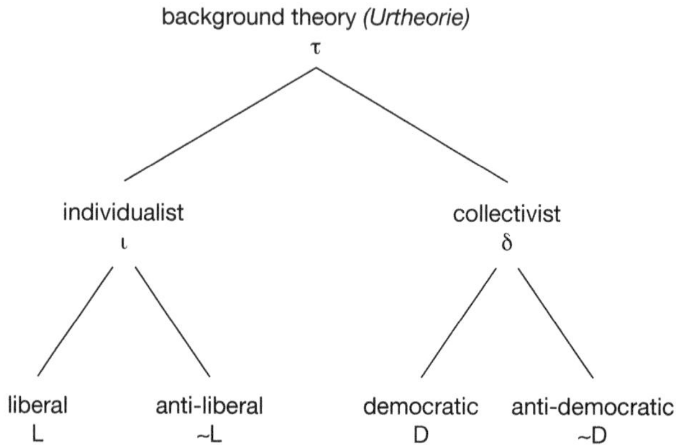

Exercise set 22.7

1	(1)	$\tau \subset \iota, \delta$	$Ps(\tau)$
	conclusion	$\tau \subset \iota, D, \sim D$	$Ps(\delta)$
2	(1)	$\tau \subset \iota, \delta$	$Ps(\tau)$
	(2)	$\tau \subset L, \sim L, \delta$	$Ps(\iota)$
	conclusion	$\tau \subset L, \sim L, D, \sim D$	$Ps(\delta)$

Chapter 23

Exercise set 23.1

1 A: $\{[L^{\kappa} \rightarrow (I^{\sim p}\sim\gamma^{r}C^{v} \rightarrow B)] \cdot L^{\kappa} \cdot I^{\sim p}\sim\gamma^{r}C^{v}\} \Rightarrow B$
A: $(L^{\kappa} \cdot I^{\sim p}\sim\gamma^{r}C^{v}) \propto B$

2 A: $\{[L^{\kappa} \rightarrow (I^{\circ}\sim\gamma^{r}C^{v} \rightarrow B)] \cdot L^{\kappa} \cdot I^{\circ}\sim\gamma^{r}C^{v}\} \Rightarrow B$
A: $(L^{\kappa} \cdot I^{\circ}\sim\gamma^{r}C^{v}) \propto B$

3 Z: $\{[L^{\kappa} \rightarrow (I^{p}\sim\gamma^{\sim r}C^{v} \rightarrow \sim B)] \cdot L^{\kappa} \cdot I^{p}\sim\gamma^{\sim r}C^{v}\} \Rightarrow \sim B$
Z: $(L^{\kappa} \cdot I^{p}\sim\gamma^{\sim r}C^{v}) \propto \sim B$

4 Z: $\{[L^{\kappa} \rightarrow (I^{p}\sim\gamma^{\sim r}C^{v} \rightarrow \sim B)] \cdot L^{\kappa} \cdot I^{p}\sim\gamma^{\sim r}C^{v}\} \Rightarrow \sim B$
Z: $(L^{\kappa} \cdot I^{p}\sim\gamma^{\sim r}C^{v}) \propto \sim B$

Chapter 24

Exercise set 24.1

1 A: $\{[L^{\eta} \rightarrow (I^{p}{\sim}H^{r}{\sim}\chi \rightarrow B)] \cdot L^{\eta} \cdot I^{p}{\sim}H^{r}{\sim}\chi\} \Rightarrow B$
A: $(L^{\eta} \cdot I^{p}{\sim}H^{r}{\sim}\chi) \propto B$

2 A: $\{[L^{\eta} \rightarrow (I{\sim}H^{r}{\sim}\chi \rightarrow B)] \cdot L^{\eta} \cdot I{\sim}H^{r}{\sim}\chi\} \Rightarrow B$
A: $(L^{\eta} \cdot I{\sim}H^{r}{\sim}\chi) \propto B$

3 Z: $\{[L^{\eta} \rightarrow (I^{p}{\sim}H^{\sim r}{\sim}\chi \rightarrow {\sim}B)] \cdot L^{\eta} \cdot I^{p}{\sim}H^{\sim r}{\sim}\chi\} \Rightarrow {\sim}B$
Z: $(L^{\eta} \cdot I^{p}{\sim}H^{\sim r}{\sim}\chi) \propto {\sim}B$

4 Z: $\{[L^{\eta} \rightarrow (I^{p}{\sim}H^{\sim r}{\sim}\chi \rightarrow {\sim}B)] \cdot L^{\eta} \cdot I^{p}{\sim}H^{\sim r}{\sim}\chi\} \Rightarrow {\sim}B$
Z: $(L^{\eta} \cdot I^{p}{\sim}H^{\sim r}{\sim}\chi) \propto {\sim}B$

Exercise set 24.2

1	(1)	$\iota \subset L, {\sim}L$	Ps(ι)
	conclusion	$\iota \subset L^{\kappa}, L^{\eta}, {\sim}L$	Ps(L)
2	(1)	$\tau \subset \iota, \delta$	Ps(τ)
	(2)	$\tau \subset L, {\sim}L, \delta$	Ps(ι)
	conclusion	$\tau \subset L^{\kappa}, L^{\eta}, {\sim}L, \delta$	Ps(L)
3	(1)	$\tau \subset \iota, \delta$	Ps(τ)
	(2)	$\tau \subset L, {\sim}L, \delta$	Ps(ι)
	(3)	$\tau \subset L, {\sim}L, D, {\sim}D$	Ps(δ)
	conclusion	$\tau \subset L^{\kappa}, L^{\eta}, {\sim}L, D, {\sim}D$	Ps(L)

Exercise set 24.3

2	(1)	$\tau \subset \iota, \delta$	Ps(τ)
	conclusion	$\tau \subset L^{\kappa}, L^{\eta}, {\sim}L, \delta$	Th(ι)
3	(1)	$\tau \subset \iota, \delta$	Ps(τ)
	(2)	$\tau \subset L^{\kappa}, L^{\eta}, {\sim}L, \delta$	Th(ι)
	conclusion	$\tau \subset L^{\kappa}, L^{\eta}, {\sim}L, D, {\sim}D$	Ps(δ)

Exercise set 24.4

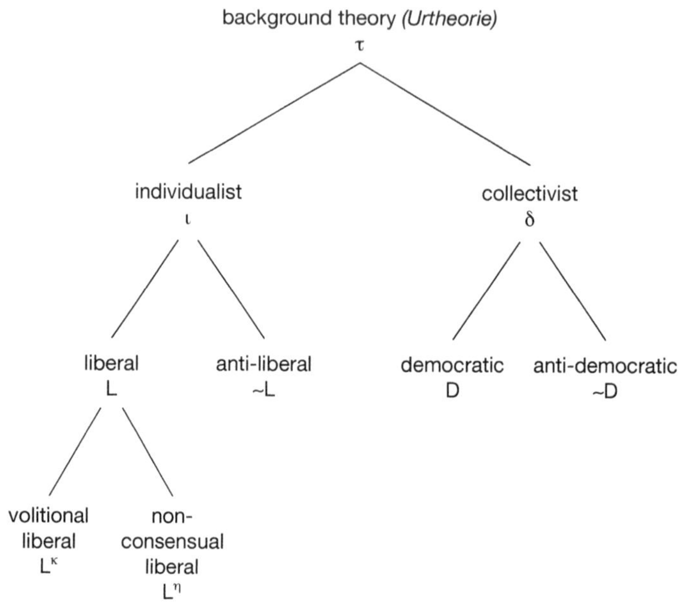

Chapter 25

Exercise set 25.1

1 $Z: \{[\sim L \rightarrow (IH^{r}\sim C^{\sim v} \rightarrow \sim B)] \cdot \sim L \cdot IH^{r}\sim C^{\sim v}\} \Rightarrow \sim B$
$Z: (\sim L \cdot IH^{r}\sim C^{\sim v}) \propto \sim B$

2 $A: \{[\sim L \rightarrow (I^{\sim p}\sim\gamma^{r}C^{\sim v} \rightarrow B)] \cdot \sim L \cdot I^{\sim p}\sim\gamma^{r}C^{\sim v}\} \Rightarrow B$
$A: (\sim L \cdot I^{\sim p}\sim\gamma^{r}C^{\sim v}) \propto B$

3 $A: \{[\sim L \rightarrow (I^{p}H^{\sim r}\sim C^{\sim v} \rightarrow B)] \cdot \sim L \cdot I^{p}H^{\sim r}\sim C^{\sim v}\} \Rightarrow B$
$A: (\sim L \cdot I^{p}H^{\sim r}\sim C^{\sim v}) \propto B$

Chapter 26

Exercise set 26.1

1 $Z: \{[D^{\sim v} \rightarrow (SH^{r}\sim C^{\sim v} \rightarrow \sim B)] \cdot D^{\sim v} \cdot SH^{r}\sim C^{\sim v}\} \Rightarrow \sim B$
$Z: (D^{\sim v} \cdot SH^{r}\sim C^{\sim v}) \propto \sim B$

2 $A: \{[\sim D \rightarrow (S\sim H^{r}\sim\chi \rightarrow B)] \cdot \sim D \cdot S\sim H^{r}\sim\chi\} \Rightarrow B$
$A: (\sim D \cdot S\sim H^{r}\sim\chi) \propto B$

3 $A: \{[D^{v} \rightarrow (S\sim\gamma^{r}C^{v} \rightarrow B)] \cdot D^{v} \cdot S\sim\gamma^{r}C^{v}\} \Rightarrow B$
$A: (D^{v} \cdot S\sim\gamma^{r}C^{v}) \propto B$

Exercise set 26.2

	(1)	$\delta \subset D, \sim D$	$Ps(\delta)$
	conclusion	$\delta \subset D^{\nu}, D^{\sim\nu}, \sim D$	$Ps(D)$

Exercise set 26.3

1	(1)	$\tau \subset \iota, \delta$	$Ps(\tau)$
	(2)	$\tau \subset \iota, D, \sim D$	$Ps(\delta)$
	conclusion	$\tau \subset \iota, D^{\nu}, D^{\sim\nu}, \sim D$	$Ps(D)$
2	(1)	$\tau \subset \iota, \delta$	$Ps(\tau)$
	(2)	$\tau \subset L, \sim L, \delta$	$Ps(\iota)$
	(3)	$\tau \subset L, \sim L, D, \sim D$	$Ps(\delta)$
	(4)	$\tau \subset L^{\kappa}, L^{\eta}, \sim L, D, \sim D$	$Ps(L)$
	conclusion	$\tau \subset L^{\kappa}, L^{\eta}, \sim L, D^{\nu}, D^{\sim\nu}, \sim D$	$Ps(D)$

Exercise set 26.4

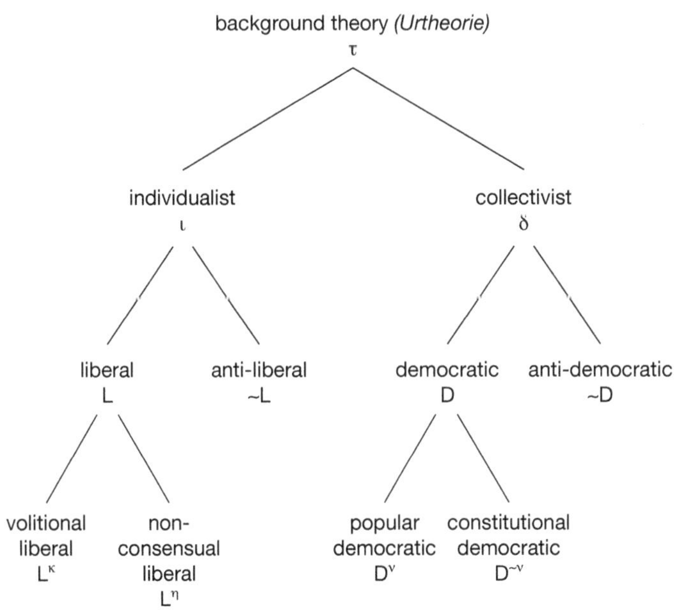

Glossary

A vertical arrow (↑) denotes a cross-reference to a separately defined term. Only one grammatical form for a term is supplied (e.g. for the term 'cause', see 'causation'). The numbers in parentheses following a definition indicate the section in which the term first appears. Definitions apply only to the model, and not necessarily to usage in other scholarly contexts.

absolute rule see **reverse translation rule, absolute**
actor [α] within a θ position↑, person or entity to whom an interest is attributed (2.1)
actor, identified expressly ascertained actor↑ (10.2)
actor, implied actor↑ who is not identified↑, but whose interests are broadly implied↑ by interests attributed to an identified actor↑ (10.2)
actor, individual [I] within a θ position↑, person or entity other than society↑, to whom an interest is attributed (5.2)
actor, non-personal [$I^{\neg p}$] individual actor↑ affected by the exercise of a right↑ by the personal actor↑ (7.3)
actor, personal [I^{p}] individual actor↑ seeking to exercise an asserted right↑ (6.1)
actor–causation reflexivity see **reflexivity, actor-causation**
actor–causation non-reflexivity see **non-reflexivity, actor-causation**
agent [ψ] person or entity who makes an argument as a party, or to whom an interest is attributed within an argument, as an actor↑ (2.2)
agent, specified most hierarchically inferior agent↑ (9.4)
agent, unspecified hierarchically superior agent↑ (9.4)
anti-liberal see **theory, paternalist**
axiom stipulation expressed in natural language (1.1)
background formula [BF] see **formula, background**
background theory see **theory, background**
breach [B] conclusion that a restriction↑ is unlawful (20.1)
causation origin of harm↑ as right-based↑ or restriction-based↑ (12.1)
causation, restriction-based see **harm, restriction-based**
causation, right-based see **harm, right-based**

claimant [A] party asserting a right↑ and challenging a restriction↑ (on behalf of the personal actor↑) (3.1)
collectivism see **theory, collectivist**
compound position see **position, compound**
conjunction [·] linkage of two or more assertions to form a compound position↑ (5.4)
consent [κ] disposition of an actor↑ to incur a harm↑ (17.1)
consent, invalid (~C) non-recognition of consent in law, either because of non-consent in fact, or regardless of consent in fact (17.1)
consent, valid (C) recognition of consent in law, either on the basis of consent in fact, or regardless of non-consent in fact (17.1)
constant symbol representing one element of discourse within the model (3.1)
constitutional democracy see **theory, constitutional-democratic**
contingent see **reverse translation rule, contingent**
corollary principle following from an axiom↑ (possibly in conjunction with some other element of the model) (3.2)
democracy see **theory, constitutional-democratic; theory, popular democratic**
democracy, constitutional see **theory, constitutional-democratic**
democracy, popular see **theory, popular democratic**
determinacy, formal degree to which assertions can be represented by θ positions↑ (3.5)
determinacy, substantive degree to which substantive values can be assigned to symbols within θ positions↑ (3.5)
formal determinacy see **determinacy, formal**
formal indeterminacy see **indeterminacy, formal**
formula [F] statement expressed in symbolic form (3.1)
formula, background [BF] general formula↑ representing a background theory↑ (21.3)
formula, general [GF] notation expressing a general form of θ positions↑ (17.4)
generality level of abstraction at which the content of a right is formulated (1.1)
harm [η] effect of the exercise of a right↑ or a restriction↑ on an actor↑ (11.1)
harm, restriction-based [$\eta^{\sim r}$] harm↑ caused by the exercise of a restriction↑ (12.1)
harm, right-based [η^{r}] harm↑ caused by the exercise of a right↑ (12.1)
identified actor see **actor, identified**
implication, broad reasoning by which a conclusion is drawn from relevant but unstated premises (10.1)
implication, strict reasoning by which a conclusion is validly drawn from stated premises (10.1)
implicature see **implication, broad**

implied actor see **actor, implied**

implied interest interest attributed to an actor↑ and thereby attributable to another actor↑ by broad implication↑ (10.3)

indeterminacy, formal degree to which assertions cannot be represented by θ positions↑ (3.5)

indeterminacy, substantive degree to which substantive values cannot be assigned to the symbols within θ positions↑ (3.5)

individual actor see **actor, individual**

individualism see **theory, individualist**

invalid consent see **consent, invalid**

liberal right see **right, liberal**

liberalism see **theory, non-consensual liberal**; **theory, volitional liberal**

marker superscript symbol attached to a principal symbol in order to give the latter a particular meaning (4.1)

non-breach [~B] conclusion that a restriction↑ is lawful (20.1)

non-liberal see **theory, paternalist**

non-personal actor [$I^{\sim p}$] see **actor, non-personal**

non-reflexivity relationship in which a person or entity represented by one symbol is not the same as a person or entity represented by another symbol (6.5)

non-reflexivity, actor–causation relationship in which the actor↑ incurring a harm↑ is not the person or entity who causes the harm (15.2)

non-reflexivity, party–actor relationship in which a party and an actor↑ are not the same person or entity (6.5)

non-reflexivity, party–causation relationship in which the party is not the person or entity who causes the harm↑ (15.3)

party–actor reflexivity see **reflexivity, party–actor**

party–causation reflexivity see **reflexivity, party–causation**

paternalism see **theory, paternalist**

personal actor see **actor, personal**

popular democracy see **theory, popular democratic**

position notation form comprising the party symbol preceding a colon together with the assertion or assertions which follow it (3.1)

position, compound θ position↑ consisting of two or more conjoined assertions (5.4)

position, simple θ position↑ containing one assertion (5.4)

postulate formula↑ setting forth the possible values↑ of a variable↑ (2.3)

rapport relationship of reflexivity↑ or non-reflexivity↑ between persons or entities represented by two distinct symbols within a θ position↑ (6.5)

reflexivity relationship within a θ position↑ in which a person or entity represented by one symbol is the same as a person or entity represented by another symbol (6.5)

reflexivity, actor–causation [θ: $I^p\eta^r$] relationship in which the actor↑ causing a harm↑ is the person or entity who incurs it (can only be the personal actor↑) (15.2)

reflexivity, party–actor relationship in which a party and an actor↑ are the same person or entity (6.5)

reflexivity, party–causation relationship in which the party is the person or entity who causes the harm↑ (15.3)

recognition incorporation or application of a right↑ within a corpus of liberal rights (1.1)

respondent [Z] party challenging a right↑ and seeking or defending a restriction↑ (on behalf of the personal actor↑) (3.1)

restriction (formal concept) any means by which a person or entity impedes the right-seeker (personal actor↑) in, or penalises the right-seeker (personal actor) for, the exercise of an asserted right↑ (1.2)

restriction-based causation see **harm, restriction-based**

restriction-based harm see **harm, restriction-based**

reverse translation rule rule for translating from a symbolic formula↑ into natural language (4.2)

reverse translation rule, absolute reverse translation rule↑ applied regardless of context or usage (6.5)

reverse translation rule, contingent reverse translation rule↑ applied unless context or usage dictate or permit otherwise (6.5)

right see **right, liberal**

right, liberal (conventional concept) right recognised within a conventional corpus of civil rights and liberties (1.1)

right-based see **harm, right-based**

right-based causation see **harm, right-based**

right-based harm see **harm, right-based**

right-seeker see **actor, personal**

simple position see **position, simple**

singular agent agent↑ construed to be only one person or entity (4.4)

society [S] total body of individuals within a jurisdiction, to whom an interest is attributed within a θ position↑ (8.2)

specified variable see **variable, specified**

specified agent see **agent, specified**

substantive determinacy see **determinacy, substantive**

substantive indeterminacy see **indeterminacy, substantive**

symbol, inclusive symbol collectively representing all possible values↑ of the corresponding variable↑ (4.1)

symbol, strongly exclusive symbol representing only one value↑ of the corresponding variable↑ (4.1)

symbol, weakly exclusive variable↑ representing one or more of its possible values↑ (4.1)

theorem [Th] formula↑ stating a set of values↑ of a symbol derived from one or more postulates↑; by extension, formula stating a set of values of a symbol derived from one or more postulates or other theorems (9.3)

theory, anti-democratic [~D] collectivist theory↑ attributing to society↑ irrelevant (right-based) consent to incur a harm↑ as a basis for finding a breach↑ (26.3)

theory, background [τ] theory presupposed by a β position↑ (21.1)

theory, collectivist [δ] background theory↑ adducing the interests of society↑ as a basis for finding breach↑ or non-breach↑ (22.2)

theory, constitutional-democratic [$D^{\sim v}$] collectivist theory↑ attributing to society↑ invalid, non-volitional consent↑ to incur a harm↑, as a basis for finding non-breach↑ (26.2)

theory, individualist [ι] background theory↑ adducing the interests of an individual actor↑ as a basis for a finding of breach↑ or non-breach↑ (22.1)

theory, non-consensual liberal [L^{η}] individualist theory↑ attributing to an individual actor↑ irrelevant consent↑ to incur an insufficient harm↑ as a basis for a finding of breach↑ or non-breach↑ (24.1)

theory, paternalist [~L] individualist theory↑ attributing to an individual actor↑ invalid consent↑ to incur a sufficient harm↑ as a basis for a finding of breach↑ or non-breach↑ (25.1)

theory, popular democratic [D^{v}] collectivist theory↑ adducing volition↑ of society↑ as a basis for a finding of breach↑ or non-breach↑ (26.1)

theory, volitional liberal [L^{κ}] individualist theory↑ adducing volition↑ of an individual actor↑ as a basis for a finding of breach↑ or non-breach↑ (23.1)

unspecified agent see **agent, unspecified**

unspecified variable see **variable, unspecified**

valid consent see **consent, valid**

value constant↑ which can be represented by a variable↑ (2.3)

variable symbol able to represent one or more of a set of constants↑ or other variables (2.2)

variable, specified most hierarchically inferior variable↑ (9.4)

variable, unspecified hierarchically superior variable↑ (9.4)

violation see **breach**

volition will of an actor↑ in giving or omitting to give consent↑ to incur a harm↑ (19.1)

volitional liberalism see **theory, volitional liberal**

Notes

Introduction

1 *R v. Brown* [1993] 2 All ER 75.
2 1997-I Eur. Ct H.R. 120.
3 The term *liberal rights discourse* is examined further in Chapters 1 and 3. For now, it can be understood to refer to:

1 substantive arguments (i.e. arguments on the merits, as opposed, say, to procedural or jurisdictional points), which are or could be,
2 adduced either in support of, or in opposition to,
3 any assertion that a liberal right must be recognised or applied.

Some notes on that definition:

a In Section 1.1, we will adopt a preliminary concept of *liberal right* aimed at avoiding any circularity which might arise under (3).
b As examined further in Section 1.3, the definition assumes a contentious framework. Although assertions about whether a right should be 'recognised or applied' will be analysed in judicial contexts, the model would also be relevant to disputes about rights in non-judicial (e.g. legislative or popular) fora, in so far as there is genuine disagreement about a right.
c The distinction in (3) between 'recognising' and 'applying' a right mostly reflects conventional usage. In Section 1.1, we will see that it is rarely important for our model.

4 See, e.g. Akkermans *et al.* 1999; Lebreton 1999; van Dijk and van Hoof 1998; Bleckmann 1997; Jacobs and White 1996; Robert and Duffar 1996; Bailey *et al.* 1995; Harris *et al.* 1995.
5 Horn 2001: 93–6. Cf. Cotterrell 1989: 38–41.
6 Holmes 1963: 5 (first published in 1881).
7 Ayer 1952: 85 (first published in 1935).
8 Ayer 1952: 79. These insights were already current, having built upon the work of Frege, Russell, Whitehead and Wittgenstein.
9 Ayer 1952: 87.
10 Ayer 1952: 85–6.
11 Cf. Horn 2001: 96–7.
12 See, e.g. Freeman 2001: 15–19; Bix 1999: chs 1, 2; Cotterrell 1989: ch. 8; Kaufmann 1994a, 1994b.
13 Cf. Alexander 1998; Neumann 1994.

14 Kelsen 1979: 216–20 (noting the concurring views of Kalinowski, Klug and Tammelo).
15 Cf. text accompanying note 6 above.
16 Soeteman 1989, Hage 1996, cf. van Hees 1995.
17 Rhodes and Pospesel 1997.
18 Meier 2000.
19 The word 'deontic' comes from the Greek *deon*, meaning 'obligation'. For a concise historical and conceptual synthesis of deontic logic, see Kalinowski 1972.
20 Von Wright 1963, 1951.
21 Hohfeld 1946.
22 For a brief bibliography of representative studies, see Simmonds 2001: xxviii–xxix.
23 See, e.g. Sumner 1987: ch. 2. Cf. Kramer 2000.
24 Cf. Saunders 1990 (proposing a fully formalised account of Hohfeldian analysis).
25 Cf. Heinze 2002: ch. 14 (arguing, in the US context, that there is no formal difference between the arguments in *Plessy v. Ferguson* and *Brown v. Board of Education*).
26 Similarly, I have suggested elsewhere that deontic analysis can be deployed usefully in the analysis of legal discourse, independently of any validity-testing function. Heinze 2003b; Heinze 2002: ch. 4.
27 See Steiner and Alston 2000: chs. 4, 15 (discussing controversies surrounding those claims).
28 See, e.g. Harris *et al.* 1995: 19–22, 284–5.
29 In a classic exposition, Carnap makes a point particularly appropriate for this book, as economy of expression, rather than validity testing, will be the principal role of the symbolic notation form.

> [An] advantage of using artificial symbols in place of words lies in the brevity and perspicuity of the symbolic formulas. Frequently, a sentence that requires many lines in a word-language (and whose perspicuity is therefore slight) can be represented symbolically in a line or less. Brevity and perspicuity facilitate manipulation and comparison and inference to an extraordinary degree. [. . .] Had the mathematician been confined to words and denied the use of numerals and other special symbols, the development of mathematics to its present high level would have been not merely more difficult, but psychologically impossible. To appreciate this point, one need only attempt to translate into the word-language e.g. so elementary a formula as '$(x + y)^3 = x^3 + 3x^2y + 3xy^2 + y^3$' ('The third power of the sum of two arbitrary numbers equals the sum of the following summands: . . .').
>
> (Carnap 1958: 2)

30 Heinze 2002 (acquaintance with that work is unnecessary for the present one).
31 Heinze 2004.
32 Excerpts from the Convention appear in Appendix 4. In this book, primary reference is made to the *Publications of the European Court of Human Rights* and to the *Decisions and Reports of the European Commission of Human Rights*. Court judgments not yet published in the former collection are cited with reference to the *European Human Rights Reports*. Texts of Court judgments can also be located at http://www.dhcour.coe.fr/hudoc/ or http://www.echr.coe.int. For an edited collection which contains many of the cases examined in this study, including judgments in extenso and summaries of separate opinions, see Lawson and Schermers 1999. For briefer case summaries, see Berger 1998. Where citations refer to the Convention both prior and subsequent to the Protocol 11 changes, citation is made to both versions.
33 Unless otherwise indicated, translations into English are mine and are not official.

1 Rights and restrictions

1 See, e.g. Robertson and Merrills 1996: 2–7.
2 GG article 5(1) ('[D]ie Freiheit der Berichterstattung durch Rundfunk und Film [wird] gewährleistet. Eine Zensur findet nicht statt.').
3 GW article 7(3) ('Er is geen voorafgaand toezicht op de inhoud van een radio- of televisieuitzending.').
4 See, e.g. Tribe and Dorf 1991: 50–8 and *passim*; Tribe and Dorf 1990.
5 Under article 25(1) of the Convention at the time when *Laskey* was brought, i.e. prior to entry into force of Protocol 11, the Commission was authorised to receive applications only from parties 'claiming to be the victim of a violation . . . of the rights set forth in the Convention or the protocols thereto'. That rule now applies to the Court under article 34. Cf. also the current article 28 (on declarations of inadmissibility).
6 See Section 20.1, this volume.
7 112 Eur. Ct H.R. (ser. A) (1986).
8 Article 12 provides: 'Men and women of marriageable age have the right to marry and to found a family, according to the national laws governing the exercise of this right.'
9 112 Eur. Ct H.R. (ser. A) (1986) at 23–4, paras 49, 50.
10 Ibid. at 25, para. 54.
11 See, e.g. Akkermans *et al.* 1999: 161–2; Berka 1999: 139; van Dijk and van Hoof 1998: 730–47; Bleckmann 1997: ch. 18; Robert and Duffar 1996: 121–3; Bailey *et al.* 1995: ch. 4.
12 The full text of articles 2, 3 and 15 appears in Appendix 4. Article 4(1) prohibits forced or compulsory labour. Article 7 prohibits *ex post facto* criminal punishments.
13 103 Eur. Ct H.R. (ser. A) (1986).
14 On the passing of that role from a private individual, Mr Kreisky, to the Austrian state, see Section 3.1, this volume.
15 Article 10 of the European Convention provides in pertinent part:

> 1. Everyone has the right to freedom of expression. This right shall include freedom to hold opinions and to receive and impart information and ideas without interference by public authority [. . .].
> 2. The exercise of these freedoms, since it carries with it duties and responsibilities, may be subject to such formalities, conditions, restrictions or penalties as are prescribed by law and are necessary in a democratic society [. . .] for the protection of [. . .] morals, for the protection of the reputation or rights of others [or] for preventing the disclosure of information received in confidence.

16 See Sections 18.1, 19.3, this volume.
17 See note 15 above. See also ECHR articles. 2(2), 4(3), 7(2), 8(2), 9(2), 11(2).
18 See, e.g. Harris *et al.* 1995: 17.
19 See, e.g. ECHR Protocol 2, article 1(1). Cf. van Dijk and van Hoof 1998: 264–6.
20 In view of the focus on arguments adduced in substantive rights disputes, the corpus to be examined includes only judgments on the merits of disputes, without reference to issues of procedure or jurisdiction. Arguments will be drawn from published judgments, even, in some cases, if they differ from the parties' original oral or written submissions; and even if those submissions themselves change over the course of litigation. A broader corpus, embracing written or oral pleadings, or decisions of lower courts or bodies, would provide further instances for applying the model, but in no way bears upon its structure.

21 The analysis would apply equally to quasi-judicial bodies such as the Human Rights Committee of the United Nations, constituted under ICCPR article 28 and authorised to receive individual complaints under the first Optional Protocol to the International Covenant on Civil and Political Rights.

22 See ECHR article 45(1) (formerly article 51(1)) (providing that the Court shall give reasons for its judgments). Cf. van Dijk and van Hoof 1998: 218.

23 See ECHR article 45(2) (formerly article 51(2)) (providing that judges may deliver individual opinions). Cf. van Dijk and van Hoof 1998: 218.

24 See, e.g. Bailey *et al.* 1995: 5, 6.

25 Cf. Section 8.3, this volume.

26 As set forth in ECHR article 35. Cf. van Dijk and van Hoof 1998: ch. 3; Harris *et al.* 1995: ch. 23.

27 ECHR article 35(3). Cf. van Dijk and van Hoof 1998: 162–5; Harris *et al.* 1995: 627–8.

28 Cf. Chapter 3, note 4.

29 See, e.g. *Lochner v. New York*, 198 US 45 (1905).

30 As noted earlier, no knowledge of symbolic logic is being assumed. It should be apparent as an intuitive matter that the argument is formally valid, i.e. if the premises are true, then the conclusion must be true. (On that definition of validity, cf. Chapter 3, note 10). Nevertheless, those familiar with symbolic logic may want a demonstration. (The ordinary-language version is less cumbersome without quantifiers, but a symbolic rendering can usefully quantify those elements required to attain the concluding formula. The question whether the premises are true is a separate one, to which we next turn.)

$\mathrm{R}x$	=	x is an individual right	$\forall$	=	universal operator
$\mathrm{I}x$	=	x protects an individual interest	$\rightarrow$	=	conditional operator
$\mathrm{L}x$	=	x is subject to the rule of law	$\cdot$	=	conjunctive operator
$\mathrm{B}x$	=	x is a liberal right	$\therefore$	=	conclusion

1	$(\forall x)(\mathrm{R}x \rightarrow \mathrm{I}x)$	thesis 1 (premise)
2	$(\forall x)[(\mathrm{R}x \cdot \mathrm{I}x) \rightarrow \mathrm{L}x]$	thesis 2 (premise)
3	$(\forall x)[(\mathrm{R}x \cdot \mathrm{I}x \cdot \mathrm{L}x) \rightarrow \mathrm{B}x)$	thesis 3 (premise)
4	flag a	flagging step (universal generalisation)
5	$\mathrm{R}a \rightarrow \mathrm{I}a$	1, universal instantiation a/x
6	$(\mathrm{R}a \cdot \mathrm{I}a) \rightarrow \mathrm{L}a$	2, universal instantiation a/x
7	$(\mathrm{R}a \cdot \mathrm{I}a \cdot \mathrm{L}a) \rightarrow \mathrm{B}x$	3, universal instantiation a/x
8	$\mathrm{R}a$	assumption
9	$\mathrm{I}a$	5, 8, conditional elimination
10	$\mathrm{R}a \cdot \mathrm{I}a$	8, 9, conjunction introduction
11	$\mathrm{L}a$	6, 10, conditional elimination
12	$\mathrm{R}a \cdot \mathrm{I}a \cdot \mathrm{L}a$	10, 11, conjunction introduction
13	$\mathrm{B}a$	7, 12, conditional elimination
14	$\mathrm{R}a \rightarrow \mathrm{B}a$	8–13, conditional introduction
	$\therefore\ (\forall x)(\mathrm{R}x \rightarrow \mathrm{B}x)$	14, universal generalisation

31 We will assume that thesis 1 holds despite differing views on the nature of the individual interest protected. For example, a choice theorist maintains that the interest protected is the individual prerogative to exercise or not to exercise the right. By contrast, a benefit theorist believes that the interest protected is a substantive good which can accrue to the right-holder. See, e.g. Kramer *et al.* 2000; Steiner 1994: 59–73.

32 In postulating an absolute sovereign, this thesis is positivist in a classical ('pre-Hart') rather than a contemporary ('post-Hart') sense.

33 See Section 23.5, this volume.
34 Cf. Sections 17.5 and 26.2 this volume.
35 Mill 1974.
36 Hart 1963; Devlin 1959.
37 Heinze 1998: 465–6.
38 Hart 1961: 124 (original emphasis).
39 See, e.g. Dworkin 1986, 1985, 1977.
40 Cf. Heinze 2003a.
41 See Section 3.5, this volume.
42 This is not to say that all members of the critical-realist grouping *do* make such a claim. But if they do not, then that further supports the observation that they have no dispute with the idea that the *fact* of open texture in no way precludes the possibility of a determinate *analysis* of it. The view that a theory of open-endedness must itself be open-ended would entail a paradox: if an analysis of open texture must itself be open-ended, then *that* open-endedness would have to accommodate, among its competing viewpoints, the viewpoint that open texture is *not* open-ended. Declining to accommodate that viewpoint would mean that it is not open-ended.

2 Overview of agents

1 See Sections 5.3 and 6.5, this volume.
2 See Section 9.4, this volume.

3 Parties

1 Cf. ECHR article 34 (formerly article 25) (providing that '[t]he Court may receive applications from any person, non-governmental organisation or group of individuals claiming to be the victim of a violation by one of the High Contracting Parties'). Cf. van Dijk and van Hoof 1998: 46.
2 See, e.g. van Dijk and van Hoof 1998: 60–1.
3 ECHR article 34 (formerly article 25). Cf. van Dijk and van Hoof 1998: 23.
4 It is because actions before such international bodies must be brought against states that the concept of 'third-party applicability' (*Drittwirkung*) has acquired particular significance in human rights law. Through that doctrine, states may incur liability under international treaties for failing to protect certain individual interests which fall within the scope of those treaties, even where encroachments have been caused by private persons or entities rather than government bodies or officials. See, e.g. van Dijk and van Hoof 1998: 22–6. For example, the case of *X and Y v. The Netherlands*, 91 Eur. Ct H.R. (ser. A) (1985), concerned a woman aged 16, who had lived in a privately-run home for mentally handicapped children, where she was the victim of a sexual assault. The woman's father brought a complaint against the government for failing to provide adequate legal remedies. The Dutch authorities pointed to provisions of Dutch law which do impose criminal liability for various kinds of sexual assault or sexual offence. They maintained that stricter penalties had not been introduced because, in situations concerning individuals of the woman's age, more severe legal penalties might 'lead to unacceptable paternalism and occasion an inadmissible interference by the State with the individual's right to respect for his or her sexual life' (ibid. at 12, para. 25). The Court nevertheless found a violation of the article 8 privacy right, not on the basis of any affirmative act of any government body or official, but rather through the government's failure to provide

adequate legal recourse (ibid. at 13–14, paras 29–30). For our purposes, X and Y would count as the claimants, and the Dutch state as the respondent.

5 ECHR article 33 (formerly article 24). Cf. van Dijk and van Hoof 1998: 40–4.

6 See, e.g. Section 13.1, this volume. Note also that, in Chapters 23–6, both parties will be able to make arguments presupposing liberal, paternalist or democratic theories, but certain specific versions of those theories are possible only for the claimant, and others only for the respondent.

7 See Chapter 20, this volume.

8 Cf. Section 3.4, this volume.

9 See Section 19.8, this volume.

10 See, e.g. Priest 2000: 5; Guttenplan 1997: 26; Rhodes and Pospesel 1997: 5; Hodges 1977: 55. As those and other writers commonly note, that description is rough. For a thorough account, explaining the reliance of validity on form, see, e.g. Sainsbury 1991: ch. 1. For present purposes, the rough description will suffice.

11 As opposed, say, to 'unknown' or 'unknowable'. Cf. Malinowski 2001.

12 On the concepts of acceptable and unacceptable harms, see Chapter 11, this volume.

13 On transparent and opaque contexts, see, e.g. Taylor 1998: ch. iv. Classic examinations appear in Quine 1960: 143–51; Quine 1953: 142–3.

14 Aside from self-contradictory statements, a party could make silly or absurd ones, like 'We should prevail because green elephants can fly.' As a practical matter, such arguments adduce no legally cognisable interests, and are thus discounted from any balancing of rights against restrictions. The status of statements made by insane witnesses, for example, are relevant to other areas of law, but not to that balancing of substantive interests. As a theoretical matter, the Axiom still applies, as it would simply mean that the party has adduced an extraordinarily weak argument.

15 In some instances, such statements may be purely rhetorical. If it is already acknowledged that the claimant *did* assert *x*, then, in a sarcastic or polemical way, one might exclaim 'The claimant *would* assert that!' or 'The claimant *had* to assert that!' If it is clear from the context that such a locution only rhetorically states what the claimant does in fact assert, then it can be treated as we are treating indicatives.

16 Another way of making the point is as follows. In modal logic, a statement like '*x* is possible' is commonly analysed through recourse to 'possible world' semantics. The statement '*x* is possible' is construed to mean 'There is a possible world in which *x* obtains or is true.' That construction allows the logician to introduce a truth value. Similarly, for our analysis, we can stipulate that, for any θ position, our model assumes some possible world in which the party makes the assertion attributed to it. Of course, in modal logic, possible world semantics do not answer the question as to what is 'possible' or 'necessary'. For example, do we admit any imaginable world? Or only one in which some laws of physics apply? Or only one in which *our* laws of physics apply (whatever that means)? Possible world semantics merely provide a means of assigning truth values, assuming stipulated answers to such questions, i.e. stipulated meanings for 'possible' and 'necessary'. The logician who responds 'yes' to the first question, admitting *any* imaginable world, can then assign truth values, even if, as a separate matter, others might doubt whether that really is the best way to define the concepts of possibility and necessity. Similarly, for our model, we can analyse a θ position for the structure of *p*, while leaving as a distinct matter the question whether the party does, did, will, can, would or should make that argument. We assume a possible world in which the party does assert *p*, solely for purposes

of ascertaining the formal structure of p. On that reading, the Hypothetical Case Corollary could be formulated as follows: *A party is assumed to make any assertion attributed in some possible world to that party in a θ position*. The question of what plausibly constitutes a 'possible world' for liberal rights discourse would lie outside the model. On possible world semantics, see, e.g. Hughes and Cresswell 1996: 21; Konyndyk 1986: 16–17 .

17 Cf. Section 9.7, this volume.

18 Cf. Section 13.8, this volume.

5 The individual actor

1 Similarly, the distinction is important for the analysis of other features of legal argument, such as pleading. See, e.g. Rhodes and Pospesel 1997: 214–18.

2 Cf. Section 18.3, this volume.

3 260-A Eur. Ct H.R. (ser. A) (1993).

7 The non-personal actor

1 This principle is commonly known as the 'law of contradiction' (or the 'law of non-contradiction') (Detlefsen *et al.* 1999: 60).

2 This use of the negation function raises the question of the relationships between concepts of negation, mutual exclusion, contrariness and contradiction. In abstraction, nothing about the term 'personal actor' intrinsically implies that any actor who is not a personal actor is thereby necessarily a non-personal actor. The set of things that are 'not the personal actor' could include guppies, asteroids or Martians. More realistically, other kinds of actors might be imagined, e.g. actors who neither exercise, nor incur the effects of, the right (such as certain witnesses, or lawyers and judges, or persons having nothing to do with the whole affair). In other words, if we were to include all conceivable beings, or all conceivable actors, there would be many possible contrary terms to the term 'personal actor'. However, under the Axiom of Individual Actors, we are admitting as an individual actor only a personal actor or a non-personal actor. Only within that expressly limited domain of actors can we designate the personal and non-personal actors as a mutually exclusive pairing. Of course, those unhappy with using a contradictory to represent what might appear to be a contrary could, throughout the rest of the book, simply substitute $I^{\sim p}$ for, say, I^q, without any change in meaning resulting.

3 There is one sense in which the analogy to an utterance such as 'Madrid is the capital of Spain' does not hold. The utterance 'Madrid is the capital of Spain' could be called a 'proposition' in the familiar sense that it 'affirms' something. In ordinary conversation, such a statement is commonly made with the intention of expressing its truth. The symbols 'p' and '~p', and the symbols I^p and $I^{\sim p}$, are not propositions in that sense: the utterance 'Mr Lingens', by itself, does not affirm anything. Of course, we could say that these symbols do in fact assume unstated propositions, such as 'Mr Lingens *exists*'. But we can also avoid confusion merely by stating as a matter of definition that, for purposes of our model, the symbol Ip is meant to refer only to the personal actor; and the symbol $I^{\sim p}$ is meant to refer only to the non-personal actor, without either symbol, in itself, representing anything more.

4 For an analysis of party–actor reflexivity involving states as parties to disputes, see Section 8.4, this volume.

8 Society

1 24 Eur. Ct H.R. (ser. A) (1976).
2 Ibid. at 7–8, paras 9–13. See also ibid. at 13–17, paras 27–34.
3 Ibid. at 8–10, paras 14–19.
4 Ibid. at 15, 24–5, paras 31, 52.
5 Cf. e.g. UDHR, article 29(2): 'In the exercise of his rights and freedoms, everyone shall be subject only to such limitations as are determined by law solely for the purpose of . . . meeting the just requirements of morality, public order and the general welfare of a democratic society.'
6 45 Eur. Ct H.R. (ser. A) (1981).
7 Article 8(2) sets forth a limitations provision similar to that of article 10(2), including a 'protection of morals' clause which was that invoked in *Handyside*.
8 45 Eur. Ct H.R. (ser. A) at 13–14, 23–5, paras 25, 60, 62.
9 Ibid. at 12–14, 22–3, paras 24–6, 56–9.
10 Ibid. at 12–14, 23–4, paras 23–5, 60.
11 1997-I Eur. Ct H.R. 120, 132–3, paras 40–4.
12 See Section 1.3, this volume (on government action *ultra vires*).
13 106 Eur. Ct H.R. (ser. A) (1986).
14 184 Eur. Ct H.R. (ser. A) (1991).
15 1998 Eur. Ct H.R. —— ; 27 EHRR 163 (1998). But see note 18 below.
16 The European Court examined the complaints principally under the article 8 right to privacy.
17 Cf. *Sheffield and Horsham*, 27 EHRR at 168, paras 16–19.
18 *Rees*, 106 Eur. Ct H.R. (ser. A) at 17–18, paras 42, 44; Cossey, 184 Eur. Ct H.R. (ser. A) at 16, para. 39. Those issues were also raised in *Sheffield and Horsham* and in *B v. France*, 232-C Eur. Ct H.R. (ser. A) (1992), but receive more emphasis in *Rees* and *Cossey*.
19 These received particular attention in *B v. France*, 232-C Eur. Ct H.R. (ser. A) at 49, para. 47. See also ibid. at 60 (Matscher, J., dissenting), at 61, para. 16 (Pinheiro Farinha, J., dissenting), at 63, 64–5 (Pettiti, J., dissenting) and at 69, 74, para. 3.2 (Morinella, J., dissenting).
20 116 Eur. Ct H.R. (ser. A) (1987).
21 Ibid. at 25, para. 59.
22 Under the European Convention, the possibility of a complaint brought as an *actio popularis* is in theory possible within the context of inter-state complaints. Van Dijk and van Hoof 1998: 40. However, under the rule governing the right of individual complaint, it is effectively precluded. Van Dijk and van Hoof 1998: 46, 52.
23 24 Eur. Ct H.R. (ser. A) (1976) at 8, 27, paras 11, 57 (noting also the endorsement of this view by a minority of Commission members).
24 Ibid. at 28, para. 57.
25 Ibid. at 22, para. 48.
26 Ibid. at 26, para. 54.
27 'The competent authorities in Northern Ireland, the Isle of Man and the Channel Islands may, in the light of local conditions, have had plausible reasons for not taking action against the book and its publisher, as may the Scottish Procurator-Fiscal. [. . .] Their failure to act . . . does not prove that the judgement of [the English court] was not a response to a real necessity' (ibid.).
28 45 Eur. Ct H.R. (ser. A) (1981) at 20–1, 22, 23–4, paras 49, 56, 60.
29 Ibid. at 22, 23, paras 56, 58.
30 Although the Court does not formally abide by any doctrine of *stare decisis*, its judgments draw strongly on prior case law for purposes of explaining the Court's adherence to, or departure from, its own precedents. See, e.g. Merrills 1993: 12–16.

9 Theorems and proofs

1 On controversies surrounding concepts of group rights, see, e.g. Steiner and Alston 2000: ch. 15; Heinze 1999b; Heinze 1999c.
2 298 Eur. Ct H.R. (ser. A) (1994).
3 Ibid. at 10–14, paras 10–11.
4 Ibid. at 17, para. 19.
5 In the government's view, this interest encompassed an internationally binding obligation incumbent upon Denmark as party to the International Convention on the Elimination of All Forms of Racial Discrimination. See 298 Eur. Ct H.R. (ser. A) at 18–19, 20, paras 21, 27.
6 Ibid. at 20, para. 27. See also ibid. at 29–30, para. 5 (Ryssdal, Bernhardt, Spielmann and Loizou, JJ, dissenting) and ibid. at 31 (Gölcüklü, Russo and Valticos, JJ, dissenting).
7 On the question of implied interests and implied actors, see Chapter 10, this volume.

10 Implication and implicature

1 Grice 1975.
2 Cf. Chapter 3, note 9, this volume.
3 103 Eur. Ct H.R. (ser. A) (1986) at 25, para. 37.
4 Ibid. at 28, para. 45.
5 For example, differences in the level of abstraction at which similar sentences are pitched, respectively, in English, French, German and Dutch, could result from the sheer fact that there is no perfect overlap in the usage of the English *one*, the French *on*, the German *man* and the Dutch *men*.
6 1997-I Eur. Ct H.R. 120, 142, para. 61. Cf. the Court opinion, ibid. at 133, para. 45.
7 Ibid. at 142, para. 60.
8 103 Eur. Ct H.R. (ser. A) at 26, para. 42.

11 Two harm axioms

1 Cf. Heinze 1998: 465–6.
2 24 Eur. Ct H.R. (ser. A) at 14, 24–5, paras 29, 52 (1976).
3 Ibid. at 13–18, 24–8, paras 27–35, 52–9.
4 45 Eur. Ct H.R. (ser. A) at 23–4, paras 60–1 (1981).
5 Ibid. at 19–21, paras 46–9. See also ibid. at 29, 30, para. 3 (Zekia, J., dissenting), and at 39, 43–4, paras12–14 (Walsh, J., partially dissenting).
6 10 Eur. Comm'n H.R. Dec. and Rep. 100 (1977).
7 Ibid. at 107, para. 24(3).
8 Ibid. at 111, para. 30. See also ibid. at 118, 120, para. 7 (Mr Fawcett, dissenting).
9 1997-I Eur. Ct H.R. 120, 124, 127–8, 131–2, paras 8–9, 22–33, 37–9. See also excerpts from Opinion of the Commission, ibid. at 138–9, paras 43–4, and at 147–8 (Mr Loucaides, dissenting).
10 Ibid. at 126–7, 128–9, 132–4, paras 19–21, 25–31, 40–50.
11 169 Eur. Ct H.R. (ser. A) (1989).
12 Protocol 1, article 1 provides in part:

> Every natural or legal person is entitled to the peaceful enjoyment of his possessions. No one shall be deprived of his possessions except in the public interest. . . .

> The preceding provisions shall not, however, in any way impair the right of a State to enforce such laws as it deems necessary to control the use of property in accordance with the general interest.

13 169 Eur. Ct H.R. (ser. A) at 9–13, 27–9, paras 11–26, 50, 52, 54.
14 Ibid. at 21–3, 27–30, paras 35–6, 50, 53, 55.
15 25 Eur. Ct H.R. (ser. A) (1978).
16 Article 3 provides that '[n]o one shall be subjected to torture or to inhuman or degrading treatment or punishment'.
17 25 Eur. Ct H.R. (ser. A) at 40–54, paras 92–132.
18 In view of later developments, Britain did not seek to rebut all of Ireland's allegations. In this and later discussions of the case, we will consider the case only with respect to those allegations which the United Kingdom either did contest, or might have contested, in particular, as set forth in 25 Eur. Ct H.R. (ser. A) at 110, 115–31, paras 12–36 (Sir Gerald Fitzmaurice, J., separate opinion).
19 25 Eur. Ct H.R. (ser. A) at 65, para. 162.
20 26 Eur. Ct H.R. (ser. A) (1978).
21 Ibid. at 7, para. 10.
22 Ibid. at 16, para. 32. See also ibid. at 22 (Sir Gerald Fitzmaurice, J., separate opinion).
23 Ibid. at 15–17, paras 30–5.
24 247-C Eur. Ct H.R. (ser. A) (1993).
25 Ibid. at 53, 58–9, paras 9, 29.
26 Ibid. at 59–60, paras 31–32.
27 See, for Tyrer, the notoriously provocative arguments of Judge Sir Gerald Fitzmaurice, 26 Eur. Ct H.R. (ser. A) at 22, and *Costello-Roberts*, 247-C Eur. Ct H.R. (ser. A) at 64 (Ryssdal, Thór Vilhjálmsson, Matscher and Wildhaber, JJ, partly dissenting).
28 1996-VI Eur. Ct H.R. 2260.
29 Ibid. at 2266, 2278, paras 14–16, 60.
30 Ibid. at 2277–8, para. 59.
31 161 Eur. Ct H.R. (ser. A) (1989).
32 Ibid. at 36–7, para. 93.
33 Ibid. at 37–9, paras 94–9.
34 10 Eur. Comm'n H.R. Dec. & Rep. 100, 113, para. 37 (1977).
35 Ibid. at 118, 119, para. 4 (Mr Fawcett, dissenting).
36 23 Eur. Ct H.R. (ser. A) (1976).
37 Protocol 1, article 2 provides that '[n]o person shall be denied the right to education. In the exercise of any functions which it assumes in relation to education and to teaching, the State shall respect the right of parents to ensure such education and teaching in conformity with their own religious and philosophical convictions'.
38 Ibid. at 18–20, paras 36–43. See also ibid. at 31 (Verdross, J., separate opinion).
39 23 Eur. Ct H.R. (ser. A) at 10, 27, paras 20, 54.
40 324 Eur. Ct H.R. (ser. A) (1995).
41 Article 2 reads in part:

> 1. Everyone's right to life shall be protected by law. [. . .]
> 2. Deprivation of life shall not be regarded as inflicted in contravention of this Article when it results from the use of force which is no more than absolutely necessary:
>   (a) in defence of any person from unlawful violence;
>   (b) in order to effect a lawful arrest [. . .].

42 324 Eur. Ct H.R. (ser. A) at 51–4, paras 174–86.
43 Ibid. at 54–6, paras 187–91. See also ibid. at 65 (Ryssdal *et al.*, JJ, dissenting).
44 Ibid. at 56–62, paras 192–214.
45 176-A Eur. Ct H.R. (ser. A) (1990).
46 176-B Eur. Ct H.R. (ser. A) (1990).
47 The verb *prévue* in French more strongly implies a requirement that the law be foreseeable in its application. (Under the concluding paragraph of the European Convention, the English and French texts are equally authentic.)
48 The dispute at issue in these cases makes them particularly interesting. In a more obvious sense, the harm in question is wire tapping and, more broadly, invasion of privacy. Within the context of adjudication, however, disputes are not always so straightforward. The precise harm at issue in these cases arises not directly from conduct in the physical world, but rather is closely tied to the wording and application of a legal text. The purely formal concept of harm set forth in the Claimant and Respondent Harm Axioms can accommodate that dispute more easily than can a substantively determinate concept of harm.
49 See Introduction, note 28; Chapter 3, note 4, this volume.
50 106 Eur. Ct H.R. (ser. A) (1986) at 21 (Bindschedler-Robert, Russo and Gersing, JJ, dissenting).
51 184 Eur. Ct H.R. (ser. A) (1991) at 20 (Bindschedler-Robert and Russo, JJ, dissenting).
52 *Rees*, 106 Eur. Ct H.R. (ser. A) at 10, 16; *Cossey*, 184 Eur. Ct H.R. (ser. A) at 9.
53 232-C Eur. Ct H.R. (ser. A) at 49–53, paras 49–61.
54 32 Eur. Ct H.R. (ser. A) (1979).
55 Article 6(1) provides that '[i]n the determination of his civil rights and obligations . . . everyone is entitled to a . . . hearing . . . by [a] tribunal established by law.'
56 32 Eur. Ct H.R. (ser. A) at 14, para. 25.
57 Ibid. at 14–16, para. 26.
58 91 Eur. Ct H.R. (ser. A) at 12–13, paras 24–7.
59 See, e.g. Card *et al.* 1998: 144–9.
60 See, e.g. Dias 1989: 959–64.
61 See note 9 above.
62 On this point, see Section 18.1, this volume.

12 Causation

1 Harris *et al.* 1995: 40–1. See also van Dijk and van Hoof 1998: 319–20. See also the discussion of *Osman v. United Kingdom* later in this chapter.
2 1996-IV Eur. Ct H.R. 2195.
3 Ibid. at 2201, paras 15–17.
4 Ibid. at 2205–8, paras 35–47.
5 3 Eur. Ct H.R. (ser. A) (1961).
6 145-B Eur. Ct H.R. (ser. A) (1988).
7 258-B Eur. Ct H.R. (ser. A) (1993).
8 Article 5(1) provides in part:

> Everyone has the right to liberty and security of person. No one shall be deprived of his liberty save in the following cases and in accordance with a procedure prescribed by law:
> (a) the lawful detention of a person after conviction by a competent court;
> [. . .]

(b) the lawful arrest or detention of a person effected for the purpose of bringing him before the competent legal authority on reasonable suspicion of having committed an offence or when it is reasonably considered necessary to prevent his committing an offence or fleeing after having done so; [. . .].

9 Article 5(3) provides that '[e]veryone arrested or detained in accordance with the provisions of . . . this Article shall be brought promptly before a judge or other officer authorised by law to exercise judicial power and shall be entitled to trial within a reasonable time or to release pending trial'.
10 Article 5(4) provides that '[e]veryone who is deprived of his liberty by arrest or detention shall be entitled to take proceedings by which the lawfulness of his detention shall be decided speedily by a court and his release ordered if the detention is not lawful'.
11 [1992] 4 All ER 559.
12 Ibid. at 562.
13 Ibid. at 562–66.
14 1998 Eur. Ct H.R. —— ; 29 EHRR 245 (2000).
15 As a school teacher, the individual was indeed performing a public function, but was not, as to the issues relevant to the dispute, deemed to have been clothed with state authority such as that assumed by state officers in cases such as *McCann*, *Tyrer*, *Aksoy*, or the Northern Ireland cases. See 29 EHRR at 284–5, 286–7, paras 107, 115–16.
16 See, e.g. van Dijk and van Hoof 1998: 22–6; Harris *et al.* 1995: 19–22.
17 29 EHRR at 286, para. 115.
18 Ibid. at 286–7, para. 116.

13 The basic harm symbols

1 H and ~H are variables since they have inferior values. See Section 14.1, this volume.
2 For the same reason cited in note 1 above, $\sim\gamma$ counts as a variable.
3 Cf. Section 4.1, this volume.
4 One possible source of confusion can be eliminated immediately. Under $Ps(\eta = H)$, the possibility of $\eta = \gamma$ is not excluded. Indeed, it is implied. One might then argue that, under $Ps(\gamma = \sim H)$, it is tautologically true that $\gamma = \sim H$. Therefore, we can combine $Ps(\eta = H)$, which implies $\eta = \gamma$, with $Ps(\gamma = \sim H)$, which tautologically implies $\gamma = \sim H$, to reach an absurd conclusion: if $\gamma = H$, then $\gamma = \sim H$. However, that error cannot in fact occur. $Ps(\eta = H)$ requires $\eta \neq \sim H$, and thus cannot combine with $Ps(\gamma = \sim H)$.
5 *Hamlet* III.iii, 36–72 (Blakemore-Evans 1974: 1166–7).
6 Cf. Sections 3.5 and 9.7, this volume.

15 Right-based harm

1 See, e.g. van Dijk and van Hoof 1998: 82–95; Kastanas 1996; Yurow 1996.
2 24 Eur. Ct H.R. (ser. A) at 22, para. 48 (1976).
3 Ibid. at 23, para. 49.
4 Ibid.
5 45 Eur. Ct H.R. (ser. A) at 23–4, para. 60 (1981).
6 See Harris *et al.* 1995: 7–9. See also van Dijk and van Hoof 1998: 77–80.
7 45 Eur. Ct H.R. (ser. A) at 12–14, 23–4, paras 23–5, 60.
8 Ibid. at 23, para. 60. Cf. van Dijk and van Hoof 1998: 87.

9 295-A Eur. Ct H.R. (ser. A) (1994).
10 *Jersild*, 298 Eur. Ct H.R. (ser. A) at 21–6, paras 25–37 (1994).
11 *Otto-Preminger*, 295-A Eur. Ct H.R. (ser. A) at 20–1, para. 49.
12 Ibid. at 23–5 (Palm, Pekkanen and Makarczyk, JJ, dissenting). See also excerpts from the Opinion of the Commission, ibid. at 31.
13 298 Eur. Ct H.R. (ser. A) at 29–30 (Ryssdal, Bernhardt, Spielman and Loizou, JJ, dissenting), and at 31 (Gölcüklü, Russo and Valticos, JJ, dissenting). See also excerpts from the Opinion of the Commission, ibid. at 40–2 (Mr Jörundsson, dissenting, noting, in addition to a link to racial discrimination generally, the possibility of individual offence to members of racial minorities), and ibid. at 44–5 (Mrs Liddy, dissenting).
14 Cf. Heinze 1999a: 328–35; Heinze 1999d.

16 Restriction-based harm

1 25 Eur. Ct H.R. (ser. A) at 78–9, para. 207 (1978).
2 145-B Eur. Ct H.R. (ser. A) at 27–8, para. 48 (1988) (emphasis added).
3 Ibid. at 42.
4 Ibid. at 44–5, para. 3.

17 The concept of consent

1 See, e.g. Stauch *et al.* 1998: 105, 127–35.
2 See, e.g. for England and Wales, Sexual Offences Act 1956, s. 5. Cf. Card 1998: 235.
3 See, e.g. Stauch *et al.* 1998: chs 3, 4.
4 See, e.g. Card 1998: 144–9; Dias 1989: 959–64. See also Stauch *et al.* 1998: 105.
5 See, e.g. for the United Kingdom, *Gillick v. West Norfolk and Wisbech AHA* [1986] AC 112. Cf. Stauch *et al.* 1998: 167–79.
6 45 Eur. Ct H.R. (ser. A) at 11–14, paras 22–6.
7 Ibid. at 13, para. 25.
8 See Section 15.1, this volume.
9 See Section 25.2, this volume.
10 See Section 23.3, this volume.
11 Cf. Section 13.4, this volume.
12 The elimination of a possible source of confusion cited in Chapter 13, note 2, applies here *mutatis mutandis*. Under Ps(κ = C), the possibility of $\kappa = \chi$ is implied. One might then argue that, under Ps(χ = ~C), it is tautologically true that χ = ~C. Therefore, we can combine Ps(κ = C), which implies $\kappa = \chi$ with Ps(χ = ~C), which tautologically implies χ = ~C, to reach an absurd conclusion: if χ = C, then χ = ~C. However, that error cannot occur. Ps(κ = C) requires $\kappa \neq$ ~C, and thus cannot combine with Ps(χ = ~C).

18 Harm and consent

1 As opposed to *giving* valid consent, as explained in Section 18.2.
2 Card 1998: 144–9; Dias 1989: 959–64.
3 See, e.g. for England and Wales, Sexual Offences Act 1956 s. 1.
4 See, e.g. Sexual Offences Act 1956 s. 5. Cf. Card 1998: 235.
5 That observation may seem counterintuitive. It would appear that an assertion of valid consent is compatible with an assertion of insufficient harm. However, the two each form part of distinct positions, rather than being one unified position. See Section 18.3.

6 45 Eur. Ct H.R. (ser. A) at 18, para. 40.
7 Cf. Section 23.2, this volume.
8 The personal actor would of course take the same view, hence the more inclusive formula, A: $\alpha^{\circ}{\sim}\gamma^{r}C$.

19 Volition

1 Cf. Section 18.3, this volume.
2 CE 17/02/1988, époux Camara, 1988 AJDA 329, 366.
3 Loi no. 76–1181 of 22 December 1976.
4 Cf. Lebreton 1999: 271–72.
5 24 Eur. Ct H.R. (ser. A) at 25, para. 52 (1976).
6 Ibid. at 27, para. 57.

20 Breach

1 Detlefsen *et al.* 1999: 114.
2 Detlefsen *et al.* 1999: 5.
3 Detlefsen *et al.* 1999: 25.

23 Volitional liberalism

1 59 BverfGE 275 (1982).
2 'Everyone has the right to free development of his personality in so far as he does not violate the rights of others or offend the constitutional order or the moral code.' ['Jeder hat das Recht auf die freie Entfaltung seiner Persönlichkeit, soweit er nicht die Rechte anderer verletzt und nicht gegen die verfassungsmäßige Ordnung oder das Sittengesetz verstößt.'] (GG art. 2(1)).
3 59 BVerfGE at 276.
4 The attribution to Voltaire appears to be apocryphal, having first been identified in an English-language work about Voltaire published in the early twentieth century. See Bartlett 1955: 362, n. 4.
5 Section 4 of Law no. 1672/1939 (Greece). See 260-A Eur. Ct H.R. (ser. A) at 20–1, para. 16. Cf. Greek Constitution of 1975, which provides in part:

> Article 3
> (1) The dominant religion in Greece is that of the Christian Eastern Orthodox Church. The Greek Orthodox Church, which recognises as its head Our Lord Jesus Christ, is indissolubly united, doctrinally, with the Great Church of Constantinople and any other Christian Church in communion with it (*omodoxi*). [. . .]
>
> Article 13
> (2) [. . .] The performance of rites of worship must not prejudice public order or public morals. Proselytism is prohibited. [. . .]

6 260-A Eur. Ct H.R. (ser. A) at 8–9, para. 10 (1993). Cf. ibid. at 20–1, para. 16.
7 Ibid. at 8–9, 20–1.
8 *Jersild*, 298 Eur. Ct H.R. (ser. A) at 14, para. 12; *Otto-Preminger-Institut*, 295-A Eur. Ct H.R. (ser. A) at 8–9, para. 11.
9 Cf. the more paternalist argument in Section 25.2, this volume.
10 1996-VI Eur. Ct H.R. at para. 61.
11 HR 9 January 1987; NJ 1987.

24 Non-consensual liberalism

1 59 BVerfGE at 276 (italics added) ['Der mündige Bürger müsse . . . sein Risiko selbst beurteilen und sein Verhalten danach ausrichten können.'].
2 128 Eur. Ct H.R. (ser. A) (1987).
3 ECHR article 12 provides that '[m]en and women of marriageable age have the right to marry and to found a family, according to the national laws governing the exercise of the right'.
4 128 Eur. Ct H.R. (ser. A) at 17, para. 35.
5 Ibid. at 17–18, para. 36.
6 Ibid. at 18, para. 37.
7 Ibid.
8 Ibid. at 17–18, para. 36.
9 Ibid.
10 Cf. Jacobs and White 1996: 321–2.
11 *Kruslin*, 176-A Eur. Ct H.R. (ser. A) at 22–5, paras 30–6; *Huvig*, 176-B Eur. Ct H.R. (ser. A) at 54–7, paras 29–35.

25 Paternalism

1 59 BVerfGE 275, 278 (1982).
2 Cour d'Appel de Paris, 6 November 1997, 1998 Dalloz 122.
3 1997-II Eur. Ct H.R. 619.
4 247-C Eur. Ct H.R. (ser. A) at 55, para. 17 (1993). See also ibid. at 55–6 paras 18–20 (on state supervision of corporal punishments).
5 Ibid. at 52–3, para. 9. See also ibid. at 64 (Ryssdal, Thór Vilhjálmsson, Matscher and Wildhaber, JJ, partly dissenting).

26 Democracy

1 128 Eur. Ct H.R. (ser. A) at 17, para. 35.
2 Ibid. at 11–12, para. 17 (citing the opinion of the Swiss Federal Court).
3 Ibid. at 16–17, para. 33.
4 Ibid. at 13–14, para. 24.
5 Ibid. at 16–17, para. 33 (noting that the mere retention by a state of an otherwise outmoded view does not perforce justify a finding of a Convention violation).
6 59 BVerfGE 275, 276 (1982).

27 Conclusion: a roomful of scholars

1 As set forth in Section 13.7, this volume.

Bibliography

Akkermans, P.W.C., C.J. Bax and L.F.M. Verhey, 1999, *Grondrechten: Grondrechten en grondrechtsbescherming in Nederland*, Deventer: Tjeenk Willink.

Alexander, Larry, 1998, 'The Banality of Legal Reasoning', *Notre Dame Law Review* Vol. 73, pp. 517–33.

Ayer, Alfred Jules, 1952, *Logic, Truth and Logic*, New York: Dover.

Bailey, S.H., D.J. Harris and B.L. Jones, 1995, *Civil Liberties: Cases and Materials*, 4th edn, London: Butterworths.

Bartlett, John, 1955, *Familiar Quotations*, 13th edn, Boston: Little, Brown & Co.

Berger, Vincent, 1998, *Jurisprudence de la Cour Européenne des droits de l'homme*, 6th edn, Paris: Sirey (available in translation in several languages).

Berka, Walter, 1999, *Die Grundrechte: Grundfreiheiten und Menschenrechte in Österreich*, Vienna: Springer.

Bix, Brian, 1999, *Jurisprudence: Theory and Context*, 2nd edn, Oxford: Sweet & Maxwell.

Blakemore-Evans, G., ed., 1974, *The Riverside Shakespeare*, Boston: Houghton Mifflin.

Bleckmann, Albert, 1997, *Staatsrecht II – Die Grundrechte*, 4th edn, Cologne: Carl Heymanns.

Card, Richard, Rupert Cross and Philip Jones, 1998, *Criminal Law*, 14th edn, London: Butterworths.

Carnap, Rudolph, 1958, *Introduction to Symbolic Logic and its Applications*, W.H. Meyer and J. Wilkinson, trans., 1958, New York: Dover.

Cotterrell, Roger, 1989, *The Politics of Jurisprudence*, London: Butterworths.

Detlefsen, Michael, David McCarty and John Bacon, 1999, *Logic from A to Z*, London: Routledge.

Devlin, Patrick, 1959, *The Enforcement of Morals*, Oxford: Oxford University Press.

Dias, R.W.M, ed., 1989, *Clerk & Lindsell on Torts*, 16th edn, London: Sweet & Maxwell.

Dworkin, Ronald, 1977, *Taking Rights Seriously*, Cambridge, MA: Harvard University Press.

——, 1985, *A Matter of Principle*, Cambridge, MA: Harvard University Press.

——, 1986, *Law's Empire*, Cambridge, MA: Harvard University Press.

Freeman, M.D.A., 2001, *Lloyd's Introduction to Jurisprudence*, 7th edn, London: Sweet & Maxwell.

Grice, H. Paul, 1975, 'Logic and Conversation', in Peter Cole and Jerry L. Morgan, eds, *Syntax and Semantics*, Vol. 3, New York: Academic Press, pp. 41–58 [reprinted in A.P. Martinich, ed., *The Philosophy of Language*, 3rd edn, Oxford: Oxford University Press, ch. 11].

Guttenplan, Samuel, 1997, *The Languages of Logic*, 2nd edn, Oxford: Blackwell.

Hage, Jaap, 1996, *Reasoning with Rules: An Essay on Legal Reasoning and its Underlying Logic*, The Hague: Kluwer.

Harris, David J., M. O'Boyle and C. Warbrick, 1995, *Law of the European Convention on Human Rights*, London: Butterworths.

Hart, H.L.A., 1961, *The Concept of law*, Oxford: Oxford University Press.

—— , 1963, *Law, Liberty and Morality*, Oxford: Oxford University Press.

Heinze, Eric, 1995, *Sexual Orientation: A Human Right*, Kluwer: Dordrecht.

—— , 1998, 'Victimless Crimes', in *Encyclopedia of Applied Ethics*, Vol. 4, pp. 463–75.

—— , 1999a, 'Principles for a Meta-Discourse of Liberal Rights: The Example of the European Convention on Human Rights', *Indiana International & Comparative Law Review* Vol. 9, pp. 319–94.

—— , 1999b, 'The Construction and Contingency of the Minority Concept', in D. Fottrell and B. Bowring, eds, *Minority and Group Rights in the New Millennium*, The Hague: Martinus Nijhoff, pp. 25–74.

—— , 1999c, Book Review (of I. Schulte-Tenckhoff, *La Question des peuples autochtones*), *Netherlands Journal of International Law* Vol. 46, pp. 269–76.

—— , 1999d, Book Review (of E. Kastanas, *Unité et diversité: Notions autonomes et marge d'appréciation des Etats dans la jurisprudence de la Cour européenne des droits de l'homme*), *Modern Law Review* Vol. 63, pp. 155–8.

—— , 2002, *The Logic of Equality*, Aldershot: Ashgate.

—— , 2003a, 'Open Texture and the Patterns of Legal Theory' (forthcoming).

—— , 2003b, 'The Logic of Standards of Review in Constitutional Cases' (forthcoming).

—— , 2004, *The Logic of Constitutional Rights*, Ann Arbor: University of Michigan (forthcoming).

Hodges, Wilfred, 1977, *Logic*, London: Penguin.

Hohfeld, Wesley N., 1946, *Fundamental Legal Conceptions as Applied in Judicial Reasoning*, New Haven: Yale University Press [republished in an edition by David Campbell and Philip Thomas, eds, 2001, Aldershot: Ashgate].

Holmes, Oliver Wendell, 1963, *The Common Law*, Boston: Little, Brown & Co.

Horn, Norbert, 2001, *Einführung in die Rechtswissenschaft und Rechtsphilosophie*, 2nd edn, Heidelberg: Müller.

Hughes, G.E. and M.J. Cresswell, 1996, *A New Introduction to Modal Logic*, London: Routledge.

Jacobs, Francis G. and Robin C. White, 1996, *The European Convention on Human Rights*, 2nd edn, Oxford: Oxford University Press.

Kalinowski, Georges, 1972, *La Logique des normes*, Paris: Presses Universitaires de France.

Kastanas, Elias, 1996, *Unité et diversité: Notions autonomes et marge d'appréciation des Etats dans la jurisprudence de la Cour européenne des droits de l'homme*, Brussels: Bruylant.

Kaufmann, Arthur, 1994a, 'Rechtsphilosophie, Rechtstheorie, Rechtsdogmatik', in A. Kaufmann and W. Hassemer, eds, *Einführung in Rechtsphilosophie und Rechtstheorie der Gegenwart*, 6th edn, Heidelberg: Müller Juristischer Verlag, ch. 1.

—— , 1994b, 'Problemgeschichte der Rechtsphilosophie', in A. Kaufmann and W. Hassemer, eds., *Einführung in Rechtsphilosophie und Rechtstheorie der Gegenwart*, 6th edn, Heidelberg: Müller Juristischer Verlag, ch. 2.

Kelsen, Hans, 1979, *Allgemeine Theorie der Normen*, Vienna: Manz.

Kennedy, Duncan, 1982, 'Legal Education as Training for Hierarchy', in D. Kairys, ed., *The Politics of Law*, New York: Pantheon Books, pp. 40–61.

Konyndyk, Kenneth, 1986, *Introductory Modal Logic*, Notre Dame: University of Notre Dame Press.

Kramer, Matthew, 2000, 'Rights without Trimmings', in M. Kramer, N. Simmonds and H. Steiner, eds, *A Debate over Rights*, Oxford: Oxford University Press, pp. 7–111.

Lawson, R.A. and H.G. Schermers, 1999, *Leading Cases of the European Court of Human Rights*, 2nd edn, Nijmegen: Ars Aequi Libri.

Lebreton, Gilles, 1999, *Libertés publiques et droits de l'homme*, 4th edn, Paris: Armand Colin.

Malinowski, Grzgegorz, 2001, 'Many-Valued Logics', in L. Goble, *The Blackwell Guide to Philosophical Logic*, Oxford: Blackwell, pp. 309–35.

Meier, Christian, 2000, *Der Denkweg der Juristen*, Münster: LIT Verlag.

Merrills, J.G., 1993, *The Development of International Law by the European Court of Human Rights*, Manchester: Manchester University Press.

Mill, John Stuart, 1974, *On Liberty*, G. Himmelfarb, ed., Harmondsworth: Penguin.

Neumann, Ulrich, 1994, 'Juristische Logik', in A. Kaufman and W. Hassemer, eds, *Einführung in Rechtsphilosophie und Rechtstheorie der Gegenwart*, 6th edn, Heidelberg: Müller Juristischer Verlag.

Priest, Graham, 2000, *Logic: A Very Short Introduction*, Oxford: Oxford University Press.

Quine, Willard van Orman, 1953, *From a Logical Point of View*, 2nd edn, Cambridge, MA: Harvard University Press.

—— , 1960, *Word and Object*, Cambridge, MA: MIT Press.

Rhodes, Robert E. and Howard Pospesel, 1997, *Premises and Conclusions: Symbolic Logic for Legal Analysis*, Upper Saddle River, NJ: Prentice Hall.

Robert, Jacques and Jean Duffar, 1996, *Droits de l'homme et libertés fondamentales*, 6th edn, Paris: Montchrestien.

Robertson, A.H. and J.G. Merrills, 1996, *Human Rights in the World*, 4th edn, Manchester: Manchester University Press.

Sainsbury, Mark, 1991, *Logical Forms*, Oxford: Blackwell.

Saunders, Kevin W., 1990, 'A Formal Analysis of Hohfeldian Relations', *Akron Law Review* Vol. 23, pp. 465–506.

Simmonds, Nigel E., 2001, 'Introduction', in Wesley N. Hohfeld, *Fundamental Legal Conceptions as Applied in Judicial Reasoning*, 2001, Aldershot: Ashgate, pp. ix–xxix.

Soeteman, Arend, 1989, *Logic in Law*, Dordrecht: Kluwer.

Stauch, Marc, Kay Wheat and John Tingle, 1998, *Sourcebook on Medical Law*, London: Cavendish.

Steiner, Henry J. and Philip Alston, 2000, *International Human Rights in Context*, 2nd edn, Oxford: Oxford University Press.

Steiner, Hillel, 1994, *An Essay on Rights*, Oxford: Blackwell.

Sumner, L.W., 1987, *The Moral Foundation of Rights*, Oxford: Oxford University Press.

Taylor, Kenneth, 1998, *Truth and Meaning*, Oxford: Blackwell.
Tribe, Laurence and Michael Dorf, 1990, 'Levels of Generality in the Definition of Rights', *University of Chicago Law Review* Vol. 57, pp. 1057–1080.
——, 1991, *On Reading the Constitution*, Cambridge, MA: Harvard University Press.
van Dijk P. and G.J.H van Hoof, 1998, *Theory and Practice of the European Convention on Human Rights*, 3rd edn, The Hague: Kluwer Law International.
van Hees, Martin, 1995, *Rights and Decisions: Formal Models of Law and Liberalism*, The Hague: Kluwer.
von Wright, Georg Henrik, 1951, 'Deontic Logic', *Mind* Vol. 60, pp. 1–15 [reprinted in G.H. von Wright, 1957, *Logical Studies*, London: Routledge, pp. 58–74].
——, 1963, *Norm and Action*, London: Routledge & Kegan Paul.
Yurow, Howard Charles, 1996, *The Margin of Appreciation Doctrine in the Dynamics of European Human Rights Jurisprudence*, The Hague: Martinus Nijhoff.

Index

For Product Safety Concerns and Information please contact our EU representative GPSR@taylorandfrancis.com
Taylor & Francis Verlag GmbH, Kaufingerstraße 24, 80331 München, Germany

www.ingramcontent.com/pod-product-compliance
Ingram Content Group UK Ltd.
Pitfield, Milton Keynes, MK11 3LW, UK
UKHW022215190926
475702UK00003B/374

* 9 7 8 0 4 1 5 3 0 0 5 6 8 *